MW01504937

THE POST-SECULAR IN QUESTION

The Post-Secular in Question

RELIGION IN CONTEMPORARY SOCIETY

Edited by Philip S. Gorski, David Kyuman Kim,
John Torpey, and Jonathan VanAntwerpen

A joint publication of the Social Science Research Council
and New York University Press

NEW YORK UNIVERSITY PRESS

New York and London

www.nyupress.org

Library of Congress Cataloging-in-Publication Data

The post-secular in question : religion in contemporary society / edited by Philip Gorski . . . [et al.].

    p.   cm.

  Includes bibliographical references and index.

  ISBN 978-0-8147-3872-6 (cl : alk. paper)

  ISBN 978-0-8147-3873-3 (ebook)

  ISBN 978-0-8147-3874-0 (ebook)

  1. Religion and sociology.   2. Post-secularism.   I. Gorski, Philip S.

BL60.P593   2012

200.9'051—dc23

2011044707

New York University Press books are printed on acid-free paper, and their binding materials are chosen for strength and durability. We strive to use environmentally responsible suppliers and materials to the greatest extent possible in publishing our books.

Manufactured in the United States of America

10 9 8 7 6 5 4 3 2 1

References to Internet websites (URLs) were accurate at the time of writing. Neither the author nor New York University Press is responsible for URLs that may have expired or changed since the manuscript was prepared.

Contents

CHAPTER ONE

The Post-Secular in Question

Philip S. Gorski, David Kyuman Kim, John Torpey,
and Jonathan VanAntwerpen

Are we living in a post-secular world? That question has surged onto the academic agenda, marked by the increasing scholarly use of the notion of the "post-secular." From the writings of Jürgen Habermas on the role of religion in public life to a host of more theoretical reflections on religion in contemporary society, the idea of the post-secular has acquired increasing currency in contemporary academic discussions.[1] The outpouring of books and journal articles on the topic signals an important shift in scholarly thinking about religion and secularism. Yet it should also give us pause; the term has at times been used uncritically, and we should be wary of its deployment simply to signal a <u>contested claim</u> about the <u>resurgence of religion.</u> That said, there is no doubt that the notion raises a number of important issues concerning both the place of religion in twenty-first-century society and its status as an object of study in the academy.[2]

Why the renewed interest in religion? The notion of the "post-secular"—suggesting that we have left a secular era behind—implies a tectonic shift in the Zeitgeist. But here some caution is in order. Amid the proliferation of "post-" terms in recent academic discourse, it is important to consider whether the concept of the post-secular refers to an actual shift in the social world, or whether its growing deployment results, instead, from a zealous need to detect epochal turning points in every minor twist of the historical road. (The brief career of "post-nationalism"—a term that garnered much attention in the social sciences just a decade ago but now appears wildly overdrawn—provides a cautionary tale.[3]) The inquiries into and assessments of the postmodern that have had staying power were engaging, in part, because they called sharply into question the ethical and epistemological certitude and purported superiority of the modern project. In other words, the disputes over postmodernism revolved around the naming of a diminishing and even dying core of modernity—Fordist capitalism (e.g., Jameson, Harvey); truth, rationality, and knowledge (e.g., Foucault, Lyotard, Feyerabend); European culture and Orientalism (e.g., Said); and so on.[4] The development of postmodern discourse is instructive for making sense of the post-secular, insofar as postmodernism can be read in at least two different ways. In one reading, postmodernism claims that modernity is over and hence that we live in a "postmodern" era; in another view, postmodernism insists that the universalistic claims associated with modernity can no longer be sustained without demurral.

And so it goes with the post-secular. At the turn of the twenty-first century, Peter Berger argued that "the world is just as furiously religious as it ever was, and in some places more so than ever."[5] While some would claim that there has been a simple resurgence of religion, Berger saw both continuity and upsurge. In so doing, he was reversing his earlier judgment of the matter: earlier in his career, he had been one of the main promoters of secularization theory. Bearing in mind such shifts in the thought of a major sociologist and social thinker like Berger, we ask: Is it the social scientists' vision that is crooked, while the historical road is straight? To what other constructive narratives about the secular and the religious do scholars and everyday people alike appeal in order to help make sense of the world?

The question of the post-secular poses two lines of inquiry: first, determinations about the state of religiosity in the world; second, understanding the new ways that social scientists, philosophers, historians, and scholars from across disciplines are and are not paying attention to religion. In other words, the question is: Which world has changed—the "real" one or the scholarly one? To some degree, the contributors to this book argue that the answer is "both." By many measures, there is, in fact, a religious resurgence of global dimensions, but this resurgence is not taking place with much uniformity around the globe.[6] Rather, it is taking many forms—not all of which fit into an easily codifiable definition of "religion." The recent outpouring of academic work on religion in the social sciences and philosophy is partly a response to this resurgence—but only partly. A growing unease with

"Enlightenment fundamentalism" and broadening skepticism about scientific naturalism in many quarters have also made it easier for many academics to take religion seriously again.[7] In the context of claims about religious resurgence, the essays in this volume grapple with the legacies of secularism and secularization theory, the contested categories of religion and the secular, and the diverse claims associated with the concept of the post-secular.

In the remainder of this introduction, we offer an overview of the shifting patterns of scholarly attention to religion; the relations between the religious and the secular; the history of philosophical and social scientific understandings of religion; disciplinary differences in the study of religion; and a brief consideration of the future prospects for the social scientific study of religion.

Patterns of Scholarly Attention to Religion:
Causes, Connections, Consequences

The Iranian revolution, the Moral Majority, the Pentecostal explosion, the post-socialist Buddhist revival,[8] faith-based initiatives, communal violence, the politics of the veil, the inconclusive "Arab spring," and, of course, 9/11: In retrospect, it is not difficult to understand why religion has found its way back to a central place on the scholarly agenda over the last decade. More puzzling, perhaps, is why religion took so long to return, and why it was pushed to the margins in the first place. (Disciplines such as religious studies and, to a lesser degree, anthropology—for which religion has always held center stage—are notable exceptions.) While the contributors to this volume all share this perplexity, they propose different answers.

On one account, the collapse of structural functionalism in the social sciences precipitated the marginalization of religion.[9] Under the reign of Talcott Parsons in sociology—a dominant mode of the ancien régime of modernization theory in the social sciences—"norms" and "values" were seen as the woof and warp of social order, and religion as their raw materials. But by the 1960s, the old regime had met with a general rebellion, and other approaches and perspectives began displacing structural functionalism. Among the new approaches and perspectives was the amalgam of Marx and Weber known as "conflict theory," which highlighted the role of "power" and "interests" in social life while relegating religion to the category of "ideology," when not ignoring it altogether.[10] Allies in revolution, "neo-Marxism" and "left

Weberianism" became enemies in power. Social scientists found common ground with philosophers, perhaps most distinctively in the discourse generated by the Frankfurt School. It is perhaps not so surprising, then, that Habermas has played such a pivotal role in these revolutions of thought.[11] The ensuing debate over the nature of social class, the "relative autonomy" of the state, and, more broadly, the relative importance of capital and states in determining the fundamental shape of modern social phenomena "in the last instance" was eventually superseded in another palace coup known as "the cultural turn."[12] The renewed attention to culture in history and the social sciences beginning in the late 1980s reopened the door for the return of religion.[13] Religion could now be conceived not merely as an "ideology" but as "a cultural structure," "a social organization," or "a movement frame," among other things.[14] Let us call this the "post-Parsons interpretation."

An alternative view holds that the erasure of religion from the social scientific agenda actually occurred a good deal earlier, during the opening decades of the twentieth century, and resulted from the retreat of religious conservatives from public life and the declining influence of religious elites and institutions on higher education—which is to say, from the secularization of public life and academic institutions. Just as Baptist congregations withdrew into their "hard shells" and Congregationalist ministers were banished to divinity schools at the turn of the twentieth century, the academy saw the eventual formation of departments of "religious studies."[15] Subsequently, religion was rendered invisible—and risible—to many academic researchers. On this account, the return of religion to the scholarly agenda is traceable to the upsurge of "public religions" in the late 1970s and to the prodigious inflow of foundation monies for scholarly pursuits related to religion in the decades that followed (as documented by John Schmalzbauer and Kathleen Mahoney in chapter 9 in this volume).[16] Notwithstanding the prodigious efforts of Robert Bellah—and, in a different vein, Peter Berger—in shoring up the sociology of religion in the American academy, this disciplinary formation remained an outlier for researchers and institutions alike.[17] One might call this the "secularization interpretation" of the decline of religion's perceived importance in the social sciences.

A third view maintains that the return of religion to the academic agenda is an interesting but minor subplot in the recent history of higher education, whose main story line is the increasing marginalization of the humanities and social sciences within the modern research university.[18]

Because universities are increasingly reliant on private and public largesse, and because such funding goes disproportionately to research in the natural sciences, engineering, and medicine, little of this money finds its way to researchers working on religion. Accordingly, while there may be some upsurge of interest in religion on American college campuses today, it is likely to be and to remain quite limited. This might be dubbed the "materialist interpretation."

Yet another interpretation suggests that the decline in overall scholarly attention to religion correlates with a decline in individual religious commitments among social scientists (there was not much room for decline among philosophers). If the rise of the social sciences was closely connected to religiously motivated reform projects—such as the Social Gospel, for instance—and if some form of religious belief was still quite common just a few generations ago, most social scientists have now moved to a position somewhere "beyond belief." Personal irreligion intersects with scholarly insecurity, as Robert Wuthnow has argued, insofar as social scientists have a certain anxiety about the scientific status of their disciplines, which leads them to distance themselves from religion. It is possible that these forces combined to reduce academic attention to religion in the social sciences. This might be referred to as the "secular intellectual interpretation."

Whatever the causes of this scholarly inattention to religion—and they are many and varied—the consequences are clear enough: some of the most important features of modern life have been misapprehended or ignored entirely.[19] States and bureaucracies, revolution and reform, voluntary associations and social movements, human and civil rights, corporations and welfare states—these and many other building blocks of Western modernity have religious genealogies.[20] Whatever differences they may have in terms of approach, the contributors to this volume share the view that it is impossible to make sense of the world without taking account of religion and that a social science inattentive to religion cannot hope to be adequate to the realities that it seeks to elucidate.

The essays gathered here thus address a number of urgent issues concerning how scholars approach religion today. They ask: What is the place of religion in the contemporary academic scene? How and when did religion decline as a matter of scholarly concern? How does the scholarly status of religion vary according to location in the institutional field of higher education? How are research and teaching on religious matters funded, and what impact do funding patterns have on what gets studied? Inevitably, among the central themes of their reflections are the nature of the religious, the increasingly contested character of the secular, and their interrelations.

Relations between the Religious and the Secular: New Understandings of an Old Distinction

Throughout the twentieth century, the "dominant paradigm" in the social scientific study of religion was secularization theory.[21] Over the last two decades, the "secularization thesis"—roughly, that modernization undermines religion—has been subjected to searching reexamination.[22] While the old orthodoxy still has its defenders, particularly in Western Europe, the general drift of the commentary, especially in North America, has been moving in the direction of skepticism, particularly with regard to two key predictions of the secularization paradigm: that religion would undergo decline, and that it would become subject to privatization.[23] In truth, the fate of "churchly religion" (let alone personal spirituality) has been far more varied and complex than secularization theory suggested, even in secularism's Western European strongholds.[24] Meanwhile, the place of religion in public space and debate is now the subject of energetic and sometimes vitriolic debates, among pundits and philosophers alike.[25] Witness the ongoing debate about integrating Muslims in Western Europe, or the intellectual combat between "separationists" and "accommodationists" in courtrooms and law schools in the United States. In this atmosphere, secularization theory looks more like a partisan political program than a "value-free" social theory. The view that reason would replace religion and, more fundamentally, that reason is opposed to religion—the conventional wisdom among right-thinking intellectuals just a generation ago—is now being called into question. Perhaps it was the secularists rather than the religionists who were blinded, not by darkness, but by *les lumières* of Enlightenment reason. While many assumed that religion was an ailing patient in the back wards of historical development, it was engaged in a worldwide revival tour.

Be that as it may, we should not be too quick to equate today's religious resurgence with a "de-secularization of the world." As José Casanova and others have rightly emphasized, secularization theory actually consists of at least three analytically distinguishable hypotheses: (1) the decline of religious belief; (2) the differentiation of religious and nonreligious spheres;

and (3) the privatization of religious commitments.[26] In Casanova's view, the decline and privatization theses must be rejected, but the differentiation thesis is essentially correct. There are good reasons to think that religion is, in fact, less central to the governing institutions of the societies of Latin Christendom (d.b.a. "the West") than it was five hundred years ago and that, at least at this level, the secularization thesis makes some sense, and not only in Western Europe. If anything, the line "between church and state" is even more sharply drawn in the United States, at least in terms of legal principles and often in terms of institutional arrangements as well.[27] As regards individual beliefs and public engagement, however, the United States is perhaps the least secular country in the West. Indeed, one of the reasons that the secularization thesis has come to seem so dubious is the "anomalous" status of the United States, a clear outlier by most metrics.[28] From a global perspective, however, it is Western Europe that stands out as "the exceptional case," while the United States appears strikingly "normal."[29] Little wonder, then, that the staunchest defenders of the secularization paradigm are to be found in Western Europe, where its predictions have the greatest empirical traction, as John Torpey discusses in chapter 11 in this volume.

As Talal Asad and others have noted, the terms "religious" and "secular" can really be understood only in relation and opposition to each other. Thus, any redefinition of the secular necessarily involves a redefinition of the religious, and vice versa. For example, an expansive definition of religion, such as Durkheim's or Luckmann's, will find religion everywhere, even in putatively secular and mundane activities, such as professional sports or solitary walks.[30] Conversely, an expansive definition of secularity, such as Wilson's or Bruce's, will find secularity everywhere, even in churches and synagogues.[31] To wit, by imposing a particular definition of the subject, it is possible to predetermine the outcome of the debate. Nor is this the only complication. For one thing, the liminal space between the religious and the secular is now occupied—indeed, has long been occupied, as Courtney Bender shows in chapter 3—by a third category: the spiritual.[32] Yet the meaning of this category is also highly contested, outside the academy and, increasingly, inside the academy as well. Some define spirituality in opposition to "organized religion," but what, then, should we make of Tibetan prayer bells in suburban megachurches or of "Bu-Jew" rabbis on college campuses? Others define spirituality in opposition to scientific rationalism, but how, then, can we explain card-carrying cosmologists who cite the Kabala or, for that matter, the mystical reverence for nature among "new atheists" like Richard Dawkins and Christopher Hitchens? The difficulty here, as so often in the social sciences, is that the "categories of analysis" we use in our academic writing are also "categories of practice" that are contested in public debate.[33] Whatever our intentions, then, our definitions are never really "neutral." Of course, old hands in the study of religion are well versed in these difficulties and are quick to add the appropriate caveats and qualifications to their definitions. Whence concepts such as "lived religion," "believing without belonging," and "invisible religion," which draw our attention to the limitations of a "churchly" definition of religiosity?[34] But even sophisticated typologies such as these become fraught when transported outside the context of Abrahamic traditions. Greater attention to Asian religion, for example, complicates another set of conceptual categories that are used to stabilize the meaning of religion—categories such as "belief," "orthodoxy," "community," "philosophy," "intellectual," and "science." As Richard Madsen shows in chapter 2, it is not clear that the category of "religion" really has much purchase in the Chinese context.

Coming to Terms with Religion

Is there something about religion that necessarily escapes the analytical frameworks of the social sciences but that finds better expression among philosophers and historians? Historically, social scientists have been of two minds on this question. On the one hand, those who embrace the skeptical and materialist epistemologies that arose during the Scottish and French Enlightenments (e.g., with Hume and d'Holbach), particularly the monist-materialism that Jonathan Israel has christened the basis of the "radical Enlightenment," are apt to answer in the negative.[35] From this perspective, which has roots that extend back through the neo-Epicureanism of Hobbes and Bayle to the atomistic materialism of Lucretius and Democritus, religion is a chimera rooted in ignorance and fear.[36] The "scientific atheism" of classical Marxism belongs in this lineage (though Marx's own views on this subject were more complicated), as does much orthodox secularization theory, including the recent work of Norris and Inglehart, which traces religious belief to "existential insecurity."[37] On the other hand, those more influenced by Kantian and neo-Kantian epistemologies, who maintain the sharp distinction between scientifically comprehensible "phenomena" and experientially inaccessible "noumena"—between "things of experience" and "things-in-themselves"—and the strong emphasis on the limits of human understanding that follows, will be more inclined to answer in the affirmative. Because the two "founding fathers" of the contemporary sociology of religion—Durkheim and Weber—were both so strongly influenced by neo-Kantianism (the "spiritualist" neo-Kantianism of Renouvier, on one side, and the southwest German school of Rickert, on the other), most Anglo-American sociologists of religion are inclined to answer this question in the affirmative.[38] Weber's famous remark that he was "religiously unmusical" captures the sense of a potentially impassable divide between the rational, logical mind and the putatively ineffable qualities of religious experience. In this view, social scientists can study the ideas, rituals, practices, and institutions that make up *la vie religieuse* even if they may personally experience religious life as more noumenal than numinous, more incomprehensible than awe-inspiring. As much as he admired the ethical conviction and consistency of Tolstoy, Weber himself was unwilling to make the "sacrifice of the intellect" that he believed religious commitment necessarily required.[39] It should be added that this way of seeing things is easily reconciled to certain—namely, "liberal" and "spiritualist"—forms of religiosity, which emphasize inner experience, ethical commitment, and social change more than, say, rational theology, communal belonging, and doctrinal orthodoxy. This is the conception of religious experience that arises out of the Romantic appropriation of Kant by Schleiermacher and then finds its way into the Anglo-American world along various paths, including Emersonian spirituality, Kierkegaardian fideism, and Victorian moralism.[40] On such a reading, the social sciences can even function as a "negative theology" of sorts, a purifying agent that helps to identify nonreligious accretions to religion—that is, the various ways in which history, culture, power, and interests have tarnished and corrupted the core truths and messages of a pristine religiosity accessible only through the authentic experiences of religious virtuosos, past and present. H. Richard Niebuhr combined theology and social theory in precisely this way.[41]

And yet, the neo-Kantian dispensation had costs as well as benefits. On the positive side of the ledger, by explicitly bracketing the question of religious truth, and by implicitly distinguishing the ineffable truth of religion from its sociocultural contaminants, the neo-Kantian approach marked off certain aspects of religious life as susceptible to sociological analysis (dogmas, rituals, hierarchies, communities, and so on) and made possible a scientific sociology of religion that was not just a scientistic critique of religion. This enabled a modus vivendi that maintained that certain forms of religion (read "observable" and "verifiable") are appropriate objects of analysis for sociology. On the negative side of the ledger, this modus vivendi also presumed that religious belief was somehow irrational, that faith cannot be founded on reason, and, in the Weberian version, that all "value commitments"—religious and secular—are grounded in subjective experience and not subject to objective analysis.[42] Social science, in Weber's phrase, was to be "value free." This claim has been much criticized from within the social sciences, of course, by those who argue that the value commitments of social scientists affect not only the kinds of questions the individual researcher asks, as Weber had claimed, but also the sorts of answers he or she gives; that individual values always lead to subjective "biases" of various sorts; and that these biases, moreover, cannot be fully neutralized or controlled by methodological procedures. Interestingly, this line of argument also gave rise to a corresponding theology. Protestant theologians and philosophers from Cornelius Van Til to John Frame followed suit and turned the tables on positivistic versions of social science, arguing that all worldviews, the scientific worldview included, rest on unprovable and untestable "presuppositions" whose prima facie validity is no more and no less "testable" than the divine revelations of historic religion.[43] More recently, neo-Aristotelian and neo-Thomist philosophers and theologians such as Alasdair MacIntyre and Jacques Dupuis have elaborated an even more radical critique of the neo-Kantian dispensation.[44] Drawing on the Aristotelian argument that human beings have a certain telos, and also working from the premodern theory of natural law elaborated by the Scholastics (not to be confused with the modern theory of natural rights initiated by Grotius), MacIntyre and company critique subjectivist, "emotivist," and "therapeutic" forms of ethics, arguing that the nature of "the good life" and "the good society" is rationally and even objectively determinable.[45] In this regard, they are moral realists. Put plainly, they contend that the physical constitution and intellectual capacities of human beings are such that we can "flourish" and achieve genuine "well-being" only in certain sorts of societies and not in others.

From the other angle, theology and religious sensibility unabashedly entail ethical considerations that social scientific ideas of objectivity and "value-freedom" have tended to banish from the social sciences. If the latter remain committed to a stance that insists that it cannot engage hermeneutically with moral postures, however, is it not condemned to viewing religion forever from "the outside"? One senses a need for that Gadamerian "fusion of horizons" that would allow both the religious person and the (secular) social scientist to make themselves mutually comprehensible to each other.[46] Indeed, Gadamer's insistence that presuppositions are always operative in inquiries, whether scientific or moral, is a methodological correction that has gained widespread acceptance. The status of ethics in the social sciences immediately comes into play in any serious rethinking of their relations with religion—a problem that Gorski addresses, in connection with Durkeim's sociology, in chapter 4.

Is such a "fusion of horizons" really possible? Or must the conversation between the religiously inspired person and the secular social scientist be a dialogue of the deaf, an endgame of foregone incommensurability? The primary question, however, is whether or not these realms can be so neatly cordoned off from each other. Religious people are not necessarily dogmatists (though they may be, of course). Schools of theology exist precisely to hash out the meaning and consequences of the fine points of "dogma." Assuming that all (or at least much) theological thought is subject to communicative discourse, how different is the religious from the social scientific? How one assesses the possibilities for a constructive dialogue between religion and the social sciences depends on the understanding each has of itself and of the other. If the social scientist understands "religion" as an irrational response to fear, and if the religionist understands "social science" as premised on an arbitrary set of presuppositions, then little dialogue is possible. By contrast, if the social scientist understands religion as a rational interpretation of telos and cosmos, and the religionist understands social science as a search for the best society, then the two can walk hand in hand. Somewhere between these extremes, one finds something like Habermas's recent conversation with Cardinal Ratzinger (now Pope Benedict XVI).[47] Habermas insists religions must accept elements of modernity, particularly the fact of religious pluralism, the leading role of science in making sense of the world, and the constitutional-democratic organization of the polity. Nonetheless, he concedes that historic/positive religious traditions retain a sense of unredeemed utopian promise that may have been lost with the development of more secular ideas of salvation, and that modern, secular societies therefore lost a vital moral resource.[48]

In many cases, the opening of the academy to the study of religion has been accompanied by a growing openness to the contributions of self-consciously religious scholars. This trend is perhaps most evident in writing on the history of religion, but important strides toward a renegotiation of relations with religious worldviews have occurred in philosophy and other disciplines as well. While some will view this development with equanimity or even enthusiasm, others will undoubtedly worry that the inclusion of religious perspectives in the academy may undermine the wall of separation so arduously erected between faith and reason. Needless to say, the apparent rapprochement between science and religion has provoked gales of hostility from those who regard them as twain that ne'er should meet.

Disciplinary Differences in the Study of Religion

American higher education had its roots in the training of clergy and other professionals, and it thus bore a deep religious imprint. But while it once dominated the ethos of the college or university, the scholarly study of religion has since come to be distributed across a variety of different disciplines and schools. Today, seminaries have only a tenuous connection to mainstream academic life. Divinity schools connected to universities are administratively and often geographically separate from colleges of arts and sciences. Furthermore, departments of religion or religious studies are often ghettoized in relation to other disciplines. Even within the discipline of the so-called study of religion, heated debates continue over whether religious studies should also include the study of theology. The animosity that often characterizes these debates arises from precisely the questions raised earlier in regard to the possibility of conducting value-free (read "scientific") research on religious phenomena. In the context of the discipline of religious studies, advocates of a value-neutral study of religion, like McCutcheon, argue that theology and theologians are too overtly normative in their concerns.[49] There is no small amount of irony in attempts by scholars within religious studies to meet supposedly scientific standards of inquiry in their efforts to reform the discipline, while at the same time a broad range of scholars from political theory and literary studies, for example, are turning to the productive possibilities of political theology. The emergence of a substantial literature in political theology is only partially indebted to the revival of interest in the work of Carl Schmitt. The translation of Giorgio

Agamben's corpus into English, along with the widening influence of the philosophico-theological work of Hent de Vries (see his contribution, chapter 5) and the prolific Slavoj Žižek have proved to be fountainheads for the new discourse on political theology.[50]

Among the dominant social scientific disciplines, research on religion is a thriving specialty in history departments and is well established if somewhat marginal within sociology. Whether it has maintained its centrality in anthropology in recent years is open to debate. Despite the increasing interest in questions of Islam in the field, research on religion has only a weak toehold in political science.

Disciplinary differences extend further, to the matter of *what* exactly is studied when religion is the object of examination. Political scientists are interested chiefly in the impact of religion on the struggle for the acquisition of power. An influential outlier of sorts is in the subfield of political theory and political philosophy, in which the work of Michael Walzer, Charles Taylor, Michael Sandel, Bonnie Honig, and William Connolly, among others, has long focused on religion.[51] Sociologists concentrate on the following: varying rates of participation in religious practices, rituals, and institutions; the interrelationships among religious beliefs and other kinds of behavior; the nature and aims of religiously inspired movements; and the place of religion in public life. Anthropologists, relying principally on ethnographic methods, tend to be more attuned to the peculiarities and meanings of religious experience in specific settings, cultural formations, and traditions. Historians have worked on almost all of the issues addressed above but are perhaps particularly invested—as befits their métier—in questions concerning the origins and declines of various religious movements and practices.

Against this background, it is not hard to diagnose a certain balkanization of the study of religion that divides up the object of study in ways that reproduce the fault lines among the different fields themselves. (A notable exception: determinations about these methodological and disciplinary foci begin to break down somewhat when turning to the serious consideration of the importance of gender and hierarchy in analyzing religious life.) This fragmentation and marginalization helps to reinforce the notion that religion is a relatively insubstantial part of scholarly life. Meanwhile, interdisciplinary studies are often merely "multidisciplinary" rather than truly syncretic and synthetic. This is a problem, however, not just in the study of religion but in interdisciplinary scholarship generally; the problem of overcoming "multidisciplinarity" in the study of religion is the problem of overcoming disciplinary boundaries in general. Yet it should also be said that "interdisciplinarity" often simply serves as an excuse for a lack of rigor.

At the same time, there seems to be a reorientation of disciplines afoot, whereby sociological forms of thinking are popping up in a variety of neighboring disciplines. So, however, are more utilitarian, or economistic, forms of thinking, particularly in the methodologically individualistic, rational-choice mode. Political science has become wildly smitten by this mode over the past two decades. Will these developments at the epistemological level result in greater coherence in the study of religion (or anything else)? Is interdisciplinary scholarship on religion—which, like the study of migration, seems to be interdisciplinary in nature—any more likely to be successful than that in other areas? Reflection on earlier patterns of scholarly attention to religion, as represented in this volume, will be indispensable in addressing these kinds of questions.

Prospects for the Social Scientific Study of Religion

Against the background of these considerations, this book points toward new directions in the social scientific study of religion by interrogating the concept of the post-secular. It does so on both historical and theoretical grounds. One major problem, clearly, is to make sense of the rhythms of past social scientific attention to religion. How, for example, did secularization theory come to be so dominant and unquestioned (until, say, the 1980s) that there seemed little need to spell it out in any great detail? This is an urgent question insofar as much of the world was not behaving according to its dictates, even as the theory was being articulated. While one can understand why European scholars might conclude that the theory helped them to account for their own situation, its relevance to the American scene has always been problematic at best. How did a theory that had so little to say to American conditions nonetheless become hegemonic in the United States? We are not the first to note that the idea of secularization has been as much "a program" as it has been an empirically observable reality. The problem is to determine when, where, and why that program came to be realized and how stable it is.

From a theoretical perspective, can we define "religion" in a Weberian "ideal-typical" manner that makes the phenomenon more amenable to social scientific analysis? Some think that this would be misguided, taking away from religious phenomena their unavoidable historical and cultural specificity, and hence robbing us of an important pathway to understanding. Moreover, the barriers separating the religious from the secular are increasingly regarded as fluid, and the view that the two spheres are simply mutually constitutive seems to be on the ascent. But is it possible to study religion if one can't say what it is with some degree of consistency?

Next, the turn to discussion of the post-secular has raised the question of the place of religion in social science scholarship more generally. How much of social life can we understand if we exclude religion from our analyses? Is religion crucial to understanding major social change, or not? The Weberian project was pitched on the scale of "universal history" and intended to make sense of the ways in which religious worldviews facilitated or hampered certain historical developments. Because his ultimate concern was with explaining the rise of modern capitalism in Europe, Weber was unashamedly Eurocentric in his conception of this project. This approach now appears to cast other traditions in an unnecessarily unflattering, as well as inaccurate, light. A more decentered analysis of the ways in which religion may shape behavior is called for today, eschewing an implicit directionality of development. Was ascetic, sectarian Protestantism *really* the central reason that the West emerged from the pack in the early modern period, ultimately outstripping its competitors in dramatic fashion? Is Western religiosity playing that role again—perhaps elsewhere in the world?

Religion has proved remarkably hardy, despite many reports of its death. The present moment offers an unusual opportunity for rethinking the dominance of secular assumptions in the self-understanding of the social sciences and beyond. We have witnessed a number of turns in the academic disciplines in recent years—linguistic, cultural, institutional, historical—that have heralded substantial shifts in the ways in which many scholars have conceived of what they are doing. Taken together, the essays in this volume suggest that we may now be in the throes of a turn toward renewed engagement with religion as well. This volume addresses the most urgent and compelling questions concerning religion's place in the social sciences and beyond by way of a sustained and critical examination of the notion of the post-secular.

Notes

1. Jürgen Habermas and Joseph Ratzinger, *Dialectics of Secularization: On Reason and Religion* (San Francisco: Ignatius Press, 2006); Jürgen Habermas, "Religion in the Public Sphere," *European Journal of Philosophy* 14 (2006):1–25; Jürgen Habermas and Eduardo Mendieta, *Religion and Rationality: Essays on Reason, God and Modernity* (Cambridge: Polity, 2002). For a helpful overview of various uses of the term "postsecular," see John D. Boy, "What We Talk about When We Talk about the Postsecular," *The Immanent Frame*, March 15, 2011, http://blogs.ssrc.org/tif/2011/03/15/what-we-talk-about-when-we-talk-about-the-postsecular/.

2. That same question prompted an exploratory workshop at the Social Science Research Council (SSRC) in June 2007 on the status of religion in contemporary culture, society, and politics as well as in the work of the contemporary social sciences. A conference at Yale University exploring the post-secular followed a year after the initial SSRC workshop on religion and public life. This volume brings together revised versions of papers presented and discussed during these gatherings.

3. David Jacobson, *Rights Across Borders: Immigration and the Decline of Citizenship* (Baltimore, MD: Johns Hopkins University Press, 1996); Yasemin Nuhoğlu Soysal, *Limits of Citizenship: Migrants and Postnational Membership in Europe* (Chicago: University of Chicago Press, 1994); Damian Tambini, "Post-National Citizenship," *Ethnic and Racial Studies* 24 (2001): 195–217; Martin J. Matustik, *Postnational Identity: Critical Theory and Existential Philosophy in Habermas, Kierkegaard, and Havel* (New York: Guilford Press, 1993).

4. Michel Foucault, *The Order of Things: An Archaeology of the Human Sciences* (New York: Pantheon, 1970); Edward W. Said, *Orientalism* (New York: Vintage, 1979); Jean-François Lyotard, *The Postmodern Condition: A Report on Knowledge* (Minneapolis: University of Minnesota Press, 1984); Paul Feyerabend, *Farewell to Reason* (London: Verso, 1988); David Harvey, *The Condition of Postmodernity: An Enquiry into the Origins of Cultural Change* (Oxford: Blackwell, 1990); Fredric Jameson, *Postmodernism, or the Cultural Logic of Late Capitalism* (Durham, NC: Duke University Press, 1991).

5. Peter L. Berger, "The Desecularization of the World: A Global Overview," in *The Desecularization of the World: Resurgent Religion and World Politics* (Washington, DC: Ethics and Public Policy Center; Grand Rapids, MI: W. B. Eerdmans Pub. Co., 1999), 2.

6. Peter L. Berger, *The Desecularization of the World: Resurgent Religion and World Politics* (Washington, DC: Ethics and Public Policy Center; Grand Rapids, MI:

W. B. Eerdmans Pub. Co., 1992); Emile F. Sahliyeh, *Religious Resurgence and Politics in the Contemporary World* (Albany: State University of New York Press, 1990). For a historical account of this phenomenon, see Jonathan Israel, *The Radical Enlightenment: Philosophy and the Making of Modernity, 1650–1750* (New York: Oxford University Press, 2002).

7.   Ernest Gellner, *Postmodernism, Reason and Religion* (London and New York: Routledge, 1992).

8.   Richard Madsen, *Democracy's Dharma* (Berkeley and Los Angeles: University of California Press, 2007).

9.   For an excellent overview of these developments, see Hans Joas, Wolfgang Knöbl, and Alex Skinner, *Social Theory: Twenty Introductory Lectures* (Cambridge and New York: Cambridge University Press, 2009).

10.   Randall Collins, "Conflict Theory and the Advance of Macro-Historical Sociology," in G. Ritzer, ed., *Frontiers of Social Theory* (New York: Columbia University Press, 1990), 68–87.

11.   One need look no further in Habermas's corpus than to his *Theory of Communicative Action* (vol. 1, *Reason and the Rationalization of Society*, and vol. 2, *Lifeworld and System: A Critique of Functionalist Reason*), in which he gives an account of the fate of normative concerns in light of the effects of Weberian secularization theory (vol. 1) and the emergence of discourse ethics out of Durkheim's notion of "the linguistification of the sacred." See Jürgen Habermas, *The Theory of Communicative Action*, trans. Thomas McCarthy, 2 vols. (Boston: Beacon Press, 1984–1987).

12.   On arguments on the relative autonomy of the state, see Fred L. Block, *Revising State Theory: Essays in Politics and Postindustrialism* (Philadelphia: Temple University Press, 1987); Peter B. Evans, Dietrich Rueschemeyer, and Theda Skocpol, *Bringing the State Back In* (Cambridge and New York: Cambridge University Press, 1985); Ralph Miliband, *The State in Capitalist Society* (London: Weidenfeld & Nicolson, 1969); Nicos Poulantzas, *Political Power and Social Classes*, ed. and trans. Timothy O'Hagan (London: NLB and Sheed & Ward, 1973). For discussions of the cultural turn, see Jeffrey Alexander and Philip Smith, "The Strong Program in Cultural Theory: Elements of a Structural Hermeneutics," in Jonathan H. Turner, ed., *Handbook of Sociological Theory* (*Handbooks of Sociology and Social Research*) (New York: Springer, 2001), 135–150. Victoria E. Bonnell, Lynn Avery Hunt, and Richard Biernacki, *Beyond the Cultural Turn: New Directions in the Study of Society and Culture* (Berkeley: University of California Press, 1999); Frank Parkin, *Marxism and Class Theory: A Bourgeois Critique* (New York: Columbia University Press, 1979); George Steinmetz, *State/Culture: State-Formation after the Cultural Turn* (Ithaca,

NY: Cornell University Press, 1999); Erik Olin Wright, *The Debate on Classes* (London and New York: Verso, 1989).

13. Terrence J. McDonald, *The Historic Turn in the Human Sciences* (Ann Arbor: University of Michigan Press, 1996).

14. Given the disputed character of the concept of religion and the potential breadth of the concept of culture, it is remarkable that the "cultural turn" has lacked almost any attention to religion.

15. Mark Juergensmeyer, "Beyond Words and War: The Global Future of Religion," *Journal of the American Academy of Religion* 78, no. 4 (2010): 882–895.

16. A good deal of this funding is already said to be drying up, however, threatening whatever gains may have been made in the scholarly understanding of religion and in the institutionalization of related academic research.

17. For classic statements of their respective brands of the sociology of religion, see Robert Bellah, *Beyond Belief: Essays on Religion in a Post-traditional World* (Berkeley: University of California Press, 1991), and Peter L. Berger, *The Sacred Canopy: Elements of a Sociological Theory of Religion* (New York: Doubleday, 1967).

18. George M. Marsden, *The Soul of the American University: From Protestant Establishment to Established Nonbelief* (New York and Oxford: Oxford University Press, 1994); Julie A. Reuben, *The Making of the Modern University: Intellectual Transformation and the Marginalization of Morality* (Chicago: University of Chicago Press, 1996).

19. For an extended discussion of this problem, see Philip S. Gorski, "The Return of the Repressed: Religion and the Political Unconscious of Historical Sociology," in Julia Adams et al., eds., *Remaking Modernity: Politics, History, and Sociology* (Durham, NC, and London: Duke University Press, 2005), 161–189.

20. Philip S. Gorski, *The Disciplinary Revolution: Calvinism and the Rise of the State in Early Modern Europe* (Chicago and London: University of Chicago Press, 2003); Gorski, "The Protestant Ethic and the Bureaucratic Revolution," in Charles Camic, Philip Gorski, and David Trubek, eds., *Max Weber's Economy and Society: A Critical Companion* (Palo Alto, CA: Stanford University Press, 2005), 167–296; Sigrun Kahl, "The Religious Roots of Modern Poverty Policy: Catholic, Lutheran, and Reformed Protestant Traditions Compared," *European Journal of Sociology* 46 (2005): 91–126; Philip Manow, *Religion und Sozialstaat: Die konfessionellen Grundlagen europäischer Wohlfahrtsstaatsregime* (Frankfurt am Main and New York: Campus, 2008); Peter Stamatov, "Activist Religion, Empire, and the Emergence of Modern Long-Distance Advocacy Networks," *American Sociological Review* 75

(2010): 607–628; Michael Walzer, *The Revolution of the Saints: A Study in the Origins of Radical Politics* (New York: Atheneum, 1968); Charles Taylor, *Sources of the Self: The Making of Modern Identity* (Cambridge, MA: Harvard University Press, 1992); Michael P. Young, *Bearing Witness against Sin: The Evangelical Birth of the American Social Movement* (Chicago: University of Chicago Press, 2006).

21. Olivier Tschannen, *Les théories de la sécularisation* (Geneva: Droz, 1992).

22. Roger Finke and Rodney Stark, *The Churching of America, 1776–1990: Winners and Losers in Our Religious Economy* (New Brunswick, NJ: Rutgers University Press, 1992); Philip S. Gorski, "Historicizing the Secularization Debate: Church, State, and Society in Late Medieval and Early Modern Europe, ca. 1300–1700," *American Sociological Review* 65 (2000): 138–167; R. S. Warner, "Work in Progress toward a New Paradigm for the Sociological Study of Religion in the United States," *American Journal of Sociology* 98 (1993): 1044–1093.

23. Steve Bruce, *God Is Dead: Secularization in the West* (Oxford and Malden, MA: Blackwell Publishers, 2002); Ray Wallis and Steve Bruce, "Secularization: The Orthodox Model," in S. Bruce, ed., *Religion and Modernization* (Oxford: Oxford University Press, 1992), 8–30. The "differentiation thesis," by contrast, still enjoys broader acceptance.

24. Grace Davie, *Religion in Modern Europe: A Memory Mutates* (Oxford: Oxford University Press, 2000); Andrew M. Greeley, *Religion in Europe at the End of the Second Millennium: A Sociological Profile* (New Brunswick, NJ: Transaction Publishers, 2003). Philip S. Gorski and Ateş Altınordu, "After Secularization?" *Annual Review of Sociology* 34 (2008): 55–85.

25. Richard Dawkins, *The God Delusion* (New York: Mariner Books, 2008); Daniel Dennett, *Breaking the Spell: Religion as a Natural Phenomenon* (New York: Penguin, 2007); Sam Harris, *The End of Faith: Religion, Terror and the Future of Reason* (New York: W. W. Norton, 2004); Christopher Hitchens, *God Is Not Great: How Religion Poisons Everything* (New York: Twelve, 2009). For a different take on religion and public life, see Jim Wallis, *God's Politics: Why the Right Gets It Wrong and the Left Doesn't Get It* (San Francisco: Harper, 2006).

26. José Casanova, *Public Religions in the Modern World* (Chicago: University of Chicago Press, 1994).

27. Edwin S. Gaustad, *Church and State in America* (New York: Oxford University Press, 2003); Philip Hamburger, *Separation of Church and State* (Cambridge, MA: Harvard University Press, 2002).

28. R. S. Warner, "Work in Progress Toward a New Paradigm."

29. Peter L. Berger, Grace Davie, and Effie Fokas, *Religious America, Secular Europe?: A Theme and Variation* (Aldershot, England, and Burlington, VT: Ashgate, 2008); Grace Davie, *Europe, the Exceptional Case: Parameters of Faith in the Modern World* (London: Darton, Longman & Todd, 2002).

30. Emile Durkheim, *The Elementary Forms of Religious Life*, trans. Carol Cosman (Oxford and New York: Oxford University Press, 2001); Thomas Luckmann, *The Invisible Religion: The Problem of Religion in Modern Society* (New York: Macmillan, 1967).

31. Bruce, *God Is Dead*; Bryan R. Wilson, "Secularization: The Inherited Model," in P. E. Hammond, ed., *The Sacred in a Secular Age* (Berkeley: University of California Press, 1985), 9–20.

32. Catherine L. Albanese, *The Spirituality of the American Transcendentalists: Selected Writings of Ralph Waldo Emerson, Amos Bronson Alcott, Theodore Parker, and Henry David Thoreau* (Macon, GA: Mercer University Press, 1988), and Albanese, *A Republic of Mind and Spirit: A Cultural History of American Metaphysical Religion* (New Haven, CT: Yale University Press, 2007).

33. Pierre Bourdieu et al., *The Craft of Sociology: Epistemological Preliminaries* (Berlin and New York: Walter de Gruyter, 1991).

34. Courtney Bender, *Heaven's Kitchen: Living Religion at God's Love We Deliver* (Chicago: University of Chicago Press, 2003); Grace Davie, *Religion in Britain since 1945: Believing without Belonging* (Oxford: Blackwell, 1994); Luckmann, *The Invisible Religion*.

35. Michael J. Buckley, *At the Origins of Modern Atheism* (New Haven, CT: Yale University Press, 1987); Jonathan Israel, *A Revolution of the Mind: Radical Enlightenment and the Intellectual Origins of Modern Democracy* (Princeton, NJ: Princeton University Press, 2010); and Israel, *Radical Enlightenment*.

36. Michael Allen Gillespie, *The Theological Origins of Modernity* (Chicago: University of Chicago Press, 2008); Catherine Wilson, *Epicureanism at the Origins of Modernity* (Oxford: Clarendon Press; New York: Oxford University Press, 2008).

37. Wendy Brown, "The Sacred, the Secular and the Profane: Charles Taylor and Karl Marx," in Michael Warner, Jonathan VanAntwerpen, and Craig Calhoun, eds., *Varieties of Secularism in a Secular Age* (Cambridge, MA: Harvard University Press, 2010), 88–104; Pippa Norris and Ronald Inglehart, *Sacred and Secular: Religion and Politics Worldwide* (Cambridge and New York: Cambridge University Press, 2004).

38. Thomas Bürger, *Max Weber's Theory of Concept Formation: History, Laws, and Ideal Types* (Durham, NC: Duke University Press, 1976); Mark Sydney Cladis, *A*

Communitarian Defense of Liberalism: Emile Durkheim and Contemporary Social Theory* (Stanford, CA: Stanford University Press, 1992); Steven Lukes, *Émile Durkheim: His Life and Work, a Historical and Critical Study* (New York: Harper & Row, 1972); Guy Oakes, *Weber and Rickert: Concept Formation in the Cultural Sciences* (Cambridge, MA: MIT Press, 1988).

39. Max Weber, "Science as a Vocation," in *From Max Weber: Essays in Sociology*, ed. H. H. Gerth and C. Wright Mills (New York: Oxford University Press, 1958),129–158. Leo Tolstoy, *A Confession and Other Religious Writings*, trans. J. Kentish (New York: Penguin, 1988).

40. Gary J. Dorrien, *The Making of American Liberal Theology: Crisis, Irony, and Postmodernity, 1950–2005* (Louisville, KY: Westminster John Knox Press, 2006).

41. H. Richard Niebuhr, *The Social Sources of Denominationalism* (New York: Henry Holt and Co., 1929).

42. Max Weber and Edward Shils, *The Methodology of the Social Sciences* (New York: The Free Press, 1949).

43. John M. Frame, *Apologetics to the Glory of God: An Introduction* (Phillipsburg, NJ: P & R Publishing, 1994); Cornelius Van Til, *Pierre Teilhard de Chardin: Evolution and Christ* (Nutley, NJ: Presbyterian and Reformed, 1966).

44. Alasdair C. MacIntyre, *After Virtue: A Study in Moral Theory* (Notre Dame, IN: University of Notre Dame Press, 1981); MacIntyre, *Whose Justice? Which Rationality?* (Notre Dame, IN: University of Notre Dame Press, 1988); and MacIntyre, *Three Rival Versions of Moral Enquiry: Encyclopedia, Genealogy, and Tradition; Being Gifford Lectures Delivered in the University of Edinburgh in 1988* (Notre Dame, IN: University of Notre Dame Press, 1990).

45. Richard Tuck, *Natural Rights Theories: Their Origin and Development* (Cambridge and New York: Cambridge University Press, 1979); Richard Kraut, *What Is Good and Why: The Ethics of Well-Being* (Cambridge, MA: Harvard University Press, 2007); Iris Murdoch, *The Sovereignty of Good* (New York: Schocken Books, 1971).

46. Hans Georg Gadamer, *Truth and Method* (New York: Crossroad, 1989).

47. Habermas and Ratzinger, *Dialectics of Secularization.*

48. Jürgen Habermas, "Faith and Knowledge," in *The Future of Human Nature* (Malden, MA: Polity, 2003 [2001]), 101–115.

49. Russell T. McCutcheon, *Critics Not Caretakers* (Albany: State University of New York Press, 2001).

50. For central texts, see Giorgio Agamben, *Homo Sacer: Sovereign Power and Bare Life* (Stanford, CA: Stanford University Press, 1998); Agamben, *State of Exception* (Chicago: University of Chicago Press, 2005); Hent de Vries, *Philosophy and the*

Turn to Religion (Baltimore, MD: Johns Hopkins University Press, 1999); de Vries, *Minimal Theologies: Critiques of Secular Reason in Adorno and Levinas* (Baltimore, MD: Johns Hopkins University Press, 2005); and de Vries, *Political Theologies: Public Religions in a Post-Secular World* (New York: Fordham University Press, 2006). Slavoj Žižek, *The Puppet and the Dwarf: The Perverse Core of Christianity* (Cambridge, MA: MIT Press, 2003); Slavoj Žižek and John Milbank, *The Monstrosity of Christ: Paradox or Dialectic?* (Cambridge, MA: MIT Press, 2009); Slavoj Žižek, Eric L. Santner, and Kenneth Reinhard, *The Neighbor: Three Inquiries in Political Theology* (Chicago: University of Chicago Press, 2006).

51. Michael Walzer, *The Revolution of the Saints* and *Exodus and Revolution* (New York: Basic Books, 1986); Charles Taylor, *Sources of the Self* and *A Secular Age* (Cambridge, MA: Harvard University Press, 2007); William E. Connolly, *The Augustinian Imperative: A Reflection on the Politics of Morality* (Thousand Oaks, CA: Sage, 1993), *Why I Am Not a Secularist* (Minneapolis: University of Minnesota Press, 2000), and *Capitalism and Christianity, American Style* (Durham, NC: Duke University Press, 2008); Bonnie Honig, *Democracy and the Foreigner* (Princeton, NJ: Princeton University Press, 2003) and *Emergency Politics: Paradox, Law, Democracy* (Princeton, NJ: Princeton University Press, 2009).

What Is Religion? Categorical Reconfigurations in a Global Horizon

Richard Madsen

Conundrums of an Expanding Horizon

When Matteo Ricci and his Jesuit confreres arrived in China in the late six-teenth century, they encountered an intellectual culture full of sophisticated "teachings" (*jiao*), elaborated through centuries of scholarly discourse, and a social life structured according to meticulously elaborated "rituals" (*li*). None of this fit neatly into the categories these European priests used for articulat-ing the beliefs and practices of their Catholic faith. The "teachings"—which included the teachings of the scholars (what we now call "Confucianism"), the teaching of the Dao (which we now call Daoism), and the teachings of the Buddha (which we now call Buddhism)—were not necessarily about supernatural entities. They were ways of thinking about a natural world that had empirically visible and invisible components (not that different in principle, though different in substance, from a natural science that explains visible phenomena by reference to non-observables). The "rituals" were not segregated into specifically religious institutions. The great state rituals were an integral part of imperial politics. Community festivals, centered on local temples, combined commerce and local politics with enactment of legends and imprecations of spirits—so much so that it is almost impossible to tell where one begins and the other ends. Family rituals, like funerals, were expressions of status, wealth, and power as well as expressions of belief in a world beyond the present.[1]

The categories used by the Jesuits initially did not make much sense to the Chinese either, and the Jesuits attracted hostility based on allegations that they were out to undermine the Chinese political and social order. Gradually, however, both sides learned to speak to each other. Ricci and some of the other Jesuits, extremely talented linguists, learned to read, write, and speak Chinese well enough to win the respect of highly educated late-Ming scholar-officials.[2]

Xu Guangqi, one of the most brilliant scholars and eventually the highest-ranking official, akin to a prime minister, in the Ming court, became a friend of Ricci's, and together they translated Euclid's *Elements of Geometry*, in the process coining the Chinese terms that are used to this day for "line" and "point." Xu Guangqi became a convert to the Catholic faith and opened doors for the Jesuits, enabling them to extend their missionary work to the Chinese elites. But what did he see in this "foreign teaching" (*yang jiao*) of the Jesuits? Was it—to use our modern terms—"religion" or "science"? Xu Guangxi was very interested in acquiring intellectual tools for better measuring natural phenomena (he edited the Chinese rural almanac into the form in which it is still used today) and adopting technology (he advocated new methods of casting cannons for use in defense against invading Manchus). The Jesuits gave him some of these tools, together with their doctrines about the true God. He accepted both. But the Jesuits did not demand any sacrifice of the intellect or any fundamental moral conversion. Xu Guangqi's embrace of Catholic teaching, Jesuit style, was probably less religious than what we commonly mean by conversion today, and his appropriation of Euclid was probably less a matter of pure scientific reason than we would assume it is today.[3]

The Jesuits, on their part, took the teachings and rituals of the scholar-officials (based on the "new learning" of the Song dynasty, which synthesized certain ideas attributed to Confucius and his disciples with ideas derived from Buddhism) to be not at all inconsistent with the Catholic claim to revelation of the one true God. The Jesuits portrayed the scholars' neo-Confucian (a modern term not in use then) teachings as a kind of admirable natural philosophy promoting good morals and a harmonious social order. The Chinese would have to abandon none of these teachings and rituals in order to become followers of the true God. On their part, the scholar-officials who befriended the Jesuits assured them that Chinese teachings were concerned only with this-worldly affairs and contained no religion. This may have been true for the most highly educated, elite scholar-officials. But what about all of the icons of powerful spirits that filled the temples of villages, towns, and cities? What about the elaborate ceremonies for calling on the intercession of these spirits or for placating and warding them off? All of this, a mixture of Daoist and Buddhist as well as Confucian teachings and practices, was central to the lives of at least 99 percent of the population. This, the scholarly elites assured the Jesuits, didn't really count. It was just the confused beliefs of ignorant people. The Jesuits helped invent a name for it: *mixin*, "superstition."[4]

The Jesuit missionaries had European religious rivals, Dominicans and Franciscans, who tended to work closer to the grass roots. There, they discerned plenty of religion—false religion. As they saw it, conversion to the true faith had to entail a complete turning away from such false teachings. They accused the Jesuits of having compromised the Catholic faith by tolerating Chinese beliefs and practices that constituted false religion. The result was the infamous "rites controversy," which was decided against the Jesuits in the early eighteenth century by Pope Clement XI and resulted in the emperor consigning Catholic teaching to the status of a "heterodox teaching" (*xiejiao*) and prohibiting Catholic missionary work in China.

This dispute is an early and classic example of the problems that arise when the horizons of a culture expand.[5] Such expansion takes place under two conditions: first, new forms of communication enable people in one culture to encounter the ways of life and thought of another, and, second, one or both sides are cognitively and morally vulnerable to the effects of the new encounter. One can have the first condition without the second. For example, if one society invades and subdues another through overwhelming power, it is not necessarily morally vulnerable to the new experiences it has gained. The hegemonic society's elites can just dismiss the other's strange customs as primitive and inconsequential. The elites in the invaded society may feel pressured to acquiesce in this condescension and to imitate the beliefs and values of the superior country in order to overcome their weakness and acquire its power. The powerful society in effect has pulled the weaker society into its own horizon. But if the power relationship is relatively symmetrical, if one society encounters another on a relatively equal footing, the cognitive frameworks of both may be vulnerable to destabilizing reinterpretation. The horizons—the scope of possibility of thought and feeling and belief—of both may expand.

This is what happened to the Jesuits and their Chinese interlocutors in the sixteenth and seventeenth centuries. The categories of Counter-Reformation Catholic philosophy and theology were inadequate for grasping the richness of Chinese teachings and rituals. The European categories could not be used to determine unambiguously whether the Chinese were practicing religion or not. This led to disputes (inflamed by institutional rivalries between Jesuits and their competitors) that could be settled only by papal fiat. On the Chinese side too there was confusion about how to understand the moral and intellectual status of the teaching of Catholic missionaries.

Something analogous is happening today when Western scholars try to make sense out of religious cultures in non-Western societies. There are serious disputes not about how to explain certain religious phenomena but about how to define and classify the phenomena themselves. What is this we are looking at? What should we call it? Where does it fit in our mental world? The category disputes cannot be resolved by gathering more information. More information simply intensifies the disputes. The parties in disagreement merely argue past one another.

But doesn't it make a difference that the categories used today for understanding or misunderstanding religion cross-culturally are secular categories, the categories of a supposedly objective social science, rather than the theological categories that were used in the sixteenth century by the Jesuits and their rivals? Perhaps this does not matter as much as social scientists might like to think.

To a significant degree, the sixteenth-century Jesuits thought they were applying worldly categories, not strictly theological categories, to understanding Chinese culture. The worldly categories were of course more closely and more explicitly intertwined with theological discourse than social scientific categories are today. We claim to differentiate our supposedly objective social scientific concepts from our private faith. We claim to have neutral definitions of religion to which atheists as well as adherents of any particular faith could agree. Yet I will argue that our current most commonly used social scientific categories, especially those defining "religion" and the "secular," have been deeply shaped by Western Protestant theological concepts and are still connected with unspoken assumptions about the constitution of the world and the meaning of history—assumptions that are empirically unverifiable and virtually theological.

Disputes about how to handle cross-cultural relations are then too often resolved through arbitrary power plays. In discussing these problems, I will focus mainly on European and American relations with China, because that is what I know best. But I believe that the confusions that spring from expanding horizons are affecting international relations more generally, including, certainly, American relations with the Islamic world.

Today, expanding moral and cognitive horizons are the result not so much of new information—modern communications and modern research have long made available a glut of information about every culture in the world—but of a new vulnerability (at least among elites in Europe and North America) to that information. During the Cold War, the American super-power and its close allies could set the terms for their relationships with the "underdeveloped," non-Western world. North Atlantic intellectuals could write off the beliefs and customs of the non-Western world as forms of back-wardness that would someday surely be overcome by Western-style moder-nity. The preferred framework for understanding such societies was "mod-ernization theory." This assumed that development required a process of economic and political rationalization—that is, an open, self-equilibrating market economy and a technocratically managed bureaucratic state—which would require a separation of religion from economics and politics and its relegation to a sphere of private belief. The rise of new centers of wealth and power in Asia and the Middle East, the breakdown of the American political economy, and the vulnerability of American political power to "asymmetric warfare" waged by weaker countries—all make it less possible for American and European elites to dismiss non-Western cultures as primitive cultures that will eventually be overtaken by modernity. This makes Western intel-lectual horizons vulnerable to these cultures. It lets encounters with those cultures shake up the categories that Western elites have used to understand the world. This often leads, among intellectuals at least, to a weakened faith in the eternal validity of the foundations of their own cultural traditions, which in turn leads to the loss of a stable yardstick with which to assess the Other. Anxieties over this often take the form of harsh public debates over "cultural relativism."

As the expansion of horizons takes place, one of the first categories to be shaken up is religion. Religion is not as central to the discourse of Western intellectuals as it was in the time of Ricci and his fellow Jesuits (although the current "post-secular" discussion argues that it should become more central). Now, the modern social sciences shape most Western "religious studies." As a social science category, "religion" is supposedly agnostic about the ultimate truth of any religious faith. It is separated from other parts of social life, like the economy or polity, and usually considered to be of lesser importance than "secular" matters. It is usually defined in terms of private beliefs in supernatural realities. Research is carried out to show why different beliefs fare better in a religious marketplace.[6] Sometimes research is done to trace the effects of particular beliefs on some aspect of economics or politics. But up until recently, there hasn't been much attention paid to these effects. In 2006, the *American Political Science Review* marked its centenary by publishing a content analysis of articles it had published in the past one hundred years. Prior to 1960, only a single article had treated religion as an independent variable. In the next half century, there were only three other articles (after 1980, when the Iranian revolution and the rise of the religious right in the United States increased the attention paid to religion by observers of international and domestic politics) that put religion at the center of empirical analysis.[7]

Now, however, religion has moved closer to the center of Western consciousness. Global religious movements and religious transformations are becoming too obvious and in some cases too politically consequential to ignore. But there is confusion not only about how to explain this but about what it is that has to be explained.

Take, for example, the frustrations of Western social science when it comes to understanding today's remarkable religious revivals in China. Standard sociology of religion defines religion in terms of subjective beliefs about the supernatural—a matter of individual conscience and consciousness. Such beliefs lead adherents to join congregations of like-minded believers and eventually to create institutions that regulate such associations. This corresponds to a Protestant Christian notion of religion. Determining how and why different kinds of people adopt a preference for different beliefs— what determines the "religious market" for beliefs—becomes a matter for sociological research.[8] How to protect the rights of individual believers to practice their personal faith while keeping them from imposing their beliefs on others becomes an issue for political theory. How different forms of belief might influence believers' spending or saving habits or their proclivity for consistent hard work becomes an issue for economics. One can link the genealogy of such concerns to Durkheim's theories about the sacredness of the modern individual and Weber's theories about the Protestant origins of Western modernity.[9]

But how can one apply such perspectives to modern China, where (contrary to common social scientific predictions in the 1960s and 1970s that a combination of modernization and Communist oppression would obliterate religion) there has been an efflorescence of activities that involve elaborate rituals and myths about good and bad spirits, healing practices that don't fit the paradigm of allopathic medicine, and, sometimes, renewed discussion of ancient texts as part of a deep search for moral meaning? Such activities do not seem purely economic or political or instrumentally social. But many of them are not religious, by the standard definitions of Western social science. They are, first of all, less matters of private belief than public practice. They are rituals that constitute various forms of community life, encompassing villages, or networks of villages, or even whole ethnic regions, like greater Tibet. Those who take part in common rituals seem to have a wide variety of personal understandings about their meaning and a variety of motivations for practicing them. The organization of these forms of activity helps to create and legitimate various forms of political authority and gives structure to matters of economic exchange. The recent development of these practices seems connected with the collapse with another kind of quasi-religious practice—the veneration of Chairman Mao (complete with rituals, recitation of sacred texts, and reports of miracles) that had mobilized the Chinese masses during the Cultural Revolution.

The ritual activities flourishing in China today are often directed not toward otherworldly salvation but toward gaining good health and economic prosperity in this life. Like Chairman Mao in days gone by, the beings venerated in myth or celebrated in ritual today are not really set apart from this world. They are once-living beings with all the virtues and vices found among most humans, and though generally invisible now, they intermingle with their living families and communities, continuing to provide moral examples and to influence mundane affairs.[10]

These activities do not fit into our standard Western social scientific categories of the secular or the religious. They do seem very this-worldly, and that would make them "secular," but they involve the practicing of rituals and telling of myths that at least partly fit our definitions of the religious. They also challenge political as well as intellectual categories in the West. Thus, many local temples in China are nexuses of economic and political power.

Their leadership consists of a committee of the most influential members of the community, and they may carry out extensive economic development projects. Sometimes they are directed by retired Communist Party secretaries, who may actually acquire more power (and money) as temple bosses than they did as political officials.[11] Even some local Catholic communities function in a similar way.[12] Though not completely religious, these local community organizations are not completely political or economic. They defy the standard analytic distinctions Western social scientists use to delineate religion, politics, and economics. It then becomes impossible to carry out a research agenda that would trace the influence of religion on politics or economics. One is confronted with realities that look religious, political, or economic depending on one's point of view but which cannot be broken down into separate components. The same could be said of social life in much of the rest of Asia and indeed in much of the rest of the world outside of the West.[13]

The inability to make analytic distinctions within our present theoretical frameworks leads to practical consequences in international affairs. Is Tibetan Buddhism, for example, a set of privately held religious beliefs that should be protected in the name of universal standards of freedom of conscience, or is it a political movement that threatens the Chinese state by demanding autonomy within China? Is the Dalai Lama a spiritual or a political leader? Where scholars of comparative religion see a religious leader, Chinese political officials see a rival political leader. The Chinese government, officially legitimated through a Marxist, atheist ideology, nonetheless claims the right to take control of Tibetan monasteries and even to determine the reincarnated successor to the Dalai Lama. If one defines religion in the supposedly neutral terms of Western science, Tibetan Buddhism seems to be a genuine religion that would fall under the protection of international declarations of religious freedom. But from the Chinese government's perspective, one is dealing here with a political entity that must be negotiated with by political leaders and confronted with political power. There are many valid reasons to be appalled at the Chinese government's demonization of the Dalai Lama and its subjugation of the Tibetan people. But to frame this problem simply in terms of a discourse about religious freedom will fail to capture the complexities of the Tibetan problem and will not help to create a workable solution to the oppression of the Tibetans.

These are just a few examples of how the opening of new global horizons is now forcing us to name things anew and to alter the frames of reference that give names their meaning.

Narratives Fit for a Global Horizon

Around the world and throughout history, social relationships have been built on shared common meanings—shared symbols for dialogue and dispute about common identities and purposes. "Rational choice" theorists notwithstanding, these meanings can never be reduced to calculations by individuals of how to maximize wealth and power. In modern Western cultures, these shared meanings are articulated (as Max Weber suggested) into specialized spheres for politics, kinship, art, morality, and erotic satisfaction—a field of "warring gods."[14] In many other cultures and periods of history, however, the differences among these spheres of meaning are not as articulated, and, indeed, sometimes they are completely fused. In the modern West, the term "religion" commonly refers to a distinct sphere of life that is connected to but also in tension with other spheres. This term doesn't fit with societies in which such differentiations haven't taken place (or even those in which believers are trying to erase differentiations that have taken place). Yet there certainly is a dimension of meaning in all these cultures that points beyond the practical tasks of everyday life—a dimension that corresponds at least in part to what we today call "religion." If we want to understand this dimension, we have no other choice but to start with conceptual tools that we have developed for the purpose of understanding religion in our own society, even as we aspire to transcend them.

But then, in studying this religious dimension cross-culturally and cross-temporally, we need to make a choice about how high to fly or how deep to dive. By "diving deep," I mean plunging into a micro-detailed description of all the filigreed layering that constitutes the religious-aesthetic-economic-political life of a particular community in a particular place and time. An excellent example of this is Kenneth Dean's account of the festivals that have been revived (or reinvented) in Fujian, China, after having been suppressed during the Cultural Revolution.

> This opens another way of thinking about ritual activities in contemporary Fujian. They produce a world in which the Cultural Revolution both happened

and did not happen. It is not that these ritual practices are remnants or survivals from an earlier time. It is not simply that ritual practices are at once continuous and discontinuous with their past—despite the radical break with the Cultural Revolution, for instance, ritual practices appear renewed. Events like the Cultural Revolution are what allow for ritual practices to serve as a site for the construction of alternative modernities, for modernity's productive failure. While there is no doubt that ritual activities can be interpreted as archaic subterranean forces that subvert the imposition of modern totality, we think that there is another dimension to ritual, another temporal dimension—a looping or spiraling that allows for the folding of worlds with other worlds. This temporality is not merely cyclical, returning constantly to the same point of departure. Its looping or spiraling enables complication, fabulation, or "creative involution." The play of historical continuity and discontinuity in Fujian ritual is not only that of rupture and reinscription (alternative modernity) but also that of folds, loops, and spirals (fabulation and "incomposable" worlds).[15]

Dean here describes contemporary Chinese rituals as a folding of worlds within each other. The people who are carrying around images of local gods in elaborate processions and sacrificing animals and conducting séances and burning huge quantities of incense—these people are also fully invested in the modern market economy (which is where they get the money for these expensive rituals). They work in fancy new office buildings and have the most modern cell phones and watch television programs from around the world on flat screen TVs, and they use computers. All of these activities are folded together with rituals that Western social scientists once thought had been consigned to a "traditional" way of life in the past. But Dean goes beyond the detailed descriptions of local, contextually specific ethnography. He tries to develop a language that expresses the radical particularity of his case. He does this by allowing the linear language of analytic social science to break down into metaphors about folds and spirals and neologisms about "incomposable" worlds.

Such writing, common among postmodern cultural theorists, often has the intended effect of shocking our cognitive frameworks into imagining multidimensional social realities that combine tradition and modernity, religion, economics, and politics in kaleidoscopic shifts that cause the dimensions to flicker into view in constantly changing combinations as the reality is turned around in the mind's eye. As often with postmodern theory, however, the enfolding of language sometimes turns into a conceptual knot, which cuts the theorist off from communication with anyone outside of a narrow scholarly enclave and makes any kind of comparative study virtually impossible. The intricacy into which these linguistic worlds are enfolded makes it difficult to link the particular rituals that Dean describes with those found in other areas of China—or with forms of life that are not so interfolded.

Pushed to an extreme, this can dissolve the religious world into an incoherent mélange of particularisms. But the human mind looks for order, and the social sciences have usually promised to earn their keep by finding conceptual coherence in the face of apparent empirical chaos. Although the expansion of our horizons has indeed destabilized the conceptual frameworks that once underpinned that coherence, the challenge for the social sciences, I believe, is not to give up the quest for coherence but to find better ways of achieving it. So we must fly high enough to see beyond the particularities of different forms of cultural practice.

But how? For some social scientists (more likely in sociology and economics than in cultural anthropology), "flying high" means to abstract some common religious essence that is supposedly present in all cultural forms. Sometimes, this is called "religiosity," and the task then becomes to find out how, under different "religious market" conditions, this religiosity leads to belonging in different groups.[16] The problem is that this religiosity sometimes seems suspiciously like a Western Protestant understanding of religion—a profound feeling of faith deep within one's heart that leads to voluntary association in religious congregations. But this oversimplifies the vast array of cultural practices found throughout the world. For example, many of the Chinese villagers practicing the rituals described by Kenneth Dean may not have any deep personal faith in the presence of the gods. They may participate in rituals because that is what you do when you have been born into a particular community and when you want to celebrate your connections—belonging without belief. Flying high shouldn't lead one to assume that the topography below is flat.

In my view, the best approach is that demonstrated by Robert Bellah in his magisterial new book, *Religion in Human Evolution*.[17] Bellah does indeed fly high, not by abstracting from the particular complexities of human culture but by positing a grand narrative that produces complexity. It is like an account of the earth's geological development that tells how continents became separated, mountains arose, deserts were formed, and so forth. But in Bellah's case, it is an account of the landmarks of human cultures, of the many different ways of finding and celebrating larger meanings to quotidian existence. Bellah's grand narrative extends from the Big Bang down through the evolution of hominoids to the development of the enduring cultural legacies of Israel, Greece, India, and China in the so-called axial age. His accounts of the development of Hebrew monotheism, Greek philosophy, Indian Buddhism, and Chinese Confucianism are full of historical detail, and he sees their development as the result of myriad historical contingencies. They are presented as extremely different in substance, although roughly similar in degree of complexity. Thus, in Bellah's narrative, one cannot simply compare these different forms of religion-culture but can see them as arising from similar processes of cultural development—which, in Bellah's rendering, however, does not necessarily make them morally superior to what came before.

What they have in common is that they are all forms of symbolic activity, and it is the capacity to use and to develop symbols that makes possible the development of human culture. But there are many kinds of symbols and many phases of their development. Bellah distinguishes between broad classes of symbolic development that are expressed in ritual, myth, and theory. The earlier kinds form the condition for the emergence of the development of the later ones, but "nothing is ever lost," and the latter never completely supersede the former. Thus, even when the self-reflexive theoretic develops, it always remains embedded in ritual and myth.[18]

One can connect the developments of ritual, myth, and theory with that of institutions that both enable and depend on them. The various "chapters" of this grand story could stand alone. They represent unique configurations of symbolic practices and institutional structures. Yet the grand narrative enables Bellah to create a coherent and compelling story that unifies an enormous repository of scholarship.

I would argue that this narrative approach is the best way to make intellectual sense out of the vast variety of constantly changing religious cultures that confronts us today. One could also develop mid-level narratives instead of the grand narratives Robert Bellah and Charles Taylor have written. For example, besides describing (however "thickly") the rituals of Chinese village temple worship as Kenneth Dean has brilliantly done, one could show how the interactions between Chinese and Western histories in the twentieth and twenty-first centuries have given those rituals and beliefs their particular shape. And one could show how those same interactions have challenged the ways in which people in Western societies have thought about religion and practiced it.

Part of the narrative can show that in certain particular contexts there has arisen a category of "religion," through which people have sought to name some commonality in particular configurations of ritual, myth, and theory found in different places. In China, for example, Chinese intellectuals borrowed the category of "religion" from the West, and it was used to refer to intellectually articulated forms of Buddhism and Daoism—and to distinguish these from "superstition," another term borrowed from the West that referred to the popular rituals found in village temples. But the narrative could go on to say that in other contexts, the category of "religion" starts to break down as people discover the full dynamic complexity of these different configurations. So today the boundary between "religion" and "superstition" begins to be seen as arbitrary.[19]

An approach based on narrative commits us to diving deep into the rich particularities of human life. The specific symbolic forms of ritual, myths, and theoretical critique are almost infinitely variable as are the relationships among them. Such an approach warns us that the categories used in broad comparative research are always in danger of being frozen—reified—if they are not constantly challenged by the micro-details of closely observed ethnography.

Yet, while careful description shows us the particular differences among religious practices, a narrative approach shows their connections in common origins. For example, in a recent paper, I argued that in the United States some forms of religion that seem radically dissimilar can actually be seen as being connected through origins in a common cultural logic of individualism. And one could make a similar argument that some very dissimilar forms of Chinese religion, such as Pentecostal Christianity and folk Daoism, have also taken shape through common interaction with more communitarian forms of Chinese culture.[20]

This narrative approach can help us avoid facile judgments about the value of all those complex cultural practices that we sometimes call "religion." Much ink has been spilled trying to evaluate whether religion has been good or bad for human flourishing. In its various dimensions, it has been both, with many gradations in between. The kind of analysis I propose can give us a way of describing the full range of the negative and positive contributions of these practices to harmony and conflict, to conservation of the past and innovation in the future. Rituals often bind people together in face-to-face solidarity, but they have also set up conflicts between in-groups and out-groups. Myths provide a narrative justification for rituals and also enable larger solidarities, which have set the stage for larger-scale conflicts between in- and out-groups. The critical reflexivity of the theoretic, which first emerged in what Karl Jaspers calls the "axial age" of the first millennium BCE, has created universal visions of transcendent reality that potentially could unite all of humanity under common spiritual principles.[21] But the universal visions of prophets have quickly been reabsorbed into particular configurations of ritual and myth that have created new exclusive in-groups and sometimes led to intensified fanaticisms and wider conflicts. Furthermore, although ritual and myth are generally conservative, the critical-theoretic breakthroughs made by prophets have certainly impelled radical movements toward imagining and creating new worlds. Yet these breakthroughs have often been mummified by their reabsorption into ritual and myth and become justifications for rejections of further change.

Finally, this narrative approach does not at all assume that religious activity can be separated from other forms of human life. Sometimes it does; sometimes it doesn't. Ritual and myth at least are usually deeply blended into economic and political affairs. In China, for example, the food ritually sacrificed to the ancestors provides a good feast for living family members— in the past, often the only occasion when poor people could add meat to their diets. Myths about sage-kings become part of the ideology for a certain style of emperorship. The prophetic critiques of the axial age provided insight and impetus for separating religious vision from mundane life, but the extraordinary degree of separation that we know in North America and Europe today is a relatively recent development in one part of the world.

Theological Anxieties

The social scientific category of religion is like the canary in the coal mine. Its distress is the first sign of an impending change in atmosphere. On the barely visible boundaries of our horizons is something like theology, a set of fundamental, improvable assumptions about the nature of the world and the direction of history. Of all Western social scientific categories, the category for religion is most closely connected with these. Although better theoretical tools for comparing religious action cross-culturally may help us confront the historical challenges of new global horizons, they are not in themselves sufficient for reestablishing cultural equilibrium—that is, an attitude of confidence in our collective capacity to discern what is truly valuable in our traditions and how to adapt them to the fluid history of a multicultural world. In the end, empirical confusion is connected to quasi-theological questions.

I say quasi-theological because the fundamental assumptions about the nature of the world and the direction of history that are being called into question are not necessarily articulated in "God-talk." As Charles Taylor has shown, in our modern Western "secular age," even believers in a transcendent reality have to recognize that it is intellectually and morally plausible to live with a non-theological or even anti-theological "immanent frame"—and vice versa.[22] Indeed, modern Western culture can be characterized in terms of a particular dialectic between faith and doubt. But with the expansion into a global horizon, the West's forms of dialogue about the immanent and transcendent are themselves thrown into confusion.

One recent expression of this confusion is the debate that started in the 1990s over the late Samuel Huntington's article and book on the "clash of civilizations."[23] Huntington's thesis was that the new lines of military conflict in the post–Cold War world would be between Western Christian, Asian Confucian, and Arab Islamic civilizations. Western civilization, having risen to power on the basis of values rooted in a (Protestant but largely secularized) Christian heritage, would now have to confront other wealthy and powerful societies arising from different and incompatible religious heritages. Huntington meant to arouse anxiety among American leaders about a supposed fundamental challenge to Western identity. He succeeded. An inconclusive debate on the thesis continues to this day, and some proponents of the thesis in the Bush administration used it to justify their global war on political Islamist movements. (Huntington himself rejected this use of his work.) The thesis was unsupported and unsupportable by empirical evidence. It gained its rhetorical power by evoking the assumption that Western values were incompatible with other values. Though expressed in terms of the "immanent frame," this derives from theological assumptions: Western identity has its origins in a jealous God, who will tolerate no other gods before Him.

Rejoinders to the Huntington thesis are, in the end, arguments based less on empirical research and more on alternative theologies. One can take the position that there can be multiple revelations. (Perhaps without being aware of it, the Jesuit China missionaries of the sixteenth and seventeenth centuries were pointing toward such a position. This was one of the reasons the Pope rejected them in the end.) The one God has been revealed in many different guises in many different societies, and all of these guises are more or less adequate and inadequate. This would imply that an ecumenical sort of moral and religious universalism is possible. We are in the end all the same, and we can become enriched through our differences and find moral common ground while still retaining our particular historical images of God. Another quasi-theological response would be polytheism. There isn't any one true God, the basis for unity of the human race. There are multiple gods, which hold sway in different areas and whose contentions ultimately decide the fate of mortals.

Although they represent unverifiable assumptions about the ultimate reality of the world, these quasi-theologies can establish a mood and set a direction for empirical research. The clash-of-civilizations vision inspires and sustains a Weberian-style agenda of uncovering the cultural forces that make civilizations different and demonstrating the religious bases for the West's historical ascendency.[24] A polytheistic theology might sustain something like postmodern scholarship. And the notion of multiple revelations could lead to an investigation into world history like that proposed by Karl Jaspers, who wrote about the rise of parallel, history-shaping visions of transcendence in Israel, Athens, India, and China during the first millennium BCE. One's choice of one or another of these empirical research agendas for comparative research would depend on a (usually unconscious) embrace of one of these quasi-theological visions.

If one believes that there is no unifying spiritual destiny for human life—that what we have in common are symbol-making capacities that we can use to construct an infinite multitude of identities and affiliations—then we might emphasize the ritual and mythic parts of this framework. From this vantage point, religion often looks like an immense variety of particular practices that can never coalesce. While criticizing earlier scholars such as Max Weber and Michel Granet for trying to uncover an underlying logic to Chinese religion, some contemporary anthropologists express admiration for the sheer creativity of Chinese polytheism. In southern China, some communities worship more than a thousand gods, and their religious landscape is like that of ancient Greece, with its pantheon of deities that reflected in a larger-than-life way the full range of human virtues and vices.[25] There is an implication that if the West could learn to be more like this, we wouldn't have the monotheistic fanaticism that provokes crusades. In the West, various New Age movements take this to heart, although they appropriate their polytheism in terms of Western cultural forms of expressive individualism.[26]

If one is or wants to be committed to a belief or hope that there is a unifying spiritual destiny for the human species, one might tilt the emphasis toward those sparks of prophetic insight that took place during the axial age and that form a permanent, if often repressed, heritage of the Abrahamic faiths as well as Buddhism, Confucianism, and philosophical universalism. Religious movements to this day still draw upon those transcendent visions in order to overcome the constant pull of ritual and myth toward parochialism.[27]

If one is committed to a monotheistic orthodoxy, one may make the case that the prophetic breakthroughs of the axial age that led to the religious foundations of one's own culture were more complete and more transcendent than breakthroughs that happened elsewhere. One can, for example, search for the ways that Greek philosophy was more universalistic than, say, Confucian philosophy. Or one can make the case that the Protestant Reformation fulfilled the biblical promise of transcendence more fully than anything that happened in the Islamic world—and make the case that the Islamic world needs to undergo a similar kind of reformation if it is to become fully modern.[28]

Finally, one might look to the reachings toward transcendence that began in the axial age, and have been periodically renewed ever since, as signs of universal human yearning toward a common but ever elusive goal. Here, one would emphasize the potential for breakthroughs toward transcendence that have occasionally, often unpredictably, become actualized in religious life in all the major civilizations since the axial age—and critically reflect on the tension that always exists within communities between wanting to express and wanting to repress this yearning. One could also emphasize the ways in which this yearning always seems to push beyond the language that makes it possible. "Words strain, crack and sometimes break, under the burden, under the tension. . . ."[29] Then the narrative of the development of religions in history becomes a story about a search for meaning that is always necessary but never able to be satisfied. A *Waiting for Godot* in which human tragedy and comedy intermingle in infinitely varied ways.

But movement along any of these paths requires the settlement of accounts about one's ultimate concerns, something that worldly research alone cannot resolve. The restoration of spiritual equilibrium after the expansion of global horizons may depend on confluences of cultural currents beyond our control. For all of our efforts to take control of our destiny, we still have to watch and wait.

Notes

1. Mayfair Yang, ed., *Chinese Religiosities* (Berkeley: University of California Press, 2008).

2. George H. Dunne, SJ, *Generation of Giants: The Story of the Jesuits in China in the Last Decades of the Ming Dynasty* (Notre Dame, IN: University of Notre Dame, 1962); Jonathan Spence, *The Memory Palace of Matteo Ricci* (New York: Viking Penguin, 1984); George Minamiki, *The Chinese Rites Controversy: From Its Beginnings to Modern Times* (Chicago: Loyola University Press, 1985); D. E. Mungello, ed., *The Chinese Rites Controversy: Its History and Meaning* (Sankt Augustin, Germany: Monumenta Serica, 1994); and Donald F. St. Sure, SJ, trans., *100 Roman Documents concerning the Roman Rites Controversy (1645–1941)* (San Francisco: Ricci Institute, University of San Francisco, 1992).

3. If one sharply distinguishes "faith"—a belief in things unseen—from an instrumental scientific reason that uses empirical research to discover systematic means for getting better control over one's world, then Xu Guangqi's conversion doesn't look like pure faith. Xu Guangxi accepted the Jesuit teaching at least in part because he thought it could give him intellectual tools with which to improve agriculture and create better military technology. But there was certainly more than intellectual rationality at stake here. Acceptance of the Jesuit teaching involved a significant change in worldview—and, for that matter, in moral discipline. To become a Catholic, Xu Guangxi had to give up his concubines and remain faithful to one wife.

4. Kristofer Schipper, *The Taoist Body* (Berkeley: University of California Press, 1993), 16.

5. Hans-Georg Gadamer, *Truth and Method*, trans. J. Weinsheimer and D. G. Marshall, 2nd rev. ed. (New York: Crossroad, 1989).

6. A good example of what counts as "mainstream" sociology of religion is Rodney Stark and William Sims Bainbridge, *A Theory of Religion* (New Brunswick, NJ: Rutgers University Press, 1996). This highly influential work exemplifies the approach outlined in the above paragraph. Many of the chapters in this book, in contrast, represent challenges to the mainstream view.

7. Kenneth D. Wald and Clyde Wilcox, "Getting Religion: Has Political Science Rediscovered the Faith Factor?" *American Political Science Review* 100, no. 4 (Nov. 2006): 523–529.

8. A good example of this approach applied to China is Fenggang Yang, "The Red, Black, and Grey Markets of Religion in China," *Sociological Quarterly* 47 (2006): 93–122.

9. Emile Durkheim, *The Elementary Forms of Religious Life*, trans. Karen E. Fields (New York: The Free Press, 1995); Max Weber, *The Protestant Ethic and the Spirit of Capitalism*, trans. Talcott Parsons (New York: Charles Scribner's Sons, 1958).

10. Lizhu Fan, James Whitehead, and Evelyn Whitehead, *Sociology of Religion—Religion and China* (Beijing: Current Affairs Press, 2010); cf. also Fenggang Yang and Graeme Lang, eds., *Social Scientific Studies of Religion in China: Methodologies, Theories, and Findings* (Leiden and Boston: Brill, 2011).

11. Adam Chau, *Miraculous Response: Doing Popular Religion in Contemporary China* (Stanford, CA: Stanford University Press, 2006)

12. Richard Madsen, *China's Catholics: Tragedy and Hope in an Emerging Civil Society* (Berkeley: University of California Press, 1998).

13. For that matter, there are aspects of Western religious culture, such as some forms of evangelical Christianity that have been fused with local economic, political, and social life in the American South, that fit this "non-modern" or "non-Western" model. However, the theoretical straitjackets of mainstream social science make it difficult to recognize these forms.

14. Max Weber, "Religious Rejections of the World and Their Directions," in *From Max Weber*, ed. H. H. Gerth and C. Wright Mills (New York: Oxford University Press, 1947), 329-359.

15. Kenneth Dean and Thomas Lamarre, "Ritual Matters," in *Traces 3: Impacts of Modernity*, ed. T. Lamarre (Hong Kong: Chinese University of Hong Kong Press, 2003), 257–284.

16. See the many works influenced by Rodney Stark and William Sims Bainbridge, *A Theory of Religion*.

17. Robert N. Bellah, *Religion in Human Evolution* (Cambridge, MA: Harvard University Press, 2011).

18. This of course is controversial. Philosophers committed to the Enlightenment project, such as Jürgen Habermas, would want to argue that theoretical reason can supersede ritual and myths, although some of the essential truths expressed by the latter can be translated into rational-theoretic terms. But other prominent

philosophers, such as Charles Taylor, would agree with Bellah that the modern theoretic does not lose its connections to ritual and myth.

19. See Peter Van der Veer, "Smash Temples, Burn Books: Comparing Secularist Projects in India and China," in *Rethinking Secularism*, ed. Mark Juergenesmeyer, Craig Calhoun, and Jonathan VanAntwerpen (New York: Oxford University Press, 2011), 270-281.

20. See Lian Xi, *Redeemed by Fire: The Rise of Popular Christianity in Modern China* (New Haven, CT: Yale University Press, 2010).

21. Karl Jaspers, *The Origin and Goal of History* (New Haven, CT: Yale University Press, 1953).

22. Charles Taylor, *A Secular Age* (Cambridge, MA: Harvard University Press, 2007).

23. Samuel J. Huntington, "The Clash of Civilizations?" *Foreign Affairs* 72:3 (Summer 1993): 22–49.

24. Hans Joas, "The Axial Age Debate as Religious Discourse," in *The Axial Age*, ed. Robert N. Bellah and Hans Joas (Cambridge, MA: Harvard University Press, forthcoming 2012); Heiner Roetz, "The Axial Age Theory between Philosophy and Religion, Sociology, and History: With a Look at the Normative Discourse in Axial Age China," in Bellah and Joas, *The Axial Age*.

25. Kenneth Dean, "Local Ritual Traditions of Southeast China: A Challenge to Definitions of Religion and Theories of Ritual," *Social Scientific Studies of Religion in China*, ed. Yang and Lang, 133-162.

26. Richard Madsen and Elijah Siegler, "The Globalization of Chinese Religions and Traditions," in *Chinese Religious Life*, ed. David A. Palmer, Glenn Shive, and Philip L. Wickeri (New York: Oxford University Press, 2011), 227–240.

27. Richard Madsen, "The Future of Transcendence: A Sociological Agenda," in Bellah and Joas, *The Axial Age*

28. Roetz, "The Axial Age Theory."

29. T. S. Eliot, *Burnt Norton*, in *Four Quartets* (1944).

CHAPTER THREE

Things in Their Entanglements

Courtney Bender

> . . . we must begin with things in their *complex entanglements* rather than
> with simplifications made for the purpose of effective judgment and action;
> whether the purpose is economy or dialectical esthetic or moral. The sim-
> plifications of philosophic data have been largely determined by apolo-
> getic methods, that is by interest of dignifying certain kinds and phases
> of things. So strong is this tendency that if a philosopher points to any
> particular thing as important enough to demand notation, it is practically
> certain that some critic will shift the issue from whether the denoted thing
> is found to be as he has described it to be, to the question of value.
> —John Dewey, *Experience and Nature*

Few aspects of social life seem more entangled within the project of modernity than religion. This is evident, if nowhere else, in the current far-rang-
ing discussions about religions, the secular, and the post-secular within the
social sciences and humanities. But while such entanglements now seem
self-evident, this was not the case even fifteen years ago.[1] What has trans-
pired to make religion such a lodestone, and such an interesting problematic
for the social sciences once more? What, furthermore, might sociology contribute to these renewed discussions?[2] Dewey's phrases encourage us to consider answering this question with an approach that takes religion's entanglements as a productive empirical and methodological beginning point.

Taking the post-secular seriously either as a mode of theorizing religion or as a statement of the "realities" of the role of religion in social worlds should be followed (more frequently than it has been) with empirical studies and methodological stances that tackle the various entanglements (theoretical, methodological, or empirical) where religion and the secular take shape in the modern world.

The observation that prompts this paper is that while sociologists have begun to embark on a project of retheorizing religion and the secular—with great positive effect—most empirical research on religion does not incorporate these theoretical turns into its methods or choices of sites to study. To put it simply, most studies of religion, whether qualitative or quantitative, historical or comparative, begin and end in unambiguously, obviously, religious spaces. There are few studies of religion in settings, spaces, or interactions that are not religious, and likewise rarely any formal discussion of the ways that sociologists identify the groups, actors, traditions, or the like that effectively frame religion's boundaries. Given that most scholars are understandably not interested in internecine squabbles about the meaning or definition of religion, or in troubling standard analytic categories, we should nonetheless acknowledge that one of the consequences of the post-secular turn, and many of the questions that it elicits, revolve around precisely these issues.

In this essay, I use a series of fragments from recent research to advocate for a modest and entirely non-novel direction for future research, wherein sociologists studying religion pay attention to the ways that choices about field sites (broadly defined) simplify and answer questions about religion's location in modern life—before our theoretical projects begin to even take shape. With these fragments, I suggest what such a turn might look like and how focusing on the inevitable and present historical, scholarly, and empirical entanglements that shape our scholarly work might add new ideas, sites, and theoretical frames to the work that we do.

To begin with, things in their "complex entanglements" means, then, that we are aware from the outset that the ability to observe some groups, individuals, and experiences (or practices, discourses, and institutions) as religious and others as not religious marks us as participants in an ongoing set of procedures wherein these distinctions are made real. This is, in part, what the post-secular turn already takes into account. As many have noted, religion and secularity are a relational pair, with each taking on its peculiar but very real potency in social life in different historical national and state contexts. Analyses, studies, and theories of the dynamic interaction between religion and the secular furthermore challenge scholars to proceed with their analysis in a way that takes these dynamics into account as partially constitutive of their own research. In other words, post-secular studies do not lead researchers to a new, less problematic, less historically shaped, less politically embedded analytic of "religion" but rather demand that scholars approach religion and the secular with the understanding that these complex dynamics are constitutive of both.

The value of these studies is clear. Yet, as we can also see, the theoretical insights have not on the whole altered sociological apprehension of their subject in the world. With few exceptions, sociologists who study religion or the secular continue to conduct empirical inquiries in what we might call self-evidently religious communities, practices, objects, texts, and traditions. There are, of course, many issues to consider in choosing the appropriate analytical space where we conduct our research. Yet it seems likely that taken-for-granted modes of determining the best place to study or understand religion—and its positions in modern life—currently limit our collective ability to seek satisfactory answers to the questions posed by the post-secular turn. Beginning with self-evidently religious places and individuals may indeed show us some of the complex dynamics of religious-secular binaries, but they do not offer ways of theorizing or analyzing some of the more challenging aspects of modern religion, especially those elements that seem to thrive "outside" of the milieus and spaces that are normally deemed religious.

From Complexity to Entanglement

As this volume's introduction notes, over the last decades, ethnographic and historical research has generated a critique of earlier frameworks for studying religion by highlighting the complexity of religious practice and identity, shaped in dynamic interactions between communities, individuals, secular structures, and religious traditions. Recent ethnographic analyses of living religious communities contribute greatly to our shared understandings of how religion in modern life is embodied, ritualized, and practiced, both in relation to religious traditions and authority and, likewise, within unequal interactions with secular structures and discourses. To note two well-known examples, both R. Marie Griffith's and Saba Mahmood's research with religious women (in the United States and Egypt, respectively) demonstrates how religious women shape their experiences together and separately, not only in dynamic conversation with a religious tradition and set of practices, but also as part of an implicit and explicit critique of secular conceptions of agency and freedom.[3] Such complex cases of religious self-formation not only make different kinds of religious activity visible to us but also challenge directly many of the implicit notions of belief, agency, identity, and religion that are loaded into social scientific approaches to religion.[4]

Such studies obliquely raise questions about the spaces of religious production. In calling attention to the dynamic shaping of religion within interactions with secular meanings and interests, they also suggest a variety of additional settings in which scholars can evaluate the shape of religion in modern life. These go beyond the settings that are prima facie religious and that anchor all but a few recent ethnographies of religion in modern life.[5] An approach that begins with entanglements designates the shifts that studies focused on religious complexity often speak to yet do not follow out. It can lend itself to study of the kind of religious actions and meanings that are shaped or produced in a range of secular institutions, discourses, and practices. It may, in addition, lead to further reflection on the interactive processes (or entanglements) of academic and lay understandings of both the religious and the secular. The questions posed by the post-secular turn are as much about method as they are about theory and should enter into our considerations: How do we know what is religious, and how do we know where religions and religiosities are located, observed, reproduced? How do our procedures for choosing demonstrate a tangled space of religion naturally observed and religion analytically represented?

A further reason for focusing on entanglements emerges in Gauri Viswanathan's observation that "secularism, in defining itself against religion, has contributed to homogenizing religion's variegated history." This history, she writes, "nonetheless continues to exert influence in subtle, oblique ways that escape the secular understanding."[6] With this in mind, beginning with entanglements allows us to write and speak of the developments and alterations that secularism has made to the "oblique and variegated history" of heterodox religions including not only the "homogenizing" effects, on one hand, but the powers to create "new" spiritual forms, on the other. Viswanathan notes that certain secular forms have a role in creating new forms of religious surplus that are often marked (or experienced) as heterodox and enchanted. These forms do not easily become enfolded into either religious or secular divisions: they are claimed by neither, recognizable as neither (or potentially as both). These histories, for Viswanathan, are spaces for exploration of religion's and secularity's resonant power.

Three fragments from recent work on spirituality in the United States demonstrate how these methodological moves shift the mode of inquiry about religion in modern life.[7] I conducted this research in Cambridge, Massachusetts, between 2001 and 2003, and traced the institutional and organizational spaces where individuals could learn to practice spirituality. Although most sociological study of "spirituality" focuses on its individualistic character, I wanted to investigate how and where people learned to be religious individuals and to trace (so far as possible) the institutional and organizational dynamics of American-style "spirituality." Cambridge was my choice of setting both for matters of convenience and because it was (and is) a heterogeneous, urban, and liberal city: a place where I expected I would find diverse activities and networks. As I note in the volume based on this research, Cambridge's history of institutions and groups invested in "spiritual" explorations was not an initial interest but became more so as I conducted research. I began to investigate further how the genealogies of sociological concepts such as spirituality and experience shaped my investigations and those of others as well. Briefly put, my opening question of how spirituality is organized prompted questions about why spirituality chronically figures as such a disorganized, nonsocial thing in both public discourse and scholarly research. Answering these questions led to sites of entanglement, sometimes unexpectedly.

Each of the following fragments introduces a different set of entanglements encountered during research. Individually, they denote different places where practice, theory, and definitions relationally take shape through designations of either distinction or similarity. Read together, these fragments highlight distinct yet interlinked practices and conceptions that give power to a milieu in which "spirituality" takes particular shape as a naturally present category for Americans, including American scholars.

First Fragment: How "Spirituality" Appears Disentangled from Religion in Sociological Discourse

A first fragment considers how "spirituality" and "religion" so rarely appear to be entangled in sociological discourse. Although studies of "religion and spirituality" make it very clear that these terms are not necessarily oppositional (while many claim to be "spiritual but not religious," many more claim to be "spiritual *and* religious"), in sociological literature, "religion" indicates communal identity and interactions, authority, and tradition, and "spirituality" indicates individual experience, novelty, and antiauthoritarian impulses.[8] How did spirituality become autonomous as an analytical concept, and what (or whose) purposes does its autonomy serve? These questions are all the more perplexing as we see that spirituality, while emerging in sociological discourse as an autonomous social fact, is nonetheless difficult to locate in social processes or groups.

The autonomy of "spirituality" is built on two notions of religion that are endemic to our conceptions of both religion and modern society: first, that individuals can in fact have socially and culturally unmediated religious experiences and, second, that modern Western societies can be distinguished from others for exhibiting higher degrees of institutional differentiation and "rationalization." Individuals are able to move between spheres and institutions, and those spheres or institutions are increasingly organized according to nonoverlapping lines of discourse, rationality, and purpose. The secularization and restriction of the production of religion to the sphere of the religious—a central narrative in the story of sociology—articulates that any religious activity, action, or purpose located "outside" of the religious institutional field is an import (for example, carried by individuals or groups) rather than as (alternatively) produced or embedded within the discourse, practices, or structures of nonreligious fields.[9] Within this framework, the resonance of a concept of the "spiritual" as religiosity organized and reproduced within individual consciousness reinforces attention to (or dependence on) the individual's experience and autonomy as a source of religious production within increasingly differentiated, secular social fields.

The logic that links modernity, religious individualism, and spirituality is apparent within many of the recent treatments of spirituality, but we can also turn to classical formulations in sociology to find this at work.

For example, Troeltsch's church-sect theory also includes a "third type" of Christian organization, the "mystic," which "has no impulse towards organization at all." This type is uniquely interesting to Troeltsch: while he sees that the impulse to individual mysticism is present throughout Christian history, modernity and its challenges shift the relationship between individual and institutional authority and present the new potential for mysticism to break free of religious institutions. No longer embedded in the structure of the church, it offers a new trajectory. According to Troeltsch, however, this potential, without grounding in institutions, leads to religious individualism and a-religion.[10]

Troeltsch views "individualistic mysticism" as fundamentally antagonistic to the "real nature of Christianity." He argues that its links with "Romanticism" and other theories favored by the liberal, educated classes are troublesome, not because they emphasize individual experience per se (as many other forms of "Christian mysticism" did through history), but rather because they "possess neither the sense of solidarity nor the faith in authority which this requires."[11] He continues, "In its depreciation of fellowship, public worship, history and social ethics this type of 'spiritual religion,' in spite of all its depth and spirituality, is still a weakened form of religious life." It "must be maintained in its concrete fullness of life by churches and sects, if an entirely individualistic mysticism is to spiritualize at all. Thus we are forced to this conclusion: this conception of Christianity . . . assumes the continuance of other and more concrete living forms of Christianity as well."[12]

These concerns are not Troeltsch's alone, nor are they disconnected from other aspects of his theory (and those of others) of religion's declining place in a secular modern world. The receding place of religion means not that institutional religious authority loses its public authority over individuals but that religion now furthermore no longer influences or intersects other fields. Law, science, economics, the arts, and other fields of human life become "demystified" as they develop their own rational bases for verification and legitimacy.[13] This narrative of institutional secularization was reinforced by the development of a variety of concepts including, arguably, the concept of a noninstitutionally derived mystical identity. Troeltsch and others believed that mysticism led to an evacuation of religious identity and toward individual secularity. As this has not been the evident consequence of the turn toward mystical spirituality, we might renew the question about whether mystical identities are produced and look for the sites of their production. As such, we can question whether the development of the "mystical" in sociological analysis provided a way of explaining the types of religious and enchanted activity (practice, production) that flourished in what scholars designated as secular. That is, we might consider whether it became possible to observe the religious practices produced or sustained within secular institutions as mere residue or shadows of a vibrant religious past, on the one hand, or, on the other, as imports by individuals who carried religious ideas into secular spaces (which in turn were deemed weak, given the view that they could be sustained only by a link to "concrete living forms" of religious institutions).

When we begin, in contrast, with the observation that spirituality in the United States is shaped through and within religious discourses and practices that are produced within numerous institutional fields including the religious and the secular, we move far from the description of spirituality as a perennial product of disconnected individuals. It is, rather, a set of historically embedded, reproduced, and changing ideas. We can pin scholarly neglect of these elements not on spirituality's esoteric or subterranean nature but rather on predominant theoretical logics of secularization that implicitly and explicitly deflect sociological attention from the continued circulation of religious meanings, yearnings, and imaginations in spaces understood to be secular.

Fieldwork investigating the active production of spirituality took me to medical and alternative medical practitioners and settings, the arts (both "professional" and "amateur"), and various religious institutions and groups. The institutional fields (medicine, the arts, religion) have undergone profound and complicated changes over the past century and have frequently been the sites of inquiry into secularization and (in different ways) the secular. Whatever we can say about them now, it is hardly disputable that mainstream medical groups and associations currently embrace modalities that were for several generations *explicitly deemed* to be wholly in error. Likewise, while the field of the arts itself was erected in distinction from "religious art," artists and art historians have in recent years questioned the validity, reality, or worth of presuming that the field is "spiritually" arid: a current resurgence in interest in the "spiritual" in modern art among art professionals is another indicator. These changes are real, even if recent events also remind us that such changes are not unidirectional, final, or complete.[14]

Absent a robust vocabulary and historical sensitivity to these changes, or ways to talk about these changes as unfinished projects of secularization, inquiries like this certainly might sound like claims for the re-sacralization of social life. This is not the intention. Rather, I would suggest that we begin with the possibility that these spaces have not fully finished their stated business of secularization and trace instead the spaces where various secular reformulations were accomplished and where they became amenable to the production of religious, transcendent, or enchanted actions, practices, and engagements.

Focusing on the manner in which the religious (or what we have herein been calling the "spiritual") is not only lived but produced within nonreligious "sectors" or "fields" lays open numerous settings for investigation and contributes to further investigation not only of religion's entanglements in social life but also of the sociological considerations of religion's entanglements with civic virtue and politics. Michael Schudson argues that the standard, normative view of "civil society" understands civil action only as those acts that are sustained over time, collective, and require work and are not self-interested. Subsequently, this view of civic life remains within a narrow and normative frame. He asks what civic life might look like if we were to include acts that are transitory and singular, the "individual (and insufficiently collective)," the "cheap and convenient," and the "self interested." Rather than bemoaning the lack of the civic, in other words, we need to take a closer look at the types of persons and institutions that we expect are necessary for societies like ours to thrive and compare them closely and in relation to those institutions that may in fact be shaping the civic, albeit in ways that do not conform to our expectations.[15]

Schudson's contrarian argument provokes similar investigation into the shape of the religious, especially as we have long held positive associations between civic and religious life. Religious groups, like their civic counterparts, are generally defined as communities sustained over time and, at least insofar as they are non-profit, not self-interested. In contrast, the "spiritual" appears as individual, self-interested, cheap (or, at least, for sale), and transitory. Studying "spirituality" does not require that we embrace "individualism" or "convenience" as religious goods. But it does raise questions about how sociologists over many generations have reproduced certain practices of distinguishing religion from other kinds of actions and organizations and how such distinctions have mattered not only to sociological analysis but, more broadly, to scholarly and lay evaluations of the religious and its proper political mobilization.

Second Fragment: The Surprising Sociological Career of "Religious Experience"

A second set of entanglements comes into view when we observe that American religious historians have long argued that "contemporary spirituality" is deeply entwined with American metaphysical, harmonial, and spiritual religious traditions.[16] Although most of these studies remain focused on nineteenth- and early twentieth-century materials, a number evocatively suggest how contemporary projects carry on these traditions. More importantly, many of these studies suggest that these traditions have been carried forward by both religious professionals and the academic study of religion as much as they are by popular religious practices. These studies point repeatedly to a much broader set of histories and, likewise, to a much less stable institutional space in which investigations of contemporary spirituality might take place.

Some of these pasts were evident to me as I continued my research: in traversing the spaces of early twenty-first-century Cambridge, Massachusetts, I frequently brushed against living examples of spirituality's nineteenth- and twentieth-century antecedents. Increasingly aware of these historical fragments and their resonance with Cambridge's local stories and architecture, I nonetheless wondered whether these histories mattered to the people I met at the Seven Stars esoteric bookshop or whom I witnessed "soul singing" at a local arts festival. How, if at all, did Cambridge's past explorations and experiences matter to the present lives of those I interviewed? For whom did it matter, for example, that hundreds of mesmerists practiced in and around Boston in the 1800s, or that William James had taken to the stand to defend their right to practice?[17] Did the people who attended an occasional lecture at the Spiritualist Temple or who enrolled at yoga classes at the Theosophical Society think about these places or why the activities they pursued were so frequently lodged in these settings? Most of my informants appeared to be uninterested in these pasts, and while some were aware of various historical figures and knew a bit about them, they seemed quite tangential to my interviewees' immediate interests. When my informants mentioned these figures, it was not to place themselves within a shared historical tradition but rather to call attention to mystical bonds that connected them, ahistorically, as seekers of perennial and esoteric "truths."

Rather than recover the "lost" history of contemporary American spirituality via my work in Cambridge, I began to inquire further into how, and why, this past is so regularly lost and recovered by scholars. Further, I began to inquire into what is at stake in the processes that recombine and rejoin strains of American religiosity to either historical or perennial narratives.[18] A key element in these processes, for both scholars and practitioners (for whom the past similarly comes into view and disappears), was the representation of religious experience. Experiences of multiple kinds—including numinous, unexpected experiences, mystical experiences of "flow," and daily synchronicities, dreams, and the like—shaped the worlds in which spiritual practitioners lived. People worked to embody and elicit felicitous circumstances for experience, and they read and lived relationships with others as well as their politics and their aesthetic sensibilities through experiential lenses. They pondered the meaning of their individual experiences, discussing their meanings and arguing about their authenticity with friends and fellow travelers. As they did so, they also debated whether such experiences can be initiated through individuals' actions. Their practices of narrating, embodying, and interpreting experience signaled their participation within a tradition. These practices, focused on the immediacy of experience and a perennial truth underlying any particular experience, positioned individuals within a tradition of experience that flourished in part by minimizing attention to their own historical pasts.

These religious practices have been difficult to locate sociologically, given that with few exceptions sociological analysis of spirituality and religious experience mirrors spiritual practitioners' claims that their conceptions and practices are self-generated and individualistic. Sociologists who study spiritual practitioners using individually centered research tools (either interviews or survey methods) have little leverage in critically assessing the degree to which individualistic narratives reflect or capture the social worlds in which such narratives and expressions become most salient; spiritual practitioners' claims in turn reinforce sociological assumptions that there is little payoff in studying the "lived religious practices" or social worlds of spiritual practitioners.[19] Arguably, our collective scholarly view that contemporary spirituality is more akin to a "condition" than a "tradition" (a view that many spiritual practitioners will wholeheartedly share) is at least in part a consequence of the methods we have chosen for studying it.

While my larger project mapped out many of the practices of experiential spirituality, we might turn here to consider the consequence of sociology's interesting uses of a particular frame of religious experience. At first blush, it appears that sociologists have ceded the territory of religious experience to other disciplines (for example, psychology). Although sociologists do not study religious experience, a particular notion of religious experience sometimes surfaces within sociological writings as an event that stands outside the sociological purview. The historical development of "religious experience" as an ambiguous, individual event inaccessible to sociological investigation presents an opening for sociologically meaningful "religious individualism" to emerge and take shape as a category of religious expression. We can pay attention to the impact of particular formations of religious experience on sociological understandings of religion.

The individual, nonmediated religious experience that figures prominently in contemporary spiritual practice and in sociological discussions of religion is a "relatively late and distinctively Western" concept.[20] Over the past century, scholarly and popular understandings of "religious experience" have been transformed into naturally, biologically or psychologically occurring events. The varied strains of scientific investigation into "religious experience" make it difficult to chart a single trajectory in this development. But we might for the moment consider how even recent scientific investigations of religious experience are shaped by earlier theological responses to Enlightenment critiques of religion. In response to Enlightenment arguments that highlighted the deficits of religious argumentation for explaining the natural world or grounding moral reasoning, theologians began to identify the site of religious authority in the heart rather than the head. Religious experience and its outcomes, located in the emotions and other religious "organs," became the key site from which religious authority developed. Various thinkers identified the core of religion, embedded in these sensory and experiential parts of the human body and psyche, as distinct from and unassailable by reason. Martin Jay notes that the transformation shifted a broadly based, European notion of religion as "*adherence* to belief, either rational or willed, in certain propositions about God and His creation" to a *property* or *condition* "understood as devotional or pious behavior derived from something akin to an emotionally charged, perceptual experience of divinity or the holy."[21]

A number of philosophical arguments developed around this concept of the uniqueness of experiential authority, as did a number of protective strategies that inoculated experience from exterior critique: philosophers and hermeneuticists argued that the only true knowledge about an experience was the experience itself. Sociologists and other observers could arguably interpret an experience account, but the experience "itself" remained impervious to evaluation or explanation. This fundamental distinction between an experience and its account continues to operate in sociological analyses of religious experience (a point I will return to below). Arguments for the existence of irreducible religious experiences suggested that experience was the proper focus of psychology, and experimental psychological and psychical tools became the proper means of evaluation. Modern psychological techniques and apparatuses made it possible to observe and document experiences and frequently to elicit or prompt similar experiences. By the end of the nineteenth century, a captivated public was enthralled by the "new" sciences of psychology and medicine that were developing as means of testing and "proving" experiential knowledge of the divine.[22] Many religious liberals embraced science, presuming that scientific studies would demonstrate that a "'true religion' was 'religion in general' and that authentic religious experience and naturalistic theories of religion were compatible."[23] The increasingly materialistic bent of psychological research soon dashed the hopes of many. Religious experience was written into the narrative of psychology and studied as naturally occurring, non–socially instigated events.

Developing views of religious experience in psychology and theology, popularized and disseminated by William James, Hugo Munsterberg, F. H. W. Meyers, and others, were taken up by sociological contemporaries. Both Ernst Troeltsch and Joachim Wach's religious typologies identify "mystical" religion that emerges from noetic individual experience and note that this origin point makes it difficult to organize in robust social forms. Wach, for example, notes that mysticism "points to a type of religious experience . . . that concerns the individual and innermost self. . . . We feel justified in stating that 'isolation' is constitutive of mystical religion." Wach cites Rudolph Otto's understanding of numinous religious experiences when he argues that religious experience is "ultimately uncommunicable" and thus "generates" a kind of religion that is not social at its base. Individual religious experiences thus have the ability to shape religious organization and, consequentially and importantly, mark the ground on which religious regeneration and revolution can take place.[24]

As antique as these ideas may seem, they continue to surface in sociological writing. Peter Berger argues in *The Heretical Imperative* that religious movements emerge from religious experiences that take place outside of the sociological gaze. Religious experiences are impervious to social and cultural analysis: "[r]eligious experience . . . *comes to be* embodied in traditions, which mediate it to those who have not had it themselves and which institutionalize it for them as well as for those who had." The process through which raw, analytically inaccessible religious experiences are translated and domesticated into specific cultural-historical traditions is "a constant in human history." Berger likewise states that all religious traditions and cultures are based on original experiences of this kind. Drawing on Otto and others, Berger argues not only that experiences are constitutive of religion but also that these elements of religious life are always beyond the reach of sociological investigation.[25]

Not all sociologists take this approach (or are as concerned about religion's origins), yet a similar concept of a pre-cultural experience emerges in other studies in which the distinction between a psychological experience and a cultural account of it still holds. Thus, even as sociologists criticize psychology's individualistic definition of religious experience, its focus on abnormal and peak experiences, and its oversimplification of the role of social groups and cultures in shaping religious experience,[26] most sociological studies of religious narratives preserve a pre-cultural religious experience by invoking a strong analytical distinction between a religious experience and its cultural account.[27] As one critic has recently observed, this approach to experience sets up a proper boundary of sociological analysis, freeing scholars to analyze "the mystical claims of religion in terms of social realities, yet refus[ing] to push the reasoning to its limit by asserting that these claims are mere social realities," so that "what can be considered as the distinctive and central dimension of religion— its claims pertaining to the supernatural realm—cannot be grasped by sociology, or that [sociology's] findings may have nothing to do with the reality of those claims."[28] Religious experience remains an important site where sociologists locate the boundary on which they can perform sociological agnosticism and mount "non-reductive" interpretations of religious phenomena.

Individual religious experiences continue to surface in sociological accounts of religion, yet without being the actual object of sociological attention. Thus we come to see the ways that individual religious experience surfaces to signal the "end" of religion in recent studies of spirituality or the "spiritual but not religious." The phenomenological reality of individual religious experience emerges as a background concept that allows for spirituality to take place, as a viable expression, "outside of" social or historical formations. There is not much distance between Joachim Wach's description of mysticism and Bellah and colleagues' representation of Sheila Larson's Sheilaism in *Habits of the Heart*. Among the dozens of articles that cite "Sheilaism" as shorthand for religious individualism, most agree with Bellah that Sheila's religion and her experience mark her as a *bricoleur* in an indeterminate shopping mall of faith; personal experience leads to personal selection of religious goods, religious expressions, and self-determination.[29] That said, given that we have reasons to continue to investigate the impact of various complicated genealogies and changing practices of "religious experience" in various academic fields, it behooves us to return to the question of individual spirituality as it has developed in relation to these naturalized understandings of experience in the social sciences in closest conversation with sociology.[30]

The entanglements engaged in concepts and experiences of religious experience, psychology, and religious individualism are differently noted by social scientists and spiritual practitioners. Let's consider how we might analyze spirituality if we did not have the category of the self-generated (or divinely generated) religious experience in our tool kit. Without it, the typology of the "spiritual but not religious" would take on a quite different meaning, and the entanglements of individual spiritual practitioners in various histories, traditions, and institutional engagements would be brought to the fore. In inquiring into the ways that such concepts are practiced in scholarly research, we would quickly bring into view a number of metaphysical and mystical "traditions" in the United States produced in relation to both religious and nonreligious institutions. With this in mind, sociologists would be much less likely to uncritically employ the religious and spiritual concepts (including perennialism and individual experience) practitioners use in analyses. Sociologists likewise might consequently open up their methodological and theoretical focus in order to address a wider range of practices and settings in which religion is reproduced, including a focus on modes of narration and practice that are at odds with commonplace historical narration and its secular temporal structures.

Third Fragment: Mystical Cosmopolitanism and the Spirits of Politics

A third fragment from my fieldwork presents another articulation of religious entanglements that emerge when we ask how some of these spiritual strains are wrapped into particular conceptions of U.S. politics. As my own interests in marking and imagining Cambridge as a spiritual landscape took sharper focus, I became even more aware of how my informants' spiritual projects turned their attention away from the places where they lived day to day, including Cambridge. This is not to say that they were not actively engaged in institution building, civic activities, and community events—many were actively involved in various projects and initiatives—but they did not talk about Cambridge as a place of significance.[31] I was thus excited when Annette, a newcomer, mentioned in a small group meeting that she had moved to Cambridge because she felt "drawn" to the region for reasons she did not understand. She told us that her journey had started with her divorce, after which she had spent two years at Esalen, a spiritual community in Big Sur, California. Coming to the end of her time there, she consulted with her spiritual guides about her next move. Cambridge and Portland, Oregon, were the cities that continued to emerge in dreams and meditations. She moved to Cambridge without knowing anyone or having a single lead for a job. She had since made friends, found a temporary job, and was searching for the reason or person that had drawn her there. As she had already lived in Sedona, Arizona, and at Esalen, two of the best-known spiritual centers in the United States, I was curious about whether she would mention Walden Pond or Concord, transcendentalism, or other "connections" to the region's metaphysical history in her Cambridge chapter.

Annette, however, resolutely told me that Cambridge's draw was a person, not a place. She was not that interested in history, she told me.

She was committed to topographically spiritual landscapes, not historical ones, and she found Cambridge to be spiritually uninteresting, compared with the desert's panoramic skies and Esalen's natural warm baths. Her attempts to find nature in Cambridge were dissatisfying. As it happened, Annette and I frequently traveled on the same nature path that cut through parks and wooded areas on the way to the subway. I tried talking with her about the trail, but each time I heard a litany from her about nature's absence.

Annette's view that "nature" and the earth's "spiritual energies" existed somewhere else, outside of Cambridge, was shared by her friends. They reinforced the view of Cambridge's aridity by retelling stories about their journeys to far-flung places, regional "power spots," and national forests. Many of my respondents had visited the pink rocks of Sedona, and a few had traveled to Britain's Glastonbury or identified Morocco, India, or other distant places as sites of spiritual significance.[32] Faye, for example, told me that her experience of visiting Mayan ruins presented her with a strong sense of "homecoming." She was not certain if this was because she had been a Mayan in a previous life or because of the ruins' position on a naturally occurring energy field that had a special ability to connect her to greater astral realities. No matter, stories of homecoming always took place somewhere other than where my respondents lived. Cambridge had no vibrational pull. The town's energetic aridity was further played out in pilgrimages to nationally or internationally known power spots and trips to regional power spots such as Stonehenge USA in Salem, New Hampshire, a two-hour drive north of Cambridge and the site of yearly solstice rituals, an activity organized and advertised by Mika and attended by hundreds from the Boston metro area.

"Stonehenge USA" is a relatively recent designation for a formation of rocks that resembles (on a miniature scale) the famous English site. Respondents told me that the site was built several thousand years ago by European settlers. The builders were "probably Celts," Faye said, adding that these ancient builders had "ancient dowsing" technologies and used those techniques to locate places for their ritual and astronomical sites. Until quite recently, the site had been "forgotten" and "buried," but it was recently opened to the public after the state of New Hampshire bought the farm where it is located and converted it into a public park. It was at that point, Faye and Mika both told me, that scientists and archaeologists became interested in the site and determined that it was the work not of Native Americans but rather of "ancient European" settlers. It was not without some sense of irony that I listened to the ways that this story of European labor seized the imaginations of modern Cantabridgians of European descent and the sighs of relief (sotto voce) because there would not be a tussle over the spot with other indigenous people who might lay claim to it. Even within the story of a "natural" and "ancient" and scientifically given type of power spot, narratives of authority and other kinds of claims to "power" and ownership continue to be refracted.

Driving two hours north of the city to participate in rituals at a "natural" power spot identified by "ancient" and forgotten people presented yet another opportunity to mark Cambridge as a secular place devoid of any particular importance. The recent and recoverable past of the flourishing of metaphysical religions in Cambridge or Boston did not hold my informants in thrall. As if to drive this point home, Faye and Wes began offering spiritual walking tours soon after I moved away from Cambridge. Excited to hear this, I e-mailed Wes about his plans and about the route. He told me that the tours wound along the banks of the Charles River and highlighted the "very old trees" that he and Faye had identified as having "strong" energies.

While scholars describe and analyze the practices that spiritual practitioners use to sacralize landscapes, they have paid far less attention to the ways that these sacred places relate to or transform individuals' understandings and experiences of their towns, cities, homes, and neighborhoods and how the experience of powerful sacred sites marks everyday settings as devoid of particular kinds of power and meaning. To the shopworn question of how contemporary spirituality shapes a response to the feelings of alienation that attend modernity, we must necessarily ask how contemporary spiritual practitioners build such alienation into their projects and are thus actively producing motifs of belonging.[33]

The social and religious practices of Cambridge's contemporary spiritual practitioners compose at least one set of ways that cosmopolitan imaginaries take root.[34] This cosmopolitanism is not merely "imagined" or "thought" but embedded in chronotopically inflected practices that allow them to take up places in the world that are at a distance from *every* place.[35] This social imaginary, conveyed in practices and concepts of religious experience, allowed the varieties of people who gathered in the parlor of the Swedenborg

Chapel on the eve of what many worried (correctly) would be drawn-out wars in Iraq and Afghanistan to work out their own uncertain place in these affairs. Uncertainty was indeed in the air. Earlier in the day, thousands of high school students had walked out of the public schools in Cambridge, Somerville, and Arlington to protest the impending intervention in Iraq. Even with my office windows closed to the cold air outside, I could hear their noisy shouting as they walked toward Boston. I received a reminder e-mail from Cathy, one of the leaders of the mystical experiences discussion group, about that evening's meeting, that included a few sentences about the student protest her son had joined. She was proud of his decision to be an "activist who stood for love and justice."

As we stood around in the chapel's parlor, drinking tea and waiting for the discussion group to begin, a few people noted that more people than usual were showing up and that it must be because of Iraq. Eric and Marcy searched for extra chairs, and Crystal worried that we might run out of sage, which the group burned to "smudge" or purify the room at the beginning of the meeting. We started late, but with almost twenty in attendance, many more than the usual group of nine or ten. I wondered how it would be possible to have everyone share and still end on time. Eric seemed to be worrying about the same thing, and after we all sat down, he rushed through his typical description of the group's style. He then led a "chakra meditation." Usually, Eric would lead an initial meditation through each of a person's chakras, which he described as points of energy aligned vertically along the spine from base to crown, slowly noting each chakra's "color" and "spin" and encouraging us to breathe slowly in order to enliven these internal energy points. But on this night, his group meditation was perfunctory, and he quickly "passed the group's attention" over to Cathy. Cathy took a moment before speaking.

Cathy's soft voice immediately changed the pace of the proceedings. She breathed deeply and then said in a soft voice, "Take a few more deep breaths to feel yourself connected to that chakra, the crown, the white light that is coming down, and connecting you to it. Now imagine that this white light is coming down over your body; you are pulling it down over your crown, your head, your eyes, your neck, and down over your body, until you are bathed in this white light, this source of love, universal love."

We sat in silence, eyes closed, as Cathy continued, "Now, with your mind's eye, turn your attention to the crescent moon that is shining brightly in the western sky. It is often used, the crescent moon, as a symbol for Islam." After a few moments of silence, Cathy then directed, "Now we are going to connect our energies together and send them to the Middle East. In a moment, we are going to move our energies toward the center of the circle, and we are going to use our energies together to send a beam of light and love to the Middle East. Now imagine, you are moving your energy, the light that is around you, to the middle, and it is mingling and intermingling with all of the others' together. And now we are going to send that light up, into the night sky, and across the world, and it is going to shine down on Iraq, and we are going to send our love to the people of Iraq, to the people who live there, and we are going to acknowledge their love, their existence, their beauty, and we will ask them to acknowledge ours. Now just rest for a moment, feeling that love sent there, bathing that country with this universal light."

We sat in silence for a few more minutes, and then Cathy's voice broke in again, "And now, if you feel comfortable, we are going to take this light, and we are going to direct it to someone who is in power, and who is taking part in what is going on in world events. It could be someone in this country, someone in some other part of the world whose heart is filled with hate and anger. And we are going to take this light, and we are going to connect our light and love to their heart chakras. Take a moment to do that. Don't be afraid—you are safe, enveloped in the white light, and no one can harm you."

In a few minutes, Cathy "brought us back," first to the group light beam, and then back into our individual bodies, and finally asked us to open our eyes. People opened their eyes, and a few stretched. Eric looked around, and told the people around the circle that the tradition was to "go around the circle and say what we got from the meditation." Over the next half hour, people in the room elaborated on what they had seen and felt as they traveled out of their bodies to other places in the world, often speaking out of turn and shaping a conversation that was quite unlike the normal, serial expressions that Eric preferred. The result was more of a building momentum, and conversation, than what typically occurred, despite the fact that half of the people in the room were newcomers.

Crystal was the first one to speak. "I just felt so much euphoria in this room, especially when all of our energies were pulling together in the middle, it was like—*wow*, look what we can do together. And I was just—feeling that energy and being a part of it, and all that love. So thanks, Cathy and Eric." She seemed to be finished but then turned to address Cathy directly. "Oh—and I wanted to say that when you invited us to send our love to someone who was full of hate? I was really glad that you said, 'Don't have any fear, don't be scared,' because I was feeling a bit concerned. Thanks for reminding me that I was bathed in light. Then I could do it."

Paula interrupted. "Yes—that was really great. When we are asked to imagine a person, I thought of George W. Bush. I always think of him as a child, like a little boy, immature and childish. So when Cathy said to send him love, I thought of him as a baby and sent my love to him as a child. But also, when you said that we should send our love to the people of Iraq, it was really vivid. I felt like I was zooming in. I actually saw a mother and a child together, and she was holding the child in front of what looked like their house. At least, I think it was. It was so vivid though. . . . I really felt a really strong connection to her, and them. To the real people who are there. And I thought, this is what it is about, sending our love and our power to them, because it is the mothers and children in Iraq. They're the ones who have the power."

When it came to my turn, I followed the established pattern, thanking Eric and Cathy for a "relaxing" meditation and remarking that Cathy's reference to the moon was quite nice, as I had been enjoying the moon on my walk to the chapel. "Can you still see it out there?" Cathy asked, turning to look out the window. She turned back and addressed Crystal's opening comment. "You know, the reason I said 'don't be afraid' is because when I was doing the visualization, the person who leapt to mind immediately was Saddam Hussein. And when I connected to his heart, I felt a real prick, like a sharp needle. It hurt. And so that's why I said 'don't be afraid' because I was afraid, and I needed to remember that I was in the light in order to go into his heart."

Annette jumped in, saying, "I thought about Saddam Hussein too, but just like Paula, I thought of him as a baby, as a child, about sending love to him as a child. That was easier than sending love to him as a grown-up man. I remembered that he was a child once, that we were all children once. That was a much easier way to send love to him."

Changing the subject somewhat, Annette continued, "You know that visualization, it really connected with me. I've been thinking about being an agent of peace in my life. I've had the feeling that that's what I'm supposed to be, so the fact that, that you made it clear that I'm not just to be peaceful in my own life, but also giving peace to the clients and people I see at my job, and my coworkers, and also in the world, that we can work together to make peace, that is really powerful. So now I see why I've been going around being a person of peace these last few days."

Annette shifted the subject to her work life, and on this cue, and as if arising from a slumber, Steve and John, two middle-aged men, shook off their lethargy and sat up straight. Steve asked Eric, "We don't have to talk about world events, do we?" Several people gave a resounding "no," and Steve told us all that he was a newcomer to the group and a friend of John's. "John recommended that I come, because I have a really high-anxiety, stressful job. And I haven't been sleeping well, and I have been trying to meditate and read on my own. But it's not really easy to do that on your own." I noticed several people nodding as he continued. "So, anyways, I told John about it, and he told me that we should come tonight, that it's helped him a lot, and well—that was the most peaceful I've felt in a long time. I don't know when I've felt like that before—I think I maybe fell asleep, I was so relaxed. And if I did, I apologize. That's what I have to say. It's not about world events; I wasn't really paying attention to that part."

John, always the least loquacious, stared shyly at the floor with his hands cupped in his lap. He added only, "Yeah—it's like Steve said, it's really a good thing to do the meditations. I always go into a deep trance with the chakras. So I want to commend you, Eric, for the work you do." Eric took the praise with a smile and for a change did not tell us the story about how he does the visualization on the train every morning on his way to work. Instead, he praised Cathy, telling her the "visualization was really powerful. I felt, really, this powerful pull into the vortex of our energy together. It was just so much energy—and I felt myself moving over the world, and I saw the globe glowing as our light went out around the world."

It was only at the very end of the evening that Kevin, another newcomer, spoke. "When we were turning our energy there, I felt—I got the feeling I was that there was already lots of light and energy there. That there was enough, that they didn't need any more of ours there. The people there also have lots of light, in the Middle East, in Iraq. And I also had the distinct impression that there is a sage in the Middle East—someone who is of that tradition, in the Middle East, or in Iraq, who feels the same way we do, who has the same feelings and is working for peace—and that was good to have that feeling that that person is there."

All who were gathered nodded and agreed that they too hoped there was a "sage" who would bring peace to the Middle East, missing Kevin's quiet attempt to rebuke the logic embedded in these visions. While the mystics gathered in the space of the chapel were hoping for peace and justice, and Cathy's visualization led us through familiar tropes of critique of U.S. foreign policy and warmongering, the entire ritual reproduced a spiritualized imperialism, in which those in the United States could travel quickly and effortlessly to other parts of the world, lift up spiritual children and "real" women and children from the lock of spiritual and religious tyranny, enter into others' hearts, and then return untouched to the familiar. The worst that one could suffer was a "prick" from an evil heart, but even this terror could be overcome by the protection provided by a shield of mystical light. Eric's ability to "zoom around" the world, to observe the globe from outside, was not an unfamiliar to metaphysicals. Nor, for that matter, was the discursive claim that "love" and "light" represent a strong spiritual Esperanto allowing mystics to not only encounter but *enter into* the hearts of unknown others. These hearts, at least in their pure, childlike, and uncorrupted versions, were familiar and recognizable to the equally good-hearted individuals gathered in the Swedenborg Chapel parlor.

In several recent articles, Bryan S. Turner posits the importance of cosmopolitan virtues of "ironic distance" but adds that "[i]rony may only be possible once one has already had an emotional commitment to a place. . . . Perhaps irony without patriotism may be too cool and thin to provide for identification with place and with politics." He notes, thus, "cosmopolitanism does not mean that one does not have a country or a homeland, but one has to have a certain reflexive distance from that homeland."[36] Turner's call for an ironic distance depends on particular religious and secular constructs aligned in relation to the nation. It would appear at first that Turner's vision of cosmopolitanism presents a critique of the highly cosmopolitan, postnationalist visions that metaphysicals hope for and, to some degree, participate within.

Yet metaphysicals in Cambridge—all cosmopolitan, all "homeless"—do not become nation-less, despite their zooming around. Indeed, in some respects, their zooming around represents the recovery of a particular kind of cosmopolitanism that drinks deeply from transcendental wells that conjoin the American and the universal in powerful, complex practice. These mystical visualizations present an opportunity to think about the ways that many "cosmopolitan virtues" are resonant with the chronotopes elaborated within the various projects of nineteenth- and twentieth-century mystics and metaphysicals and that are fused at present with particular concerns and legacies that mark "American" people as those without culture, without past, and thus perhaps without society at all. This theme is hardly new: Svetlana Boym argues that in the nineteenth century, "nostalgia was perceived as a European disease." Nations that "came of age late and wished to distinguish themselves from aging Europe developed their identity on an anti-nostalgic premise; for better or worse they claimed to have managed to escape the burdens of historical time." Hence, early Americans "perceived themselves as 'Nature's Nation,' something that lives in the present and has no need for the past," leading to the nationalization of progress and the "American dream."[37]

While such broad cultural sketches of the metaphysical projection of an always-unfolding national culture that never quite finds its home might sound strange, these spiritual imperialisms form understandings of home and nation that are always unfolding, always coming into being. The homeless present and the post-national future are reproduced in numerous ways throughout metaphysical communities, serving to displace attention to the very specific notions of America that emerge. Jeffrey Kripal, for example, urges readers to imagine Esalen as a project to claim or reclaim a different, deeply mystical mode of Americanness. "Can we reclaim that which we have lost? More specifically, can we revision 'America' not as a globally hated imperial superpower, not as a 'Christian nation' obsessed with . . . arrogant apocalyptic fantasies abroad and discriminatory 'family values' at home, not as a monster consumer of the world's ever-dwindling resources, but as a universal human ideal yet to be fully realized, as a potential yet to be actualized, as an empty and so creative space far more radical and free than the most patriotic or religiously right among us have dared to imagine?" He continues, asking at the end, "Are we ready for a radically American mysticism, for an 'America' *as* mysticism?"[38]

The question of whether we are ready for "America as mysticism" is put to us too late, if Cambridge's mystics are any gauge. Their spiritual imaginaries and the landscapes that they traverse show that America already figures as mysticism: one that, in characterizing the future as borderless, free, and filled with love and light, finds itself deeply entangled with ongoing American projects of political and cultural expansion.

Concluding Thoughts

The fragments offered here highlight different, non-commensurate entanglements, in which theoretical concepts and religious practices that are shaped and molded in various half-forgotten conversations from earlier projects take shape and expression in new ways. I have noted how several such entanglements shape what we collectively understand "spirituality" to be at this moment, and I have suggested that we would do well to place an understanding of those entanglements within our studies, whether of spirituality or religion or the secular. Each fragment has, in this respect, presented a site or position that might be fruitfully considered beyond my immediate project of figuring the spiritual. In the first, I argued that we might ask if what we have called "spirituality" is not to some degree religion out of place. In the second, I viewed the shaping of contemporary spirituality through the lens of one of its key logics, namely, experiential projects (and practices) that are mediated by and gain their authority from the social sciences and natural sciences. In the third fragment, I moved into fieldwork to consider how the practices of spiritual self-formation are shaped by and respond to certain political projects and, in turn, actively contribute to some strains and claims that translate American virtues and subjectivities into universal human qualities. These felt, experienced translations and interpretations are all the more powerful insofar as they remain tangled and hidden behind articulations of the spiritual as having no history, having no practice, and having no set of operating theologies.

I have argued that beginning with a question of how and where religion is entangled—conceptually, practically, and institutionally—orients sociological questions about religion in new directions, ones that are consistent with our broader post-secular turn. This approach is not one that demands, requires, or is content with genealogical analyses of the terms we use. Rather, it builds on such considerations, providing new avenues of analysis that are not stymied by unreflexive methodological adoption of the terms we wish to analyze. This approach likewise does not necessarily draw scholars away from the field sites and subjects that we designate as religion. On the contrary. Yet they will prompt a stronger empirical assessment of the varying degrees of differentiation that things marked "religion" and "the secular" enjoy.

This approach to entanglements may similarly prompt attention to aspects of religious social life (and likewise social theory) that have not received much sociological scrutiny of late. The enduring focus in the sociology of religion on religion in public life—including issues of civic participation, civil society, political participation, and the role of religion in (reasoned) public debate—runs on one axis of interest shaped by secularization, namely "belief or reason." But there are others to consider, including, as Gauri Viswanathan suggests, the axis of "belief or imagination." This is an important frame for analyzing religion, one that may well offer us better coordinates for engaging the imbrication of religion in medicine and science, the various religious fantasies and investigations that are currently fashioned in neuroscientific discourse and popular literature, and connections between religion, politics and the arts that go beyond the old saw of the culture wars. Tracing these actions requires attention to additional theoretical and empirical entanglements, including, as Viswanathan notes, the axis of "belief and imagination" that takes shape around the frames of enchantment and disenchantment. If historian Michael Saler is right that academics have "enchanted themselves with the spell of disenchantment, but that spell appears to be breaking," then our discussion of "post-secular explorations" will require a renewed focus on this key concept and its entangled effects.[39]

Notes

The author thanks Paul Lichterman, David Kyuman Kim, Jonathan VanAntwerpen, José Casanova, Philip Gorski, and John Torpey for comments on earlier presentations and drafts.

1. For example, in the 1991 introduction to *Comparative Social Research*, Craig Calhoun wrote: "It is hard, from the vantage point of the 1990s, to remember how central religion seemed to the founding social scientists of the seventeenth through early twentieth centuries. . . . Major works on religion remain compartmentalized. Whatever the opinions of specialists, these books do not capture the imagination of whole disciplines, reorient social theory or reshape the broader questions of researchers. This is not, of course because religion has altogether lost

its capacity to move the citizens of modern societies. . . . But the presumption of unbelief is so basic to much of modern academe that it is hard for scholars to take religion altogether seriously—especially in the study of advanced industrial societies" (ix–x).

2. For example, Jürgen Habermas, "Religion in the Public Sphere," *European Journal of Philosophy* 14 (2006): 1–25. Despite ongoing contributions to the scholarly study of "secularization," American sociologists have been late to the wide-ranging scholarly debates revolving around "formations of the secular," with a few notable exceptions, such as José Casanova, "Rethinking Secularization: A Global Comparative Perspective," *Hedgehog* (2006): 7–22; and Christian Smith, ed., *The Secular Revolution: Power, Interests, and Conflict in the Secularization of American Public Life* (Berkeley: University of California Press, 2003). The literature in this cross-disciplinary conversation continues to grow, in religious studies (Janet Jakobsen and Ann Pellegrini, *Secularisms* [Durham, NC: Duke University Press, 2007]), anthropology (most notably Talal Asad, *Formations of the Secular* [Stanford, CA: Stanford University Press, 2003], David Scott and Charles Hirschkind, eds., *Powers of the Secular Modern: Talal Asad and His Interlocutors* [Stanford, CA: Stanford University Press, 2006]; Saba Mahmood "Secularism, Hermeneutics, and Empire," *Public Culture* 18, no. 2 [2006]: 323–347), history and philosophy (Charles Taylor, *A Secular Age* [Cambridge, MA: Harvard University Press, 2007]; William Connolly, *Why I Am Not a Secularist* [Minneapolis: University of Minnesota Press, 2000]; Akeel Bilgrami, "Two Concepts of Secularism," *Yale Journal of Criticism* 7 [Spring 1994]: 211–227), and literature (Vincent Pecora, *Secularization and Cultural Criticism: Religion, Nation and Modernity* [Chicago: University of Chicago Press, 2006]; Gauri Viswanathan, "Secularism in the Framework of Heterodoxy," *PMLA* 123, no. 2 [2008]: 465–476). My sense is that while sociologists have much to gain by reading across disciplines and adopting others' approaches, sociology should also in tandem consider its own disciplinary histories in engaging the question of religion.

3. Representative texts include Robert Orsi, *Between Heaven and Earth* (Princeton, NJ: Princeton University Press, 2005); R. Marie Griffith, *God's Daughters: Evangelical Women and the Power of Submission* (Berkeley: University of California Press, 1997); Charles Hirschkind, *Ethical Soundscape* (New York: Columbia University Press, 2007); Saba Mahmood, *Politics of Piety* (Princeton, NJ: Princeton University Press, 2004).

4. Talal Asad, *Genealogies of Religion* (Baltimore, MD: Johns Hopkins University Press, 1993); Tomoko Masuzawa, *The Invention of World Religions* (Princeton, NJ: Princeton University Press, 2005); Tracy Fessenden, *Culture and Redemption:*

Religion, the Secular and American Literature (Princeton, NJ: Princeton University Press, 2007).

5.   The editors of this volume raise this point both in support and in critique of qualitative scholarship on religion. See a similar critique in Courtney Bender, *Heaven's Kitchen: Living Religion at God's Love We Deliver* (Chicago: University of Chicago Press, 2003), ix–x. A number of recent studies are taking the question of entanglements much more seriously. Some exemplary texts include Leigh Schmidt, *Consumer Rites* (Princeton, NJ: Princeton University Press, 1995); R. Marie Griffith, *Born Again Bodies: Flesh and Spirit in American Christianity* (Berkeley: University of California Press, 2004); Christopher White, *Unsettled Minds: Psychology and the American Search for Spiritual Assurance, 1830–1940* (Berkeley: University of California Press, 2008); Pamela Klassen, *Spirits of Protestantism: Medicine, Healing, and Liberal Christianity* (Berkeley: University of California Press, 2011); and Kathryn Lofton, *Oprah: Gospel of an Icon* (Berkeley: University of California Press, 2011).

6.   Viswanathan, "Secularism in the Framework of Heterodoxy."

7.   Courtney Bender, *The New Metaphysicals: Spirituality and the American Religious Imagination* (Chicago: University of Chicago Press, 2010).

8.   "Spirituality" is bedeviled not by a lack of specific definitions but by an almost endless proliferation. As noted, many of the social scientific studies of "spirituality" begin with a commonsense view of spirituality as feelings, emotions, and moral values that extend beyond or are (or can be) in other ways uncoupled from religious institutions. This use of "spirituality" or "spirit" first appears in sociological literature in the late nineteenth century, when "spirituality" is coupled with "morality" and distinguished from specific religious creeds. Such use is not unique to sociology, but its persistence is notable. Daniel Vaca and Courtney Bender, "The Spiritual in Sociology," manuscript, Columbia University Department of Religion.

9.   There are many examples; one recent one is elaborated by Nancy Ammerman in "Religious Identities and Religious Institutions," in *Handbook for the Sociology of Religion*, ed. Michele Dillon (New York: Cambridge University Press, 2003), 207–224.

10. Ernst Troeltsch, *The Social Teachings of the Christian Churches* (Louisville, KY: Westminster John Knox Press, 1992), vol. 2, 800.

11. For an interesting treatment of James's theoretical influence on Troeltsch, which includes extensive quotations from Troeltsch's published memorial review of James's philosophy of religion, see Charles H. Long, "The Oppressive Elements of Religion and the Religions of the Oppressed," *Harvard Theological Review* 69,

no. 3 (1976): 379–412. See also Walter E. Wyman, Jr., *The Concept of Glaubenslehre: Ernst Troeltsch and the Theological Heritage of Schleiermacher* (Chico, CA: Scholars Press, 1983); and Karl-Fritz Daiber, "Mysticism: Troeltsch's Third Type of Religious Collectivities," *Social Compass* 49 (2002): 329–341.

12.   Troeltsch, *The Social Teachings of the Christian Churches*, vol. 2, 796–797, 799.

13.   To recite what we all (I think) agree on: these are not ineluctable trends but rather have taken shape in the particular social and historical conditions that they likewise help to form. Talal Asad, *Formations of the Secular* (Stanford, CA: Stanford University Press, 2003); Charles Taylor, *A Secular Age* (Cambridge, MA: Harvard University Press, 2007); Christian Smith, ed., *The Secular Revolution: Power, Interests, and Conflict in the Secularization of American Public Life* (Chicago: University of Chicago Press, 2003); David Hollinger, *Science, Jews, and Secular Culture* (Princeton, NJ: Princeton University Press, 1996).

14.   For a full discussion and citations, see Bender, *The New Metaphysicals*, chapter 2. To put this another way, to the growing literature on the historical dynamics of differentiation noted in Gorski and Altinordu's 2008 review essay (67–68) we can add an emergent literature on the co-reconstruction of psychology and religion in the United States, the history and resurgence of alternative medicine, neuroscience, and "Buddhist" and "Eastern religious" traditions, and so on.

15.   Michael Schudson, "The Varieties of Civic Experience," in *The Civic Life of American Religion*, ed. Paul Lichterman and C. Brady Potts (Stanford, CA: Stanford University Press, 2008), 23–47.

16.   Numerous studies abound; many tell the story of developing and changing histories of New Age and occult religions. A developing body of recent research links these histories with mainstream currents in American cultural and political thought and expression. See R. Marie Griffith, *Born Again Bodies*; Beryl Satter, *Each Mind a Kingdom: American Women, Sexual Purity and the New Thought Movement, 1875–1920* (New York: Oxford University Press); and Leigh Schmidt, *Restless Souls: The Making of American Spirituality* (San Francisco: HarperSanFrancisco, 2005).

17.   William James gave testimony in an 1898 Massachusetts State House inquiry into whether mind-curers should be regulated, arguing against their being regulated. He said, "It is enough for you as legislators to ascertain that a large number of our citizens, persons as intelligent and well educated as yourself or I, persons whose numbers seem daily to increase, are convinced that these healing practices do achieve the results that they claim." Quoted in Reuben A. Kessel, "Price Discrimination in Medicine," *Journal of Law and Economics* 1954: 26.

18. Keeping in mind Robert Sharf's statement that it is "incumbent upon [scholars] to reject the perennialist hypothesis insofar as it anachronistically imposes the recent and ideologically laden notion of religious experience on our interpretations of premodern phenomena" (Sharf, "Experience," in *Critical Terms for Religious Studies*, ed. Mark C. Taylor [Chicago: University of Chicago Press, 1998], 98), it is nonetheless the case that those of us who study contemporary spiritual practice (unlike scholars of medieval Catholicism, pre-modern India, or even seventeenth century New England) engage in religious worlds that have been shaped by perennial and universal understandings of religious experience. There is thus nothing "inauthentic" about these forms of religious experience, and as a consequence it is incumbent to analyze the practices and strategies that develop around such theologies of experience, much as it is necessary to work to signal (if not recover) the ways that these very perennialist views have shaped our views and visions of others' religious experiences, as numerous scholars have done. See, for example, Grace Jantzen, *Power, Gender, and Christian Mysticism* (Cambridge: Cambridge University Press, 1995); James Hoopes, *Consciousness in New England: From Puritanism and Ideas to Psychoanalysis and Semiotic* (Baltimore, MD: Johns Hopkins University Press, 1989); Richard King, *Orientalism and Religion* (New York: Routledge, 1999).

19. Margaret Somers and Norbert Elias, among others, present useful correctives to this, making clear that even the most individualistic narratives and identities are social products. See Margaret Somers, "The Narrative Constitution of Identity: A Relational and Network Approach," *Theory and Society* 23, no. 5 (1994): 605–649; Norbert Elias, *The Civilizing Process* (Oxford: Blackwell Publishers, 1994).

20. Sharf, "Experience," 98.

21. Martin Jay, *Songs of Experience: Modern American and European Variations on a Universal Theme* (Berkeley: University of California Press, 2005), 80. Wayne Proudfoot identifies Schleiermacher's theological argument for religious experience as establishing the "best case" for this definition of religious experience and likewise traces the influence of Schleiermacher's thought on the hermeneutics of Dilthey, Otto, and others. Proudfoot outlines the logical inconsistencies embedded in Schleiermacher's account, demonstrating how arguments for independent, apprehendable religious experience are better understood as texts that teach the rules of the game through which religious experiences take on particular shape as uncommunicable conditions, protected from logical, rational analysis. The core of religious experience "formulated the rules for the identification of the numinous moment of experience in such a way as to prevent the

'reduction' of religious experience by its being subsumed under any explanatory or interpretative scheme. . . . If it can be explained, it is not religious experience. The criterion by which the experience is to be identified precludes certain kinds of explanation. What purports to be a neutral phenomenological description is actually a form designed to evoke or to create a particular sort of experience." In Schleiermacher's terms, and later in Otto's and others', religious experience takes place beyond or outside the realm of cognition. While a posteriori accounts of such experiences can be subject to such inquiry, the experience "itself" remains outside of this realm of investigation and falsification. Wayne Proudfoot, *Religious Experience* (Berkeley: University of California Press, 1989), 117–118.

22. See Ann Taves, *Fits Trances and Visions: Experiencing Religion and Explaining Experience* (Princeton, NJ: Princeton University Press, 1999); R. Laurence Moore, *In Search of White Crows: Spiritualism, Parapsychology, and American Culture* (New York: Oxford University Press, 1977); R. Bruce Mullin, *Miracles and the Modern Religious Imagination* (New Haven, CT: Yale University Press, 2006); Christopher White, *Unsettled Minds*.

23. Taves, *Fits, Trances and Visions*, 6.

24. Joachim Wach, *Sociology of Religion* (Chicago: University of Chicago Press, 1949), 162–165; Troeltsch, *The Social Teachings of the Christian Churches*, 2 vols. (Louisville, KY: Westminster John Knox Press, 1992).

25. Berger, *The Heretical Imperative*, 53–54.

26. While this approach paved the way for analysis of how conversion and experience are shaped within religious communities, sociologists have not employed these conceptual or cultural tools when dealing with cases of religious experience that occur outside of religious institutions. In these cases, sociologists turn to individualistic, psychological categories of "religious experience." For example, David Hay and Ann Morisy, "Reports of Ecstatic, Paranormal, or Religious Experience in Great Britain and the United States: A Comparison of Trends," *Journal for the Scientific Study of Religion* 17 (1978): 255–268; William L. MacDonald, "The Effects of Religiosity and Structural Strain on Reported Paranormal Experiences," *Journal for the Scientific Study of Religion* 34 (1995): 366–376; Roger Straus, "The Social-Psychology of Religious Experience: A Naturalistic Approach," *Sociological Analysis* 42 (1981): 157–167.

27. For example, David Yamane, "Narrative and Religious Experience," *Sociology of Religion* 61 (2000): 171–189, see 175–176. See also Omar McRoberts, "Beyond

Mysterium Tremendum: Thoughts toward an Aesthetic Study of Religious Experience," *Annals of the American Academy of Political and Social Sciences* 595 (2004): 190–203.

28. Edward Berryman, "Medjugorje's Living Icons: Making Spirit Matter (for Sociology)," *Social Compass* 48 (2001): 593–610, see 594. Sociologists who study religious experiences in groups depend on the existence of the religious experiences of nonaffiliated persons as examples of the sociologically inexplicable (nonsocial, nonreducible) aspects of religion. Thus, far from being a category of tertiary interest, the extra-sociological existence of religious experiences bolsters the sociology of religion's claims to nonreductionism. "Religious experience is certainly not the only or "natural" term to play this role, but it been an important one.

29. Robert Bellah et al., *Habits of the Heart: Individualism and Commitment in American Life* (Berkeley: University of California Press, 1985), 221, 226. The number of articles and books that take up or critique Sheilaism, or Bellah's depiction of Sheila, are legion. See, for example, Bruce Greer and Wade Clark Roof, "Desperately Seeking Sheila: Locating Religious Privatism in American Society," *Journal for the Scientific Study of Religion* 31 (1992): 346–352; Melissa Wilcox, "When Sheila's a Lesbian: Religious Individualism among Lesbian, Gay and Transgender Christians," *Sociology of Religion* 63 (2002): 497–513; Robert Fuller, *Spiritual but Not Religious: Understanding Unchurched America* (New York: Oxford, 2001), 159–162; Wade Clark Roof, *Spiritual Marketplace* (Princeton, NJ: Princeton University Press, 1997).

30. Martin Jay's *Songs of Experience* is a wonderful entry point into some of the varied histories of experience in philosophy and history.

31. One-quarter of my respondents were engaged in some aspects of the towns in which they lived, in ways that extended beyond the spiritual activities and groups in which they were involved. These activities included a range of volunteering activities and active participation in local library committees, parent-teacher associations, and even Sunday school groups. As a group, practitioners of alternative and complementary health ere most active, particularly in secular "community health" initiatives and in groups that lobbied state officials for recognition. More than half voted in the local elections in 2003, most read the *Boston Globe* daily, and about one-third said that they listened to the local public radio station's news programs on a regular basis; the rest received their news from television or the Internet.

32.	See Adrian Ivakhiv, "Nature and Self in New Age Pilgrimage," *Culture and Religion* 4 (2004): 93–118; Ivakhiv, *Claiming Sacred Ground: Pilgrims and Politics in Glastonbury and Sedona* (Bloomington: Indiana University Press, 2001).

33.	It is perhaps not surprising that the religious practices of spiritual practitioners resonate strongly with notions of "hierophany" and the "sacred center" of the sort articulated by Mircea Eliade in *The Sacred and the Profane* (New York: Harcourt Brace Jovanovich, 1959). Where Eliade considered such projects of centering and sacrality as archaic (not the province of "secular man"), it is precisely the universal and perennial concepts that are not rooted in any particular history or past that resonate and are most easily reproducible by spiritual practitioners.

34.	The empty spaces of Cambridge contribute to spiritual practitioners' "cosmopolitan imaginaries," which, Craig Calhoun notes, often fail "to recognize the social conditions of [their] discourse, presenting it as a freedom from social belonging rather than a special sort of belonging, a view from nowhere or everywhere rather than from particular social spaces." As Calhoun argues, being without culture and place is an expression of privilege: while it marks out a sense of being "neutral" or having attained a universal place, it is nonetheless a kind of belonging that takes root in a particular kind of cultural position, requiring ongoing labor to articulate and rearticulate commitments as contingent. Craig Calhoun, "'Belonging' in the Cosmopolitan Imaginary," *Ethnicities* (2003): 531–553, 532.

35.	Several historians note that the developing discourse around religious experience in the late nineteenth century opened up the possibility of a universal religion "of the spirit, not dogmatic, ecclesiastical, sacramental, or sectarian, Protestant as much as post-Protestant." American intellectual elites of the late nineteenth century interpreted the writings of German romantics, Asian philosophical texts, and their own religious encounters as providing evidence for this universal religious sensibility. Leigh Schmidt, "The Making of Modern 'Mysticism,'" *Journal of the American Academy of Religion* 71 (2003): 273–302, 287. The "ahistorical, poetic, essential, intuitive, and universal mysticism" promoted by ultra-liberal Protestants served them well. Far from serving as a privatizing and domesticating belief, it allowed elites to develop worldly engagement with religious others and in so doing to seek out the similarities among all religious traditions along lines of a protean but universal religious experiential core. Experience played an important role in shaping transnationally defined distinctions between religion and science, "Western" and "Eastern" religions, and premodern and modern Christianity and, furthermore, continues to do so. Robert Sharf, "Buddhist Modernism and the Rhetoric of Meditative Experience," *Numen* (1995): 228–283; Peter van der Veer, "Global Breathing: Religious Utopians in India and China," *Anthropological Theory* 7 (2007): 315–328.

36. Bryan S. Turner, "Cosmopolitan Virtue, Globalization and Patriotism," *Theory, Culture and Society* 19 (2002): 45–65, 57.

37. Svetlana Boym, *The Future of Nostalgia* (New York: Basic, 2001), 17.

38. Jeffrey Kripal, *Esalen: America and the Religion of No Religion* (Chicago: University of Chicago Press, 2007), 463–464, 466.

39. Michael Saler, "Modernity and Enchantment: A Historiographic Review," *American Historical Review* 111 (2006): 692–716. See also various engagements on these lines, including Dipesh Chakrabarty, *Provincializing Europe* (Chicago: University of Chicago Press, 2000); and Simon During, *Modern Enchantments: The Cultural Power of Secular Magic* (Cambridge, MA: Harvard University Press, 2002).

CHAPTER FOUR

Recovered Goods: Durkheimian Sociology as Virtue Ethics

Philip S. Gorski

Émile Durkheim envisioned sociology as a "moral science." Today, this phrase jars the ear. Among sociologists, at least, it is apt to elicit bewilderment, bemusement, denial, or dismissal. "What could Durkheim have possibly meant by it?" "Durkheim was a little woolly-headed, wasn't he?" "Aren't ethics and science two quite different enterprises?" "Frankly, what use do we postmoderns have for 'morality' anyway?" "What nonsense! You can't derive an ought from an is!" Yet that is precisely what Durkheim proposed to do—at least sometimes. His goal was not just to study morality scientifically—a goal that at least some contemporary sociologists would still endorse; in his bolder moments, he also proposed to put morality on a scientific footing—a goal that most contemporary sociologists would be uncomfortable with. The orthodox view is that sociology can and should be "ethically neutral" (Weber), and various antinomies have been advanced in order to establish and secure that neutrality: fact versus value, knowledge versus faith, objective versus subjective, material versus ideal, interests versus beliefs, and so on. The purpose of this essay is to determine what Durkheim could have meant by this unsettling phrase and whether the project it implied is a defensible one.

What was the inspiration for Durkheim's vision of a moral science? Was it Kant? Several of Durkheim's teachers were neo-Kantians, and many Durkheim scholars have noted that Durkheim's theory of morality was strongly influenced by Kant's.[1] But Kantianism was not the inspiration for

Durkheim's vision of a moral science, nor could it have been. Kant did of course propose a rational morality, free from theological presuppositions, which could and did provide one starting point for a secular, nontheistic morality, a project that Durkheim strongly supported.[2] But he certainly did not propose a *scientific* morality, based on empirical observation. On the contrary, moral rationality—in Kant's terms, "practical reason"—was utterly distinct from scientific rationality. Practical reason inhabited the ineffable world of the "noumena" and was experienced subjectively as "moral duty." Scientific rationality—in Kant's terms, "pure reason"—was oriented outward, toward the observable world of the "phenomena" that were governed by objective laws of causality.[3] Thus, while Durkheim may have found Kant a helpful ally in fending off the churchmen and creating the space for a secular—and republican—morality, Kant was of little use when it came to combating the nihilists and laying the foundations of a scientific—and sociological—morality.

Was utilitarianism then the inspiration? Certainly, no one has ever accused Durkheim of being a utilitarian. And for good reason. But it is important to note that utilitarianism does provide one possible path toward a scientific morality. If "society" is really just an aggregation of individuals, and "good" and "evil" are just religious mumbo jumbo for "pleasure" and "pain," then "morality" is nothing more or less than "the greatest good of the greatest number." Or so Bentham and others would argue.[4] This path is by now a well-trodden one. It leads to neoclassical economics and libertarian ideology. But it is a path that Durkheim resolutely rejected not only as unsociological but also as un-republican, that is, for scientific as well as political reasons.

So what *was* Durkheim's inspiration then? The principal thesis of this paper is that Durkheim's vision of "moral science" was inspired largely by Aristotelian ethics and that it anticipated many of the ideas of virtue ethics and related schools of thought and research. Insofar as it makes *eudemonia*, typically translated as "happiness" or "human flourishing," the aim and the measure of moral and social life, Aristotelianism opens the door to a social *science* of morality informed by empirical observation. Variations in human well-being, after all, are something that one can systematically study, and which contemporary psychologists *do* study, within the subfield of "positive psychology." Further, insofar as it assumes that human flourishing is strongly influenced by institutional arrangements, Aristotelian ethics points in the direction of a *social* science of morality, which goes beyond psychology. Finally, insofar as it assumes that political liberty and civic friendship are essential aspects of human flourishing, it also underwrites a *republican* sociology of morality. For all these reasons, Aristotelian ethics was much better suited to Durkheim's purposes than was Kantianism or utilitarianism.

If there is such a strong connection between Aristotle and Durkheim, though, then why has it gone essentially unnoticed, even by careful and sensitive readers?[5] The obvious answer would seem to be that Durkheim himself did not much emphasize the connection and that his interpreters were not primed to see it, since they are sociologists rather than philosophers. And this is no doubt part of the answer. But this answer also raises further questions. If Durkheim was so strongly influenced by Aristotle, why did he mention him so infrequently? As we will see, there are a number of reasons why Durkheim might have wished to downplay the Aristotelian connection. He may even have done so consciously and strategically, though that would be difficult to prove.

As a result, the philosophical roots of Durkheim's sociology were rendered invisible. They are to be found in an intellectual tradition that Durkheim himself regarded as proto-sociological, namely, what is today called "political philosophy," and, more specifically, the "civic republican" strand of that tradition, stretching from Aristotle and Cicero through Machiavelli and Harrington to Montesquieu and Rousseau. Reinserting Durkheim into that tradition, I will argue, not only helps us to better understand the Durkheimian project of a "moral science"; it may even provide us with the intellectual resources to revive it, by showing us a way beyond the hoary distinctions between "fact" and "value" or "ideals" and "interests," distinctions that Durkheim himself employed in his own academic and partisan battles, to the detriment of his intellectual project. Central to this project is recovering a robust notion of the good, which can serve as the ethical foundation for a post-secular social science.

The Aristotelian Connection

Today, it is common to distinguish three main schools of ethical thought: deontological, consequentialist, and virtue ethics. Deontological ethics is premised on the notion of moral *duty* (Greek, *deon*). The seminal formulation of this position is contained in Kant's *Groundwork of the Metaphysics of*

Morals, in which Kant first articulated his "categorical imperative": "Act only according to that maxim whereby you can at the same time will that it should become a universal law."[6] For Kant, then, to be moral was to make choices that conform to universalizable principles of right. As the moniker implies, consequentialist ethics focuses on the consequences of an individual's acts for the general good. The seminal formulation of this position is the classical utilitarianism of Jeremy Bentham, James Mill, and Henry Sidgwick.[7] In utilitarian interpretations of consequentialism—which now compete with a host of others—the general good can in principle be calculated. In Bentham's famous formula, it is simply "the greatest good of the greatest number." While deontological and consequentialist ethics are both the offspring of the Enlightenment, virtue ethics traces its lineage back to Ancient Greece (and also to Ancient China, where it arose independently). It remained the dominant school of moral philosophy in Latin Christendom until the Enlightenment. It emphasizes responsibility not simply for one's moral acts but also for one's moral character.[8] Accordingly, it stresses the role of moral education and political liberty in the promotion of practices of moral virtue. Virtue ethics had gone into eclipse by the early nineteenth century but was revived during the mid-to-late twentieth century by Anglo-American philosophers such as G. E. M. Anscombe and Martha Nussbaum.[9]

Durkheim's career coincided with the period of eclipse. But there can be no doubt that he was intimately familiar with Aristotle's thought and that he was deeply influenced by it. His youthful preparations for the admission exam for the École normale supérieure would have involved extensive reading of the Greek and Roman classics, as would his subsequent studies at the École normale itself.[10] Nor can there be any doubt that Durkheim engaged with classical philosophy during these years. One of his second-year papers at the École normale was on the Roman Stoics,[11] and his favorite teachers there were Fustel de Coulanges, a scholar of ancient history, and Émile Boutroux, an expert on ancient philosophy. Nor did the engagement with the ancients end in Paris. In his first teaching post at Bordeaux, Durkheim became close friends with Georges Rodier, an Aristotle specialist, and himself gave special lectures (alas, now lost) on the *Nicomachean Ethics* and the *Politics* to help prepare philosophy students for their final examinations.[12] It was during these years at Bordeaux (1897–1902) that Durkheim penned his French dissertation, *The Division of Labor in Society*. Its first footnote, given in the original Greek, was to the *Nicomachean Ethics*.[13] In English translation, the passage reads as follows: "When people associate with one another for the purpose of exchange, however, this kind of justice—reciprocity in accordance with proportion, not equality—is what binds them together, since a city is kept together by proportionate reciprocation."[14] Those familiar with *The Division of Labor* will instantly recognize that the cited passage is not just an ornament; it actually anticipates the core claim of the book—that simple societies are integrated by means of "mechanical solidarity" while complex ones are held together by "organic solidarity." Perhaps it was even the main inspiration for *The Division of Labor*. Durkheim himself, toward the end of his life, emphasized the profound influence of Aristotle's thought on his vision in a letter to the editor of the *Revue néo-scolastique*, in which he explained, "I owe it to my mentor, Monsieur Boutroux, who at the *École Normale Supérieure* often used to repeat to us that every science must explain according to 'its own principles', as Aristotle states: psychology by psychological principles, biology by biological principles. Very much imbued with this idea, I applied it to sociology."[15] From the beginning of his career until the end, then, the Aristotelian influence on Durkheim is quite clear.

The question at hand, however, is not whether Durkheim was influenced by Aristotle's philosophy in general but whether he was influenced by Aristotelian *ethics*. To be clear, by "Aristotelian ethics," I mean not only the *Nicomachean Ethics* but also the *Politics*, since Aristotle understood these works to be continuous with, and complementary to, each other; for him, there was no distinction between "moral philosophy" and "political philosophy." I will make the case for influence in two ways: (1) positively, by identifying parallels between Durkheim and Aristotle, and (2) negatively, by demonstrating divergences between Durkheim and, say, Kant or Bentham. I begin with the positive case, noting echoes of Aristotelian principles in Durkheim's writings.

One hallmark of Aristotle's ethics is the principle of the mean. In the *Nicomachean Ethics*, Aristotle argues that each of the virtues is "a kind of mean," specifically, "a mean between two vices, one of excess, the other of deficiency."[16] For example, "[i]n fear and confidence, courage is the mean," while "[i]n giving and taking money, the mean is generosity."

Durkheim often reasons in this way as well, most notably in *Suicide*, in which he argues that "[n]o moral idea exists which does not combine in proportions . . . egoism, altruism and a certain anomy."[17] Durkheim's central concern in this work is not with individual well-being, however, but with collective well-being. The suicide rate serves primarily as a social indicator, with high rates indicating social pathology and low rates indicating social well-being. His central argument in *Suicide* is that a good society is one that achieves the right levels of social regulation and social integration, that is, a society that sets sufficient but not excessive limits on human freedom and human autonomy by means of formal and informal social rules and ties. In other words, *Suicide* extends the principle of the mean in ethics to society as a whole. A good society is one that has neither too much integration and regulation nor too little, with the actual mean being definable only in relation to a given society.

A second distinguishing feature of Aristotle's ethics is his emphasis on *eudemonia*, or "human flourishing," and the particular conception of human nature on which it is premised. As the ambiguity of the translation suggests, *eudemonia* in Aristotle's sense is not quite the same thing as "happiness" in the modern, colloquial sense. To flourish is not simply to "feel" happy, to experience many moments of positive emotion; rather, it is to be happy in a particular way and for the right reasons. More specifically, it is to excel in, to be virtuous at, those things that set humans apart from beasts, particularly reason and speech. These are the things that constitute *human*, as opposed to animal, nature. The life of virtue, Aristotle argues, is therefore a life in accord with nature. Since human beings differ from animals in two respects, there are two paths to a virtuous life. One is the life of contemplation, which employs reason. The other is the active life of politics, which employs speech. Aristotle also identifies a third path in life, the life of pleasure, which can perhaps lead to happiness in the modern, colloquial sense but certainly not to flourishing in the specifically Aristotelian sense. For example, the "happy" person in Aristotle's sense may in fact experience considerable pain, but she or he does so for the right reasons—in the form of shame over misdeeds, say—but not for the wrong ones, such as the progress of age, the blows of fate or other events beyond her or his control. For Aristotle, it should be noted, the virtuous life is possible only within human society and, indeed, within a very particular form of human society, as we will see shortly. In his view, a happy life cannot be lived in isolation.

Durkheim, too, rejects the life of mere pleasure and argues that genuine happiness requires the regulation and reordering of our initial nature and of our inner life. "[T]he most essential element of character," he argues, is the "capacity for restraint . . . which allows us to contain our passions, our desires, our habits, and subject them to law."[18] Here, he sounds a Kantian note. For Durkheim, however, mere restraint is not enough; it must be melded with a desire for, and an attraction to, the social good of social interaction and social solidarity.[19] Here, he sounds more like Aristotle. In combining Kant and Aristotle, he again applies the principle of the mean. Virtue, he implies, is a mean between the right (law or duty) and the good ("charity" and "energy"). Only human society can supply us with such restraints and desires. Thus, it is only in human society that human beings are fully human: "deprive man of all that society has given him and he . . . becomes a being more or less indistinct from an animal. Without language, essentially a social thing, general or abstract ideas are practically impossible, as are all the higher mental functions."[20] To live outside of society, or to live as if one were not a part of society, he contends, is "contrary to nature."[21] For Kant, there was no conflict between ethical virtue and social isolation—least of all in his own life. For Durkheim, however, they were fundamentally at odds. Like Aristotle, he regarded human beings as inherently social creatures.

A third hallmark of Aristotle's ethics, and another area in which we see notable parallels with Durkheim, is the notion of *phronesis*, or "practical wisdom," and the resulting concern with moral education. Practical wisdom is not be confused with theoretical knowledge. The meaning of *phronesis* is aptly conveyed in the famous metaphor of the expert bowman. "In all the states of character we have mentioned," Aristotle says, "there is a sort of target, and it is with his eye on this that the person with reason tightens or loosens his string."[22] Virtue is like archery in that it is (i) an embodied capacity developed through (ii) training and habituation that leads to (iii) a heightened probability of "hitting the target"—that is, achieving the mean as it is (iv) defined in that context (i.e., the nature of the target). It involves body as well as mind, emotion as well as reason, and attentiveness as well as knowledge. Virtue can and must be learned, and the inculcation of virtue was in fact the principal goal of education for Aristotle; the acquisition of vocational skills or formal knowledge was strictly secondary.

Here, too, we find a number of striking parallels between Aristotle and Durkheim. The most obvious is the shared concern with moral education. Good republican that he was, Durkheim espoused the view, widespread among French intellectuals at that time, that the Third Republic needed a "secular morality" that could sustain public virtue, and he lectured on this subject before thousands of would-be schoolteachers over the years. These lectures were eventually published as a book, his little-read treatise *Moral Education*. Though he did not explicitly characterize moral knowledge as "practical wisdom," he did open these lectures by insisting that moral education was neither a science nor an art, suggesting that it was something in between, in other words, a form of practical knowledge. And he said much the same about morality itself, warning that it did not involve the application of a general principle that transcended place and time, as Kant implied, but consisted rather of concrete maxims that could be quite specific to particular societies and periods, and even to particular groups and organizations. The morality that governs the family, for instance, is quite different from that which is appropriate to political society or a business enterprise. He was, moreover, quite clear that moral education could not be taught in a purely formal or theoretical way; rather, it required repetition and habituation.[23]

The principle of the mean and the concepts of *eudemonia* and *phronesis* distinguish Aristotle's ethics, not only from modern systems of ethics, such as Kant's and Bentham's, but also from other ancient systems of ethics, such as Plato's and Epictetus's. There are further aspects of Aristotle's system, however, that are found in many other ancient systems as well—and are also echoed in Durkheim's. One is the principle of "balance," which is common to many versions of ancient political philosophy, both Greek and Roman. For the ancients—and for civic republicans in general—"balance" is a fundamental principle of constitutional architecture that is essential to a well-constructed and durable system of republican government. On this account, a good polity—a republican polity that preserves liberty—requires a balanced constitution. The "balance" in question is between opposing groups or principles, typically, the one (monarchy), the few (aristocracy), and the many (democracy). In this view, liberty emerges and endures only if these groups are relatively equal in social power and political representation. Where one is particularly strong or predominant, there will be no restraint on its passions or interests, resulting in widespread decadence and self-seeking—what the ancients referred to as "corruption"; this in turn provokes a counterreaction by the other groups and the formation of "factions" that seek only the good of their own group. Once they take hold, it was argued, corruption and factions lead to instability, decline, and, eventually, dissolution.

Durkheim did not accept the theory of balance in its traditional formulation in terms of the one, the few, and the many; instead, he attempted to reconstruct it and adapt it to modern conditions. Like the republican political philosophers of Greece and Rome, and in marked contrast to liberal contractarians such as Hobbes and Locke, Durkheim argued that polities were constituted by and through familial and social groups rather than by rights-bearing, property-holding individuals in a "state of nature."[24] However, he rejected the classical view that these groups consisted of "the one, the few, and the many." The industrialized nation-states of nineteenth-century Europe were more "complex" and "differentiated" than that. In order to overcome what he saw as the disorganized and unjust character of economic life, which allowed the few to exploit the many, he proposed a system of "corporatism," specifically, the promotion of labor unions, employers associations, and occupational groupings that would balance one another within economic society and also serve as the nucleus of a strong civil society as well. The corporations, in turn, would be balanced against the state, so that neither would gain excessive control over the individual. Like the ancients, then, he envisioned two forms of balancing—one social, the other political—but with corporate bodies, rather than social classes, as the basic building blocks. This dual system of balances would address the problems of "anomy" and "egotism," which he saw, not only as a threat to the legitimacy and durability of the Third Republic, but as the principal sources of the moral crisis of modernity *tout court*.

Another thing that Durkheimian sociology shares with ancient political philosophy is a republican conception of liberty.[25] In this conception, liberty has at least three dimensions: nondependence, self-government, and political participation. Since this conception is so different from the modern, liberal conception first popularized by Hobbes,[26] it requires some explication. For the ancients, the opposite of "liberty" was "slavery." Within the republican tradition, the idea of slavery could be understood rather broadly to include, not only chattel slavery *strictu sensu*, but all relations of servitude. On this accounting, a king's courtier was as much a slave as a domestic servant and, indeed, anyone who was without a political voice. To be free, in this sense, was to be independent of the arbitrary will of another human being. There was a second sense of slavery as well: slavery to one's own passions. On this account, a powerful person who is ruled by his emotions is not free. To be free means to subjugate the passions to reason or, more precisely, to transform them through reason. The third and final precondition of republican liberty was collective self-governance. There can be no liberty under a tyrant, even a benign or enlightened one. (It is in this regard that the republican conception is most radically at odds with the Hobbesian.) Within the Anglo-American version of liberalism, by contrast, liberty comes to be associated mainly with noninterference and negative rights—with the freedom to "do as one pleases."

Given the influence of republican thought on the French Revolution, and of the Revolution on French political culture, it is perhaps not surprising that Durkheim's conception of liberty was more republican than liberal. Durkheim flatly rejected the liberal view that a strong state endangered individual rights. Indeed, he argued that a strong state was necessary to protect individual liberties from the "repressive influences" of powerful groups.[27] He similarly repudiated the view that individual liberty consisted in doing as one pleases. "Liberty is the fruit of regulation," he argues, and "theories that celebrate the beneficence of unrestricted liberties are apologies for a diseased state."[28] "Self-mastery," he insists, "is the first condition . . . of all liberty worthy of the name."[29] His embrace of the republican conception of liberty is undoubtedly one reason liberal readers have often (mis)characterized him as a "conservative."

I now turn to the negative side of my case.

That Durkheim was hostile to utilitarianism is old news. Still, it is instructive to examine his criticisms of utilitarianism. They bear an unmistakably Aristotelian and republican imprint. The theories of the utilitarians and the "classical economists," he argues, are founded on "an impatience with all restraint and limitation" and "the desire to encourage unrestrained and infinite appetite."[30] Such an ethos, he contends, is "contrary to nature," because "man is a limited being," with certain reserves of "vital energy," and a "part of a whole," both social and natural, whereas "the egoist lives as though he were a whole."[31] The utilitarian egoist can never achieve true happiness because she or he lives "in a state of unstable equilibrium." What is more, the egoist is a threat to society because society is impossible without a certain degree of "moral discipline."[32] Nor is a lack of moral constraint to be confused with genuine power or freedom. Invoking a commonplace argument from classical philosophy, Durkheim asks us to "[i]magine a being liberated from all external restraint, a despot still more absolute than those of which history tells us. . . . Shall we say, then, that he is all-powerful? Certainly not, since he himself cannot resist his desires. They are masters of him, as of everything else."[33] Anticipating modern critiques of consequentialism, Durkheim further warns that utilitarianism is a threat to republican government and human rights as well because "it can admit of individual liberties being suspended whenever the interest of the greater number requires that sacrifice."[34] Nor are his criticisms of utilitarianism and classical economics "merely" moral and political. They are also methodological and ontological. Rightly sensing the turn toward mathematical formalism—and away from empirical research—initiated by the "marginalist revolution" in fin de siècle economics, he argues that economists are no longer interested in "what occurs in reality or . . . how stated effects derive from causes" but only in mentally combining "purely formal notions such as value, utility, scarcity, supply and demand," in this way removing their moral premises from empirical scrutiny.[35] He also criticizes their individualist and materialist ontology (which he correctly traces to the atomism of the Epicureans) on the grounds that it ignores the emergent properties and causal powers of "synthetic entities" such as social groups, collective representations, and, for that matter, the individual psyche itself.[36]

Durkheim's attitude toward Kant's moral philosophy was more ambivalent. On the one hand, he agreed with many of Kant's premises. He agreed that "duty" is one element of morality and that we experience it as rationally compelling insofar as we are rational beings. But Durkheim's agreement was also qualified, insofar as he believed that duty is only one element of morality, and that it is often not a sufficiently compelling motive for action, because we are not *just* rational beings. "[W]e are not beings of pure reasons," he argues, but "have sensibilities that have their own nature and that are refractory to the dictates of reason." In other words, we are also "emotional creatures."[37] And because we are emotional as well as rational beings, we are compelled by particular attachments as much as by universal principles. Hence, a realistic theory of morality must include attention to the good as well as the right, because "for us to become the agents of an act it must interest our sensibility to a certain extent and appear to us as, in some way, desirable [and] it is this *sui generis* desirability which is commonly called good."[38] "Thus, we must admit a certain element of *eudemonism* and one could show that desirability and pleasure permeate the obligation."[39] Here, too, the imprint of Aristotelian ethics is unmistakably conveyed by Durkheim's introduction of the concepts of *eudemonia* and the good.

The difference in their visions of morality also leads to a difference in their stances toward moral education. One of the central premises of Kantian ethics is that all normal individuals possess an inherent capacity for moral behavior. And one of the central premises of Kantian political philosophy is that the only legitimate purpose of the state is to secure the negative rights of the individual against encroachment by other individuals. From this perspective, "A state that employs the instruments of right for purposes of a politics of virtue and moral education . . . oversteps the boundaries of legitimate lawful regulation."[40] Durkheim, by contrast, was a forceful advocate for a "politics of virtue" and indeed the chief architect of the system of "moral education" established under the Third Republic. While Kant and Durkheim both claimed to be republicans, they clearly understood republicanism quite differently—Durkheim in a more classical fashion, Kant in a more liberal one. Durkheim also found Kant's method of transcendental deduction unsatisfying and for much the same reasons that he found the mathematical formalism of the classical economists unsatisfying: because it is unempirical and ahistorical.[41] Durkheim did find Kantian moral philosophy to be empirically accurate insofar as it captured a key historical development, namely, the sacralization of abstract individuality, which Durkheim saw as the distinguishing feature of modern morality. However, it was not empirically grounded, and it mistook a historical moment for a moral universal. His criticism of Kantian ethics is therefore quite similar to the criticism of Kantian epistemology that he develops in *The Elementary Forms*: it represents a historically developed capacity as a transcendentally deduced faculty. But the most fundamental error in Kant's approach to morality, in Durkheim's view, was its attempt to seat morality in an abstracted and presocial "subject." For Durkheim, the abstract morality of moral philosophers was not to be confused with the practical morality of social actors, nor was the source of morality to be found in the transcendental faculties of the individual but in their embedded social relations. For Durkheim, morality was social through and through. Durkheim was quite far from being an unvarnished neo-Kantian; indeed, one could claim that he is better categorized as a neo-Aristotelian *avant la lettre*—or perhaps as a crypto-Aristotelian.

The Connection Denied?

Having established the connection between Durkheim and Aristotle, we can now reflect on why it has received so little attention. The most obvious reason, as noted earlier, is that Durkheim did not much emphasize it himself, which is not to say that he suppressed it altogether. Aristotle is mentioned by name at least once in all four of Durkheim's "canonical" works (i.e., *The Division of Labor, Suicide, Rules*, and *The Elementary Forms*), though less frequently than Kant and Comte, if also more frequently than, say, Rousseau and Montesquieu.

But why was Durkheim so loath to acknowledge his debts to Aristotle, and why have his interpreters been so slow to recognize them? To answer the first question, we must put Durkheim's life and work back into context, the context of both academic and party politics during the Third Republic. To answer the second, we must put Durkheim's work into the context of its reception in mid-twentieth-century America.

In 1879, when Durkheim was (finally) admitted to the École normale, "sociology" and "social science" were present in public discourse and in some private research institutions, but they were not yet institutionalized in the French system of higher education. Durkheim spent much of his life ensuring that they were and in the form that he envisioned. To this end, he had to battle on two fronts: first, against academic traditionalists and conservatives within the faculties of letters, particularly philosophers, such as his archrival, Henri Bergson; and second, against representatives of competing visions of sociology and social science, such as Gabriel Tarde and Frédéric le Play. Of course, these battles were largely "political" and even bureaucratic ones over policies and posts, but the weapons were often intellectual. In order to secure the organizational autonomy of sociology, it was necessary for Durkheim to demonstrate the empirical reality of the social and to defend his own conception of it. All of Durkheim's early works can be read as strategic "moves" in this game. This is not the place to replay that game in its entirety, move by move. For us, two aspects of it are of particular interest: his strategies vis-à-vis his two chief rivals, namely, academic philosophy and Catholic sociology.

His first move vis-à-vis philosophy was his Latin dissertation, translated as *Montesquieu and Rousseau: Forerunners of Sociology*. Durkheim opens by reclaiming "social science" as a French enterprise, rather than an English or German one, and then by tracing its origins, not to Saint-Simon or Comte, but to Montesquieu and Rousseau.[42] In this way, he sought to soothe nationalistic insecurities, which were particularly deep following the defeats of the Franco-Prussian War (1870–71) and particularly sensitive as regards philosophy, a field the Germans clearly dominated, while laying claim to a more respectable pedigree by disowning the would-be father of French sociology, Auguste Comte, whose excesses and eccentricities were well known, even notorious, in favor of other better-behaved and more legitimate founders. But if sociology was in the same lineage as Montesquieu and Rousseau, then how was it different from philosophy? If there was so much continuity, then where was the break? Durkheim marked this difference by deploying the distinction between "art" and "science." "Even Aristotle, who devoted far more attention than Plato to experience, aimed at discovering, not the laws of social existence, but the best forms of society."[43] In order to secure the autonomy of sociology, then, Durkheim played a double game. On the one hand, he sought to legitimate the new discipline by inserting it into a more honorable lineage, the tradition of republican political philosophy from Aristotle to Montesquieu. On the other hand, he sought to demarcate the new discipline by arguing that sociology was concerned with "the laws of social existence."

This double game led to certain difficulties. The distinction between science and art was useful for marking sociology's jurisdiction off from philosophy's, but it was threatening to Durkheim's vision of sociology as a "moral science" in the strong sense, that is, as a diagnostic and even prescriptive science of social morality, which was concerned precisely with "the best forms of society." How did Durkheim resolve this tension? In truth, he didn't. Instead, he simply flip-flopped between the strong and weak versions of his program as the (political) context required. When the context demanded a clear distinction between sociology and philosophy, he adopted the weak version of his program, as in this passage from his 1900 essay "Sociology in France in the Nineteenth Century": "The fact is that art, even methodical and reflective art, is one thing and science is another. Science studies facts just to know them, indifferent to the applications to which its ideas can be put. Art, on the contrary, deals with them only in order to know what can be done with them."[44] In the weak program, social science was a pure science without practical application. By contrast, when the context demanded a clear assertion of the public relevance of social science, he invoked a different metaphor, that of the diagnostician or pathologist, as in his 1904 essay "The Intellectual Elite and Democracy." "Just as a great physiologist is generally a mediocre clinician, a sociologist has every chance of making a very incomplete statesmen." In the weak version of moral science, on the one hand, sociology completely abstains from practical recommendations; in the strong version, on the other hand, it simply abstains from political leadership, though not, it should be emphasized from party politics per se. It is "good that intellectuals be represented in deliberative assemblies," Durkheim contends, because "their culture permits them to bring to deliberations elements of information which are not negligible."[45]

While Durkheim sometimes preached the weak program, the truth is that he mostly practiced the strong program.[46] With the exception of *The Rules of Sociological Method*, all of his major works contain practical prescriptions for the moral ills of French society as he diagnosed them. *The Division of Labor* proposed organization of and cooperation between employers' associations and labor unions as a remedy for the lack of economic regulation (the "anomic division of labor"), which Durkheim saw as the root cause of the economic volatility of French capitalism, a proposal that he elaborated further in *Professional Ethics and Civic Morals*. *The Elementary Forms of the Religious Life* proposed the establishment of "civic cults," national rituals, and holidays that would sustain social solidarity. *Moral Education* outlined a practical program of . . . moral education, which would create the virtuous citizens the Third Republic required.

However, Durkheim never entirely succeeded in setting forth a coherent justification for his strong program of moral science as a diagnostic and prescriptive science. His most sustained effort in this direction is to be found in chapter 3 of *The Rules*, in which he seeks to ground the strong program in a distinction between "health" and "sickness" and "the normal" and "the pathological." "For societies, as for individuals, health is good and desirable; sickness, on the other hand, is bad and must be avoided. If therefore we find an objective criterion, inherent in the facts themselves, to allow us to distinguish scientifically health from sickness in the various orders of social phenomena, science will be in a position to throw light on practical matters while remaining true to its own method."[47] But how does one determine whether a particular society is "healthy" or "ill"? One obvious solution would be to define "healthy" as "flourishing." Durkheim's use of the adjectives "good" and "desirable" to describe "health" in the passage just cited suggests that he may have at least considered a *eudemonistic* definition of health. So does his proposal, a few pages later, that we define health as "consisting in the joyous development of vital energy." Here, health is not just normality but flourishing. In the end, however, Durkheim turns away from this solution. Instead, he attempts to ground his program in another distinction, one between "the normal" and "the pathological." The results are far from satisfactory. The problem is that what is "normal" is not necessarily "good" or "desirable." Crime and suicide, for example, are "normal" parts of social life but certainly not "good" or "desirable" ones. Durkheim is not unaware of the difficulty. In *Moral Education*, for instance, he avers that "for a great nation like ours to be truly in a state of moral health it is not enough for most of its members to be sufficiently removed from the grossest transgressions—murder, theft, fraud. . . . Society must, in addition, have before it an ideal towards which it reaches."[48]

But what is this ideal to be, if not *eudemonia* or virtue? We are thus confronted with a new version of our original question. Why did Durkheim retreat from the more promising, Aristotelian justification of his strong program and choose the less propitious, functionalist justification? At least part of the answer is probably to be found at the intersection of academic and partisan politics under the Third Republic. Crudely speaking, one can distinguish three broad currents or political tendencies during this period: conservative Catholics, moderate republicans ("radicals"), and socialists. Though friendly with many socialists, particularly those of a syndicalist bent, Durkheim did not accept the central goals of Marxian socialism. He did not favor state control of the means of production or a dictatorship of the proletariat. But he allied with the socialists—and against the conservative Catholics—on the two most controversial issues of the day: the secularization of the French educational system and the Dreyfus affair. Nonetheless, there were other, perhaps less salient issues on which Durkheim's position was actually closer to that of the Catholics than of the socialists, particularly his high valuation of social order and economic peace. But as often happens to political centrists during culture wars of this sort, Durkheim found himself excoriated by hardliners from both sides. While the arch-conservative Peguy reckoned him among "the party of the intellectuals" (i.e., the left-wing secular republicans or "radicals"), the radical socialist Sorel placed him in the "neo-Scholastic party" (i.e., among the conservative Catholic nationalists).[49] It is the latter accusation that concerns us most—and that may have concerned Durkheim most as well—because it reveals the broader political stakes that would have been involved in any public identification with Aristotle.

There were narrower academic stakes as well that would have been important to Durkheim. Among the various schools contending for dominance of French sociology were the followers of Frédéric le Play, a conservative Catholic of neo-Scholastic sympathies who advocated cooperation between labor and capital and paternalistic employer policies as the remedy for class conflict and economic exploitation, a position that became the official doctrine of the Catholic Church following Leo XIII's promulgation of *Rerum novarum* in 1891. In an earlier encyclical, *Aeterni patris* (1879), issued in the second year of his papacy, it should be noted, Leo had also made neo-Thomism the official theology of the Catholic Church and used all of the considerable means at his disposal to see that it was taught and observed by Catholic intellectuals and priests.

Thus, the charge of "neo-Scholasticism," which may seem bizarre or gratuitous to us, was actually quite explosive, all the more so because it was not altogether unfounded. The patron saint of the neo-Scholastics, after all, was Thomas Aquinas, whose life's work had been to reconcile faith and reason and, more concretely, Christian theology and Aristotelian philosophy. Aquinas's oeuvre includes twelve commentaries on Aristotle, many of which are still read today, and Aquinas's ethics and metaphysics were deeply influenced by "the Philosopher." Building on the *Nicomachean Ethics*, Aquinas made the so-called function argument—that to be fully human is to develop those capacities that are distinctively human, namely, reason and speech—into the philosophical foundations of a rationalistic theological ethics. Aquinas's metaphysics were likewise premised on Aristotle's. Neither man's system is easily summarized—or, for that matter, easily understood. What is important in this context is that both systems were radically at odds with the materialistic, reductionistic, and atomistic ontologies that had first been advanced by the Epicureans, reappropriated by seventeenth-century neo-Epicurean skeptics, like Hobbes, and then developed into a full-blown anti-theistic materialism by Diderot and d'Holbach. For instance, both Aristotle and Aquinas argued (1) that "form" was as real as "matter"; (2) that particular combinations of form and matter resulted in "composite entities" whose qualities and properties were dependent on their constituent elements but were not reducible to them; and (3) that the real "substance" of an entity was not its constituent parts but the "essence" that resulted from their combination. In other words, they anticipated modern theories of symbolic forms, emergent properties, and natural law.

It is not difficult to see the parallels between the neo-Aristotelian tradition of metaphysics and the Durkheimian vision of sociology. The parallels emerge with particular clarity in Durkheim's theory of "collective representations." To recall, Durkheim argues that (1) collective representations are every bit as real as individual ones; (2) collective representations emerge from interactions between individuals over time, and while they can exist only in and through individual minds, they have properties and powers not reducible to individual minds; and (3) they are, in some deep sense, the essence of a society without which "society" as we understand it simply would not exist. Nor are these parallels between scholastic metaphysics and Durkheimian sociology accidental. Recall that Durkheim's nickname at the École normale was "the metaphysician." His beloved teacher, Émile Boutroux, was a neo-Aristotelian who drew on the notion of "composite entities" to develop a theory of emergent properties. And Durkheim himself would draw heavily on Boutroux's work in developing his own theory of collective representations. Of course, the correlation between Durkheim's and Aquinas's views was almost certainly spurious in that both could be traced back to the same source: Aristotle.

So while Sorel's charge of neo-Scholasticism was surely overblown, it seems likely that Durkheim's sociology drew not only on Aristotle's ethics but also on his metaphysics. But deny it Durkheim did, and on more than one occasion. In *Suicide*, for instance, he somewhat disingenuously and incoherently insisted that "there is some superficiality about attacking our conception as scholasticism and reproaching it for assigning to a social phenomenon a foundation in some vital principle or other of a new sort. We refuse to accept that these phenomena have as a substratus the conscience of the individual, we assign them another; that formed by all the individual consciences in union and combination. There is nothing substantival or ontological about this substratus, since it is merely a whole composed of parts. But it is just as real, nevertheless."[50] This may not have been full-blown scholasticism, but it *was* substantive and ontological as Durkheim himself surely knew, if not in a strongly scholastic sense. Indeed, he admitted as much in a later essay, in which he emphasized that "Metaphysical problems, even the boldest ones which have wracked philosophers, must never be allowed to fall into oblivion, because this is unacceptable. Yet it is likewise undoubtedly the case that they are called upon to take on new forms. Precisely because of this we believe that sociology, more than any other science, can contribute to this renewal."[51] What, after all, was Durkheim's famous claim that "society is a reality *sui generis*" if not an ontological claim? The problem was that he could not forthrightly concede this without playing into the hands of his political and academic rivals. In short,

Durkheim had to abstain from certain theoretical moves that might have endangered his political position.

In sum, Durkheim distanced himself from Aristotle for at least two reasons: first, in order to assert the intellectual autonomy of sociology from philosophy and, second, in order to maintain his political distance from Catholic conservatives. There may have been a third reason as well: among the "modern" French philosophers of Durkheim's era, Kant's stock was much higher than Aristotle's. And yet, the distancing was not complete. Durkheim also stressed the continuities between social theory and political philosophy, especially political philosophy of a civic republican sort. Further, his commitment to moral education and corporatist economics did appear conservative to libertarians and socialists. This double game or balancing act did introduce certain tensions and aporias into the heart of Durkheim's sociology. This was most evident in his (failed) attempt to recast *eudemonia* in terms of normality; flourishing and normality are not the same thing.

Durkheim's sociology might have developed differently in another context. Imagine that sociology's main intellectual competitor is economics, rather than philosophy. Imagine that religious conservatives are radical individualists of a Protestant sort, and political liberals are radical individualists of a secular sort. And imagine, finally, that Aristotle's stock is higher than Kant's among academic philosophers and theologians. In short, imagine that Durkheim is working in the contemporary United States. In that context, he would have no good reason to downplay the Aristotelian connection. On the contrary, it might serve him well. Why, then, have American sociologists been so slow to reconceive Durkheim's sociology as a sociology of the good? It is to that question that I now turn.

The reception of Durkheim in American sociology can be divided roughly into three phases.[52] In the first, which spanned the early decades of the twentieth century, Durkheim's work was generally misunderstood when it was not simply ignored. Albion Small's 1902 review of the French version of *The Division of Labor* focuses exclusively on the corporatist approach to the social problem that Durkheim advanced in his new preface.[53] There is no discussion whatsoever of the changing nature of solidarity and corresponding changes in law, leading one to wonder whether Small actually read beyond the preface. Be that as it may, he summarily dismisses Durkheim for giving too little recognition to the role of "interests" and conflicts in social life. With the first translation of *The Elementary Forms* in 1915 and then of

The Division of Labor in 1933, followed by *The Rules* in 1938, Durkheim's work became much more widely known and, judging from the reviews, also much better understood.[54] But this does not mean it was well received, even by the translators themselves. Thus, George Simpson's introduction to *The Division of Labor* is quite critical of Durkheim's "social realism."[55] Similarly, in his introduction to *The Rules*, George Catlin takes Durkheim to task for "confusing" science and ethics.[56] While there was growing recognition of Durkheim's role in establishing French sociology, there was also considerable mistrust of the "French School," a mistrust that was common to laissez-faire individualists, such as Sumner, as well as to socialist sympathizers, such as Simpson, who disliked Durkheim's emphasis on social harmony and his aspirations toward a moral science.

In the second phase, which spanned the middle decades of the twentieth century, Durkheim's work came to be seen through a Parsonsian lens and with mixed effects. On the one hand, *The Structure of Social Action* transformed the American Durkheim from the leading representative of the "French School" into one of the founding fathers, a status he still enjoys today. There was a flurry of translations during the 1950s, and by the early 1960s, all of Durkheim's major works, and many of his minor ones, were available in English. On the other hand, the enormous influence of structural functionalism in the social sciences during these years, in both the United States and the United Kingdom, meant that these translations received little attention, with the notable exception of *Suicide*. Lewis Coser recounts that "Those of us who went to graduate school in the 1930s, 1940s and 1950s were largely led to see in Durkheim the father of most structural explanation in sociology. Hence, *The Division of Labor in Society*, *The Rules of Sociological Methods* as well as *Suicide* were the works we were encouraged and required to study."[57] Ironically, then, the structuralist reading of Durkheim had the effect of obscuring the moral dimension of his thought.

More ironically still, it was precisely the revolt against Parsonsianism beginning in the late 1960s, inspired partly by a critique of Parsons's emphasis on social norms, that opened the door to a fuller understanding of Durkheim's work, based on a more complete reading of his oeuvre. This third phase of Durkheim's reception runs from the early 1970s until the present. Coinciding as it did with the rediscovery of civic humanism by intellectual historians,[58] on the one hand, and the renaissance of virtue ethics,[59] on the other, one might have anticipated that the third phase would have also involved a greater appreciation of Aristotelian themes in Durkheim's work, and indeed it did, though only to a very limited degree. Thus, the most cited major work of this period, Steven Lukes's intellectual biography of Durkheim, makes only fleeting mention of Aristotle and does not count him among the major influences. The influence of "classical philosophy" receives somewhat greater attention in several communitarian interpretations of Durkheim written by non-sociologists.[60] As its title suggests, Douglas Challenger's *Durkheim through the Lens of Aristotle* places the connection front and center, and anticipates many of the arguments of this paper, but it has been almost completely ignored within sociology, registering fewer than a dozen citations as of this writing.[61] In retrospect, it is clear that the main upshot of third-wave work on Durkheim has been a revitalization of the sociology of culture, not a recovery of the sociology of the good. *The Elementary Forms* is now seen as Durkheim's chef d'oeuvre; his works on moral education and civic life, meanwhile, continue to be ignored by most sociologists if, indeed, they are known at all.

Why has the Aristotelian influence on Durkheim remained hidden for so long? In part, curricular reform and intellectual specialization are the causes. The classics are no longer part of the core curriculum at most American high schools and universities as they were in Durkheim's day. They are not even part of the core curriculum in most undergraduate and graduate social science programs. They are to be encountered, if at all, in survey courses on philosophy or political theory. Were he writing today, Durkheim would not really need to renounce the Aristotelian influence because many of his readers probably would not detect it.

This is not to say that a more Aristotelian Durkheim would have met with a more positive reception. There would have been considerable resistance to such an enterprise. The professionalist faction within early American sociology wished to distance itself from practical enterprises such as teacher education and social welfare, not to mention "religious sociology" and "Christian sociology," which it viewed as threats to its agenda of establishing sociology as a pure science in the core of the research university.[62] It also wished to distance itself from any politics of virtue or moral education, terms that had been co-opted by conservative reformers during the nineteenth century. The Durkheimian agenda of a moral science was very much at odds with these goals. So other Durkheims were created. *The Division of Labor* became a functionalist work. *Suicide* became a positivist work. And *The Elementary Forms* became a work of cultural sociology. Not that these readings are wrong. But they are partial. If the "essence" of a thing is in the whole, rather than the parts, then such readings surely miss the essence of Durkheim's work. For all of these books are moral science with a practical intent, a point that comes out that much more clearly when all of the parts are included in the whole.

Conclusion: Post-Secular Durkheim

This essay has advanced three theses. The first is that Durkheim was a neo-Aristotelian of sorts. I say "neo" because Durkheim was well aware that Aristotle's ideas could not be mechanically applied to modern societies. The chief differences between the ancient city-state and the modern nation-state, as Durkheim saw it, were two: (1) a more complex "division of labor" that could not be captured by the classical distinction between the one, the few, and the many; and (2) a more egalitarian moral system that extended citizenship to all and postulated liberty and virtue as universal human capacities rather than elite privileges. Viewed in this way, Durkheim's sociology fits squarely into the evolving lineage of civic humanism, from Aristotle to Montesquieu, and placed alongside the work of other thinkers who sought to adapt the classical tradition of political thought to the modern age, such as Adam Ferguson, Alexis de Tocqueville, Benjamin Constant, Madame de Staël, and, for that matter, James Madison and Thomas Jefferson.

Why has the Aristotelian influence been so little noticed? The answer proposed here—and this is the second thesis—is that Durkheim himself downplayed it for reasons of academic and partisan politics. He wished to draw a sharp line between sociology and philosophy and between his politics and social Catholicism, and a public association with Aristotle would have blurred these boundaries. Alas, the ruse succeeded all too well. Later generations were ill equipped to see the Aristotelian influence and were, in any event, more inclined to see Durkheim as something else, not as a neo-Aristotelian, but as a "French sociologist," a "functionalist," or a "sociologist of culture."

What, finally, is to be gained from recovering the neo-Aristotelian Durkheim? As Freud reminds us, the repressed always returns: as symptoms. The double repression of the Aristotelian underpinnings of Durkheimian sociology is no exception to this rule. Perhaps the most debilitating symptom of all has been functionalism. The roots of the disorder can be traced back to chapter 3 of *The Rules*, in which Durkheim retreats from a positive ideal of human flourishing and seeks to establish his moral science on a pseudo-biological concept of "normality," turning from the function argument à la Aristotle to a quasi-functionalist argument à la Spencer. It was a fatal move that derailed sociology for the better part of two generations. To be sure, the blame cannot be pinned on Durkheim alone. He had his accomplices on this side of the Atlantic as well, with Talcott Parsons being the chief culprit.

Functionalism was put to rest nearly three decades ago—or, rather, exiled to Germany, where it lives on in the new guise of "systems theory." All attempts to revive it on this side of the Atlantic have thus far failed. But while there is no reason to regret this, there are perhaps some reasons for nostalgia. Functionalism *did* at least provide a certain language, however inadequate, for talking about the social good. Apart from Marxism, post-functionalist sociology finds itself quite bereft of a moral vocabulary, and graduate training in the field often serves as kind of moral *un*-education, in which students are taught to transform their moral convictions into researchable problems (a good thing) before sloughing them off altogether (a bad thing).

Durkheim's sociology contains a strong critique of the neo-Kantian and utilitarian "solutions." Against the neo-Kantians, it contends that there are *objective* sources of morality that derive from human sociality itself. We *desire* the common good because of the emotional returns that moral action generates in the social side of our personalities. Against the utilitarians, it argues that infinite pleasure is not the same as individual well-being and that moral obligation remains psychologically compelling even when it conflicts with "natural" inclinations. Recasting "altruism" or "honor" as "preferences" merely defers the problem without solving it.

Durkheim's sociology also suggests a possible alternative: a theory of the good. Indeed, his major works contain an implicit theory of the good (modern) society. This theory is articulated and elaborated across Durkheim's oeuvre, and I can provide only the barest of sketches in this context. In *The Division of Labor*, the good (modern) society is one in which the structural interdependencies between individuals are intellectually recognized, morally valorized, and politically organized. In *Suicide*, the good (modern) society is one in which the goods of individual autonomy and liberty are properly balanced with the goods of group solidarity and moral regulation. In *Professional Ethics and Civic Morals*, the good (modern) society is one in which there is a robust civil society that can mediate between the individual and the state and establish a proper balance between individual rights, group solidarities, and regulatory power. In *Moral Education*, the (good) modern society is one that forms its offspring, not simply into good workers, but also into good citizens, by inculcating public virtues. Finally, in *The Elementary Forms*, the good (modern) society is one that reproduces and revitalizes its core values by means of civic rituals and celebrations.

These prescriptions are admittedly vague. But a neo-Aristotelian moral science would of course be a practical science that would be somewhat vague in its results, however exact it might be in its methods. It can help to conceptualize the mean or "target" that one is aiming for, but it is not the means or "bow" itself. And vague is not wrong. On the contrary, contemporary work on "hedonics," "positive psychology," and "the sociology of happiness" suggests that Durkheim's conclusions were essentially correct. Income above a certain level (ca. $10,000 per capita) does *not* increase aggregate levels of happiness within a society. Personal well-being and even longevity are much more strongly influenced by the density of social ties than by the size of one's paycheck. And participation in rituals does have measurable effects on individual contentment.

Of course, Durkheim's is not the only vision of sociology. But neither is his the only case of repression. With the exception of Tocqueville, all of the "founders" of modern sociology entered into more or less the same strategic trade-off: in order to distance themselves from religion and philosophy, they cut themselves off from moral and political philosophy. The result, however, was not an "objective" science independent of moral concerns. Rather, it was a moral science predicated on a thin morality—one that came to valorize equality and autonomy above all else—a morality that is publicly denied and typically performed in negative terms, as a critique of all inequality and, more generally, of all power. It is in no small part this lack of moral depth and seriousness that leads many laypeople to dismiss the discipline out of hand.

How might we recover this lost depth and seriousness? One strategy might be to undo the double repression that was the side effect of the "secular revolution," in which early sociology was swept up, by reconnecting the discipline to the traditions of moral and political philosophy out of which it initially arose, traditions that have real depth and seriousness. This is not to say that sociology should merge with philosophy or that it should become a stalking horse for civic republicanism—though worse outcomes are imaginable. Rather, it is to say that it should seek to bring the rigor of its methods to bear on the study of human flourishing,and pose the results of its researches against the moral naïveté of radical individualism, so as to recover the good from the closet.

Notes

1. Emile Durkheim and Anthony Giddens, *Emile Durkheim; Selected Writings* (Cambridge: Cambridge University Press, 1972), 3.

2. Immanuel Kant and Mary J. Gregor, *Critique of Practical Reason*, Cambridge Texts in the History of Philosophy (Cambridge and New York: Cambridge University Press, 1997).

3. Immanuel Kant, Paul Guyer, and Allen W. Wood, *Critique of Pure Reason*, The Cambridge Edition of the Works of Immanuel Kant (Cambridge and New York: Cambridge University Press, 1998).

4. Jeremy Bentham and ebrary Inc., "An Introduction to the Principles of Morals and Legislation" (Kitchener, Ont.: Batoche, 2000), http://site.ebrary.com/lib/yale/Doc?id=2001956; Philip Beauchamp and Jeremy Bentham, *The Influence of Natural Religion on the Temporal Happiness of Mankind*, Great Books in Philosophy (Amherst, NY: Prometheus Books, 2003).

5. Robert N. Bellah, ed., *Emile Durkheim on Morality and Society* (Chicago: University of Chicago Press, 1973); Jeffrey C. Alexander and Philip Smith, eds., *The Cambridge Companion to Durkheim* (Cambridge and New York: Cambridge University Press, 2005); Steven Lukes, *Émile Durkheim: His Life and Work, a Historical and Critical Study*, 1st U.S. ed. (New York: Harper & Row, 1972). Emile Durkheim, *On Morality and Society: Selected Writings*, The Heritage of Sociology (Chicago: University of Chicago Press, 1973); Mark Sydney Cladis, *A Communitarian Defense of Liberalism: Emile Durkheim and Contemporary Social Theory*, Stanford Series in Philosophy (Stanford, CA: Stanford University Press, 1992); Ernest Wallwork, *Durkheim: Morality and Milieu* (Cambridge, MA: Harvard University Press, 1972). The one important exception to this is Douglas F. Challenger, *Durkheim through the Lens of Aristotle: Durkheimian, Postmodernist, and Communitarian Responses to the Enlightenment* (Lanham, MD: Rowman & Littlefield Publishers, 1994). Challenger's book anticipates many of the arguments of this paper, though I am not wholly in agreement with his interpretation. In particular, unlike him, I do not regard Durkheim's attempt to reconceive *eudemonia* in terms of normality as successful.

6. Immanuel Kant and Mary J. Gregor, *Groundwork of the Metaphysics of Morals*, Cambridge Texts in the History of Philosophy (Cambridge and New York: Cambridge University Press, 1998).

7. John Stuart Mill and George Sher, *Utilitarianism*, 2nd ed. (Indianapolis, IN: Hackett Publishing, 2001); Henry Sidgwick, *The Methods of Ethics*, 7th ed. (Chicago: University of Chicago Press, 1962).

8.   David Carr and J. W. Steutel, *Virtue Ethics and Moral Education*, Routledge International Studies in the Philosophy of Education 5 (London and New York: Routledge, 1999); Stephen D. Carden and ebrary Inc., "Virtue Ethics: Dewey and MacIntyre," in *Continuum Studies in American Philosophy* (London and New York: Continuum, 2006), http://site.ebrary.com/lib/yale/Doc?id=10224799.

9.   Richard Taylor, *Virtue Ethics: An Introduction*, Prometheus Lecture Series (Amherst, NY: Prometheus Books, 2002); Roger Crisp and Michael A. Slote, *Virtue Ethics*, Oxford Readings in Philosophy (Oxford and New York: Oxford University Press, 1997).

10.   Terry Nichols Clark, *Prophets and Patrons: The French University and the Emergence of the Social Sciences* (Cambridge, MA: Harvard University Press, 1973), 22, 39; Antoine Prost, *L'école et la famille dans une société en mutation*, ed. Louis-Henri Parias, vol. 4, *Histoire générale de l'enseignement et de l'éducation en France* (Paris: Nouvelle librairie française, 1968).

11.   Lukes, *Émile Durkheim*, 53.

12.   Ibid., 104–106.

13.   Emile Durkheim and W. D. Halls, *The Division of Labor in Society*, 1st U.S. ed. (New York: Free Press, 1984), 7 n. 1.

14.   Aristotle, *Nicomachean Ethics*, trans. Roger Crisp (New York: Cambridge University Press, 2000), 89; 1133a.

15.   Emile Durkheim and Steven Lukes, *The Rules of Sociological Method*, 1st U.S. ed. (New York: Free Press, 1982), 259.

16.   Aristotle, *Nicomachean Ethics*, 30–31.

17.   Emile Durkheim, *Suicide: A Study in Sociology* (New York: Free Press, 1951), 321.

18.   Emile Durkheim, *Moral Education: A Study in the Theory and Application of the Sociology of Education* (New York: Free Press of Glencoe, 1961), 46.

19.   Ibid., 96.

20.   Emile Durkheim, *Sociology and Philosophy* (Glencoe, IL: Free Press, 1953), 55.

21.   Emile Durkheim, *Professional Ethics and Civic Morals*, International Library of Sociology and Social Reconstruction (Glencoe, IL: Free Press, 1958), 60. Careful readers will notice that Durkheim's language mixes Aristotelian terms ("character" and "the good") with Kantian ones ("law" and "duty"). However, his use of a function argument—the claim that the human good involves the realization of human nature, defined as that which sets humans apart from animals—and his emphasis on human sociality put him squarely in the neo-Aristotelian camp.

22.   Durkheim, *Suicide*, 103; Aristotle, *Nicomachean Ethics*.

23.   Indeed, the analysis of ritual and religion contained in *The Elementary Forms* suggests that embodied morality is actually prior to codified morality, both phylogenetically and

phenomenologically, and that moral conviction is effective only to the degree that it is undergirded by collective emotion.

24. Durkheim, *Professional Ethics and Civic Morals*, 45.

25. Philip Pettit, *Republicanism: A Theory of Freedom and Government*, Oxford Political Theory (Oxford: Clarendon Press; New York: Oxford University Press, 1997); Quentin Skinner, *Liberty before Liberalism* (Cambridge and New York: Cambridge University Press, 1998).

26. Quentin Skinner, *Hobbes and Republican Liberty* (Cambridge: Cambridge University Press, 2008).

27. Durkheim, *Professional Ethics and Civic Morals*.

28. Durkheim, *Moral Education*, 54.

29. Ibid., 45.

30. Ibid., 36.

31. Ibid., 51, 71.

32. Ibid., 69; Durkheim, *Professional Ethics and Civic Morals*, 10.

33. Durkheim, *Moral Education*, 44.

34. Durkheim, *On Morality and Society*, 46.

35. Durkheim and Lukes, *The Rules of Sociological Method*, 179.

36. Durkheim, *Sociology and Philosophy*, 1–30. Here, Durkheim's position anticipates that of contemporary "critical realists," such as Andrew Sayer, Roy Bhaskar, and Margaret Archer.

37. Durkheim, *Moral Education*, 109.

38. Durkheim, *Sociology and Philosophy*, 36.

39. Ibid., 44–45.

40. Durkheim, *Professional Ethics and Civic Morals*, 345; Wolfgang Kersting, "Politics, Freedom, and Order: Kant's Political Philosophy," in *The Cambridge Companion to Kant* (New York: Cambridge University Press, 1992).

41. Durkheim and Lukes, *The Rules of Sociological Method*, 179.

42. Emile Durkheim, *Montesquieu and Rousseau: Forerunners of Sociology* (Ann Arbor: University of Michigan Press, 1960), 1.

43. Ibid., 4.

44. Durkheim, *On Morality and Society*, 4.

45. Ibid.

46. Durkheim's strong program of moral science is not to be confused with Jeffrey Alexander's strong program of cultural sociology. On the contrary, Alexander's strong program is closer to Durkheim's weak program.

47. Durkheim and Lukes, *The Rules of Sociological Method*, 86.

48. Durkheim, *Moral Education*, 13.

49. Durkheim, *On Morality and Society*, xxxviii.

50. Durkheim, *Suicide*, 319.

51. Durkheim and Lukes, *The Rules of Sociological Method*, 237.

52. Lewis A. Coser, "Review: [Untitled]," *American Anthropologist* 76, no. 4 (1974).

53. Albion Small, «Review: *De La Division Du Travail Social* by Emile Durkheim," *American Journal of Sociology* 7, no. 4 (1902).

54. John Donaldson, «Review: Emile Durkheim on the Division of Labor in Society by George Simpson,» *Annals of the American Academy of Political and Social Science* 173 (1934); Émile Benoît-Smullyan, "Review: The Rules of Sociological Method: By Émile Durkheim; Sarah A. Solovay; John H. Mueller; George E. G. Catlin," *American Sociological Review* 3, no. 4 (1938); J. P. Lichtenberger, "Review: *The Elementary Forms of the Religious Life* by Emile Durkheim," *Annals of the American Academy of Political and Social Science* 66 (1916).

55. Emile Durkheim, *The Division of Labor in Society* (New York: Free Press; London: Collier Macmillan, 1933).

56. Emile Durkheim et al., *The Rules of Sociological Method*, 8th ed., The University of Chicago Sociological Series (Chicago: University of Chicago Press, 1938).

57. Lewis A. Coser, "The Revival of the Sociology of Culture: The Case of Collective Memory," *Sociological Forum* 7, no. 2 (1992): 365.

58. Bernard Bailyn, *The Ideological Origins of the American Revolution*, enl. ed. (Cambridge, MA: Belknap Press of Harvard University Press, 1992); J. G. A. Pocock and ebrary Inc., "The Machiavellian Moment: Florentine Political Thought and the Atlantic Republican Tradition," Princeton University Press, online book, http://site.ebrary.com/lib/yale/Doc?id=10035914.

59. Alasdair C. MacIntyre, *After Virtue: A Study in Moral Theory* (Notre Dame, IN: University of Notre Dame Press, 1981).

60. Cladis, *A Communitarian Defense of Liberalism*; Dominick LaCapra, *Émile Durkheim: Sociologist and Philosopher* (Ithaca, NY: Cornell University Press, 1972); Wallwork, *Durkheim*.

61. Based on a "Cited References" search of social science titles in Web of Science, August 18, 2010.

62. Christian Smith, "Secularizing American Higher Education: The Case of Early American Sociology," in *The Secular Revolution* (Berkeley: University of California Press, 2003); Olivier Tschannen, *Les théories de la sécularisation*, Travaux de droit, d'économie, de sciences politiques, de sociologie et d'anthropologie, no. 165 (Geneva: Droz, 1992).

CHAPTER FIVE

"Simple Ideas, Small Miracles": The Obama Phenomenon

Hent de Vries

"A Good Crazy"

It needs no proof that the 2008 election of Barack Obama as the forty-fourth president of the United States represented in the eyes of many "a magical transformative moment . . . the symbolic culmination of the black freedom struggle, the grand achievement of a great collective dream," in other words, "a seismic event."[1] And what, mostly in Europe, was called the "Obama effect"—including its, perhaps, inevitable disappointments—has not ceased to cause wonder as to the fate of the political in what is not just a post-9/11 era of global politics but, in the eyes of many, also the dreamlike, if very tentative, beginnings of a post–civil rights era and post-racial phase in American culture.

It is no accident, then, that Obama, in the very speech that launched him onto the national and then international stage, appealed not just to "simple ideas" but also to "small miracles" in formulating his agenda of "hope" and "change." Nothing less would do and be required. And in the subsequent speeches and writings in which he would map his route to national prominence, indeed, the presidency, he tapped into the deepest intellectual and spiritual resources that the American dream had stored, reclaiming a past of which William Faulkner had written that it "is not dead. In fact, it's not even past."[2]

From this past, Obama confessed in his autobiography, *Dreams from My Father*, he conjured up "a series of images, romantic images of a past I have never known," alluding to scenes and sounds such as "the sit-ins, the marches, the jailhouse songs"[3] of the civil rights movement and also, even deeper down, the experiences from the African continent and his father's native Kenya, just as he drew on motifs and motivations steeped in the tradition of so-called American Transcendentalism and Emerson's "Self-Reliance," the theological legacy and Christian Realism in political matters inspired especially by the writings and teachings of Reinhold Niebuhr.

However, these innovative turns to tradition did not so much suggest a choice between, say, "memory" (let alone "the nostalgia of the Party of Memory"), on the one hand, and "hope" (let alone a party that would pretend to own this hope at every turn), on the other, but the surprising—and, we should add, somewhat anachronistic—possibility of bringing memory and hope into one single, unified perspective while allowing their respective aspects and elements to retain their distinctive political meaning and force.[4]

Some have speculated that this "double vision" (a term I borrow from Sari Nusseibeh) had everything to do with Obama's early experience of and extensive meditation upon the question of race (in Kloppenburg's words, "the color line, 'two-ness,' and double consciousness"[5]). Others have located it elsewhere.

Be this as it may, Obama clearly was a master in telling and universalizing his own story. In the words of his best biographer:

> He learned to make it an emblematic story: my story is *your* story, an *American* story. Obama was not suggesting that he was unique; there are many millions of Americans with complex backgrounds and identities, criss-crossing races, nationalities, origins. But Obama proposed to be the first President who represented the variousness of American life.[6]

He was able to do so, this author continues, because he was able to "change styles without relinquishing his genuineness: a more straight-up delivery for a luncheon with business people in the Loop . . . ; echoes of the pastors of the black church when he was in one," crafting his speech "to fit the moment," as only a "multilingual" person—a person, rather, who could speak in more than one key and gear, a so-called shape-shifter—could do.[7]

This said, Obama's eventual election remained in the eyes of many, not least the "giants" of the civil rights era, "a kind of miracle": "It could only be a miracle that white Americans, even white Southerners, were prepared to at last vote for a black man."[8] In the words of one of Martin Luther King

Jr.'s former colleagues, Joseph Lowery, one of the founders of the Southern Christian Leadership Conference, who introduced Obama's speech at
Brown Chapel in Selma, his possible election would be "a *good* crazy." Invoking the metaphor of trains and railways (a subway) in order to sketch the
odds—the mechanism and its technologies—that human boundless frailty
and immeasurable courage are up against, he noted:

> When Harriet Tubman would run up and down the underground, she was
> as crazy as she could be—but it was a *good* crazy. And when Paul preached to
> Agrippa, Agrippa said, "Paul, you're crazy." But it was a *good* crazy.
>
> And I'm saying today we need more folks in this country who've got a
> good crazy. You can't tell what will happen when you have the good crazy
> folks going to the polls to vote. . . .
>
> Let me tell you what *good* crazy can do. The other day in New York,
> a man on the platform of the subway had a good crazy. He looked down
> between the tracks and saw a brother, prostrate, doomed by an oncoming
> train. And he jumped down in the middle of the tracks. And I asked a friend
> of mine, I said, Go out there and measure how deep it is. The deepest mea-
> surement they've given me is twenty-six inches. Ain't no way in the world for
> one man to get on top of the other in twenty-six inches, and the train go over,
> and the only thing it touched, left a little grease on his cap. . . .
>
> That *same* God is here today. Something crazy may happen in this coun-
> try. Oh Lord![9]

At least as interesting as these "crazy" comments, which initially seemed
to take all the spotlight away and seemed unlikely to properly set the stage
for Obama's attempt in Selma to claim the mantle of the civil rights movement—proclaiming his membership in the "Joshua generation" that, unlike
Moses, would "get to the Promised land"—Lowery's parable spoke in fact to
the heart of the matter. Nothing but a "good crazy" would make this happen,
if anything did. Yet to wager this much, the rewards could be enormous. As
Remnick writes:

> Through most of Lowery's five-minute speech, Obama had a faraway look,
> but as Lowery started waving his hands, as his homily went into overdrive, as
> it got funnier, as it became clearer that the really "good crazy" notion behind
> it all was the possible election of a black to the Presidency, Obama started
> laughing and clapping like everyone else. As Lowery stalked away, with the

laughter and applause still booming, Obama's face split into an enormous grin. The stage was not merely set; it was as if Lowery had set it ablaze.[10]

For reasons having to do with his remarkable biography and personal temperament, Obama represented and represents—perhaps more than any other presidential candidate or political leader in the Western world at this particular juncture in time—a post-multicultural, post-identitarian, post-partisan, and, indeed, post-secular form of politics, whose operating concepts and fundamental categories we have, perhaps, not yet fully gauged.

A decisive factor in Obama's effectiveness, to put all my cards on the table, I take to be his "political theology," by which I understand a theologically inspired, informed, and inflected politics, characterized, first of all—and, somewhat paradoxically (since, erroneously, one would not associate this with "theology" or even with "political theology")—by its "deep pragmatism." This essay explains what this means, drawing on some of the intellectual resources cited in Obama's published writings, notably the thought of Reinhold Niebuhr, key speeches made during the campaign, and important presidential declarations issued since his election.

What's in a Name?

To start out with just one and far from fortuitous example of the logic of "reset," it may be useful to recall the following anecdote. On December 9, 2009, the *Chicago Tribune* reported that then president-elect Obama had boldly declared that his presidency should be seen as "an opportunity for the U.S. to renovate its relations with the Muslim world, starting the day of his inauguration and continuing with a speech he plans to deliver in an Islamic capital." The article went on to note:

> And when he takes the oath of office Jan. 20, he plans to be sworn in like every other president, using his full name: Barack Hussein Obama.
>
> "I think we've got a unique opportunity to reboot America's image around the world and also in the Muslim world in particular," Obama said . . . , promising an "unrelenting" desire to "create a relationship of mutual respect and partnership with countries and with peoples of good will who want their citizens and ours to prosper together." The world, he said, "is ready for that message."

The metaphor of rebooting, together with the *Chicago Tribune*'s sense that the mere pronunciation of a single and simple proper, especially *middle*, name might signal the almost immediate transformation of a whole landscape—as an at once risky and lifesaving or salutary shibboleth—are among the most interesting motifs to reflect on when it comes to understanding the Obama phenomenon, including the resistance and, in part, manufactured discontent it inevitably generates and invites.

Lest we forget, two years into his presidency, Obama and his team would find themselves still or yet again "struggling with the perception of 'otherness'." The fact that Obama's first interview with a foreign news agency was with the Al Arabiya Arab television network (on January 26, 2009), a Dubai-based station and rival of the independent, Qatar-based network Al Jazeera, only underscored his determination to make a gesture, to "reboot." Whether the world was ready for that message remains to be seen to this day. Responses have been mixed, to say the least.

But, then, perhaps is it just an unwarranted and fundamentally dogmatic assumption that a world would need to be prepared and ready in the first place for such a transformation to take effect, if not unconsciously, then at least at a subliminal level and one that is not always fathomed or accounted for by the political commentary of the day? Could one shape or reshape the world in a better image one has of it (or thinks one can offer to it, if only given a chance, sufficient hope)? And did "Obama"—by which I mean not just the person and the candidate, the then junior senator from the state of Illinois, but the *total phenomenon* that he or his name and campaign came to represent and embody—have what it takes to bring this about?

Many knowledgeable commentators have sought to lower expectations, especially where the United States' relationship with the Muslim world is concerned. Even his impressive speech to the Turkish parliament on April 6, 2009, may not have done the trick for many, although his repeated statement that the United States never was and never will be at war with Islam (a doctrine already espoused by the Bush administration) was amplified by his admission that the country he represented was neither a Christian nor a Jewish nor a Muslim nation, which certainly resounded a novel theme, as did his administration's subsequent attempt to rid America's security interests from the term and language of "terror," especially "war on terror."[11]

Hence, for all their informed judgment, the cautious commentators seeking to lower our expectations may have been wrong, if only because under the new dispensation that is ours, things simply no longer work the same way, and expectations—just as past hurts, injuries, injustices, and insults—may well count for nothing when a genuine new tone is struck, a page is turned, or when a new image is painted or, rather, an old one is painted all over again.

The metaphor of rebooting suggests as much. For one thing, it implies that, in a digital age dominated by global media, impressions and perceptions, even cause and effect, operate in unexpected, often inversely proportional, ways (with minimal gestures having maximal impact, while grandstanding claims and aspirations go largely unnoticed). For another, it means that while all accumulated active memories may be wiped clean (this, after all, is what the computer metaphor of "pressing the reset button" suggests), a nation's or democracy's basic language system, that is to say, its hardware and software, must remain intact for this rebooting—and, hence, the enabled emergence of possible new memories—to have any chance of success at all.

For more than one reason, the digital computer metaphor for the change in America's overall political culture and global "image"—namely, that of rebooting it—is informative in that it reveals a dramatically new aspect of how presidential, partisan, and post-partisan as well as grassroots politics and social activism must operate from now so as to have any noticeable radius and, hence, also impact. Even though these changes had been long in preparation, it may well turn out to be hallmark of a whole new—post–Cold War and also post–baby boomer—generation, whose precise influence on the political process (namely, by altering its rules) and culture wars (namely, ending them, precisely, by rendering them obsolete) will define our times in ways we have only barely begun to realize.[12]

Not only did the reference to "rebooting" or "resetting" America's "image" underscore what so many noted during his astounding campaign, namely, that Obama's team outperformed all others in part through its far more resourceful use of new technological media.[13] His subsequent administration would immediately claim for itself the mantle of the first Internet presidency (with its website recovery.gov detailing and tracking the spending of its first stimulus package, and with the president and his surrogates following up his major speeches and decisions with constant personalized e-mailings[14]). The metaphors of "rebooting" and "resetting" also recalled the peculiar *temporality* that politics had assumed under a global regime of 24/7 news cycles and digital media, which can, indeed, "reboot" or "reset" representations and reputations in real time, if not with the snap of the finger or press of a button, then at least with an *instantaneousness* whose *eventfulness* and quite *special effect* seemed to border upon the *miraculous*.

Creating maximal differences with seemingly minimal efforts, reducing to an absolute minimum the maximal pressure from the outside world of vested interests, opponents, and media, in short, subverting the relationship and proportion between cause and effect—as if politics were the art of creating something out of nothing (ex nihilo, as it were), of showing that the powers that be do amount to nothing, really—all this was part and parcel of Obama's way of contributing to what he so often called his "improbable story." It seemed that a different distribution of force or forces now worked across all relevant (economic, juridical, diplomatic, and cultural) domains that mapped out new terrains and modalities in which politics—and especially geopolitics—had to learn to operate and find their way.

Of course, the metaphor was never without risk. No metaphor is. In digital parlance, one resets or reboots an operating system, a computer's software, if it has gotten stuck in a loop or has been infected by a virus. And these technical terms, to say nothing of the latter possibility's uncanny bio-political associations, may not be too helpful in the attempt to diagnose what's wrong with the status quo or what should be done about it.[15] Indeed, the politics of the clean slate, or tabula rasa, has a far from reassuring track record, associated as it is with a long, unfortunate history of—totalitarian—revolutions that, almost without exception, ended badly. Should we go there again and trade the unspectacular politics of incremental reforms for carte blanche revolutions, assuming that in-between revolts yield no viable institutional option?

The new reality that Obama, more precisely, the "Obama phenomenon," presents is not so much one of good intentions or lofty, otherworldly aspirations—and, as a matter of fact, can be seen largely as a return to age-old American values of patriotism and common sense, to the American "character" and its tradition of self-reliance, precisely as it discards unrealistic claims based on cynically twisted versions of American exceptionalism that marked the Bush era—as it is that of a ruthless, yet somehow also strangely "deep," form of pragmatism that uses the intellectual, symbolic, and affective resources of power to new effect.

Not the least interesting aspect of Obama's campaign was its pairing of what I am tempted to call a "political theology" with a smart and calculated use of technological media, just as it succeeded in giving new attention and importance to the special effectiveness—not without some miraculous qualities, to press the point even further, relying on what, at one point, he called "small miracles"—of genuine events, whether those of crises (and there are plenty) or their solutions (and there would be no fewer, if only intelligence, inventiveness, and courage were brought to bear on the crises in question, trusting they would be met with a stroke of luck, nothing short of divine grace, in turn).

Moreover, Obama seemed to have realized that in order to address any one of the most burning issues, one needed to tackle—at the very least be mindful of—all and, hence, address and repair *all at once*. Indeed, I take this "simple idea" to epitomize his politics of "small miracles." After all, a politics that knows when and where and how to capture moments and their momentum breaks away—in its very principle and intent, if not always execution— from the gradualism of piecemeal engineering as well as from the infinite approximation of infinite tasks, both of which were so central to the reformism of European social democracy and American liberal progressivism, but also of religious socialism, the Social Gospel, and liberation theologies, as earlier generations of politicians and activists understood them and put them into practice, with mixed results. "This time" seemed to dictate a different rhythm, an at once more dreamlike and relentless "deep pragmatism," whose central suppositions and directives will interest us here.

Although Obama seems to realize that the older politico-theological models no longer work under present global conditions, marked by the expansion of markets and media, each of which affects the inner workings of all nations, not least the one that is still considered the most powerful on earth, his solution is everything but revolutionary or unprecedented. It is the peculiar mixing and dosage or timing of continuity and discontinuity, of the old and the new, of acceleration and patience, that marks his style and tactics and that has allowed him to formulate and now implement a strikingly novel model, again, of "deep pragmatism."[16]

Established and even conservative pundits (David Brooks and George F. Will among them) were quick to admit that Obama carried a different promise and might well be the only candidate who would be able to pull the United States out of the ever deepening hole it had been consistently digging for itself during the Bush years, in full denial and unwilling to learn.

It is clear that a singular phenomenon or constellation of phenomena, and not just Obama's persona and everything it did or did not evoke, was all of a sudden able to trigger a tidal wave of perceptual change, of changing attitudes, charting new avenues of thought and unexpected courses of action. Indeed, for all his insistence that "old habits" (partisanship in Washington but also, more innocuously, lighting up an occasional cigarette) die hard, the agenda of Obama and his team seemed to experiment with a different kind of political future, whose perspective tens of millions were willing to give the benefit of the doubt, if not their unconditional and long-lasting enthusiasm.

This said, one can only be surprised at how quickly and easily especially liberal and independent voters seem not to have realized what they voted for, venting unrealistic or blind expectations of a candidate who had been abundantly clear about the main lines of his approach and basic political intuitions and instincts. What were they thinking when they let their projective imaginings loose on the blank screen with which Obama was so often—and so often wrongly—identified? Was their ideal that of a politics without negotiation, without built-in corrections and adjustments or changes of course, an ethics without tactics, as it were? Were they unable to measure the impacts of—or stay faithful to—an event whose arithmetic was anything but a simple calculation, keeping scores, as was the case during the zero-sum games of the theoretical political models of old, but obeyed an altogether different temporal and economic logic instead?

"Like an Odyssey Except in Reverse"

And so "a black man with a funny name"—a name that, not so much the first, given name (namely, Barack, from *baraka*, "the blessings of God"[17]), but the middle and family names (namely, Hussein and Obama), became overnight, in the wake of 9/11, an inevitable and "irresistible target of mocking websites from overzealous Republican operatives" who targeted his Muslim name, spread false rumors about his alleged faith, and childishly punned on "Obama"/"Osama"—a man by many considered "a long shot," was elected by a respectable margin, supported by a majority of new voters and independents, and given what seems an even greater political mandate, sustained by favorable public approval ratings, with no initial hint that would they sink soon.[18] Further, even though they did eventually—and inevitably—there seemed no doubt that Obama's political clout was, at least for some time, *supra-numerary* (as certain contemporary so-called post-continental philosophies tend to say of genuine "events," political and other, that are ultimately inexplicable in terms of the preceding conditions and situations in which they happen to occur, gratuitously, miraculously, spectacularly). In other words, his mandate was symbolic, carried by associations that carried with them their political risks as well.

Obama's sharp insight into the fact that merely respecting tradition—namely, citing his full name, Barack Hussein Obama, during the swearing-in ceremony at his official inauguration on January 20, 2009—would all by itself send a powerful symbolic tidal wave through a world by now, perhaps, "ready for that image," thus indicating that world politics need no longer play by the same old rules but could wager on a greater net public, indeed, global gain. A radically new logic of political events and actions, including their consequences (that is to say, affects and effects)—albeit long in preparation—had apparently reached a level of explicitness that forced most pundits and commentators, activists and scholars, to reconceive their basic assumptions and to adjust to a novel (or, merely, newly realized) order of things in which anything, perhaps *everything*, was possible in principle, if not in fact.

To stay with our example of the power and risks, not of nomenclature, but of a more singular *naming*, not only would Obama's mention and use of his middle name—not defiantly, rubbing it in, but precisely, pronounced as a simple matter of fact, paradoxically claiming that he was not going to make a "statement" out of it but just follow procedure as all presidents before him did—ipso facto send a remarkable signal; he also predicted (no doubt rightly) that the world would know how to take and read it, namely, as nothing less than an epochal shift, epitomized here, again, by a simple act of declaring one's (as one says) "Christian" name. As if any further proof were needed, Obama had demonstrated, as he did time and again during his "improbable" run, that he knew how to work the rhetoric and iconic role of political language and imagery, in this case, how to read and use a shibboleth (saying "Barack," "Hussein," or, for that matter, "Obama"), thereby signaling something deeply significant, with huge consequences, without being all too specific or explicit about it.

The fact that Supreme Court justice John Roberts garbled the text of the oath, thus causing Obama to misspeak as well—with the embarrassing result that the Obama White House took no chances and asked both to redo this portion of the swearing-in ceremony, albeit this time behind closed doors and out of sight of television cameras—does not so much contradict but only confirm the symbolic-iconic importance of the meaning and pronunciation of names, of given and spoken words, onstage and offstage. Words, after all, are our bonds, much more so than theories of the social contract and models of deliberative democracy as well as institutions of political liberalism would like to believe. Such words and bonds are signs, the writing on the wall, even when no one is there to see or read.

And yet, the world seemed to understand and get the message. Not so much the given Muslim name (especially, "Hussein") would matter—after all, Obama is a devout Christian and, I will argue, *a subtle political theologian in a decidedly Protestant vein*, at that—but the fact that the U.S. presidency just had come to embody a promise that most of the rest of the world (and least of all the European nations that cheered his campaign most enthusiastically) could not even begin to dream of. The singular circumstance and outcome of the U.S. presidential election, everybody seemed to realize, mattered somehow even more than any additional promise of bringing together the most ethnically and culturally diverse administration in the history of the nation (a promise, we now know, only barely fulfilled). A homecoming and exodus at once, it was "like an odyssey except in reverse."[19]

Sources of Inspiration

There is no doubt that Obama's outlook is steeped in part in the particular American experience, the journey of black churches, the civil rights movement and its aftermath, and not just from the moment he joined the Trinity United Church of Christ, led by Reverend Jeremiah Wright Jr., on the South Side of Chicago. Until then, a variety of vaguely religious influences (from the Methodist, Baptist, and Unitarian Universalist beliefs of his grandparents, the "secular humanism"[20] and the distanced anthropological view of religion that characterized his mother, to the Catholicism of his Indonesian missionary school, up to the "folk Islam"—as he writes, "a brand of Islam that could make room for remnants of more ancient animist and Hindu faiths"[21]—he had encountered in his stepfather, Lolo) held sway over the quest for meaning and belonging that marked the first half of his life. These influences never coalesced into a single coherent set of beliefs, leaving an imprint of distinct, yet seemingly unrelated, virtues and values, all of which he would seek to place within a broader perspective and more consistent narrative whole later on. Until he was able to do so, such apparently dispersed elements and forms of faith would merely help Obama to unmask and ward off the comprehensive salvific and soteriological doctrines—such as the "nationalism" of the Chicago-based Nation of Islam led by Louis Farrakhan—that he soon realized came with too big a price (or remained too unspecific and practically useless, which is to say that could all too easily "thrive as an emotion and flounder as a program" and thus end up as "just" or "loose talk"[22]).

Yet none of these earliest religious and spiritual influences, taken in isolation or combination, explain what makes Obama's theology—least of all, his political theology—tick at their deepest. Neither one of them, nor their sum total, offers us any keys to understanding what I have called his deep pragmatism. Indeed, it is fair to say that Obama would not have become the effective and truly transformational—that is to say, more than simply post-partisan, multicultural, post-racial, but genuine twenty-first-century—candidate for the presidency that impressed and continues to impress friend and foe alike, if his persona and personal faith, like his social and political sensibilities, were just made up of these added and superimposed layers of cultural heritage. Not the least interesting aspect of the Obama phenomenon is that it has taught us to literally see that, politically speaking, *culture is no longer what matters*. It is what he, eclectically and pragmatically, took from—and brought to—these elements and forms of faith, while allowing them to retain their full original perspective and, indeed, historical and existential depth, that is of importance and that makes him at once so exceptional *and* exemplary, in any case, *recognizable* for so many, among his supporters and detractors, among younger voters and older observers, in this nation and abroad. Strangely and paradoxically, it is the peculiarity and, at times, idiosyncrasy of his background and outlook that make his case a *focal point* and *catalyst* for a common cause that has found almost general, near-universal appeal in virtually all segments of society and worldwide.

Obama's appeal is not that of an empty flag beneath which all can gather, nor is it a "blank screen"[23] onto which anyone can project what he or she likes; it is, rather, that of a "saturated phenomenon," *a much-awaited and needed density and intensity*, that symbolizes *a new and cool seriousness* that by its own force can usher in a "new era of responsibility" (as his first budget proposal titled its ambition). Such renewal was long overdue, and the present times of economic and other (financial, ecological, and geopolitical) crises seem ripe for it, favoring the simultaneous turning around of more than one trend. The near fatality of current problems may yet offer a greater chance of doing things—and doing them right, not one by one but, if need be, all at once.

The Singular and the Common

In the preface to the new edition of his *Dreams from My Father*, Obama expresses a certain correspondence, indeed, resemblance between his singular life story and the particular crossroads at which America finds itself, suggesting, more in particular, that "the story of my family, and my efforts to understand that story, might speak in some way to the fissures of race that have characterized the American experience, as well as the fluid state of identity—the leaps through time, the collision of cultures—that mark our modern life."[24] He also notes that the events of 9/11 and those following in its wake seem to have only magnified this point of analogy even as it made his own subsequent political success all the more unlikely, not least since a traumatized society tends to fold back onto itself, close itself off, and resort to the worst of its traditions and instincts. How, then, could Obama capture the wave that, in spite of America's subdued and somewhat regressive state, was nonetheless unstoppable in its coming? How did he succeed in riding it all the way to its provisional zenith (i.e., his decisive electoral victory and first administrative and legal successes as well as continued high approval ratings)? Finally, what else could we still expect from a turn of events that few could have predicted?

Far from indicating the seeds of a self-indulgent, let alone hagiographic, account of the subsequent role of his persona in politics, Obama's quoted words reveal that he understood himself from early on in the campaign to be a post-identitarian and, if possible, post-partisan candidate for a twenty-first century that, with its new challlenges, requires new—but also, strangely, old—skills (the apt use of powerful words, the ability to construct compelling narratives, the courage to make decisions, the tact to be patient, and so on). There is nothing pretentious or naive about this realization, nor, to be sure, should it be mistaken for a denial of the question of either partisanship or identity, let alone race, *tout court*. For one thing, Obama finds no difficulty in listing his "progressive"—indeed, Democratic—credentials in no uncertain and concise terms.[25] For another, he leaves no doubt that one could not merely decide to have a "multiracial identity," to just be an "individual"—an all-too-unrealistic, delusional stance of imagined sovereignty for which, Obama recalls, he chastised some of his middle-class black peers in his early years in college in Los Angeles.[26] The claim, therefore, indicates that the so-called politics of identity, like the entrenched agendas of political parties and ideologues, will no longer suffice to address and vehicle the great causes and crises that are upon—or still await—us. As to matters of identity, one should thus follow the biblical maxim, recited by one of young Obama's role models, namely, to "Stay awake," just as, to the question of getting things done in both life and society, Obama soon realized that he needed to cherish the value of sheer "determination" and the "willingness to endure,"[27] which his father had taught him. And as to the politics of race and of post-racial politics, the matter would be no different:

> You might be locked into a world not of your own making . . . , but you still have a claim on how it is shaped. You still have responsibilities. . . . My identity might begin with the fact of race, but it didn't, couldn't, end there. At least that's what I would choose to believe.[28]

Everything else, especially the contrary illusion that partisanship, identity, and race no longer carry their (at least, historical) weight and could from now on—even with the advent of the "new politics"—be ignored, would promise merely "a sorry sort of freedom,"[29] not one worthy of its name. It is through the singular and the particular that one achieves the common and the general. No illusion, then, should be harbored of pushing our luck even further. Aspiring to the One and the Universal—in an all-out redemptive, that is, prophetic-messianic perspective—is not an option for us. This is yet another aspect of Obama's deep pragmatism, its sense of the "tragic" and, perhaps, the "ironic," in one word, his "Christian realism" (a view he adopts from Reinhold Niebuhr and to which we will turn below).

Two Further Preliminaries

Two further provisos are in order. First, we do not capture the full significance of the Obama effect—nor its "redeeming" but less than "messianic" qualities—if we take him to be just a more accomplished, more sophisticated, and technologically savy representative of, say, Reverend Jesse Jackson's Rainbow Coalition, albeit this time no longer operating under its somewhat worn-out banner. In fact, as some commentators have noticed,

Obama's rise and success also signaled that a new generation of African American leaders (Deval Patrick, Artur Davis, Cory Booker, Michael Nutter, Harold Ford Jr., and others) had begun to make its unmistakable impact, turning a page in the history of race in this country.[30] For all the relevance and importance of the "images" and, indeed, "romantic images" of the civil rights movement, rather than of the more superficial "slogans and theories" of the day—indeed, he writes, "Such images became a source of prayer for me, bolstering my spirits, channeling my emotions in a way words never could"[31]—Obama's determination came from elsewhere and tapped into different and deeper and wider resources, which may well have carried the civil rights movement in turn. It was only from them that "a promise of redemption," of "community," and "resolve" could come.[32]

Second, we do not fully understand Obama's policy proposals on the campaign trail and his early administrative plans if we see them as just a continuation of the agenda of the so-called New Democrats during the 1990s and, especially, the Clinton years. However much he may have needed to rely on the acquired experience and competence of officials who served in Bill Clinton's two administrations, Obama's policy goals and overall governmental style are completely different. In fact, it was noted, immediately following the presentation of his first budget, that the radicality of his plans for a financial fix of the economic and banking crisis consisted precisely in the fact that it undid some of the basic tenets of the tax regulation and social and fiscal policies that had undergirded not just the policies of the last Bush administration but those implemented from Ronald Reagan onward. Obama's proposed tax code turned out to be more progressive than Clinton's. And so is his frontal tackling of the problem of energy as well as of ecological issues. All this may not be enough to make a difference nor the best the "new politics" can do, but it is certainly a start on a different track.

Further, Obama is an atypical Democrat with regard to the question of the relationship between religion and politics, church and state. For while the new administration must address a myriad of practical, worldly, indeed, secular issues, at home and globally, a central element and dimension of its thinking and planning, strategizing and tactics, seem defined by the ways in which it tries to rely—and, as it were, capitalize—on *an at once sharply observed and actively advocated realignment of religion in the public sphere.* This, nothing else, characterizes its political theology as deeply pragmatic, that is to say, as both "deep" and "pragmatic" (the latter being an epithet that others, notably Henry Louis Gates, have used in making a striking comparison between Obama's and Lincoln's overall approaches and personal styles[33]).

The latter approach is not something all liberal-secular progressivists applaud (on the contrary, they take Obama's pragmatism as too accommodating of past injustices and the forces that be), nor does it assuage the fears of religious conservatives (who mistake Obama's depth for a mere rhetorical ploy, so that one of the last titans of the Christian right, James Dobson, could accuse him of "deliberately distorting the traditional understanding of the Bible to fit his own world view, his own confused theology"[34]). Yet all these positions and strategies are, precisely, vintage Obama. But what does that mean, exactly?

The Niebuhr Connection: Christian Realism

One of the most important elements of Obama's pragmatism is the sense that "hope" can be "realistic" only if it wishes to be more than wishful thinking and whistling in the dark, just as much as "realism" without "hope" leads principally nowhere but merely brutally reaffirms whatever there is and, hence, only strengthens the powers that be. This may sound trivial, a platitude, but it is not. And if it were, this would still teach us something important.

After all, the least one can say of any truism is that it has, well, more than a ring of truth to it. And in matters political—but, perhaps, not only there—insight into the complex, some would say paradoxical or aporetic, tragic or ironic, relationship between the ideal and the real, mind and world, norms and facts, the way things ought to be and the way they are, holds the key to all. How things turn out in the end—which ideas and ideals materialize, which politics and policies succeed—depends on which side of this polarity one gives prevalence, and when and where and how.

No political calculation on the basis of supposed human self-interest and self-centeredness can do this trick (and, thereby, keep idealism from turning into "naïve idealism" or realism into "bitter realism," two formulations I take from Obama), nor is instinct, intuition, practical wisdom, or skill its sound alternative. What seems required is a bit more, and the paradoxical expression "deep pragmatism" captures nicely what it is. But where does "deep pragmatism" originate, and from which sources and traditions does it draw its strength?

It has been noted that Obama in his inspirational rhetoric and overall view of the political and policies draws much less on the legacy of the civil rights movement, of Martin Luther King Jr., not to mention Malcolm X, with their insistence on human dignity and the overcoming of victimization, than he does on the thought of the Protestant theologian Reinhold Niebuhr.

True enough, as an adolescent Obama had quenched his thirst for understanding his place in the complicated ethnic and racial landscape of the United States by reading James Baldwin, Ralph Ellison, Langston Hughes, W. E. B. Dubois, and Malcolm X—a list to which he would add Toni Morrison as well as the multivolume biography by Taylor Branch of Dr. King and the civil rights struggles—but it is clear that none of these authors would come to determine his overall take on political things at its deepest and most pragmatic level.[35] Niebuhr, more than anyone else, did.

In an interview with David Brooks in April 2007, Obama stated as much in an impromptu response:

> [Niebuhr] is one of my favorite philosophers. I take away [from his works] the compelling idea that there's serious evil in the world, and hardship and pain. And we should be humble and modest in our belief we can eliminate those things. But we shouldn't use that as an excuse for cynicism and inaction. I take away . . . the sense that we have to make these efforts knowing they are hard, and not swinging from naïve idealism to bitter realism.

It was Niebuhr who shaped Obama's subtle take on the intermingling of the principled and the factual, of what is religious and what public—call it the theological and the political—and, especially, of their respective intrinsic limits, including their potential risks and dangers, whenever they were taken in isolation but also when their respective perspectives became more congruent, overlapped, or became fixated in all too comprehensive doctrines of the theologico-political (thus producing what Henri Bergson called a "static" rather than "dynamic" religion, a "closed" rather than "open" morality or society).

Reinhold Niebuhr (1892–1971) was born in Missouri to German parents and served as a pastor in Detroit among the families of autoworkers. In an early phase of his career as a minister and a teacher, he had blended faith and socialism. He ran for Congress as the Socialist Party candidate and believed that there would be no radical social change in America without violence.[36] Yet, at the height of his career as a professor of ethics at New York's Union

Theological Seminary, the founder and editor of the liberal journal *Christianity and Society*, and as the cofounder (in 1946) of the anti-Communist lobbying group Americans for Democratic Action, he came to reject both liberal theology and the social gospel, pacifism, isolationism, and, later, Cold War–mongering, and instead espoused a more traditionalist, sadder and wiser form of Christian Realism that knew of the "tragic necessity" of limited intervention by the United States in world affairs (such as the need to defeat Hitler).

For this, the publication of Niebuhr's 1932 "socioethical and political blockbuster" *Moral Man and Immoral Society* had laid the foundation by dethroning "old-style American liberal theology"[37] once and for all. Moral virtue could occasionally be expected from individuals, Niebuhr observed here, but human collectives or groups serve merely their relentless self-interest. There was no political problem that was not first of all a matter of power. Society could and should, therefore, not be moralized as liberalism and the social gospel tradition had hoped. From here on, Niebuhr presented himself as a "pessimistic optimist" or "tamed cynic," at best.[38] Inspired more by Augustine, Luther, and Calvin than by the naive optimism of the liberal theology and Social Gospel of his day, Niebuhr became acutely aware of the "reality of systemic evil"[39] and the precarious nature of sin and grace. This necessitated further revision of the earlier view and a shift in the direction of what was called "Neo-orthodoxy" (to be distinguished from the dialectical theology and church dogmatic of Niebuhr's nemesis, Karl Barth). Much later, Niebuhr noted that the title of his earlier, widely read book should have been *The Not-So-Moral Man in His Less Moral Communities*.[40]

Niebuhr became a public figure—indeed, the most well-known American Protestant thinker, famous for his early advocacy of U.S. intervention in World War II and his no less outspoken opposition to the war in Vietnam—and appeared on the cover of *Time* magazine in 1948. His books and articles (published in journals such as the *Atlantic Monthly*, the *Nation*, and the *New Republic*) gained great influence on the formulation and implementation of social and foreign policy, shaping the views of administrators and diplomats such as the Kennedy aide and historian Arthur Schlesinger Jr., Ronald Reagan's United Nations ambassador Jeanne Kirkpatrick, and others. These policy makers had a coherent conception of America's role in the world that was strikingly different from that of the later neoconservatives (often associated with the intellectual legacy of Leo Strauss). As a regular adviser to the

State Department as well as other governmental agencies, Niebuhr had laid the foundation for this reception of his work.

Indeed, it is important to recall that Niebuhr was not only "the best known and most respected theologian in America" and a public figure who throughout the 1930s, 1940s, and 1950s spoke and appealed to a large audience—a role taken over by his friend, colleague, and protégé Paul Tillich after Niebuhr suffered a stroke in 1952—but that he, like Tillich throughout the 1960s and 1970s, was read and consulted by "enthusiastic secular followers, most of whom sought to appropriate the obvious wisdom of these theologians without their . . . theological dimension."[41]

But could this be done, without significant loss of meaning and understanding of the religious legacy involved? And if so, how, exactly, was this application and, when not instrumental, then at least strategic use of a decidedly Christian realism in matters political possible or useful, indeed, desirable? Is not every adaptation of religious insights for the purpose of theorizing the political and practicing politics, even when undertaken in a secular—say, naturalist or materialist, rationalist or utilitarian—spirit (we all know examples of this), still a tribute, indeed a contribution to the very tradition of political theology it may or may not seek to denounce or ignore? And is there not a deeply metaphysical and mystical, some would say, tragic or at least ironic ring to this historical and conceptual necessity, at times fatality, which, it should be added, is a tremendous chance (for human thought and agency) as well? This, I think, is an important question, and we are still very much at a loss to answer it compellingly.

After all, where does this leave the dimension of "depth" of which I spoke earlier? In what sense could religion—and especially Christian Realism, as Niebuhr defined it—give perspective to a public domain that, under the conditions of secular modernity (or modern secularity), seems premised on a principle of neutrality or methodological atheism, guided as it is by what Charles Taylor, in his recent book *A Secular Age*, calls an "immanent frame" of thought? To what extent could a religious realism, not just respect, but also back up and orient—inflect and, perhaps, "nudge"—the cultural sensibilities and practical responsibilities that mark our time at its most critical junctures?

Further, in what way could it guide us through the dangers of the present post–Cold War world, whose global economic and political, military and ecological conflicts and challenges are increasingly unpredictable? As long as the necessary international institutional instruments for conflict resolution are either not yet in place or not functioning as they should and were expected to, what ought to be the guidelines, the operative principle, if not blueprint, for a "progressive" presidency as it must, finally, seek to put political liberalism on a firmer footing, precisely by exposing it to wider and especially deeper horizons than the "immanent frame" is ready to acknowledge?

These are questions largely absent from the otherwise impressive volumes *Change for America: A Progressive Blueprint for the 44th President*, edited by Mark Green and Michele Jolin.[42] Timothy Gordon Ash may be right: the "worldwide conceptual cacophony" concerning the term "liberalism" has demonstrated once and for all that this "vital, never-ending debate is not just over its indispensable ingredients, but also over their form, proportion and relation to one another." Does that mean that Obama has begun restoring "the thing" while continuing to shun its "name" (i.e., "liberalism," which, Ash adds, is mostly a pejorative term in the United States since the Reagan years, when it seemed to connote something like the "unholy marriage of big government and fornication"[43]).

My hunch is that instead of speaking of Obama's progressivism rather than liberalism or, alternatively, predicting that he revitalizes liberalism (i.e., the "thing" but not the "name"), it is more illuminating to stress the balance he is able to strike between the theological reference (the invocation of religious motifs and motivations, moods and modalities), on the one hand, and a resolute, relentless realism, on the other. It is this peculiar combination, if not juxtaposition, of elements and forms of speech and acts that makes his pragmatism both deep and effective. It is the very shape and orientation of what I would not hesitate to call Obama's political theology (or theologies—after all, there may be more than one and they may not need to cohere at all times).

It is to Niebuhr that Obama returns, in the full awareness that our current global crises in finance and the economy, climate and health care, immigration and international justice, the proliferation of nuclear weapons and political instability in the Middle East, to say nothing of the violence (formerly called "terror") of non-state actors and of (formerly called "rogue") states, have little in common with the predicaments of the immediate postwar and Cold War periods that faced Niebuhr and that were defined by the mutual deterrence of a few superpowers, just as many of the national and broader preoccupations of previous administrations (first the so-called war on drugs, then the so-called war on terror) have either exhausted or discredited themselves and are in need of reformulation and more adequate objectives and alternatives.

It has been rightly noted by Paul Allen that "Obama's liberalism is not that of the perennial separation of church and state" but is, instead, "born of the public implications of Christian faith, a recognition of the moral limits of the state and the individual."[44] The resulting conception, far from being an amalgam of irreconcilable strands of thought and anything but a "confused theology," yields a coherent position that parts ways with secular humanism and its institutional and dispositional equivalents in political and cultural matters (so-called liberalism and progressive modernism being the most notable features among them), just as it keeps its distance from the dictates and mind-set of the religious right (from the perverse mixture of American exceptionalism and cynical realism of so-called neoconservatism that influenced the George W. Bush administrations), and even from the alternative ideology, still in the making, that has been attributed to the Millennial Youth or Generation We that were among his staunchest—and most effective—supporters.

Again, there is a deeper sense of the tragic or, as Niebuhr preferred to say, "ironic" fate of American history that is steeped, in part, in the biblical idea of original sin, even though it is elaborated in more heterodox terms as well, and that espouses a thorough pragmatism in the adjustment of ideas and theories—including those of theology—to the factual givens of the world of political and international affairs. In this sense, Obama's political theology steers clear of the more conservative versions of moral complacency and self-congratulatory narratives and in this may well consist its signature "realism." In Allen's words:

> Thanks to Niebuhr, Obama has thought about the human condition, in terms of our shared nature and sin, categories that most liberals have rebuked since before the 1960s. . . . Obama is positioned to give the conservative idea of self-sacrifice a liberal moral meaning it has not held since John F. Kennedy. When Obama said last year that he would tell Americans, 'Not what they wanted to hear, but what they needed to know,' he was warming up an electorate for Niebuhr-like realism. . . . Obama knows that liberalism cannot thrive on an ever-expanding laundry list of human rights and victimhood.[45]

Yet is doubtful that Obama should be seen as restoring liberalism as a value per se. Liberalism, for him, is rather a set of policies to which, he feels, we have good—pragmatic—reason to adhere or, when needed, to return. And "self-sacrifice" is hardly the sole (or most important) value around which his *deep* pragmatism revolves in the end. A host of other motifs and motivations come to mind, but what is important is the novel way—and the creative as well as receptive spirit—in which they are invoked and put to work.

When confronted with skeptical reactions to the whole business of holding office at the state or national level, Obama writes, he would appeal to

> another tradition of politics, a tradition that stretched from the days of the country's founding to the glory of the civil rights movement, a tradition based on the simple idea that we have a stake in one another, and that what binds us together is greater than what drives us apart, and that if enough people believe in the truth of that proposition and act on it, then we might not solve every problem, but we can get something meaningful done.[46]

It seems a tradition based on common sense as much as it reminds us of the insights of progressive liberalism and the social gospel and a much older legacy of "Emersonian self-reliance" and what Obama, citing the late senator Edward Kennedy, recently called "the American character."

If there is a lack of agonistics in Obama's conception of the political— and if, in that sense, he was during the campaigns somewhat of a crossover candidate (putting an end to the contentious Bush-Clinton-Bush years and the senseless animosities they fed on)—it might be found in his observation, based on traveling in his home state of Illinois, of "just how modest people's hopes were, and how much of what they believed seemed to hold constant across race, region, religion, and class."[47] It was his conviction of there being a "collective conscience" and a "common set of values that bind us together despite our differences," indeed, "a running thread of hope that makes our improbable experiment in democracy work"—all of them references to a "shared language" that had suffered under the onslaughts of the most unrelenting trends of our age: "globalization and dizzying technological change, cutthroat politics and unremitting culture wars."[48]

In the face of such pressures, what was needed was "a new kind of politics, one that can excavate and build upon those shared understandings that pull us together as Americans,"[49] in other words, a new search for—and defense of—"the common good."[50]

What matters, however, is not that Obama was the sole candidate to invoke this other tradition in explicit terms but that he *related to it differently*, just as he allowed its avowed simplicity to accrue to other elements and meanings from other traditions, including other religious and non-Christian ones. Indeed, the movement from "faith in simple ideas" to "insistence on small miracles" is the itinerary—and, indeed, political snowball effect, if not avalanche—we are tracking here.

This mode of relating to the past, to tradition, to its tragedies and ironies, accomplishments and hopes seemed precisely what makes Obama's political thinking and operative style *deep* but also broad and versatile, eminently translatable, even strategically adaptable, that is to say, *pragmatic*. It is no accident that during the 2009 campaign for the Democratic presidential nomination and then the general election, Obama seemed in the eyes of many commentators (and not just those who supported him) the only candidate who was able and willing to learn and grow from mistakes and wrong turns (of phrase and of the campaign's course). The others were merely "grasping for anything that would stick"[51] and paid the price for doing so.

As Martin Marty, the well-known Chicago theologian and éminence grise of the history of American religion as well as main editor of the famous Fundamentalism project, noted in his contribution to the *Washington Post*'s "On Faith" blog (November 11, 2008), Niebuhr's conception was based on the insight that *realism in and of itself leads to cynicism*. Only a "realistic hope" and "hopeful realism," Marty recalls, could, in this view, serve as "a caution against utopianism, naïve idealism, the claiming or bragging of rights." Niebuhr's trademark was to caution against overstating America's role in the world, reminding his readers that one always uses evil to prevent the greater evil (and, hence, confirms the inescapable fact of human sinfulness). This insight, however, led Niebuhr to an insistence on humility, not to Christian "pessimism," which would all too easily become an excuse for irresponsibility and inaction.

An often-cited passage from Niebuhr's *The Irony of American History*, published in 1952, illustrates this view:

> Nothing that is worth doing can be achieved in our lifetime; therefore we must be saved by hope. Nothing which is true or beautiful or good makes complete sense in any immediate context of history; therefore we must be saved by faith. Nothing we do, however virtuous, can be accomplished alone; therefore we are saved by love. No virtuous act is quite as virtuous from the standpoint of our friend or foe as it is from our standpoint. Therefore we must be saved by the final form of love, which is forgiveness.[52]

The Irony of American History—the book Niebuhr had originally planned to title *This Nation under God*—has been described by some as "the most important book ever written on U.S. foreign policy."[53] In the preface, Niebuhr introduces its theme as "the position of our nation in the present world situation, as interpreted from the standpoint of the Christian faith."[54] Its central theses came down to four "uncomfortable" and often forgotten "truths," aptly summarized as follows in the editor's introduction to the recent republication of the book:

> the persistent sin of American Exceptionalism; the indecipherability of history; the false allure of simple solutions; and, finally, the imperative of appreciating the limits of power.[55]

Without heeding these cautionary insights, Niebuhr claimed, American "hegemony" would merely yield a fastidious form of "imperialism" whose equation of its own Christian convictions with its existing political order would be yet another example of "idolatry,"[56] of a political no less than conceptual idolatry, that is.

Niebuhr saw the tension between individualism and the need for communality, the place of U.S. power in the world and the need to restrain it. His witnessing of the two world wars, the Great Depression, Nazi death camps, and Soviet repression led him to conclude that

> Man's capacity for justice makes democracy possible, but man's inclination to injustice makes democracy necessary.[57]

And along the same lines, he captured the internal tensions and dilemmas in a succinct and compelling way:

> To those who exalt freedom, we must declare that freedom without community is not love, but leads man to making himself his own end. To those who exalt community, we must declare that no historic community deserves the final devotion of man, since his stature and structure is such that only God can be the end of his life.
>
> Against those who make the state sacrosanct, we must insist that the state is always tempted to set its majesty in rebellious opposition to the divine majesty. To those who fear the extension of the state for the regulation of modern economic life, we must point out that their fears are frequently prompted not by a concern for justice but by a jealous desire to maintain their own power.[58]

In his reflection of the nature of national and international politics, Niebuhr relied on a conceptual rather than strictly historical distinction, namely, between Greek "tragedy" and Christian "irony." In the preface and the opening as well as concluding chapters of his book, Niebuhr explains the meaning and contemporary relevance of these technical terms for which he stipulated precise definitions, whose historical appropriateness and helpfulness for current affairs, at the beginning of the twenty-first century, one may find reason to dispute and whose overall schema Obama could be said to fill in on different terms, readjusting and reimagining it where necessary. Niebuhr insists that

> the Christian faith tends to make the ironic view of human evil in history the normative one. Its conception of redemption from evil carries it beyond the limits of irony, but its interpretation of the nature of evil in human history is consistently ironic. This consistency is achieved on the basis of the belief that the whole drama of human history is under the scrutiny of a divine judge who laughs at human pretensions without being hostile to human aspirations. The laughter at the pretensions is the divine judgment. The judgment is transmuted into mercy if it results in abating the pretensions and in prompting men to a contrite recognition of the vanity of their imagination.
>
> The Biblical interpretation of the human situation is ironic, rather than tragic or pathetic, because of its unique formulation of the problem of human freedom. . . . The evil in human history is regarded as the consequence of man's wrong use of his unique capacities. The wrong use is always due to some failure to recognize the limits of his capacities of power, wisdom and virtue. Man is an ironic creature because he forgets that he is not simply a creator but also a creature.[59]

One might be tempted to rephrase these conflicting tendencies and unfortunate reversals with the help of a different idiom and recast them in Niebuhr's version of a dialectics of religious and secular Enlightenment or a paradox of modernity of sorts. But to do so would mean missing the point, which—in his theological vocabulary—is that a profound realization of "sin" does not exclude the near-miraculous possibility of divine "grace." In Niebuhr's words, the tragic and pathetic as well as ironic elements of history all have truth to them, but the first two are "subordinated" to the third:

> Since modern technological achievements include the development of atomic energy and this development has put an almost unmanageable destructiveness

into the hands of men, [a] purely tragic view of human freedom seems to have acquired a new plausibility.

Nevertheless, a purely tragic view of life is not finally viable. It is, at any rate, not the Christian view. According to that view destructiveness is not an inevitable consequence of human creativity. It is not invariably necessary to do evil in order that we may do good. . . . There is always the ideal possibility that man will break and transcend the simple harmonies and necessities of nature, and yet not be destructive. For the destructiveness in human life is primarily the consequence of exceeding, not the bounds of nature, but much more ultimate limits.[60]

One wonders what this "ideal possibility" might be, how it announces or manifests or, indeed, reveals itself. For if what Niebuhr is speaking of is nothing less than a "small miracle," then to conceive of its ideality and possibility—let alone to realize or perceive or witness its eventful occurrence—would seem to require much more than having "simple ideas." Or is to assume this the very sign of our lack of faith, hope, and love?

Notes

1. Henry Louis Gates Jr., "Introduction," in Steven J. Niven, *Barack Obama: A Pocket Biography of Our 44th President* (Oxford: Oxford University Press, 2009), 2, 3. For the reference to the "seismic event," see "Black and White, North and South," *New York Observer*, November 26, 2009. Cited after Thomas J. Sugrue, *Not Even Past: Barack Obama and the Burden of Race* (Princeton, NJ: Princeton University Press, 2010), 12.

2. The words "The past is not dead. In fact, it's not even past" can be found in William Faulkner's *Requiem for a Nun*. Obama cites and varies them in his speech "A More Perfect Union," delivered in Philadelphia on March 18, 2008: "As William Faulkner once wrote, 'The past isn't dead and buried. In fact, it isn't even past.' We do not need to recite here the history of racial injustice in this country. But we do need to remind ourselves that so many of the disparities that exist in the African-American community today can be directly traced to inequalities passed on from an earlier generation that suffered under the brutal legacy of slavery and Jim Crow." Cited after Sugrue, *Not Even Past*, epigraphs. Cf. also David Olive, *An American Story: The Speeches of Barack Obama* (Toronto: ECW Press, 2008), 261.

3. Barack Obama, *Dreams from My Father: A Story of Race and Inheritance* (New York: Three Rivers Press, 1995, 2004), 134.

4. Cf. Harold Bloom, "Out of Panic, Self-Reliance," *New York Times*, October 12, 2008.

5. James T. Kloppenburg, *Reading Obama: Dreams, Hope, and the American Political Tradition* (Princeton, NJ: Princeton University Press, 2011), 13, cf. 16. Kloppenburg goes on to note: "Although doubtless indebted to many models, *Dreams from My Father* echoes the tone of Ellison's *Invisible Man*. Ellison's protagonist, despite repeated rebuffs and deepening disillusionment, refuses despair" (ibid., 14).

6. David Remnick, *The Bridge: The Life and Rise of Barack Obama* (New York: Vintage Books, 2011), 18.

7. Ibid.

8. Ibid., 16.

9. Ibid., 17. In his own speech, Obama picks up on the phrase in question, saying, "there is some good craziness going on" (ibid., 21).

10. Ibid., 17.

11. As was made explicit in a speech by one of Obama's national security advisers, John Brennan, in August 2009. Cf. http://www.whitehouse.gov/the_press_office/Remarks-by-John-Brennan-at-the-Center-for-Strategic-and-International-Studies/.

12. See Morley Winograd and Michael D. Hais, *Millennial Makeover: MySpace, You-Tube, & the Future of American Politics* (New Brunswick, NJ, and London: Rutgers University Press, 2008); Eric Greenberg with Karl Weber, *Generation We: How Millennial Youth Are Taking Over America and Changing Our World Forever* (Emeryville, CA: Pachatusan, 2008).

13. David Talbot, "How Obama *Really* Did It: The Social-Networking Strategy That Took an Obscure Senator to the Doors of the White House," *Technology Review*, September–October 2008. See also Tim Dickinson, "The Machinery of Hope," *Rolling Stone*, March 20, 2008, and Chuck Todd and Sheldon Gawiser, *How Barack Obama Won: A State-by-State Guide to the Historic 2008 Presidential Election* (New York: Vintage Books, 2009). Todd and Gawiser point out that Obama was the only one among the serious contenders who gave a "Why I'm running speech" (in front of the Old State Capitol in Springfield, Illinois, in February 2007) and sounded out themes to which he would then subsequently stick, allowing his campaign to constantly stay on message, both in content ("Let's be the generation," among them) and in form (returning to formal speeches whenever a critical moment in the

campaign occurred and fully aware of his strengths and belief that "There is power in words"). See also Richard Wolffe, *Renegade: The Making of a President* (New York: Crown Publishers, 2009); David Plouffe, *The Audacity to Win: How Obama Won and How We Can Beat the Party of Limbaugh, Beck, and Palin* (New York: Penguin Books, 2010); and Kate Kensi, Bruce W. Hardy, and Kathleen Hall Jamieson, *The Obama Victory: How Media, Money, and Message Shaped the 2008 Election* (Oxford and New York: Oxford University Press, 2010).

14. http://www.recovery.gov/.

15. I thank Eduardo Mendieta for drawing my attention to this point.

16. For a more systematic treatment of that phrase, see Hent de Vries, "Introduction: Why Still 'Religion,'" in *Religion—Beyond a Concept* (New York: Fordham University Press, 2008), 1–98.

17. Obama, *Dreams from My Father*, 428.

18. Ibid., viii, x.

19. Bob Dylan, cited after Remnick, *The Bridge*, 41.

20. Obama, *Dreams from My Father*, 50.

21. Ibid., 37.

22. Ibid., 202, 203.

23. Although he uses the metaphor more than once, cf. Barack Obama, *The Audacity of Hope: Thoughts on Reclaiming the American Dream* (New York: Three Rivers Press, 2006), 11.

24. Obama, *Dreams from My Father*, vii.

25. Obama, *The Audacity of Hope*, 10.

26. Obama, *Dreams from My Father*, 99–100.

27. Ibid., 97 (cf. 100), and 111, 112. Ibid.,

28. Ibid., 111.

29. Ibid., 134.

30. Niven, *Barack Obama*, 21–22.

31. Obama, *Dreams from My Father*, 134.

32. Ibid., 135, 136.

33. Henry Louis Gates Jr. and John Stauffer, "A Pragmatic Precedent," *New York Times*, January 19, 2009.

34. Cited in Lisa Miller and Richard Wolfe, "Finding His Faith," *Newsweek*, July 21, 2008.

35. Obama, *Dreams from My Father*, 85, 86. Cf. also Michiko Kakutani, "From Books New President Found Voice," *New York Times*, January 19, 2009. Obama speaks

admiringly of Malcolm X, albeit with certain reservations, in *Dreams from My Father*. See also Remnick, *The Bridge*, 228 ff.

36. Gary Dorrien, *The Making of American Liberal Theology*, vol. 2, *Idealism, Realism, and Modernity, 1900–1950* (Louisville, KY: Westminster John Knox Press, 2003), 449.

37. Ibid.

38. Robert McAfee Brown, "Introduction," in *The Essential Reinhold Niebuhr: Selected Essays and Addresses*, ed. Robert McAfee Brown (New Haven, CT, and London: Yale University Press, 1986), xi–xxiv, xi.

39. Ibid., xv.

40. Ibid.

41. Langdon B. Gilkey, "Introduction," in Reinhold Niebuhr, *Moral Man & Immoral Society: A Study in Ethics and Politics* (1932; repr., Louisville, KY: Westminster John Knox Press, 2001), xi–xxii, xii.

42. Mark Green and Michele Jolin, with Ed Paisley and Lauren Strayer, eds., *Change for America: A Progressive Blueprint for the 44th President* (New York: Basic Books, 2009).

43. See Timothy Garton Ash, "A Liberal Translation: How Obama Can Restore Meaning to a Tarnished Term," *New York Times*, January 25, 2009.

44. thestar.com, June 18, 2008.

45. Ibid.

46. Obama, *The Audacity of Hope*, 2.

47. Ibid., 7.

48. Ibid., 8.

49. Ibid., 9.

50. Ibid.

51. Todd and Gawiser, *How Barack Obama Won*, 10.

52. Reinhold Niebuhr, *The Irony of American History, with a New Introduction by Andrew J. Bacevich* (Chicago and London: University of Chicago Press, 2008), 63. Cf. Richard Wightman Fox, *Reinhold Niebuhr: A Biography*, with a new introduction and an afterword (Ithaca, NY, and London: Cornell University Press, 1996), 244–247; Dorrien, *The Making of American Liberal Theology*, 435–521.

53. Andrew J. Bacevich, "Introduction," in Niebuhr, *The Irony of American History*, ix–xxi, ix.

54. Niebuhr, *The Irony of American History*, xxiii.

55. Bacevich, "Introduction," in Niebuhr, *The Irony of American History*, ix–xxi, ix, x.

56. Ibid., xi, xii.
57. Reinhold Niebuhr, *The Children of Light and the Children of Darkness* (New York: Scribner's, 1944), ix, cited after McAfee Brown, "Introduction," xii.
58. *The Essential Reinhold Niebuhr*, 99, cf. xx.
59. Niebuhr, *The Irony of American History*, 155, 156.
60. Ibid., 157, 158.

CHAPTER SIX

Post-Secular Society: Consumerism and the Democratization of Religion

Bryan S. Turner

Introduction: the argument

In this chapter I develop a number of critical reflections on the analysis of religion in both contemporary sociology and social philosophy. This argument has several interconnected components. Sociologists and more especially philosophers have focused too much on religious belief and too little on practice. In this respect, I return to a defense of Émile Durkheim, who can be interpreted as saying that belief is always embedded in collective practices and that they become problematic and uncertain only when there are major changes in practice. I set this contrast between philosophical understanding of belief and sociological analysis of practice in the context of developing a notion that secularization has be analyzed under two headings (the social and the political), denoting categories in which the emphasis on practice turns out to be more relevant to understanding social practices than to political secularization. I defend a version of the secularization thesis by arguing that modern religion (at the social level) has become democratized and that the traditional hierarchical, literary (as opposed to visual), and ineffable features of religion have been eroded. In this version of the secularization thesis, I take a somewhat unfashionable stand in defending the work of the late Bryan Wilson, whose work is too easily dismissed by sociologists who have become enthusiastic about "the turn to religion." Finally, I criticize much of the debate around secularization and "post-secular society" for being too narrowly focused on the West.

In more detail then, there is a tendency to concentrate on religious beliefs rather than practice, and mainstream sociologists almost never look at religious objects. There is also a marked inclination to examine formal theologies, official statements of belief, and formal institutions. Obviously the intellectual champions of major religions make truth claims in their official theologies, but the emphasis of lived religion in everyday life puts practice in the foreground, organizes religious activity in terms of a calendar, and celebrates collective commitment through public events such as saints' days. We should think more seriously about belief rather than knowledge as part of the habitus of individuals and pay more attention to religion and the body, or more specifically to religious habitus and embodiment.[1] A similar argument might be developed with respect to the role of emotions in religious belief, practice, and experience. Although the sociology of the emotions has in recent years developed as an important field of contemporary research, it has not played a significant part in recent philosophical or sociological understanding of religion in modernity. My argument is that in order to understand secularization as a process, we need to attend more closely to the disruption of the religious habitus and the emotional life that sustains religion rather than take notice of any alleged crisis of belief.

Philosophical discussions of the crisis of religious belief and authority tend to ignore the investigations of social scientists, and their abstract speculations rarely refer to any actual empirical findings. Whereas Charles Taylor in *A Secular Age* happily quotes William James and ÉmileDurkheim,[2] contemporary research results rarely receive any detailed attention, and as a result thereby major social developments such as the growth of "post-institutional spirituality," the emergence of popular commercialized religion, and the spread of revivalism, including Pentecostalism and charismatic movements, are ignored.

The majority of Western sociologists and philosophers have unsurprisingly had little to say about religion outside northern Europe and the United States. The point of the post-secular debate has been in part to recognize the peculiarities of the European experience of secularization, to question the notion of American exceptionalism, and to create a dialogue with religion, especially with Islam, in the public sphere. It has become increasingly obvious that it is very difficult to generalize from the European experience in which the separation of the state and the Church in the Westphalian settlement of religious wars presupposed a history of confessional politics.

By contrast, contemporary anthropological and comparative sociological research clearly illustrate both the complexity of secularization as a process and the vitality of religion in the rest of the world, especially as a result of modern pilgrimage, religious revivalism in Southeast Asia, and Pentecostal and charismatic movements in South America and Africa. When serious attention is given to religious movements outside the West, both sociologists and philosophers have directed far too much attention to fundamentalism in general and to radical Islam in particular. The principal examples are Mark Juergensmeyer,[3] Olivier Roy,[4] and Giles Kepel.[5] There are many contemporary forms of religious revivalism and growth other than radical or political religion. One of the major developments in contemporary religions is the emergence of urban piety, especially among women. I have studied this pietization of everyday life in Malaysia among reformist Muslim groups and in Singapore,[6] where educated, literate urban women turn to pious lifestyles that have no connection with political Islam. More attention to the historical and comparative study of religion would greatly improve philosophical arguments about secularization and post-secularization.

While secularization and post-secular society are clearly issues in western Europe, religion in its various and complex manifestations is obviously thriving in many parts of Asia, Africa, and Latin America. Religious reformism in Indonesia and Malaysia, the restoration of Confucianism and Daoism in China, the vibrancy of spirit possession cults in Vietnam with the Renovation Period, shamanistic religions in South Korea, the spread of Buddhism from Taiwan to the United States, the mobilization of Tibetan Buddhism as a global model of meditation, the transformation of Hinduism outside India, and so on—these are well-known developments outside the Western world that bring into question the narrow focus of much sociological and philosophical debate. Similar accounts of Pentecostalism or charismatic movements in South America and Africa could be drawn from contemporary research.[7]

While it is now widely held that the conventional secularization thesis of sociologists such as Bryan Wilson[8] was exaggerated if not plain misguided, José Casanova prudently warns against any wholesale abandonment of the secularization thesis.[9] Having rejected earlier versions of the secularization argument as simplistic, sociologists should be careful not to commit the opposite mistake of assuming that every form of religious renewal is automatically evidence of "re-sacralization." In this respect I am sympathetic to Steve Bruce's view that Peter Berger's recantation of his own version of secularization was unwarranted.[10] The strength of religion in Africa and Asia does not automatically falsify the secularization thesis. It simply means that the constellation of causal factors that produced secularization in the West is not present in many Asian and African societies. I want to maintain in any case that there is an alternative to the simple notion of membership decline and social irrelevance, namely, that religion has been democratized through commercialization. As a result, secularization is manifest through the growth of megachurches, drive-in confessionals, buy-a-prayer, religious films, religious shopping outlets, and the sale of amulets and other paraphernalia. This view of the commercialization of lay religiosity is in fact compatible with Wilson's argument in *Religion in Secular Society*, to the effect that religion (Christianity specifically) survives in America at the cost of its contents. In adjusting to the consumer culture of postwar America, religion became a lifestyle choice. I have elsewhere called this commodification of religious belief and practice an example of "low intensity religion,"[11] by which I mean that many forms of religiosity are low on commitment, individualistic, and highly subjective. As such, these religious styles are distinctly post-institutional, and it is doubtful that they will have a lasting impact on social structure or culture. In this particular discussion, however, I shall use a somewhat different terminology, referring to much modern religiosity as do-it-yourself (DIY) religion, drawing attention thereby to the mix-and-match character of much modern belief and practice. Religion has joined modernity insofar as religious lifestyles are modeled on secular lifestyles that are promoted through a vast array of advertising strategies, growth consultancies, and financial inducements. These lifestyles circulate in religious markets that sell general spiritual rather than specific ecclesiastical services. This development has been described by a number of contemporary commentators, most notably by William Connolly in *Capitalism and Christianity American Style*, in which he perceives a close connection between conservative Christianity and modern corporate capitalism leading to an "evangelical-capitalist resonance machine."[12]

This discussion of the fortunes of religion in modernity has to be further complicated by drawing a distinction between the sacred and the religious. In historical terms, in the Judeo-Christian and Islamic traditions, there was always a foundation of the sacred as the realm of the ineffable. The sacred was situated in a hierarchical world, a great chain of being, and this sacred reality became manifest in human affairs through the communication of intermediaries—prophets, angels, mythical creatures, birds, or spirits—but the message of religion was paradoxically ultimately unspeakable. While this argument that religions have been commodified is not entirely new, it is normally applied to modern urban Christianity, whereas in the contemporary period of cultural globalization, the phenomenon of commercialized and individualized religion is widespread, embracing Buddhism in Thailand, popular Islamic preaching in Indonesia and Egypt, charismatic movements in Africa, and Pentecostalism in Latin America. The pressures toward democratization, commercialization, and the norm of individual choice are generic features of modern religious cultures.[13] While religion flourishes in its diverse popular manifestations, Thomas Luckmann has claimed in an influential article that the sacred or the transcendent in shrinking.[14] While modern religious activity is articulated around the themes of self-realization, personal autonomy, and emotional expressivity, the span of the transcendent contracts.

If we look at religion in terms of a theory of media of exchange and communication, then democratization entails the disappearance of these ancient forms of sacredness and ineffability. These intermediary systems (between the divine and the human) are breaking down or disappearing in modern societies, where the electronic media are omnipresent, devolved, and dispersed. Because communication comes from everywhere, we inhabit an information-saturated social world. In place of the ineffable character of the sacred realm, religion becomes fully available to the hoi polloi, because its message is made plain, simple, and direct through the commercialized media and popular culture. In liberal global capitalism, the ineffable hierarchy of sacred beings is being eroded by a communication system that has democratizing consequences, and the religious becomes domesticated and tamed as the sacred becomes "effable." Perhaps one could even speak here of the emergence of a democratic ontology of the sacred. In this regard, the notion of religion as yet another consumption choice and particular lifestyle is intended to capture the idea that religious hierarchies have been flattened out, with the result that divine forces are no longer ineffably remote and mysteriously distant. In an individualistic culture, the idea of choice is paramount and individuals migrate between faiths and institutions with relative ease. Just as the secular market emphasizes choice for the secular consumer and the importance of niche marketing, so does the religious market. The

American megachurch is modeled on the corporation in terms of architecture, culture, ambience, and outlook.[15]

Turning once more to Casanova's important intervention in the secularization debate, he has usefully proposed that we can think of the secularization thesis as simply a subtheme of the more general notion of modernization and that modernity involves the differentiation of the religious and the secular process. Being critical of the idea that secularization means simply the decline of religious belief and practice, Casanova identified three components of secularization: differentiation of various spheres of the social system (such as religion, polity, and market); secularization as the decline of religious belief and practice; and, finally, the marginalization of religion to the private sphere. Through a number of comparative studies, he demonstrated that secularization as differentiation is indeed the key component of modern secularization. However, an adequate sociology of religion has to evaluate these three components separately and independently. Thus, sociologists of religion were forced to review their assumptions about secularization in the 1980s with the eruption of "public religions" such as the Iranian revolution, the rise of Solidarity, the involvement of Roman Catholicism in the Sandinista revolution, and the growth of the Christian right in the United States. There is, however, one dimension that is missing from or understated in Casanova's account, namely, to use the language of Bourdieu, the place of religion in the everyday life-world (or religious habitus) and the impact of a commercial culture on the religious field. In short, Weber's idea of a necessary tension between religion and the world needs to be taken into account. Commercialization liquidates this tension, and democratization levels out the relationship between the sacred and the secular, producing a situation in which the world is flat.

In light of Casanova's account of public religions, the existing debate about secularization could be made conceptually more precise and more relevant by making a simple distinction between "political secularization" (the differentiation thesis) and "social secularization" (the commodification thesis). The former refers specifically to the issue around the historical separation of church and state (or, in more complex terms, the specialization of the subsystems of society around politics, culture, the economy, religion, and so forth). It refers to a number of institutional arrangements for the management of religion in the public domain, such as secular law versus religious laws, secular schooling versus religious schools, and the independence of the priesthood and ministry from the state. Social secularization refers to everyday religious experience, practice, and belief and to the penetration of that everyday world by the secular market and secular values. It refers to the relationships, in Luckmann's terms, between transcendence and institutionalized religion. The importance of this distinction is that social and political secularization may take different directions and have different rhythms, so to speak. We can study the intersection of political and social secularization separately.

Liberty of conscience or political secularization was the cornerstone of the conventional liberal view of tolerance in which rational citizens were free to hold private beliefs and to engage in religious practices outside the secular space of the political domain, provided these activities did not intrude on the conduct of public affairs. In the Christian West, this liberal solution emerged out of the Anglican settlement stemming from the writings of figures such as Richard Hooker, and it was given a definitive philosophical foundation in the work of John Locke. It was a political solution originally intended to settle the conflicts between Catholics and Protestants. Of course the liberal solution was never as neat as this formulation suggests. The Established Church in England and the Lutheran churches in Germany had a dominant cultural and political role in shaping the state, and the alliance between church and state was essential for securing peace in civil society. In addition, in England, the word "state" did not come into regular usage until after the 1660s, and the idea of a commonwealth was promoted to express a common experience of political life. As a result, Established churches were never enthusiastic about the idea of religious liberties, and religious groups outside the Establishment were typically regarded as heresies.[16]

It is generally agreed that this liberal settlement has broken down because modern societies have inevitably become multiethnic and multifaith as a consequence of the global migration of labor. When religion defines identity, it is difficult to sustain a simple division between the public and the private. Moreover, these religious identities are typically transnational and hence cannot be neatly confined within the national boundaries of secular citizenship. The eruption of religions in the public domain means that the secular state, often reluctantly, enters into the management of religions, especially where religious revivalism impinges on liberal tolerance. When the diversity of religions in society threatens to disrupt civil harmony, states intervene either implicitly or explicitly in the regulation of religious activities,

for example, in banning head scarves in state schools. The problems arising from religious customs and laws in relation to secular courts raise even
deeper and more complex questions about legal pluralism. For example, in
Canada and England, there have been experiments with religious tribunals
under the provisions of arbitration acts, but these have given rise to considerable public acrimony and hostility, especially from feminist lobbying groups.
The Archbishop of Canterbury's public lecture on the possibility of allowing
the spread of such tribunals in British cities provoked considerable public
opposition (Williams, 2008). Nevertheless, there are jurisprudential arguments to suggest both that legal pluralism is inevitable and that it is consistent with liberal principles provided there are appropriate safeguards to protect individual rights, especially the rights of women to equal treatment.[17]

Social secularization, by contrast, refers to many of the conventional sociological measures of religious vitality—church membership, belief in God,
religious experiences, and acts of devotion such as prayer and pilgrimage. In
this regard, there is little evidence of religious decline outside of northern
Europe. However, in this discussion, I am attempting to describe something
more than merely a decline in religious practice but rather its transformation
by the twin processes of commercialization and democratization. In this
regard, I am seeking to consider not the quantitative erosion of religion but
its qualitative transformation. In the social sphere, modernity renders religion increasingly compatible with the lifestyles and practices of consumer
society. Religion as consumption is a secular practice, and consequently the
tension between religion and the world has largely disappeared, or at least
the tension has been eroded. Because religion is submerged in the circulation of commodities as a lifestyle choice, the capacity of religion to change
societies is absent. Max Weber had argued in the Protestant ethic thesis that
the unintended consequence of the division between world and religion in
inner-worldly asceticism was to transform society because Protestantism
had become a major carrier of modern rationalization.[18] Once the tension
between the ascetic calling and the mundane world had broken down, Protestantism lost its social leverage. In my version of this Weberian argument,
the distinction between the two dimensions of secularization (the political
and the social) provides a conceptually fruitful contrast between the role of
religion in the public domain of politics (the arrival of public religions) and
its character in the social domain of civil society (the evaporation of transcendence).

In structural terms, religion, state, and market have become differentiated spheres, but it is the market that is increasingly shaping religious practice rather than religion shaping the market. The result is a qualitative rather than quantitative transformation of the religious by the economic. While Casanova's work was about differentiation and the eruption of public religions, my attention is more specifically focused on the transformations of the religious by the values, practices, and institutions of modern consumerism. Following the insights of the so-called economic interpretation of religion, with differentiation and the transformation of churches into denominations, religions have to compete with one another for influence and for customers.[19] In a competitive market, religious denominations are forced to sell their services and hence have adopted many of the practices of the secular marketplace, with the use of focus groups, commercial advertising, branding, and promotional campaigns to win new customers and maintain customer loyalty.[20] Although these marketing strategies are most obvious in the North American context, similar developments can be observed in Asia across a range of religious traditions.[21]

The study of modern religion from Western sociological and philosophical perspectives, by concentrating on a narrow understanding of secularization, often ignores the profound commodification of modern religions—the circulation of Buddhist amulets, Daoist tourist centers, shrines, and festivals, Christian holidays, global Jewish publishing, religious tourism to sacred places, the commodification of religious materials, and so on. These developments are in some respects compatible with Weber, who at the beginning of *The Sociology of Religion* observed that religions are oriented primarily to this world.[22] Religion offers the poor and despised of this world the promise of health and wealth. In this regard, modern religious commodification often answers to the precarious nature of modern life, in which globalization has seriously disrupted the price of basic commodities such as rice and soybeans. Social anthropologists have observed a significant increase in witchcraft and magical practices in African societies where the volatility of prices for everyday goods has severely disrupted day-to-day social relationships.[23] Similarly, the growth of the amulet industry in Buddhist Thailand and the revival of spirit possession in contemporary Vietnam are testimonies to the connection between the precariousness of urban life, the commercialization of religion, and the demand for fortune-telling and other magical services.[24]

Philosophy and Post-Secularism

While many sociologists have taken notice of the limitations of the conventional secularization thesis, much recent thought has been given to the idea of a post-secular world, particularly in the work of Jürgen Habermas, among others.[25] The postwar generation of European philosophers and social theorists generally neglected religion, partly because of the legacy of Marxism in European social thought and partly because the validity of the secularization thesis, especially among sociologists, appeared to be obvious. For a whole generation of European social thinkers, religion was simply not a significant aspect of postwar European modernity. It is instructive to think of various significant figures in the social sciences whose work has had little or nothing to contribute to the study of religion—Luc Boltanski, Pierre Bourdieu, Anthony Giddens, Claus Offe, Goran Therborn, and the social thinkers associated with journals such as the *New Left Review*. Although recent interpretations of Bourdieu have struggled to demonstrate the relevance of his work to the field of religion, his actual contribution was modest.[26] Norbert Elias produced one of the most influential sociological accounts of historical development in his *The Civilizing Process*, with almost no reference to the impact of Roman Catholicism on codes of everyday civilized behavior. To take another example, David Harvey has been without question one of the most influential social geographers of his generation,[27] and his work on Paris has been rightly recognized as a classic in the development of historical geography and the political economy of space. And yet, in his study of Paris, there is not a single reference to religion in general or Roman Catholicism in particular. In the United States, the situation was very different, perhaps for the obvious reason that "American exceptionalism" also meant that American sociologists had to take religion seriously—or at least more seriously. Modern American history has been very different from that of northern Europe, and hence one can think of numerous American social theorists who have given religion some serious attention—Talcott Parsons, Robert Bellah, Daniel Bell, Harvey Cox, Paul Tillich, Peter Berger, and so on.

We can understand Habermas's treatment of religion in the public domain as in part a response to the liberal philosophy of John Rawls, who, in his analysis of the conditions for a successful liberal society, confronted the modern problems of diversity and difference.[28] There appears to be a need to rethink conventional liberalism because the privatization of religion is no longer a viable political strategy in the separation of state and religion. Liberals have often embraced multiculturalism as the only appropriate response to growing religious diversity, but critics of multiculturalism have argued that it is incompatible with the principle of equality and that it fosters the growth of separate and potentially conflict-ridden communities. Recognition of the rights of minorities (such as Muslims in the United States) has to be tempered by concern for social fragmentation. For example, the problem of parallel communities is real, and in the worst case, one can image the growth of modern enclaves in societies in which there is relatively little shared culture. John Rawls, in *The Law of Peoples*, has spoken of the importance of an "overlapping consensus of fundamental doctrines" if a liberal society is to survive without internal dissent and conflict, but such a liberal consensus cannot function from a sociological point of view without a system of overlapping social groups.[29] Taking multiculturalism seriously may force us to take social solidarity seriously, namely, to take a critical look at the celebration of difference at the cost of the things that hold societies together. From a sociological point of view, multiculturalism without some powerful framework of shared interests and shared institutions cannot provide an adequate cultural framework for any complex society. Sociologists such as Robert Bellah,[30] following both Rousseau and Durkheim, proposed that American society was dependent on a civil religion. The fundamental question is whether Muslim, Hindu, and Jewish communities can sit comfortably with such a civil religion and whether, after 9/11, the prospects for tolerance within such a framework are seriously diminished.

Habermas's solution to the conflict between radical multiculturalism and radical secularism is to propose a dialogue involving the inclusion of foreign minority cultures into civil society, on the one hand, and the opening up of subcultures to the state in order to encourage their members to participate actively in political life, on the other. In order to sustain the idea of communicative rationality, it is important to open up a dialogue between the secular and the religious. Habermas's defense of the importance of public communication is well illustrated by his engagement with Joseph Ratzinger. The relatively productive nature of that encounter can be understood against the background of *Kulturprotestantismus*, in which there is in Germany a general respect for religion and religion is far more prominent in public life than is the case in, for example, the United Kingdom. Habermas's response to Ratzinger rests upon the idea that politics (the state) cannot really function without a robust civil society or without a set of shared values. The role of religion—contrary to much critical theory and contrary to the secularization thesis—may be to provide a necessary support for social life as such. A dialogue between secular and religious citizens can take place only if there is something approximating an "overlapping consensus of fundamental beliefs"; otherwise the parties will merely talk past each other. In this discussion, Habermas and Ratzinger shared their opposition to relativism, which they see as a largely destructive force. Habermas's stance can therefore be useful contrasted with the work of philosophers such as Derrida, Rorty, and Vattimo, who have all been influenced by poststructuralism and postmodernism.

In *The Future of Religion*, Rorty and Vattimo embrace the idea that faith, hope, and charity—the radical legacy of New Testament Christianity—provide a framework for values in modern society.[31] They reject the authority of the Church in general and papal authority in particular. They also forcefully argue that the Church's teachings on gender and sexual relations are hopelessly antiquated, involving an essentialist reduction of women to nature (if not to anatomy). If the Church can abandon its hierarchical and antidemocratic structures and its commitment to a sacerdotal priesthood, it could more effectively, they claim, serve the needs of modern society—or at least it would be better equipped to serve those needs. The outcome is implicitly to endorse Habermas's conciliatory position that the Christian legacy is in many ways the underpinning of modern Western civilization. However, the current crisis around the sexual abuse of minors by Catholic priests has erupted largely after the publication of these philosophical discussions, and the scandals in some respects support their attack on celibacy, priesthood, and the Church's teaching on sexuality. At another level, they may demonstrate that the principal challenge to faith is never merely doctrinal coherence but actual daily practice.

Despite the references to postmodernism, both Rorty and Vattimo can be said to be merely repeating the criticisms of religion that have their foundation in the European Enlightenment. The Enlightenment attacked the metaphysical and supernatural worldviews of religion; its practical critique was directed against ecclesiastical institutions, which were seen to be authoritarian and repressive; and it developed a philosophical, aesthetic, and moral argument against the very idea of a personal God. In these criticisms, the Enlightenment prepared the groundwork for the emergence of the science of religion by treating religion as a discrete set of beliefs and practices that could be studied as social phenomena within the framework of human reason. In particular, Immanuel Kant's *Religion within the Boundaries of Mere Reason* (1998), which was published in 1793, was a decisive turning point in Western reflection on religion. Kant did not designate an independent branch of knowledge called the "philosophy of religion," and this particular publication was a contribution to ethics, thereby escaping the censorship of the Church. Because it was not classified under "biblical theology," it could be read as an analysis of the "limits of reason."

Kant's conclusions were nonetheless radical. Human beings, as moral agents, can exercise their duties only when they are free, and in exercising these moral duties, there is no need to posit a superior being, and hence morality does not require authoritative religious presuppositions. When morality and religion become confused, the result is superstition or, worse still, idolatry, in which human beings mistakenly and naively believe they can influence God by sacrifice, petitions, and offerings. By separating morality from religion, Kant opened the door to a critical study of organized religion as the negation of human freedom. In short, Kantian philosophy prepared the way toward the interpretation of religion as alienation.

Religions of Good Fortune

The Protestant Ethic and the Spirit of Capitalism explored the unique relationship between the ascetic ethic of the pietist sects and modernity. Weber's sociology is therefore based on this basic distinction between religious orientations that satisfy mundane this-worldly needs (health and good fortune) and those morally demanding religious orientations that are concerned with the need for meaning and significance. In part, it was for this reason that Weber was hostile to Freudian psychoanalysis, because it compromised these ethical demands for a calling in the world. All forms of psychoanalytical therapy functioned merely as a form of mental hygiene.

These two aspects of the religious orientation to fortune and meaning were reflected in the very meaning of the word "religion" (*religio*), which has two somewhat distinct roots. First, *relegere*, from *legere*, means "to pull together," "to harvest," or "to gather (in)." Second, *religare*, from *ligare*, means "to tie" or "to bind together." The first points sociologically to the role of the cult in forming human membership, while the meaning of the second indicates the moral or regulatory practices of religion in the discipline of passions. In Kant's essay on religion, there is a distinction between religion as cult (*des blossen Cultus*), which seeks favors from God through prayers and gifts, and religion as moral action (*die Religion des guten Lebenswandels*) that commands human beings to reform their behavior in order to lead a morally better life. This "reflecting faith" compels humans to strive for salvation through faith rather than the possession of religious knowledge. The implication of this distinction was that Protestant Christianity was the only true "reflecting faith" and thereby the model of all authentic religious intentions.

These ideas underpinned Weber's comparative sociology of religious orientations to the world and their directions. In *The Sociology of Religion*, he distinguished between the religion of the masses and the religion of the virtuosi. While masses seek earthly comforts from religion, especially healing, the virtuosi fulfill the ethical demands of religion in search of spiritual salvation or enlightenment. The religion of the masses requires charismatic saints and holy men who satisfy basic needs, and eventually charisma is corrupted by the demand for miracles and spectacles. More importantly, Weber distinguished between those religions that reject the world by challenging its traditions (such as inner-worldly asceticism) and religions that seek to escape from the world through mystical flight (such as otherworldly mysticism). The former religions (primarily the radical Calvinistic sects) have had revolutionary consequences for human society in the formation of rational capitalism. The implication of this tradition is paradoxical. First, Protestantism is the only true religion as a reflecting enlightened faith, and, second, Protestant Christianity gives rise to a process of secularization that spells out its own self-overcoming.

When contemporary philosophers such as Rorty and Vattimo approach the issues of religion and secularization, the same underlying assumptions are present, despite their overtly anti-Kantian, postmodern standpoint. The problems of modern religion are thought to be about belief and authority, and so religious practices do not enter into the analysis. My argument borrows somewhat from both Ludwig Wittgenstein's philosophy of religion and Émile Durkheim's *The Elementary Forms* in order to claim that religion is embodied practice. Religion is not about (or not only about) abstract comprehension of doctrine, associated with listening to sermons (as a reflecting faith), but about performances in connection with our exposure to the ineffable. Durkheim's criticisms of nineteenth-century utilitarian views of religion as poor philosophy or magic as ineffective technology are well known. Wittgenstein's commentaries on religion are less so. However, his critical views of Victorian philosophy—for example, in his astute remarks on Frazer's *Golden Bough*—are instructive, and my account of practice in relation to belief receives some support from Wittgenstein's view of language and games. Like their Victorian counterparts, contemporary philosophical and theological commentary on the problems of religious belief in a secular environment concentrates on problems of knowledge rather than practice. One can argue that the paucity of shared rituals for celebrating life and recognizing death is one dimension of secularization in the West. Wittgenstein, in rejecting the view in Victorian anthropology that religion is based on error, clearly understood the importance of ritual practice in sustaining the religious life. For example, Frazer argued that people persist in trying to bring about rain through magic, despite its errors, because sooner or later it will rain. Wittgenstein objected, "It may happen, as it so often does today, that someone will give up a practice when he has seen that something on which it depended is an error. But this happens only in cases where you can make a man change his way of doing things simply by calling his attention to his error. This is not how it is in connection with the religious practices of a people. . . . What makes the character of ritual action is not any view or opinion, either right or wrong."[32] Wittgenstein concluded that religious cultures survive because their character is part of the way of life of a community that is sustained over time by constant rehearsal and that, consequently, rituals cannot be simply invented intentionally de novo. One aspect of secularization is the erosion of these collective rituals, especially around the individual life cycle and the annual calendar.

Weber's sociology of religion can also be understood as concerned with practice as much as with belief. Although Weber typically is seen to be focused on the meaning of religion, Joachim Radkau, in his biography of Weber, articulates Weber's interest in religious practice very well when he says that "the crucial point for him was the influence of religion not on people's view of the world but on their everyday lives, on human types and their conduct of life."[33] The problem of belief may be a crucial philosophical issue, but it may have little immediate bearing on the everyday conduct of religion. At the very least, we should pay attention to how belief is embedded in practice. In conclusion, Weber's sociology set out to explore historically the relationships between personality and life orders (the ways in which the everyday world is shaped and organized), namely, how personality and life orientations (asceticism and discipline, for example) are determined by particular life orders.[34] How does the particular organization of social life produce different forms of virtue such as courage or wisdom or piety? Following this notion of the virtue or normative excellence of different practices, my argument is that a commercial world is a life order that is not conducive to religious personality or spiritual excellence. Paradoxically, a world dominated by consumption requires that greed become a virtue.[35]

The Commodification of Religion

There has been considerable amount of research on how commodification and the Internet are transforming the religious lives of young people. For young Muslims, Internet use is an important means of building a consensus about, for example, whether the use of henna for cosmetic purposes is compatible with Muslim tradition or whether dating and premarital intimacies are compatible with the life of a "good Muslim."[36] Whereas the religious system of communication in an age of revelation was hierarchical, unitary, and authoritative, the system of communicative acts in a new media environment are typically horizontal rather than vertical, diverse and fragmented rather than unitary, devolved rather than centralized. Furthermore, the authority of any message is constantly negotiable and negotiated. The growth of these diverse centers of interpretation in a global communication system has produced considerable instability in the formal system of religious belief and practice. In Islam, for example, there has been an inflation of sources of authority, since through some local and specific consensus, almost any local teacher or mullah can issue a fatwa to guide a local community.[37] Because new media provide multiple channels of access and encourage discursive interaction on blogs, they bring about a democratization of knowledge and religious lifestyles. Although there is clearly a digital divide, more and more people have access to these religious sites of communication. There is a democratization of Islam in the sense that many young Muslims bypass their traditional *ulama* and imams in order to learn about Islam from pamphlets and sources, but this is equally true of other religious traditions.

There is in very general terms an important growth of religion online. In developing an account of the commodification and democratization of religion, let me return to the matter of ineffability, concentrating on the issue of communication and modern Islam. How is the Internet shaping the daily lives and religious practices of young generations? One obvious answer is that it makes the actual collective practice of religion—such as going to church or to the mosque—no longer necessary, and the result is that religion online becomes online religion. The Internet has therefore only served to reinforce the problem of authority. Within the Muslim diaspora, where young Muslims face new problems relating to personal conduct, the new Internet intellectuals create personal websites, providing religious or ethical rulings on various questions relating to religious conduct. These e-mail fatwas are not recognized by traditional shari'a courts as admissible evidence and cannot be readily enforced, but they clearly have an influence within the diaspora. They become authoritative, as users compare these rulings against other sites and e-fatwas. The debate on the Internet between multiple Muslim audiences constitutes an informal shari'a in which a communal consensus can emerge around controversial issues related to appropriate practice in new environments.

In summary, the Internet is an important technology for creating an imagined community for individuals and groups that are separated from their homelands and exist as minorities in alien secular cultures that are often hostile to Islam. These Internet sites also serve to reinforce the individualism that many observers have associated with neo-fundamentalism because, in the case of Islam, the global virtual ummah, or community of believers, is the perfect site for individuals to express themselves while still claiming to be members of a community on whose behalf they are speaking.[38] We can conclude therefore that these forms of religious communication are characterized by a principle of subsidiarity by which authority rests in the local and specific act of communication rather than in a principle of hierocracy.

These media contribute to a growing subjective individualism that is very different from the rugged ascetic and disciplined individualism of early Protestantism. This emerging religious subjectivity can be interpreted as a facet of the "expressive revolution"[39] that had its roots in the student revolts of the 1960s. In the new individualism, people invent their own religious ideas and borrow religious practices from diverse traditions. The result has been a social revolution flowing from both consumerism and individualism, and as a result, "Capitalism's success eroded class rivalries and replaced the activist and utopian mass politics of the inter-war era with a more bloodless politics of consumption and management. Goods not gods were what people wanted."[40] Consumerism helped to break down the old division between religion and the world, contributing to the contraction of the span of transcendence.

Religious lifestyles get modeled on consumer lifestyles in which people can try out religions rather like the way they try out a new fashion in handbags or shoes. In a consumer society, people want "goods not gods," and to a large extent their desires can be satisfied by consumer credit. A new industry has emerged, concerned with spiritual advice on how to cope with the modern world while remaining pious and pure. Pious lifestyles are marketed by religious entrepreneurs who need to brand their products in the spiritual marketplace.

The consequence of these developments is a growing division between traditional "religion" and modern "spirituality."[41] Globalization has brought the spread of personal spirituality, and these spiritualities typically provide guidance in the everyday world as well as subjective, tailor-made meaning. Such religious phenomena are often combined with personal therapeutic, healing services or the promise of personal enhancement through meditation. While fundamentalist norms of personal discipline appeal to social groups that are upwardly socially mobile, such as the lower middle class and the newly educated, spirituality is more closely associated with middle-class singles who have been thoroughly influenced by Western consumer values. David Martin's study of Pentecostalism also suggests that new therapies and lifestyles can be sustained through membership in Pentecostal groups in which religion and material aspiration no longer conflict.[42]

The new religions are closely associated also with themes of therapy, peace, and self-help. Of course the idea that religion, especially in the West, has become privatized is hardly new.[43] However, these new forms of subjectivity and privatized living are no longer confined to Protestantism or the American middle classes; they now have a global audience. These religious developments are therefore no longer simply local cults but burgeoning global popular religions carried by the Internet, movies, rock music, popular TV shows, and pulp fiction. I have described these new forms as pick-'n'-mix religions because their adherents borrow freely from a great range of religious beliefs and practices without any noticeable regard for coherence. It is also a new experimental context in which the iconic can also be the iconoclastic, as represented in Madonna's experimentation with both Catholic and Hasidic personae.[44]

These phenomena have been regarded as aspects of "new religious movements"[45] that are, as we have seen, manifestations of the new spiritual marketplaces. Such forms of religion tend to be highly individualistic, they are unorthodox in the sense that they follow no official creed, they are characterized by their syncretism, and they have little or no connection with institutions such as churches, mosques, or temples. They are post-institutional, and in this sense they can legitimately be called "postmodern" religions. If global fundamentalism involves the modernization of social groups who are new arrivals to global megacities, the global post-institutional religions are typical of postmodernization.

Finally, spirituality is a mobile religiosity that mobile people can transport globally to new sites where they can mix and match their religious or self-help needs without too much constraint from hierarchical authorities. It is a religious orientation that permits rapid and easy transitions between different identities, in which modern conversions tend to be more like a change in consumer brands than a searching of the soul. If the new religious lifestyles give rise to emotions, these are packaged in ways that can be easily consumed. Brand loyalty on the part of consumers in low-intensity religions is also minimalistic.

Conclusion: New Gods of Communication

In modern societies, the principal characteristics of religion are its individualism in association with the decline in the authority of traditional institutions (specifically, the church, the liturgy, and the priesthood) and a growing awareness that religious symbols are social constructs. Robert Bellah's predictions about modernity[46] have been strikingly confirmed in the growth of popular, de-institutionalized, commercialized and largely post-Christian religions. In fact, similar processes are at work in all the major religions. In a differentiated global religious market, the various segments of the religious market compete with one another for followers and resources. Bourdieu's ideas about the struggle for symbolic capital in the field of religion provide a valid sociological perspective on the volatility of this religious field. The new religions are genuinely consumerist, but while fundamentalist movements appear to challenge consumer (Western) values, they are themselves typically selling a lifestyle based on special diets, alternative education, health regimes, dress codes, pilgrimage destinations, and marriage services. The contemporary religious market is consequently highly diversified into a range of competing groups, charismatic movements, Pentecostal churches, traditional religions, spirituality, and the like, but these are all, to varying degrees, influenced by consumerism. The audiences for religious services are also differentiated by class, gender, education, region, and so forth.

The triumph of popular, democratizing, global consumer culture is now having a deep impact on the traditional, hierarchical, literate religions of the past. Perhaps the most important development in modern religion is the changing status of women; one can safely predict that women will become increasingly important in religious leadership, and not simply in liberal Episcopalian churches but in the world religions more generally.[47] Gender is a crucial feature of the new consumerist religiosity in which women increasingly dominate the new spiritualities; women will be and to some extent already are the important "taste leaders" in the emergent global spiritual marketplace.

Globalization theory has focused scientific attention on modern fundamentalism, which is seen as a critique of traditional and popular religiosity. However, the real effect of globalization has been the growth of heterodox, commercial, hybrid, syncretistic religions over orthodox, authoritative, and institutional versions of the spiritual life. The ideological effects and social consequences of these religions cannot be easily or effectively controlled by religious authorities, and they often have a greater impact than official messages, at least among the young. In Weber's terms, it is the triumph of mass over virtuoso religiosity.

Pentecostalism has prepared the lower middle classes for participation in the emerging consumer economy of Latin America, and in a similar fashion, reformist Islam in Southeast Asia provides newly urbanized people, and especially educated women, with values and practices that are relevant to life in more complex, multicultural urban and largely secular societies, in countries where international corporations have provided employment opportunities for young people willing or able to leave their villages for work in the megacities.

The habitus of the modern adherent of deinstitutionalized religion is basically compatible with the lifestyles of a commercial world in which the driving force of the economy is domestic consumption. Megachurches have embraced the sales strategies of late capitalism in order to get their message out to the public. On these grounds, one can claim that modern religions are compromised because the tension between the world and the religion is lost. We may define these developments as a form of social secularization. One can imagine that social historians will object to this argument, claiming that commercialized religion was not unknown in the Middle Ages, when pilgrimage and relics were basic elements of the economy of European societies. However, with contemporary social differentiation, the market no longer dances to the tune of the dominant religious institutions. Furthermore, these secular developments are global rather than simply local. The result is a sociological paradox or set of paradoxes. Religion has erupted into the public domain, being associated with a number of radical or revolutionary movements from Iran to Brazil and from Poland to Colombia, but at the same time, religion has been coming to terms with a variety of changes that are the consequence of commodification. More precisely, the secularization of religion has occurred through a double movement—democratization and commercialization.[48] The sense of mystery and awe surrounding the ineffable character of the sacred has been eroded by the liberal ethos of democracy, in which egalitarian, immediate, and intimate relations are valued more than hierarchical, distant, and formal relationships. Religion as an agent of social change has been further compromised by the loss of any significant contrast between the sacred and the world. Religion has specialized in providing personal services and has therefore been competing with various secular agencies that also offer welfare, healing, comfort, and meaning. In this competition, religious groups have by and large taken over the methods and values of a range of institutions operating within what we can, for want of a more sophisticated term, call "the leisure industries."

Notes

1. Bryan S. Turner, *The Body and Society* (London: Sage, 2008).

2. Charles Taylor, *A Secular Age* (Cambridge, MA: Harvard University Press, 2007).

3. Mark Juergensmeyer, *Terror in the Mind of God: The Global Rise of Religious Violence* (Berkeley: University of California Press, 2000).

4. Olivier Roy, *The Failure of Political Islam* (Cambridge, MA.: Harvard University Press, 1994).

5. Giles Kepel, *Jihad: The Trial of Political Islam* (London: I. B. Taurus, 2002).

6. Mohamed Nasir Kamaludeen, Alexius A. Pereira, and Bryan S. Turner, *Muslims in Singapore: Piety, Politics and Policies* (London: Routledge, 2009). See also Bryan S. Turner and Joy Kooi-Chin Tong, "Women, Piety and Practice: A Study of Women Religious Practice in Malaya," *Contemporary Islam* 2 (2008): 41–59.

7. David Lehmann, *Struggle for the Spirit: Religious Transformation and Popular Culture in Brazil and Latin America* (Oxford: Polity Press, 1996).

8. See Bryan Wilson, *Religion in Secular Society* (London: Watts, 1966), and Bryan Wilson, *Contemporary Transformations of Religion* (London: Oxford University Press, 1976).

9. José Casanova, *Public Religions in the Modern World* (Chicago: University of Chicago Press, 1994).

10. Steve Bruce, "The Curious Case of the Unnecessary Recantation: Berger and Secularization," in Linda Woodhead, Paul Heelas, and David Martin, eds., *Peter Berger and the Study of Religion* (London: Routledge, 2001), 87–100.

11. Bryan S. Turner, "Religious Speech: The Ineffable Nature of Religious Communication in the Information Age," *Theory, Culture & Society* 25, no. 7–8 (2009): 219–235.

12. William E. Connolly, *Capitalism and Christianity American Style* (Durham, NC: Duke University Press, 2008).

13. Bryan S. Turner, "New Spiritualities, the Media and Global Religion: *da Vinci Code* and *The Passion of Christ*," in Pattana Kitiarsa, ed., *Religious Commodifications in Asia: Marketing Gods* (London and New York: Routledge, 2008), 31–45.

14. Thomas Luckmann, "Shrinking Transcendence, Expanding Religion?" *Sociological Analysis* 50, no. 2 (1990): 127–138.

15. Stephen Ellingson, "New Research on Megachurches: Non-denominationalism and Sectarianism," in Bryan S. Turner, ed., *The New Blackwell Companion to the Sociology of Religion* (Oxford: Wiley-Blackwell, 2010), 247–266.

16. Anthony Gill, *The Political Origins of Religious Liberty* (Cambridge: Cambridge University Press, 2008).

17. Brian Z. Tamanaha, *Realistic Socio-Legal Theory: Pragmatism and a Social Theory of Law* (Clarendon: Oxford University Press, 1997).

18. Max Weber, *The Protestant Ethic and the Spirit of Capitalism* (1904–1905; London: Penguin, 2002).

19. Rodney Stark and Roger Finke, *Acts of Faith: Explaining the Human Side of Religion* (Berkeley: University of California Press, 2000). R. S. Warner, "Enlisting Smelser's Theory of Ambivalence to Maintaining Progress in Sociology of Religion's New Paradigm," in J. C. Alexander, G. T. Marx, and C. L. Williams, eds., *Self, Social*

Structure and Beliefs: Explorations in Sociology (Berkeley: University of California Press, 2004), 103–121.

20. L. R. Iannaccone, "Why Strict Churches Are Strong," *American Journal of Sociology* 99, no. 5 (1994): 1180–1211.

21. Pattana Kitiarsa, ed., *Religious Commodifications in Asia: Marketing Gods* (London and New York: Routledge, 2008).

22. Max Weber, *The Sociology of Religion* (1922; London: Methuen, 1966).

23. Jean Comaroff and John L. Comaroff, "Occult Economies and the Violence of Abstraction: Notes from the South African Postcolony," *American Ethnologist* 26, no. 3 (1999): 279–301. Jean Comaroff and John L. Comaroff, "Millennial Capitalism: First Thoughts on a Second Coming," *Public Culture* 12, no. 2 (2000): 291–343.

24. Taylor, *A Secular Age*. Fenggang Yang and Joe Tamney, eds., *State, Market and Religions in Chinese Societies* (Leiden: Brill, 2005).

25. Jürgen Habermas, *Religion and Rationality: Essays on Reason, God and Modernity* (Cambridge, MA: MIT Press, 2002). Jürgen Habermas and Joseph Ratzinger, *The Dialectics of Secularization: On Reason and Religion* (San Francisco: Ignatius, 2006).

26. Terry Rey, *Bourdieu on Religion: Imposing Faith and Legitimacy* (London: Equinox Publishing, 2007).

27. See David Harvey, *Paris: Capital of Modernity* (London: Routledge, 2003).

28. John Rawls, *The Law of Peoples* (Cambridge, MA: Harvard University Press, 1999). John Rawls, *Political Liberalism* (New York: Columbia University Press, 2003).

29. Rawls, *The Law of Peoples*.

30. Robert Bellah, "Civil Religion in America," *Daedalus* 96, no. 1 (1967): 1–21.

31. Santiago Zabala, ed., *The Future of Religion* (New York: Columbia University Press, 2005).

32. Ludwig Wittgenstein, *Remarks on Frazer's Golden Bough* (Oxford: Blackwell, 1979), 2e, 7e.

33. Joachim Radkau, *Max Weber: A Biography* (Cambridge: Polity, 2009), 185.

34. Wilhelm Hennis, *Max Weber: Essays in Reconstruction* (London: Allen & Unwin, 1988).

35. Alexander Robertson, *Greed: Gut Feelings, Growth and History* (Cambridge: Polity, 2001).

36. Roxanne D. Murcotte, "Gender and Sexuality Online on Australian Muslim Forums," *Contemporary Islam* 4 (2010): 117–138.

37. Frederic Volpi and Bryan S. Turner, "Making Islamic Authority Matter," *Theory, Culture & Society* 24, no. 2 (2007): 1–19.

38. Peter Mandaville, *Transnational Muslim Politics: Reimagining the Umma* (London and New York: Routledge, 2001).

39. Talcott Parsons, "Christianity and Modern Industrial Society," in E. A. Tiryakian, ed., *Sociological Theory, Values and Sociocultural Change: Essays in Honor of Pitrim A. Sorokin* (New York: Free Press, 1963), 33–70.

40. Mark Mazower, *Dark Continent: Europe's Twentieth Century* (London: Penguin Books, 1999), 306.

41. Paul Heelas and Linda Woodhead, *The Spiritual Revolution: Why Religion Is Giving Way to Spirituality* (Oxford: Blackwell, 2004).

42. David Martin, *Pentecostalism: The World Their Parish* (Oxford: Blackwell, 2002).

43. Thomas Luckmann, *The Invisible Religion: The Problem of Religion in Modern Society* (New York: Macmillan, 1967).

44. M. D. Hulsether, "Like a Sermon: Popular Religion in Madonna Videos," in B. D. Forbes and J. H. Mahan, eds., *Religion and Popular Culture* (Berkeley: University of California Press, 2000), 77–100.

45. James Beckford, *Social Theory and Religion* (Cambridge: Cambridge University Press, 2003).

46. Robert N. Bellah, "Religious Evolution," *American Sociological Review* 29 (1964): 358–374.

47. A. Sharma and K. Young, eds., *Feminism and World Religions* (Albany: State University of New York Press, 1999).

48. Bryan S. Turner, "Introduction: The Comparative Sociology of De-Secularization," in Bryan S. Turner, ed., *Secularization* (London: Sage, 2010), vii–xi.

CHAPTER SEVEN

Secular Liturgies and the Prospects for a "Post-Secular" Sociology of Religion

James K. A. Smith

Introduction: Imagining Religion at the End of the World

In his landmark work *Ideas Pertaining to a Pure Phenomenology*, Edmund Husserl undertook a thought experiment intended as a kind of limit case that would help elucidate the nature of consciousness. While I have no investment in his particular claims, the strategy is suggestive. Imagine, Husserl (rather blithely) suggested, the complete annihilation of the world. Imagine the utter destruction of materiality: not just buildings and trees, but animals and planets. Imagine the obliteration of the earth, the eradication of material stuff, and the annihilation of our bodies. What would be left? Could consciousness survive such a catastrophe? Oddly enough, Husserl answered "yes" to such a question: "while the being of consciousness, of any stream of mental processes whatever, would indeed be necessarily modified by an annihilation of the world of physical things, its own existence would not be touched."[1]

I would like to invite you to consider some analogous thought experiments, not in order to distill the essence of consciousness, but in order to press the traditional or received ways we think about "religion" and its correlate, "the secular."

- Let's begin with Husserl's own scenario: If the entire physical universe evaporated, would religion survive? If there were no bodies, no buildings, and no bread, could there still be "religion"? Just what sort of religion could survive such an evisceration of materiality?

- Second, let's try something a little less drastic but no less catastrophic: Imagine the harrowed world of Cormac McCarthy's novel *The Road*. Imagine what's left of a world after a disastrous incineration of almost all that we know as nature and culture. Imagine a world of unspeakable cruelty and the degradation of the human race to a cannibalistic war of all with all. Would that be a "secular" world? When humanity is reduced to "bare life" (Agamben), exposed and vulnerable and just fixated on the quotidian task of *surviving*—reduced to animality—is humanity then reduced to something less than religious? Are animals "secular"?

- Finally, let's try a slightly different, less harrowing, thought experiment: Imagine the whole world looked like the Upper West Side. Imagine that, by some catastrophe (or *eu*catastrophe, depending on your perspective), the whole world looked like the enclaves of what Peter Berger calls a "globalized elite culture."[2] Or, if you like, imagine a different kind of "destruction" of the world in which everyone is converted by the gospel of Sam Harris and Christopher Hitchens—a veritable secular eschaton that leaves us solidly ensconced in immanence. Would "religion" survive that annihilation/transformation? Would the global triumph of secularism—in which everyone reflected the ideal, cultivated, "secular" citizen—signal the obliteration of religion?

I think our received (modern) categories and conceptions of both "religion" and "the secular"—the very categories and conceptions that tend to inform both philosophy of religion and the social sciences—yield predictable answers to the questions posed by these thought experiments. For instance, recall the first Husserlian scenario: Could "religion" survive the utter annihilation of matter and bodies? Well, surprisingly enough, the religion of modernity wouldn't really miss a beat. Sure, it might be "modified," as Husserl puts it. But the "religion" of modernity—and the "religion" that is considered by sociology of religion, philosophy of religion, and much of theology—*is* a religion for disembodied minds. It is a religion of "beliefs" and "values," of representations, the stuff of minds and souls.

But the odd thing is that a lot of believers wouldn't know how to believe if they didn't have bodies. That's because they wouldn't know what to *do*. For those who practice faith, faith takes practice. And such practice is embodied and material; it is communal and liturgical; it involves eating and drinking, dancing and kneeling, painting and singing—all of which are impossible delights for a disembodied mind. Such embodied, practiced religion could never survive the annihilation of the world of bodies. Our "secular" paradigms, in this respect, are largely "intellectualist"[3]: they impose on religion a picture of human persons that reflects a distinctly modern emphasis on the cognitive—a top-heavy emphasis on beliefs, ideas, and doctrines. But why should modernity get to define the human person, and hence the shape of "religion"? Perhaps it's time for a *post*-secular account of religion along with a post-secular social science.

Rethinking the shape of religion, however, also invites us to reconsider our received assumptions about "the secular." If "religion" is defined primarily not by a set of beliefs, ideas, values, or doctrines but rather by particular, "charged," identity-forming practices,[4] then could it be the case that there are practices and institutions that have the same function and force but have slipped under our "religion-detecting radar"? Even in our third "end of the world" scenario above (in which Dawkins is pope, Hitchens is in charge of the Congregation for the Doctrine of Disbelief, and Sam Harris is president of Notre Dame), might it be the case that "religion" is still at work? Granted, certain sets of doctrines, beliefs, and ideas have been eliminated, replaced by cold, hard scientific rationality and, I take it, a universal global democracy (and I'm guessing capitalism is doing just fine in this secular eschaton). But why should we thereby conclude that there's no *religion* in this wholly "secular" world? Won't there still be powerful, identity-forming practices that implicitly articulate what counts as human flourishing? Would there not still be rituals that "carry," as Charles Taylor suggests, a fundamental orientation to the world and what matters? Indeed, wouldn't such secular rituals still function as "liturgies"—those rituals and practices that shape our attunement to what is ultimate?[5] What if humans are inescapably liturgical animals? Will a secular eschaton really be able to eliminate *liturgies*? Might "secular" liturgies be no less religious?[6]

Religion is not (just) where we've been looking for it. We need a new theoretical radar that will enable us to "pick up" religion where we don't usually see it, in two senses. First, we need to appreciate that religion "takes practice," so to speak—that religion is an embodied, material, liturgical phenomenon that shapes our desire and imagination before it yields doctrines and beliefs. Second, and precisely because of that, we also need to recalibrate our theoretical radar in order to pick up secular religion, in order to appreciate the force of secular liturgies.[7] Thus my goal is to propose a methodological shift in both philosophy of religion and sociology of religion that rejects what Taylor calls "intellectualism." The inherited intellectualist model bears all the marks of the "hermeneutical project" criticized by Mahmood: it yields "a secularized conception of religion in which religion is understood to be an abstracted category of beliefs and doctrines"; as a result, "religion's phenomenal forms—its liturgies, rituals, and scriptures—are understood to be inessential to it."[8] In contrast, I will sketch an essentially "liturgical" account of religion, drawing on Taylor, Wittgenstein, Heidegger, and Bourdieu. As an implication of this, I will argue that such a paradigm is "post-secular" in two senses: it rejects the intellectualist anthropology and epistemology that informs "secular" social sciences; and it will be primed to see certain "secular" practices *as* religious. I want to sketch a methodological paradigm for a "post-secular" sociology that is attuned to worship rather than (just) belief and is thus primed to recognize religion in practices and institutions that we generally consider "secular."[9] In short, I propose a methodological paradigm[10] that has the theoretical radar, so to speak, to pick up on "secular liturgies." Insofar as exclusive humanism has its liturgies, it remains religious.[11]

Whose "Secular?" Which "Post-Secular?"

The "secularization thesis" has fallen on hard times. Only a generation ago, social scientists confidently predicted the withering of religion in public life, but experience has proved otherwise. And just as social scientists were offering descriptive accounts of secularization, political theorists were articulating normative doctrines of secular*ism* that carved out the public sphere as a realm of "pure reason"—a space for "rational actors" who would have to leave religious belief (and other irrationalities) at the door. But of late, two movements contest both descriptive secularization and normative secularism: On the one hand, a so-called resurgence of religion in domestic and global politics has disproved the prognostications of secularization theorists. On the other hand, a postmodern and post-liberal critique of Enlightenment models of rationality (allegedly neutral and objective—and therefore "secular") has called into question the theoretical impetus of normative secular*ism*. The latter critiques (such as Nicholas Wolsterstorff's critique of Rorty and Audi,[12] Jeffrey Stout's critique of Rawls,[13] and John Milbank's

critique of "secular" social theory[14]) have called into question the epistemological foundations of secularism, suggesting—perhaps even calling for—a
"*post*-secular" age.

But here we note a first ambiguity: Is "post-secular" a descriptive term or
a normative program? If it is a *de*scriptive term, countering the secularization thesis, then we encounter some empirical questions: Is it the case that
we are entering a post-secular "era"? Is "post-secular" a name for an era that
has "got (back) religion," so to speak—having recovered from an era of secular backsliding? Is that an apt or warranted description of our contemporary
situation? Are we more religious? Have we ever really been secular?

Or perhaps "post-secular" is less a descriptor and more a normative ideal,
a *pre*scription for how society or the sciences ought to be ordered and conducted, countering normative doctrines of secularism. But what is being
advocated under the banner of the "post-secular"? Does this amount to a
covert *anti*-secularism, which itself amounts to a covert theocratic project?[15]
If the sciences are essentially secular, then wouldn't the post-secular be anti-
scientific, a worrisome retreat back into irrationality and tribal narratives?

Before taking up my constructive project, I want to utilize Charles Taylor's analysis of our "secular age" in order to clarify and make sense of "post-
secular" as both a descriptive and a normative term. His nuanced analysis of
our "secular age" reconnoiters these debates by noting the equivocation of the
term "secular." As Taylor observes, "secular" can have several connotations.[16]

1. In classical or medieval accounts, the "secular" amounted to something like
   "the temporal"—the realm of "earthly"[17] politics or of "mundane" vocations.
   This is the "secular" of the purported sacred/secular divide. The priest, for
   instance, pursues a "sacred" vocation, while the butcher, baker, and candlestick maker are engaged in "secular" pursuits.[18] Following Taylor, let's call this
   secular$_1$.

2. In modernity, "secular" refers to a nonsectarian, neutral, and *a*-religious space
   or standpoint. We'll refer to this as secular$_2$. It is this notion of secular$_2$ that is
   assumed by both the secularization thesis and normative secularism. According to the secularization theory, as cultures experience modernization and
   technological advancement, the (divisive) forces of religious belief and participation would wither in the face of modernity's disenchantment of the
   world. According to secularism, political spaces (and the constitutions that

create them) should carve out a realm purified of the contingency, particularity, and irrationality of religious belief and instead be governed by universal, neutral rationality. Secular*ism* is always secularism$_2$.

3. But Taylor helpfully articulates a third sense of the secular (secular$_3$): a society is secular$_3$ insofar as religious belief or belief in God is understood to be one option among others and thus is contestable (and contested). At issue here is a shift in "the conditions of belief," or what Peter Berger would call the "plausibility structures" of a society. As Taylor puts it, the shift to secularity "in this sense" indicates "a move from a society where belief in God is unchallenged and indeed, unproblematic, to one in which it is understood to be one option among others, and frequently not the easiest to embrace."[19] It is in this sense that we live in a secular age even if religious participation might be visible and fervent. And it is in this sense that we could still entertain a certain secularization$_3$ thesis. But this would be an account, not of how religion will wither in late modern societies, but rather of how and why the plausibility structures of such societies will make religion contestable (and contested).[20]

Now, given Taylor's taxonomy, what would it mean to speak of a "post-secular" age? First, it seems clear that what must be meant is post-secular$_2$, not post-secular$_3$. There's no turning back the clock on the shift of plausibility structures occasioned by the advent of modernity; in short, secular$_3$ is here to stay. Indeed, it is precisely an appreciation of our pluralistic situation of contested plausibility structures that engenders the critique of secularism$_2$. One might say that secularism$_2$ is a standpoint that fails to recognize the contestability of its own plausibility structures—a standpoint that just takes its standpoint to be axiomatic, "the way things *really* are." Paradoxically, secularism$_2$ fails to own up to secular$_3$.[21]

However, while the secularization$_2$ thesis has been rightly challenged, normative secularism$_2$ remains influential in public discourse (with renewed vigor in Europe) and perhaps particularly in the methodology of the social sciences. This lingering secularism is loaded into the very category of "religion" as analyzed by the social sciences, particularly when "the religious" is distinguished from or contrasted with "the political" or "the public." So while affirming Taylor's claim that we live in a "secular$_3$ age," I'm arguing for a normative post-secular$_2$ methodology. This will require articulating a more dynamic and nuanced anthropology in order to undergird social scientific study. And on this "attendant anthropology," as Mahmood describes it, Taylor can also be a guide.

We Have Never Been Secular[22]

Because we live in a secular$_3$ age, we need a post-secular$_2$ social science.

Now, if we were focused on matters of epistemology and the conditions of knowledge in the sciences, I might make the claim even stronger: there never has been a secular$_2$ social science precisely because there is no unbiased, a-traditioned, neutral, universal standpoint.[23] Our theorizing, and even our observation, begins from and is shaped by pre-theoretical commitments and is indebted to traditions of rationality. But since I have articulated this epistemological critique of "secular" social science elsewhere,[24] here I would like to take a different tack.

I suggest that our social scientific accounts of the world and our being-in-the-world need to be post-secular$_2$ by being attuned to the fact that humans are inescapably religious animals. That claim does not mean that humans inescapably believe in God, gods, or even transcendence. Rather, in claiming that humans (including social scientists!) are inescapably religious animals, I mean that humans are *liturgical* animals whose orientation to the world is shaped by rituals of ultimacy: our fundamental commitments are inscribed in us by ritual forces and elicit from us orienting commitments that have the epistemic status of belief. So to suggest that we are liturgical animals is not just to claim that we are all *believers* at some fundamental level; it is to also claim that we *become* believers through ritual formation—and such formative rituals have the status of "liturgies." This identification of religion with liturgy effects a double displacement: it displaces the site of religiosity from beliefs to practices, and it displaces the identification of religion with only transcendent or "otherworldly" models.

Religion as a "Heady" Affair: The Intellectualism of the Secular

Saba Mahmood, in a provocative essay, has recently suggested that secularism is attended by a distinct philosophical anthropology—an implicit picture of the human person.[25] And this standard, assumed picture of human persons sees religion (1) as a basically "optional" phenomenon and (2) as a primarily intellectual, propositional phenomenon.

The standard picture, we might say, sees religion as a sort of addendum to being human: *all* humans eat, sleep, breathe, have sex, wear clothes, are citizens of some nation, and engage in play. Then, in addition to that, *some* (perhaps even *many*) homo sapiens are "religious": they are "believers" who participate in religious rituals and practices, identify with religious communities, and hold religious beliefs. These beliefs and practices are generally taken to be tied to certain established traditions and institutions (Buddhism, Christianity, Islam, etc.).[26] Those who study "believers" are often those without this extra-human supplement: they are "just" human, that is, "secular." "Believers," to them, are kind of exotic; they have conspicuous growths, like two heads. From the perspective of the secular scientist, who lacks such growths (who has been "healed" of such lesions, as it were), this religious addendum is a curious supplement to being human—a kind of deformation.

But implicit in this picture and assumed in this anthropology is a microcosmic version of what Taylor calls a "subtraction story": some humans have managed to excise the religious addendum that has clung to humanity for so long and continues to cling to so many. The enlightened "secular" observers have pared down to only what is essentially human. To return to our opening thought experiments, because secularism assumes this sort of anthropology, it assumes that the Upper West Side is *not* religious. But what grounds this anthropological commitment? What is the warrant for this model of the human person and its attendant understanding of religion? What if the warrant for these anthropological assumptions actually has the epistemic status of a kind of *faith*? How does one come to believe this model? What if such anthropological assumptions are absorbed through identity-forming practices that inscribe in these "secular" observers a particular, normative vision of human flourishing—an implicit understanding of what is ultimate?[27] Then, I want to suggest, even those who *are* "secularized" (Berger's global intelligentsia) are *still* religious—and not just in some banal, Tillichian sense. I would argue that even the secularized academic who spends Sunday morning reading the *New York Times Magazine* is still shaped and formed by liturgies—what I'll call, somewhat grudgingly, "secular liturgies." But in order for such a claim to have any possible viability, we need to articulate an alternative philosophical anthropology.[28]

Social Imaginaries and Liturgical Animals

The "standard (secularist) picture" of the human person is top-heavy: it still construes religion as primarily a cognitive-propositional phenomenon, as a set of beliefs or "values" (as in "the values voter"). It is this sort of epistemological fixation that makes it possible for secularist anthropologies to see religion as an addendum, an optional supplement: clearly not all people have *those sorts* of beliefs or values; thus "religion" is not an essential feature of being human.

But what if "religion" were viewed primarily not through the cognitive lens of beliefs, values, and propositions but rather through attention to rituals, practice, and liturgy? What if we "located" religion not in the head but in the body? And what if our identities—our desires, our loves, our allegiances, our visions of the good life—were shaped *through* such embodied rituals? Then our "thickest" identity-forming rituals would have an *ultimacy* about them that we might legitimately call "religious."

Thus I want to offer a general definition of liturgies as *rituals of ultimate concern*: rituals that are formative for identity, that inculcate particular, normative visions of "the good life" and do so in a way that means to trump other ritual formations. Admittedly, this might include rituals not associated with traditional religions (e.g., rituals of Nazi fascism or other rituals of totalizing nationalism); indeed, expanding our conception of what counts as "worship" is precisely the point.[29] Our thickest practices—which are not necessarily linked to institutional religion—have a *liturgical* function insofar as they are a certain species of ritual practice that aims to do nothing less than shape our identity by shaping our desire for what we envision as the ideal of human flourishing. Liturgies are the most loaded forms of ritual practice because they are after nothing less than our hearts, our most fundamental motivations. They want to determine what we *love* ultimately. By "ultimately" I mean what we love above all, that to which we pledge allegiance, that to which we are devoted in a way that overrules other concerns and interests. Our ultimate love is what defines us, what makes us the *kind* of people we are. In short, it is what we *worship*.[30]

Consider, for example, the ritual power of the opening of a NASCAR race or an NFL football game. In a massive space thronging with people, eager for the beginning of the event, a crowd of one hundred thousand can be brought into remarkable placidity by the exhortation "Please stand for the national anthem." Like parishioners who know all the motions of the Mass by heart, these fans automatically rise together. They remove their caps and many place a hand over their heart as an artist or group sings a rendition of one of the world's most affecting national anthems, laden with military themes such that those singing it are transposed into battle, the identity of the nation being wrapped up in its revolutionary beginnings and legacy of military power. Perhaps even more importantly, this rehearses and renews the myth of national identity forged by blood sacrifice. The sounds of the anthem are usually accompanied by big, dramatic sights of the flag: a star-spangled banner is unfurled across the field by a small army of young people whose movements make it undulate as if blowing in the winds of battle, proudly defiant, almost dripping with blood in those red lines across it. And almost always, the concluding crescendo of the anthem—announcing that this is the "land of the free" and "home of the brave"—is accompanied by a flyover of military aircraft, whether the searing slice of F-15 fighter jets across the sky or the pulsating presence of Apache helicopters chugging across the stadium's air space. The presence of the aircraft has a double effect: it concretizes the militarism of the anthem and the flag while also making the scene something that is *felt*, as the sound of the jets or choppers is a kind of noise one picks up in the chest more than the ears. A crowd larger than many American cities then erupts in cheers and applause as this ritual of national unity unites even fans of opposing teams. I'm suggesting that this constitutes a liturgy because it is a material ritual of ultimate concern: through a multisensory display, the ritual moves us both powerfully and subtly and, in so doing, implants within us a certain reverence and awe, a learned deference to an ideal that might someday call for *our* "sacrifice." But this isn't conveyed as a "message" to be disseminated; it is not even the communication of "beliefs"; it is more the ritual enactment and enforcement of a story that seeps into the imagination. Such liturgies don't just, or even primarily, interact with the intellect; they operate on the level of desire.

This focus on *liturgies* stems from appreciating the centrality of *love*, and it is a focus on love that grows out of an alternative, nonintellectualist anthropology. Our current theoretical radar—whether in philosophy of religion or sociology of religion—is calibrated to register the propositional: thoughts, beliefs, ideas, doctrines. This assumes an intellectualist picture of the human person as the sort of animal that is moved to act on the basis of ratiocination and conscious deliberation. But accumulating research in philosophical anthropology (and, increasingly, in the neurosciences)[31] suggests that this intellectualist model is not the best picture for explaining human behavior, including religious behavior. Rather, an alternative paradigm indicates that precognitive modes of intentionality much more significantly shape and drive our relation to, and action in, the world. Drawing on Heidegger, Taylor, and Bourdieu, I want to sketch the shape of this affective anthropology and then go on to indicate how it ought to recalibrate our model of "religion."

Feeling Our Way Around the World: The Hermeneutics of Love in Heidegger

In light of the Gourgouris-Mahmood debate about the anthropology assumed by secularism, the early work of Martin Heidegger can be seen in a new light precisely because, almost a hundred years ago, Heidegger was already contesting the rationalist or intellectualist picture bequeathed to us by modernity (and, more immediately, by his teacher Husserl). For Heidegger, we are never simply spectators of what's "given"; indeed, he found in Husserl an implicit picture of the human person as a kind of swiveling brain on a stick, an unengaged mind that surveyed the world like a lighthouse, simply "perceiving" things as "objects." In contrast, Heidegger emphasized (1) that our relation to the world is always already a *construal*, a take on the world; and, more importantly for us here, (2) that such construal happened at a precognitive level. The first point emphasizes that to be in the world is to always already *interpret* the world; indeed, there is no world without interpretation. The world never simply appears as something given but rather is construed *as* a world on the basis of presuppositions or background "horizons" that condition (and make possible) our construal of the world.[32] But the second point emphasizes that such construal and interpretation happen on an order or register that is not cognitive or intellectual—a register that is not even, in a way, "*conscious*."[33] Thus Heidegger can suggest that the world is construed on the order of "mood." It is this strange claim that I'd like to unpack a bit.

Almost struggling for words, Heidegger argues that we find ourselves to be essentially "mooded": "Dasein always has some mood."[34] But this is not just a psychological ("ontic") matter—for example, that I find myself happy or sad, disturbed or elated. Rather, such different moods are possible because I am fundamentally *attuned* to the world on a register more akin to mood than thought. Thus he describes this as an "attunement"[35] to the world—a mode in which the world is "disclosed" but by a disclosure that eludes "knowledge." As Heidegger puts it, in attunement one understands something of the world that "one does not *know*. And Dasein cannot know anything of the sort because the possibilities of disclosure which belong to cognition reach far too short a way compared with the primordial disclosure belonging to moods."[36] So mood discloses the world for us in a primordial way; it effects a construal of the world *before* our cognitive, intellectual "knowledge" of the world comes into play. And we do an injustice to this "understanding" that is effected by mood/attunement if we require it to answer to our more familiar criteria for "knowledge." "[W]e would wholly fail to recognize both *what* mood discloses and *how* it discloses," Heidegger cautions, "if that which is disclosed were to be compared with what Dasein is acquainted with, knows, and believes 'at the same time' when it has such a mood."[37] And even if we do sometimes get a handle on our particular (ontic) moods by volitional and cognitive strategies, we shouldn't let this mislead us "into denying that ontologically mood is a primordial kind of Being for Dasein, in which Dasein is disclosed to itself *prior to* all cognition and volition, and *beyond* their range of disclosure."[38] So it's not just that mood is a kind of immature, prior disclosure that needs to be articulated and then superseded by cognitive disclosure; rather, such mooded disclosure is both primordial *and irreducible*. The heart, we might say, has reasons of which reason knows nothing.[39]

Attunement (*Befindlichkeit*, moodedness) is a precognitive mode of intentionality that discloses the world precisely because it construes the world. It effects an interpretation of the world before we even get around to "thinking" about it.[40] This mode of being in the world is "circumspective": I encounter the world not just as a collection of objects to be observed or perceived but as a world that I'm involved with. I'm after something, up to something, care about something, and am engaged in and with the world on the basis of that concern—even if I might not be able to articulate that for myself in a "cognitive" manner. In short, things *matter*.[41]

Recent work in cognitive theory on the emotions can elucidate Heidegger's intuition here. As Paul Griffiths has described it, the emotions work as "independent modular systems." In this picture, a "modular system" is one that "processes information from our senses though it remains isolated from our central cognitive system."[42] Such a modular system functions as an independent "appraisal system operating below the level of consciousness," but such appraisals need to be distinguished from (cognitive) judgments. As such, these modular systems play "a central role in our orientation in the world," effecting an independent, noncognitive construal of the world. They are not dependent on beliefs; rather, they set the agenda for beliefs and desires.[43]

The upshot is something like this: humans construe the world—and thus orient their actions and pursuits—primordially on the basis of an affective relation to what matters. We intend the world—and what matters within the world—not, first and foremost, in cognitive, intellectual ways but more fundamentally in a way that is independent of, prior to, and basically eludes cognition. And this, Heidegger emphasizes, is also true of our *theorizing*. Our theoretical and scientific investigation of the world—including the world of human behavior—is already, Heidegger says, a "dimming down" of the rich complexity of the world.[44] Our theoretical radar, calibrated to the cognitive and intellectual, lacks the nuance and complexity necessary to register the sorts of precognitive, affective "drivers" that orient our being in the world. Furthermore, Heidegger emphasizes, our theoretical investigation cannot escape what we've just seen, namely, the fundamental and irreducible impact of "mood" on how we construe the world. "Even the purest *theoria* has not left all moods behind it. . . . Any cognitive determining has its existential-ontological Constitution in the state-of-mind of Being-in-the-world; but pointing this out is not to be confused with attempting to surrender science ontically to 'feeling.'"[45]

Now why is all of this of interest to us here? What does this have to do with the notion of a post-secular philosophy of religion or sociology of religion? I would indicate just three points of contact.

First, I suggest that we think of religion more on the order of "mood" than cognition. That's not to say that there are no cognitive or intellectual elements of religion, but neither can religion be reduced to just its cognitive and intellectual artifacts. When we "dim down" religion to its cognitive and intellectual aspects—the parts of religion that can register on quantitative instruments—we can then easily restrict religion to certain kinds of beliefs and ideas and thus sequester it to a certain subset of the population. But if religion operates more on the order of mood—as a precognitive disclosure of the world and an affective construal of what matters—then Heidegger's account primes us to see something like religion operative beyond the confines of synagogue, church, or mosque.

Second, Heidegger's account also primes us to appreciate that philosophers of religion and social scientists are moody: what *matters* is determined by precognitive factors. Our theorizing cannot leave "mood" behind. In a similar way, our theorizing cannot leave behind the fundamentally affective ways that we construe what matters. And if that is to be identified as "religion," then all theorizing is religious.

Finally, Heidegger's analysis of Dasein—despite articulating a holistic anthropology that displaced the rationalism of his day—did not adequately articulate just *how* such attunement and understanding were acquired and absorbed. While Heidegger's groundbreaking analysis emphasized the significance of history—that the ego was *made* more than born—his own analyses were inattentive to the material dynamics of formation, in part because even Heidegger was insufficiently attentive to the body. It was precisely into this lacuna that the work of Maurice Merleau-Ponty strode, now engendering a growing area of research at the intersection of phenomenology and cognitive science that is particularly concerned with the bodily basis of intentionality.[46] Such research is also attentive to the bodily means of formation: that our precognitive attunement and understanding are not (merely) the hardwired product of evolutionary "natural" development but are fundamentally inscribed in us by material practices that function as formative rituals.[47] And some rituals ratchet up to "liturgies" when they inscribe in us "trumping" construals of what matters. On this point, I think Charles Taylor provides further help as I try to make my case that we are "liturgical animals."

Love Takes Practice: Taylor (on Bourdieu)

Charles Taylor, drawing on Heidegger and Wittgenstein, articulates his own critique of "intellectualism"—the working picture that sees "the human agent as primarily a subject of representations." This subject, he comments, "is a monological one. She or he is in contact with an 'ouside' world, including other agents, the objects she or he and they may deal with, her or his own and others' bodies, but this contact is through the representations she or he has 'within.'" As a result, "what 'I' am, as a being capable of having such representations, the inner space itself, is definable independently of body or other." And it is just "this stripped-down view of the subject which has made deep inroads into social science" and "stands in the way of a richer, more adequate understanding of what the human sense of self is really like and hence of a proper understanding of the real variety of human culture and so of a knowledge of human beings."[48] I would add that this especially stands in the way of an adequate understanding of religion.

"To obey a rule," on such an intellectualist account, involves an agent cognitively processing the rule, "knowing" what it means, knowing the reasons for obeying, and then consciously choosing to obey the rule—and if asked *why* one did that, one must be able to articulate reasons. In contrast, Taylor is intrigued by Wittgenstein's cryptic claim that "'[O]beying a rule' is a practice." At some point, Wittgenstein emphasizes, we can no longer give reasons for what we're doing.[49] But, Taylor insists, that doesn't mean we lack *understanding*; this doesn't mean that there isn't a certain "sense" to our actions and practices. It's just that this "sense" is unarticulated and even unarticul*able*. But, given the sorts of animals we are, even this "make[s] a kind of sense"—it constitutes "a kind of unarticulated sense of things."[50]

One can see how this "unarticulated sense" resonates with Heidegger's account of mood and precognitive understanding.[51] But Taylor's model is more attuned to the acquisition of such unarticulated understanding. In particular, he emphasizes that "this puts the role of the body in a new light. Our body is not just the executant of the goals we frame or just the locus of the causal factors which shape our representations. Our understanding itself is embodied." This constitutes a "bodily know-how" that is irreducible and "encodes" our understanding of self and world.[52] Not surprisingly, Taylor here avails himself of Bourdieu's notion of *habitus* in order provide an account of how our "background understanding" is acquired, shaped, and formed. And like Bourdieu, Taylor is attentive to *rituals*, from the micro-ritual of saying "hello" to the macro-rituals of "a political or religious movement."[53] On the one hand, such rituals have a "sense" about them that is absorbed through doing; the practices become ritualized. On the other hand, the rituals "carry" an understanding, and thus we absorb this understanding through the ritual. One can see how this resonates with what Taylor will later describe as "social imaginaries." The social imaginary is "much broader and deeper than the intellectual schemes people may entertain when they *think* about social reality in a disengaged mode."[54] Rather, the social imaginary is meant to indicate "the ways people *imagine* their social existence, how they fit together with others, how things go on between them and their fellows, the expectations that are normally met," and so on.[55] Taylor describes this as an "imaginary" in order to refer to "the way ordinary people 'imagine' their social surroundings," which is "not expressed in theoretical terms, but is carried in images, stories, and legends."[56] Most importantly, he emphasizes a dynamic relationship between understanding and practice: "If the understanding makes the practice possible, it is also true that it is the practice that largely carries the understanding."[57] Or, to put it otherwise, the understanding is "implicit in practice." As Taylor remarks, "Humans operated with a social imaginary well before they ever got into the business of theorizing about themselves."[58]

Returning to Bourdieu, Taylor emphasizes that to say that a practice or ritual "carries" an understanding within it is *not* to say that it houses a proposition that is just waiting to be articulated. The practice or ritual is not an "expression" or "application" of what is otherwise known by other means. When one "follows a rule," one is not "applying" what one cognitively knows. Rather, "the 'rule' lies essentially *in* the practice. The rule is what is animating the practice at any given time, not some formulation behind it, inscribed in our thoughts or our brains or our genes or whatever."[59] The rule exists only *in* the practice; it cannot be adequately distilled into some other cognitive, intellectual form. Similarly, a *habitus* is a bodily disposition that "encodes a certain cultural understanding."[60] The ritual doesn't "contain" or "express" an interpretation; it *is* an interpretation, an irreducible take on the world that can never be adequately articulated otherwise.

How would this make a difference in the way we conceive "religion" in sociology of religion or philosophy of religion? I note just two implications: First, most obviously, we would do well to see religion as an "understanding" or "social imaginary" that is carried in rituals and practices and inscribed through bodily practices. Second, and going beyond Taylor, I suggest that we consider "religious" those rituals that carry a sense of *ultimacy* about them; that is, we might be able to demarcate rituals of *ultimate concern*. Rituals would be rituals of ultimate concern insofar as they carry within them a sense of "what matters" (Heidegger) that would *trump* other, competing construals. In this way such rituals would be *identity-constituting*, intended to mark the practitioners as *those sorts of people*. To put it otherwise, we might simply say that some rituals are "thin" whereas others are "thick," where thick rituals are those that organize the plethora of thin, seemingly neutral practices we engage in. And if "religious" rituals are not just rituals that deal with the transcendent or the afterlife or the holy, and so on, but those rituals that mean to be *trumping* rituals, then we will begin to see "religion" even in some aspects of "the secular."

In a way, I have been trying to displace our identification of religion with "transcendence" or "the otherworldly" and, instead, connect it to matters of *ultimacy*. In addition, I have tried to show that human behavior and practice are shaped and driven by a kind of teleology that is more fundamentally affective than intellectual: that we construe and interpret our world and our place within it on a register closer to love than logic—and such orientations are inscribed and absorbed through material, communal practices. In short, we learn to love something *as* ultimate ("trumping") through rituals of ultimate concern. And it's this nexus of ultimacy and its rituals that I want to describe as "religious." The reason to employ "liturgy" in this sense is to raise the stakes of what's happening in a range of cultural practices and rituals. Insofar as they aim to shape our desire and specify our ultimate concern, they function as nothing less than liturgies. Above, we emphasized the importance of seeing what might appear to be thin practices (such as shopping at the mall, attending a football game, or taking part in frosh week at university) as, in fact, thick practices that are identity-forming and telos-laden. We need to then take that recognition one step further and recognize these thick practices as *liturgical* in order to appreciate their *religious* nature. Such ritual forces of culture are not satisfied with being merely mundane; embedded in them is a sense of what ultimately matters. Just because they are "worldly" doesn't mean that they don't function religiously. "Secular"[61] liturgies are fundamentally formative and constitute a *hermeneutic of ultimacy*.

Secular Formations

My task has been to consider the shape of a "post-secular" philosophy of religion or sociology of religion. This might simply require that these disciplines relinquish any Enlightenment claim to unbiased neutrality that is usually associated with the requirement of "secular" scholarship. In that sense, any philosophy or sociology that appreciated something like the "hermeneutic turn" would be, effectively, post-secular.[62] On this account, post-foundationalism entails post-secularism. But this seems insufficient.

I have intentionally decided not to run with this epistemological version of the argument (though I do think it is a viable approach). Instead, I am suggesting that a "post-secular" turn in the social sciences will not only be concerned with the conditions of "science"; it must also retool its conception of "religion." This stems from rejecting the intellectualist anthropology that attends secularism and opting instead for something like Heidegger's and Taylor's affective, embodied anthropology, which recognizes the central role of the precognitive and its embodied formation through ritual. Once we make that move, then even much that claims to be "secular" will be seen *as religious*—not in the sense that it is covertly concerned with transcendence or the gods or the afterlife, but insofar as we can discern secular rituals and practices, which have an affective, formative power, that shape how practitioners construe "what [ultimately] matters." Insofar as these constitute rituals of ultimate concern, I'm suggesting that we describe them as "secular liturgies." In short, I suggest that our accounts will be post-secular just to the extent that we relinquish the notion that "the secular" is *a*-religious.

But what's the upshot of this admittedly contentious and provocative suggestion? What's to be gained? I see at least two potential gains from this move: (1) it critically unmasks the naive conceit that posits any simple distinction between "the religious" and "the secular" on the basis of particular doctrines or beliefs (e.g., concerning gods or transcendence); and (2) it prompts sociologists of religion to train their eyes to see religion (i.e., formative liturgies) at work where we haven't previously been inclined to look, which should then also reshape current discussions regarding policy that naively posit a sphere of discourse or action that is a-religious. Ultimately, I want to suggest that humans are essentially liturgical animals. What's at issue, then, is not *whether* we engage in rituals of ultimate concern, but *which*. In this sense, we have never been secular. The "post-secular" would be a recognition of this fact.

I grant that my suggestion of "secular liturgies" will not be enthusiastically received. Some will protest that this feels like a kind of theological colonialism: Why can't I just let atheists be atheists and naturalists, naturalists? But of course, I am: I'm just suggesting that atheists and naturalists are still *religious*, shaped and primed by rituals that amount to liturgies. I don't mean to thereby suggest that they are "anonymous Christians" or "implicit" Catholics. I just don't think they can escape being liturgical animals. Those who resist my thesis cling to a conception of "the secular" as *a*-religious because, implicitly, they continue to operate with an "intellectualist" understanding of religion. They still tend to identify "religion" with particular beliefs and doctrines, especially beliefs and doctrines concerning gods and transcendence. But if this "attendant anthropology" is put into question, then this intellectualist picture of religion *and "the secular"* must also be put into question. It is this move, I think, that "secular" critics are unwilling to make.[63]

Notes

1. Edmund Husserl, *Ideas Pertaining to a Pure Phenomenology and to a Phenomenological Philosophy*, book 1, trans. F. Kersten (The Hague: Nijhoff, 1983), §49 (110, italics eliminated).

2. Peter Berger, "The Desecularization of the World: A Global Overview," in *The Desecularization of the World: Resurgent Religion and World Politics* (Grand Rapids, MI: Eerdmans, 1999), 10. As Berger puts it, "There exists an international subculture composed of people with Western-type higher education, especially in the humanities and social sciences, that is indeed secularized. This subculture is the principal 'carrier' of progressive, Enlightened beliefs and values. While its members are relatively thin on the ground, they are very influential, as they control the institutions that provide the 'official' definitions of reality, notably the educational system, the media of mass communication, and the higher reaches of the legal system."

3. This is Charles Taylor's term to describe models that "see the human agent as primarily a subject of representations." See Taylor, "To Follow a Rule . . . ," in *Bourdieu: Critical Perspectives*, ed. Craig Calhoun, Edward LiPuma, and Moishe Postone (Chicago: University of Chicago Press, 1993), 45–60, esp. 45–49.

4. As will become clear below, my project has resonances with Saba Mahmood's recent account of "secular religion" as articulated in "Secularism, Hermeneutics, and Empire: The Politics of Islamic Reformation," *Public Culture* 18 (2006): 323–347, esp. 341–347. For just this reason, I will be contesting Stathis Gourgouris's defense of the "secular" as a-religious. Gourgouris wants to starkly distinguish religion and secularism and yet further muddies the waters by construing Mahmood's "post-secular" approach as inherently *anti*-secular (see Gourgouris, "Detranscendentalizing the Secular," *Public Culture* 20 [2008]: 437–445). I will suggest that this stems from the fact that he fails to appreciate (1) that religious ("nonsecular") practices are *political* practices and (2) that secular practices, *because* they are identity-forming, amount to *religious* practices. In short, he too tightly identifies the religious with the transcendent—as essentially "otherworldly." See Gourgouris, "Antisecularist Failures: A Counterresponse to Saba Mahmood," *Public Culture* 20 (2008): 453–459. I will be arguing that the "religious" is essentially tied not to the transcendent or the otherworldly but to the *modes* of identity formation and the *status* of the practices that engender such.

5. I'm using the term "liturgy" here in a way analogous to its use in Christian Smith, *Moral, Believing Animals: Human Personhood and Culture* (New York: Oxford University Press, 2003), 16: "Liturgy ritually reenacts a tradition, an experience, a history, a worldview. It expresses in dramatic and corporeal form a sacred belief system in words, music, imagery, aromas, tastes, and bodily movement. In liturgy, worshipers both perform and observe, act out truth and have the truth act on them, remember the past and carry it into the future. Liturgy expresses, professes, performs, and informs. This is what religious liturgies do. It is *also* exactly what human social life more generally does with cultural moral order. All of the social practices, relations, and institutions that comprise human social life generally themselves together dramatize, ritualize, proclaim, and reaffirm the moral order that constitutes social life. Moral order embodies the sacred story of the society, however profane it appears, and the social actors are believers in social congregation."

6. This is not to say that every practice is religious; however, it does entail that a number of practices we consider "secular" function religiously precisely because they form ultimate desires—that is, they function as formative rituals of ultimacy. See my distinction between practices, rituals, and liturgies in James K. A. Smith, *Desiring the Kingdom: Worship, Worldview, and Cultural Formation* (Grand Rapids, MI: Baker Academic, 2009), 85–88. For an analysis of "secular

liturgies," see ibid., 89–129. My use of "secular" appears in square quotes here precisely because I'm employing the term in its folk usage, we might say. This will be nuanced in the next section.

7. Though I can't develop it here, I also think this helps to account for the overwhelming force of American civil religion; basically, in (Protestant) America, the devil gets all the best liturgies.

8. Mahmood, "Secularism, Hermeneutics, and Empire," 341.

9. I do so, cognizant of Gourgouris's admonition that "we have to be equally careful with ascribing to secularism a religious quality in a straightforward sense" ("Detranscendentalizing the Secular," 441). I will argue that Gourgouris, in addition to clinging to the ideal of "autonomy," also equivocates on the features of "the secular." Taylor's taxonomy will help to bring clarity to the issue.

10. As will become clear in the section "Secular Formations," I share Saba Mahmood's thesis that what's at stake in "normative secularism" is an "attendant anthropology of the subject"—that is, an assumed picture of just what sorts of animals we are. See Saba Mahmood, "Secularism, Hermeneutics, and Empire: The Politics of Islamic Reformation," *Public Culture* 18 (2006): 323–347. I think the same point is discerned (albeit from very different quarters) in Christian Smith, *Moral, Believing Animals*.

11. Though not, per Gourgouris, "in a straightforward sense" ("Detranscendentalizing the Secular," 441).

12. Nicholas Wolterstorff, "An Engagement with Rorty," *Journal of Religious Ethics* 31 (2003): 129–139; Robert Audi and Nicholas Wolterstorff, *Religion in the Public Square: The Place of Religious Convictions in Political Debate* (Lanham, MD: Rowman & Littlefield, 1997).

13. Jeffrey Stout, *Democracy and Tradition* (Princeton, NJ: Princeton University Press, 2004), 64–76.

14. John Milbank, *Theology and Social Theory: Beyond Secular Reason* (Oxford: Blackwell, 1990). For further articulation, see James K. A. Smith, *Introducing Radical Orthodoxy: Mapping a Post-Secular Theology* (Grand Rapids, MI: Baker Academic, 2004).

15. As Stathis Gourgouris seems to assume in "Detranscendentalizing the Secular" and "Antisecularist Failures, 437–445, 453–459.

16. Charles Taylor, *A Secular Age* (Cambridge, MA: Harvard University Press, 2007), 2–4, 12–15, 425–426.

17. It should be noted that this is more complicated in Augustine. For Augustine, the *saeculum* is primarily a *time*: the "age" between the Fall and the

consummation of the Kingdom (the eschaton). So technically (and Augustine is not entirely consistent on this point), the *saeculum* is not coincident with creation and temporality as such; it would represent a disfiguration of temporality after the Fall. In short, "the secular" is not equivalent to "this world" if by "this world" we mean *creation*. For instance, one could imagine the work of baking and candlestick making as vocations in a *good* creation—in a prelapsarian world. In that case, such "mundane" work would not be "secular." But if, instead, "this world" refers to the current fallen configuration of creation (as in 1 John 2:15–17; 5:19), then the *saeculum* is identical to "this world."

18. One can thus read the Reformation as refusing and obliterating the distinction by sacralizing what had been previously construed as merely "secular" (Taylor, *Secular Age*, 265–266). In short, all is sacred, or at least has the potential of being a sacred vocation if it is rightly ordered.

19. Taylor, *Secular Age*, 3. It should be noted that on these criteria, the ancient world into which Christianity emerged—and perhaps *because* Christianity emerged—would have been secular$_3$. So something like modernity may not be a necessary condition for secular$_3$. Granted, the ancient world could not yet have imagined exclusive humanism as a viable option.

20. In fact, this seems to be very similar to what Jeffrey Stout—a critic of secular-*ism*—describes as the "secularization" of political discourse: "What makes a form of discourse secularized, according to my account, is not the tendency of the people participating in it to relinquish their religious beliefs or to refrain from employing them as reasons. The mark of secularization, as I use the term, is rather the fact that participants in a given discursive practice are not in a position to take for granted that their interlocutors are marking the same religious assumptions they are." Thus participants in such "secularized" discourse "cannot reasonably . . . expect a single theological perspective to be shared by all of their interlocutors" (*Democracy and Tradition*, 97). Unfortunately, Stout seems to think that those he calls "new traditionalists" (MacIntyre, Hauerwas, and Milbank) "resent" this situation (99), as if they all longed for the reinstitution of the plausibility conditions of the Holy Roman Empire. This is a serious misreading that can't distract us here. For further discussion of Stout, see James K. A. Smith, "The Politics of Desire: Augustine's Political Phenomenology," in *Augustine and Postmodern Thought: A New Alliance against Modernity?* ed. Lieven Boeve and Mathijs Lamberigts (Leuven, Belgium: Peeters, 2009), 211–235.

21. This may help clarify Gourgouris's worry that Mahmood's critique of secularism is, in fact, anti-secularism. Parsing this is difficult, but I would suggest

that, yes, Mahmood is rejecting secularism₂ (to which Gourgouris may remain "committed"), but she is not rejecting "the secular₃."

22. I'm playing a bit on Bruno Latour, *We Have Never Been Modern*, trans. Catherine Porter (Cambridge, MA: Harvard University Press, 1993). According to Latour's analysis, the "modern" is a kind of impossible ideal of purity (10). But in fact, "modernity" is characterized by "practices," which yield hybrids rather than the desired purities. Thus, "we have never been modern." I'm going to suggest something analogous about the ideal of the "secular."

23. I suppose that Gourgouris might concede that social science could never be unbiased, neutral, and the like, and yet still affirm that social science be "secular" by being radically "immanent," by shutting down any reference to transcendence, whereas I'm suggesting that critique or social science might be radically immanent (or exclusively humanist) and still be *religious* and hence not "secular." I'm not exactly sure how to mediate these different stipulations of what's loaded into the meaning of "secular" except to say that the conditions I'm noting here—something like pure Kantian rationality—were taken to be the conditions for shutting down reference to the religious and transcendence. If Gourgouris rejects these "Kantian" criteria, I think he loses the ground for excluding the religious.

24. See James K. A. Smith, *Introducing Radical Orthodoxy*, 125–142.

25. Mahmood, "Secularism, Hermeneutics, and Empire," 330.

26. Recent research on "new religious movements" (NRMs) stretches this somewhat, perhaps, but our catalogue of NRMs doesn't include, say, capitalism. So the R in NRM is still circumscribed by the "traditional" religions in some sense.

27. As Christian Smith wryly comments, "Sociologists not only make stories but are animals who are made by their stories. No one, not even the statistics-laden sociologist, escapes the moral, believing, narrative-constituted condition of the human animal" (*Moral, Believing Animals*, 87).

28. I don't think this is just a matter of dueling, stipulative anthropologies; that is, I don't think that we're in an utterly relativist situation in which the secularist arbitrarily articulates her anthropology and the post-secularist merely offers an alternative, competing anthropological model, leaving us in a position of indifference and compelled to make some sort of unmotivated "choice" between them. Rather, I think such alternative anthropologies have to "prove themselves," as it were, by how they can account for the phenomena of human social behavior. And my wager is that the post-secular model I'm sketching does a

better job of this, and that the secularist model is inadequate not just because it is secular but because it can't do justice to the data.

29. See also Philip Kenneson, "Gathering: Worship, Imagination, and Formation," in *The Blackwell Companion to Christian Ethics*, ed. Stanley Hauerwas and Samuel Wells (Oxford: Blackwell, 2006), 53–67. Kenneson notes that since the basic feature of "worship" is "ascribing worth," then all sorts of human gatherings are "fundamentally formative" insofar as they train us to ascribe worth to certain ends (53–54). This doesn't mean that *everything* is religious or constitutes "religion." I would reserve the category "religious" (and "liturgy") for identity-forming rituals that aim to *trump* others and hold a status of ultimacy.

30. Another way of putting this is to say that liturgies are ritual practices that function as pedagogies of ultimate desire. I develop this "pedagogical" theme more fully in James K. A. Smith, *Desiring the Kingdom*. For relevant discussion, see Robyn Barnacle, "Gut Instinct: The Body and Learning," *Educational Philosophy and Theory* 41 (2009): 22–33.

31. Unfortunately, I won't be able to do justice to this growing literature in this essay. I have in mind increased conversation between phenomenology and cognitive science as seen in Shaun Gallagher, *How the Body Shapes the Mind* (New York: Oxford University Press, 2006); Mark Okrent, *Rational Animals: The Teleological Roots of Intentionality* (Athens: Ohio University Press, 2007); Mark Johnson, *The Meaning of the Body: Aesthetics of Human Understanding* (Chicago: University of Chicago Press, 2007); and Timothy Wilson, *Strangers to Ourselves: Discovering the Adaptive Unconscious* (Cambridge, MA: Harvard/Belknap, 2002).

32. See Heidegger, *Being and Time*, §32.

33. This claim has to be qualified since for Heidegger, as a phenomenologist, any mode of intending the world is a mode of consciousness. On the other hand, current parlance tends to associate "conscious" modes of intentionality with occurrent, "chosen" acts. It's vis-à-vis the latter that Heidegger's account of mood points to a sort of "unconscious" construal of the world.

34. Heidegger, *Being and Time*, §29, 173.

35. Heidegger's term for this "existentiale" is *Befindlichkeit*, translated by Macquarrie and Robinson as "state-of-mind" and by Stambaugh as "attunement."

36. Heidegger, *Being and Time*, §29, 173.

37. Ibid., 175.

38. Ibid.

39. The Pascalian allusion is not out of place; Pascal had significant impact on Heidegger's *Being and Time*. See ibid., 178.

40. Ibid., 176.

41. Ibid. Heidegger goes on to summarize: *"Existentially, a state-of-mind implies a disclosive submission to the world, out of which we encounter something that matters to us"* (177, italics in the original).

42. As summarized by Sludds, *Emotions: Their Cognitive Base and Ontological Importance* (Bern: Peter Lang, 2009), 124.

43. Ibid., 130. See also Robert C. Roberts, "What an Emotion Is: A Sketch," *The Philosophical Review* 97 (1988): 183–209.

44. Heidegger, *Being and Time*, 177.

45. Ibid.

46. What Mark Johnson refers to as "the new sciences of embodied mind" (*The Meaning of the Body*, xi). Cf. Francisco J. Varela et al., *The Embodied Mind: Cognitive Science and Human Experience* (Cambridge, MA: MIT Press, 1992).

47. I don't at all deny that there is an evolutionary basis for just how and why there is a bodily basis for "meaning." See MacIntyre, *Dependent, Rational Animals*, and Okrent, *Rational Animals*. I just mean to emphasize that "mood" and "understanding" are also inscribed by cultural systems of formation.

48. Taylor, "To Follow a Rule . . . ," 49. Interestingly, with respect to Taylor's particular account of emotions, Kevin Sludds criticizes Taylor's picture as still too cognitivist. See Sludds, *Emotions*, 131–135.

49. Ibid., 47, citing Wittgenstein's *Philosophical Investigations*, §§202, 211, 217.

50. Taylor, "To Follow a Rule . . . ," 48.

51. Taylor explicitly invokes Heidegger's parallel account of "understanding" (*Verstehen*) in this context. See ibid., 50; cf. Taylor, *Secular Age*, 172–173: social imaginaries constitute just this sort of "understanding."

52. Taylor, "To Follow a Rule . . . ," 50.

53. Ibid., 51–52. Taylor's conjunction of "political or religious" in this context hints at what I'm suggesting here: not only do religious rituals have features similar to those of "secular" (e.g., political) rituals, but secular rituals can also bear similarities to religious rituals, not in terms of transcendence but in terms of *ultimacy* and *identity formation*.

54. Charles Taylor, *Modern Social Imaginaries* (Durham, NC: Duke University Press, 2004), 23 (emphasis added).

55. Ibid. (emphasis added).

56. Ibid.

57. Ibid., 25.

58. Taylor, *Modern Social Imaginaries*, 26.

59. Taylor, "To Follow a Rule . . . ," 58.

60. Ibid.

61. I use the term loosely since one of the implications of this analysis is that, in fact, there is no secular. If humans are essentially liturgical animals, and cultural institutions are liturgical institutions, then there are no "secular" (a-religious or nonreligious) institutions. By describing them as "secular" liturgies, I'm heuristically acknowledging some common habits of thought.

62. Cf. Christian Smith's account of a post-foundationalist *and therefore* post-secular social science in *Moral, Believing Animals*, 45–61.

63. One thinks here of Gourgouris, but we might also consider Talal Asad's proposal in *Formations of the Secular: Christianity, Islam, Modernity* (Stanford, CA: Stanford University Press, 2003). See my critique in James K. A. Smith, "Secularity, Religion, and the Politics of Ambiguity: A Review Essay," *Journal of Cultural and Religious Theory* 6.3 (2005): 116–121.

CHAPTER EIGHT

Secular by Default? Religion and the University before the Post-Secular Age

Tomoko Masuzawa

The questions I explore in this essay stem from an inquiry concerning the advent of the academic secular. While it may seem utterly obvious that the modern research university is secular in its constitution and in its ethos, seldom is this constitution expressly reasoned, nor is its logic clearly articulated. In fact, there is much obscurity surrounding the historical and theoretical grounding of the secularity of the academy. This obscurity could be partly, perhaps greatly, responsible for the present state of loquacious confusion manifest in our generally erratic handling of the subject of religion. For, in the last few decades, *religion*—a topic long off the social scientific detection—has suddenly reappeared as an acutely neuralgic spot, a source of excitability that seems to surprise everyone concerned. Amid this uncertain terrain, I wish to propose the following guiding hypothesis. The regime of church-and-state separation—or more precisely, this regime in the version originating in Western nations in the late eighteenth century—has been developed and instituted in an intricate relation to what might be called the regime of "church and *school* separation." Academic secularity cannot be thought to be either a natural *pre*condition for the mission of the institution devoted to scientific inquiry or its *after*effect; rather, the academy as we know it has been deeply entangled in the production of the secular, in a relation that is at once instrumental and symbiotic.

My overall purpose—a longer-term goal—is to better understand the intricate history that produced the present regime of the secular academy.

This regime, this placid order dedicated to knowledge, research, and instruction, which we have come to assume as a precondition of the learned profession, is what we trust as a generally reliable protection against excessive interference from outside entities, whether religious or political. As with every institution, this regime must have a history, one that will reveal something more about its logic. In order to induce this revelation, I believe it is profitable to pose, not the question of how the academy has dealt with religion, but how the emergent idea of the *public*, and the modern state as an organ that claims to articulate the public's will and to ensure its polity, have procured the modern academy as a domain distinct and separate from the ecclesiastical sphere.

But what does it mean for an institution, such as the university, to be secular? Is there a particular modality of "being secular" that is especially relevant, broadly presumed, or reasonable and feasible for the academic institution? Is it a matter of the *absence of religion*? Or is it something like a condition of *safety* or *immunity from religion*, such that even religion's sundry presence, even its prevalence, would not materially affect the normal operation of the institution? Or does it boil down to the question of *parity* and *equality in treatment* with respect to certain differences that are perceived to stem from religion? These divergent norms and ideals of being secular are in turn predicated on varying understandings of what sort of thing *religion* is, whether its existence is contingent and transitory or essential and permanent, whether its influence is pernicious, beneficent, or benign, whether it is divisive, unifying, or neutral and indifferent, or, for that matter, whether or not religion is the kind of entity that can be present or absent in the first place.

In recent years it has been sporadically but multiply reported that the very *concept* of "religion" was nonexistent in the discourses of all but the modern West. Here, it is appropriate to caution against any hasty inferences and to refrain from jumping to the improbable conclusion, for instance, that all phenomena that could be conceptually circumscribed by this term—or "religions themselves," as styled in shorthand—were nonexistent elsewhere outside Europe, or that they were but figments of Western imagination. The reasonableness of this anxious warning against faulty reasoning notwithstanding, it does not absolve us from the task of deliberating on the implications of the reported fact itself. As of today, this difficult task remains yet to be undertaken, and it may be surmised that only a long series of empirical historical investigations would begin to accomplish it.

One implication that could be provisionally inferred, one that is especially relevant for the current state of uncertainty, may be the following. In the moment of contact between a non-European region and the West (whether the encounter was nakedly colonial or not), there was a scramble to calibrate the native discourse and to devise an adequate translation of the Western term "religion." In that case, it is reasonable to conjecture that, depending on the nature and the outcome of that particular struggle, each geopolitical, lingo-cultural domain would likely produce a distinct idea of what it means to be secular, and perhaps also an internally divergent assessment of the value of secular space and secular institutions. In any event, there is no justification for assuming, a priori, that the secular is always and consistently construed as aligned with the West and with the modern.

The actual unevenness of the mapping of the secular, the modern, and the West, moreover, presents an intriguing contrast with the relatively even and uniform spread of the modern university throughout the world today. The university in fact may serve as a useful focus for the consideration of the secular age—or another age *beyond* it, should that prove where we are— because it has been an extraordinarily successful institution. Having its roots in the European past, the university is now found in or near every metropole across the globe, each with a form and character that may be variable and particular yet is readily recognizable as a specimen of the same institution. Whence comes the university's success—its utility, adaptability, and versatility—that made it so ubiquitous?

This may be a difficult question to address for us academic insiders, to whom the efficacy of the university seems self-evident and not in need of any in-house assessment. By the same token, we find it difficult to explain the fundamental secularity of the academy, which is also a precondition of our vocation and, as such, something we take for granted. In order to arrive at a credible analysis, then, it seems necessary to loosen the grip of the presumptions and truisms undergirding our scholarly practice.

That, to be sure, is easier said than done. An exemplary inhabitant of the university would not imagine that one could step out of the constraints of customary practice just for a moment and just for this purpose. That said, in order to mobilize a preliminary cogitation, or, as a preamble to the examination of the history of the European and American university, in this essay, I propose to begin by taking momentary refuge in the unconventional and tread a region generally avoided by the scrupulous historian, namely, personal anecdote. My purpose here is to adumbrate a broader range of secular sensibilities that might obtain—that is, other possible modalities of being secular than the one most apparent, or supposedly dominant and seemingly familiar in the West. The point, however, is not simply to play a note of something other than the West as background noise to disturb and subliminally compromise, or compensate for, the Euro-American focus of my own interest. Rather, I aim to ring out a certain tonality of the secular that might be *unofficially* relevant—if not unofficially *operative*—in the West. My hope in this preamble, in any case, is to hint at a way of broadening the scope of historical considerations, to gain a little leeway, and perhaps to reach for additional metaphors for the modality of the secular over and above our current stock, which includes, for example, the Jeffersonian "wall of separation" and the somewhat more cautiously pluralist "buffered" individual selves.

I shall begin with a recollection of a scene in which the familiar and the uncanny are apt to meet and mingle: the university campus.

About a dozen years ago, I left a teaching position in a department of religious studies in one American university in the South and found myself at another in the Midwest, this time with a joint appointment in two departments, neither of which has "religion" in the title. Although this simultaneous uprooting from an old situation and coming to straddle two new ones— and losing "religion" in the meantime—was not without problems, at the time, this turn of events came as something of a relief, at least in one respect. I was relieved that I would thenceforward be spared a particular kind of unease that had been chronic and familiar. Previously, when I was teaching "religious studies," year after year I would meet a fresh crop of students who would arrive at the university, suitably willing and prepared to learn new things, including "religion," even if they seemed somewhat vague as to what they expected from such a course. The unease came from my anticipation of the dissonance between customary student expectation, which I was in a position to predict with fair accuracy based on past experience, and what the course was prepared to offer. Such disparity and unease, to be sure, may not be something suffered uniquely by those who teach in "religious studies" departments but is more or less shared across disciplines in the university. And, for the most part, each semester passed uneventfully for me as well, with a reasonable ratio of those who were satisfied with what they got out of the semester's work and those who were not. Yet, as I could not help but be aware, my discomfort was amplified by the knowledge that, from time to time, some student would come to me afterward—perhaps years afterward—to announce something to the effect of "Well, I entered the university as a Christian, but now I'm not sure" or, sometimes, "now I'm definitely not *that*."

I am well aware that a transformation of this sort, when it happens to a person of college age, is not be attributed to any single course or to a slate of courses; rather, it is best understood as one of those common yet not exactly foreseeable changes that tend to occur as a person recently departing from his or her place of birth becomes an adult. That said, it is also true that the faculty member in a religious studies department is more likely to hear such stories of alteration directly from the source, and, every once in a while, we would also hear from their unhappy parents. In their eyes, at least, it seems incontrovertible that the university is secular, and, much to their dismay, the teaching staff of the religious studies department turns out to be just another subtribe of secular humanists. In turn, we, and the university as a whole, do not seem keen to contest this characterization and sometimes actively embrace it, especially in the case of a publicly funded institution.

But how did the university become thus secular, and when? Was there a time in the past when it was something else—that is, *un-secular* or *pre-secular*? What is the substantive opposite of "secular"? Are we, and the university, now secular more or less by default?

I do not pose these questions rhetorically, let alone ironically. Having been reared and educated elsewhere, I arrive at such questions through a rather obscure passage of thought that warrants some self-reflection on my part, but perhaps a clarifying explanation of this passage might be moderately useful in illuminating the present state of confusion, whether one considers this state to be *post*-secular, *still* secular, or *not yet* secular *enough*. To begin, let me note that, had I not left my place of origin to have a career based in the United States, I am fairly certain that it would not have occurred to me to ask, or to worry, whether a particular institution is religious or not. I will offer an illustration.

As with many (though not a majority) of my Japanese compatriots, as a young person, I attended and graduated from a Christian school—a university, in my case. There are many such schools in Japan; most of them trace their founding to a variety of European and American missionary organizations that established small academies in the second half of the nineteenth century, offering language instruction and access to "Western learning" as their featured attractions. Then, circa 1970, as I considered my options for college education, the choice came down to two: one university located in a fashionable district in the heart of downtown Tokyo, founded by the Jesuits, and the other, a generic Protestant university with a sprawling campus on the outskirts of town, built shortly after the end of the Second World War on the site of a heavily bombed military aircraft factory with funds raised by liberal Christians from the greater New York metropolitan area. This fact—that is, that I was deciding between two *Christian* universities—might strike the reader as mildly curious, perhaps odd, since there was no trace of Christianity (neither interest, sympathy, nor affiliation) anywhere among my known kin. It may be stranger still, and more revealing, that this fact rose to my consciousness for the very first time only a few months ago as I was preparing to write this essay, four decades after the fact. Not for a moment did it occur to me then, or to my parents, to wonder or to worry whether schooling in such an institution would mold me ever so subtly into a Christian or make me any more "religious" than I natively was (or was not). And even if such an alteration were to occur, I cannot imagine my parents remonstrating against the university with any seriousness, any more than they might if I were to acquire an odd habit or hobby—saxophone playing, for example, an unlikely prospect and potentially a nuisance, but just one among countless possibilities that parents were perforce prepared to accept as their children came of age. In any event, this insouciance with regard to religion on the part of everyone concerned certainly explains the absence of any controversy, at least on *this* account, at the time of my college choice, and no doubt it is also the reason that I had never had the occasion to think about the matter in the past forty years. This lack of concern over potential "religious influence," this absence of scruples, I suppose, makes me, and my parents, certified "secularists." Or perhaps I should say more cautiously, this is at least one modality of being secular, or *secular by default*.

Lest we think such an understanding of what it means to be religious— and its opposite—is too idiosyncratic and without theoretical basis, we might remember that, in one of the most successful early twentieth-century treatises on the religions of the world, the French classicist Salomon Reinach famously defined religion as "a sum of scruples which impede the free exercise of our faculties." Even though this definition in turn earned him a comment from Eric Sharpe, that his was "the most tendentious definition of religion ever seriously put forward,"[1] Reinach was by no means alone in characterizing the essential nature of religion as a scrupulous distinction-making and obsessively correct maintenance of the regime of separation—between the holy and the unholy, the sacred and the profane, the permissible and the prohibited—distinctions that seem groundless and meaningless to those who are not party to the system. Here, one need only think of Durkheim's last major treatise, *The Elementary Forms of Religious Life*, or Freud's analogy between religious observances and the rituals of obsessional neurotics. For, from the perspective of these theorists, the lack of scrupulous attention would mark a person as the opposite of the religious personality. In any event, I cannot think of a word other than "secular" that would adequately describe this disposition of indifference, a disposition rather common among my compatriots. In the native parlance, we are, religiously speaking, "nothing."

This degree of indifference, this lack of scruples, may seem puzzling, perhaps dismaying, to some people. (It would no doubt appear so, for example, to those unhappy parents of my former students.) I should like to dwell a little more on this particular modality of being secular. To delineate further, allow me to relate another anecdote.

Earlier, when I was preparing to go abroad for the first time on a high school exchange scholarship, my father, who had himself spent a couple of years as a postdoctoral research fellow at the Johns Hopkins University some years before, gave me a piece of advice that struck me as peculiar and out of keeping with his character. His counsel amounted to this: "In America, if someone asks you what your religion is, say you are a Buddhist; don't say that you are nothing." This, to my mind, was counsel to prevaricate, and I said as much. To which he replied: "Well, it's not lying as long as it's Americans who are asking the question. Just remember not to say 'nothing'; you would be misunderstood if you did."

Soon after, I went to live with an American family for a year, sharing in much of their way of life, attending high school with their daughter, going to services at their Episcopal church on Sundays, and, most trying of all, spending a considerable amount of time watching American football. I shared in these activities with mild curiosity, mostly out of gratefulness and politeness and, when it was less than thoroughly enjoyable, in the spirit of toleration and accommodation. So I generally went along with whatever they did, including taking communion. In retrospect, I realize that it was my insufficient understanding of this particular ritual, combined with my native lack of scruples—my religious insouciance—that caused me to do what everyone else was doing without a moment's hesitation.

This, in effect, was the import of my being "nothing" religiously, despite my nominal or alleged "Buddhism." I may attempt to explain this disposition further by means of an analogy. In our world today, a significant number of people are vegetarians; some of them subscribe to a somewhat extreme form of this persuasion, in which case they are vegans or, at its most outré, raw foodies. Other people may be lactose intolerant, have peanut allergies, or abstain from consuming certain foods for many and sundry reasons. But *I* am *nothing*; I eat everything. Likewise with religion, I am nothing, I have no particular scruples, I would be comfortable going along with whatever the occasion seems to recommend.

Admittedly, my own case is but a statistical sample of one and therefore might be deemed much too anecdotal to be meaningful. Nevertheless, such an anecdote may produce a certain resonance, and thus have an amplifying effect, when it is juxtaposed with some other information, for example, the oft-cited, notoriously strange statistics that the Japanese government produces annually, with humorless nonchalance, on the so-called religious conditions of the country or, in its own words, "the survey collect[ing] data on the number of religious juridical persons [i.e., corporations], clergy and adherents, etc."[2] For a nation reputed to be overwhelmingly secular, the exceedingly large number of religious "adherents" reported year after year seems to raise questions, yet the statistics are offered without explanation.

These numbers are in turn summarized and reported by the U.S. Department of State as part of its annual *International Religious Freedom Report*. A recent report (October 2009) mentions the following facts in the "Religious Demography" section on Japan:

> The country has an area of 145,884 square miles and a population of 127.6 million. Since the Government does not require religious groups to report their membership, it is difficult to accurately determine the number of adherents of different religious groups. The Agency for Cultural Affairs reported in 2006 that membership claims by religious groups totaled 209 million persons. This number, which is nearly twice the country's population, reflects many citizens' affiliation with multiple religions. For example, it is very common for Japanese to practice both Buddhist and Shinto rites. . . .

According to the Agency's annual yearbook, 107 million persons identify themselves as Shinto, 89 million as Buddhist, 3 million as Christian, and 10 million follow "other" religions. . . .[3]

The U.S. Central Intelligence Agency (CIA) reports comparable numbers in its *World Fact Book*, with a similar note attached, allegedly to explain the strange figures:

> Shintoism [*sic*] 83.9%, Buddhism 71.4%, Christianity 2%, other 7.8%
>
> Note: total adherents exceeds 100% because many people belong to both Shintoism and Buddhism (2005)[4]

From the language of these reports, it is apparent that the U.S. government—in this context represented by the State Department and the CIA—considers the following more or less equivalent: religious "membership," "adherence," "affiliation," "practice," "self-identification," and "belonging." A customary assumption in "religious demography" today is indeed generally consistent with this language, and for the most part, it seems to represent the state of affairs adequately, with regard to most other countries. The American explanation for the palpable oddity of the case of Japan seems at least threefold. To begin, the Japanese government "does not require religious groups to report their membership." Furthermore—slightly at odds with the previous sentence—these numbers are self-reporting "claims" of religious groups (and therefore possibly inflated, it seems to imply) rather than based on the actual polling of individual citizens. But the most prominently featured explanation for the excessive numbers, mentioned both by the State Department and the CIA, is that "many people" in Japan "belong to" or "practice" more than one religion, especially Buddhism and Shinto(ism).

One other oddity of these statistics, on which neither American authority offers any comment, is that this system of data gathering would not yield any figure for those who "belong to" no religious group, "practice" no religion, or "identify themselves" as nothing or, perhaps, nothing in particular. To be sure, in a country where the figure for those who reportedly *do* adhere to some type of religion is nearly double the total population—and the government in fact recognizes well over 200,000 religious groups, of which more than 180,000 have legal corporate status[5]—to ask in addition how many people *do not* belong or practice might seem an invitation to compound redundancy upon the already absurd. Yet in view of the fact that with respect to most other nations, the State Department report duly cites the percentage of people identified as "no religion" or "not religious," and also given Japan's reputation as an overwhelmingly secular society, the absence of this category might be reason for pause, at least as a matter of theoretical, even if not practical, interest.

Some numbers of this kind are available, including surveys taken periodically by two major newspapers with national distribution. One of the most often cited is the *Yomiuri Shinbun* survey of August 2005,[6] which yielded the following results:

"Do you believe in any religion?"
    Yes: 22.9%   No: 75.4%
"Do you think religion is important for you to live a good life?"
    Yes: 35.3%   No: 60.3%

In addition, the newspaper reported that a large majority says that they visit temples, shrines, or churches at least once or twice a year.[7] Perhaps even more telling is the fact that more than 86 percent responded that they were "comfortable with having Buddhist and Shinto altars in the same house."[8] Furthermore, under the same category of questions, 92.2 percent answered that there was nothing wrong with nonbelievers visiting temples and shrines during the New Year season; 83.3 percent said the same about non-Christians celebrating Christmas.

The combined government and newspaper numbers suggest that in Japan a great majority of the population practice or belong to Shinto, a nearly equally large majority belong to Buddhism, and about the same percentage of people also do not believe in religion. Exactly how these three categories overlap and intermesh to constitute the whole is not at all clear. When the categories are made mutually exclusive, as in the case of the 1995 survey conducted by another newspaper, *Asahi Shinbun*,[9] the percentage of nonbelievers—and this category alone—does not significantly diminish:

No religion	63%
Buddhism	26%
Shinto	2%
Buddhism and Shinto	1%
Christianity	1%
Other religions	2%

It would appear that, when pressed, the majority of Japanese would choose "no religion" as the most appropriate—or the least inappropriate—description of themselves; "no religion" is their default position. And if the state of having, belonging to, and practicing no religion can be called "secular," this is a type of secularism that is generally "comfortable" in having religion—in fact, a lot of religions—surrounding the quotidian in an intimate way, with little concern about religion's possible influence or intrusion.

As is easily surmised, such a state of borderless presence and ubiquity of "religion," combined with a population that claims religion to be of little significance to them personally, makes it exceedingly difficult to maintain the statutory separation of church and state, which is very clearly written into the postwar Japanese constitution thanks to the occupying Allied Powers who drafted it, and which has been heartily embraced by the people of Japan ever since.[10] Among the handful of legal cases deliberated by the higher courts, arguably the most significant is the 1977 Supreme Court decision on the "land-pacifying ceremony" that took place in 1965 in the city of Tsu, wherein local Shinto priests were engaged at the ritual commencement of the construction of a public building, and on which occasion approximately $75 was paid out of the city coffers as honoraria and for the flowers and offerings. The Supreme Court found this action on the part of the city not in violation of the constitution, on the grounds that such rites were "conducted in accordance with general social customs," and their purposes were "entirely secular," and that, even though the ceremony's "connection to religion is undeniable," the *purpose* of the municipal government's involvement in this event cannot be considered as "assisting, promoting, or interfering with religion."[11] Not surprisingly—in view of the past collusion of political Shinto with the imperialist state militarism that led to the last war—an overwhelming majority of the political controversies and litigations concerning church-and-state separation that have risen in postwar Japan have involved Shinto. Relatively few disputes have touched on the subject of religion in relation to public education, and none that could be called prominent.

This, at first blush, is a striking contrast to U.S. history over the past two centuries, where schools have taken center stage in litigations regarding religion, so much so that it might be reasonably suggested that, from its inception in the early nineteenth-century, the development of the American public school system has been absolutely inseparable from the problem of religion.[12] The first flashpoint came in the form of "bible wars" that erupted in numerous municipalities in the mid-nineteenth century. People of all persuasions quarreled over the legality of the prescription (*or* proscription) of a traditional practice of school piety, namely, compulsory reading of a Bible passage at the beginning of the day's lessons. The courtroom quarrels often spilled into the streets and resulted in violence and prolonged unrest.[13] These events cast a long shadow, and the matter was not to be legally settled until the 1963 Supreme Court decision (*Abington School District* v. *Schempp*, 374 U.S. 203), in which it was ruled that a law requiring the reading of the Bible in public schools amounted to religious coercion and was therefore unconstitutional.

My general argument—though an unabridged articulation and substantiation of this claim would exceed the limits of this essay—would be that the advent of the regime of secularity in the American university is more adequately understood when it is considered in close connection to this highly contentious legal and legislative history pertaining to lower schools. The memory of this connection—between nineteenth-century university reform and the establishment of what used to be called common schools—appears to have disappeared around 1870, precisely at the moment when the efforts to transform the American higher education began to show the first signs of dramatic success.

American colleges that had existed before the Civil War underwent fundamental reconstitution thereafter, and numerous other institutions were newly established around the same time, with the result that, as one mid-twentieth-century observer put it, "the American university of 1900 was all but unrecognizable in comparison with the college of 1860."[14] It is also acknowledged that university reform was first successfully launched in Germany, whose example was later adopted by much of the rest of the world. No exception to the rule, the American reform owed much to the German model. As another historian observed:

> Between the time of the battle of Waterloo and the outbreak of the First World War, ten thousand students from the United States passed through the halls of German universities. This was, in a sense, the most amazing century in the history of higher education. By 1914, the American higher learning had been thoroughly Germanized, although the resultant product little resembled the university system as it actually functioned in Germany.[15]

Singularly important in this regard were not Germany's ancient universities but the more recently founded variety, especially the Universities of Halle (1694), Göttingen (1737), and, most importantly, Berlin (1810). By far the most consequential outcome of German university reform was that it irrevocably transformed and realigned the relation between ecclesiastical and educational institutions. The state's growing interest and ever more activist involvement in the matter of education, especially at the higher level, resulted in a decisive diminution of the power and authority of the church in the all-important domain of public instruction (*öffentlicher Unterricht*). Given this turn of events, it may be reasonably claimed that an important beginning of the secularization of the academy is found in Germany, amid a generally pious population, among whom strident anticlericalism of the kind we know from some French intellectual circles of the eighteenth century was not strongly present.[16]

The narrative of the advent of the modern university, however, tends to be nearly as mythical and counterfactual as the lore of its unbroken medieval legacy. A common version of this story—which became something of a "standard" version by the early twentieth century—greatly emphasizes the newly discovered mission of the university expressed as a triune ideal of research (*Forschung*), science (*Wissenschaft*), and education or cultivation (*Bildung*). Paradoxically, or perhaps providentially, the story goes, the spiritual modernity exemplified by the modern university had its first awakening not in the capital of an empire, at the apex of civilization, but in a relatively rustic, agrarian region of Europe that was not yet a nation, that is, a loose, sometimes belligerent confederation of territories that was to eventually become Germany. It is as though the spirit of modernity—of reason, freedom, and democratic confraternity—came to life precisely by eschewing the great carapace of past civilization, finding an opportunity for its first sprouting and early vigorous growth in a half wilderness, culturally speaking, in a locale where there was no imposing material statehood, economy, or industry to speak of.

It is into this story that the self-understanding of American university reform, as something of a sequel to the great German beginning, fits well. While the precedence and early stellar accomplishments of German reform are incontrovertible, the ultimate destiny of the movement, perhaps, was to be in the even wilder soil of the New World. In effect, this scenario casts the post–Civil War United States as, if not the rightful heir, at least the greatest beneficiary of what Germany had initiated. Of course, there were palpable differences between the political and economic reality of Germany in the early nineteenth century and that of the United States later in the century. But these differences at times seem to add to rather than detract from the power of this Germany-to-the–United States succession story.

It is true that in Germany the "separation of church and state"—or, more exactly put, the separation of church and the modern university as an increasingly important organ of the state—was realized through the prerogative of territorial rulers, a scenario that was not possible or desirable in the American republic. A paradigmatic case of the severance of church and university occurred in the Kingdom of Prussia, where the Calvinist Hohenzollern dynasty had long ruled over a largely Lutheran population.[17] Their pragmatic mode of governance rendered them less insistent on the strict doctrinal orthodoxy of their university faculty and rather more anxious to attenuate any sectarian differences that might cause discord and disruption within their dominion. In short, the Prussian policy of religious tolerance was a matter of necessity. Furthermore, during the reign of King Friedrich Wilhelm III, the Prussian state established a new agency, initially called the Department of Ecclesiastical Affairs and Public Instruction (Sektion des Kultus und des öffentlichen Unterrichts), later to be elevated to the ministerial level and thereafter known as the Kultusministerium. This new state agency swiftly moved to abolish the traditional sectarian consistories (or ecclesiastical senates) of various Protestant churches and replaced them with provincial regulatory bureaus, which were charged with the task of overseeing both churches and schools. Finally, in 1817, by royal decree, the Reformed Church (Calvinist) and the Lutheran Church of the domain were merged, resulting in a new communion called the Evangelical Church of Prussia.

This was the broader context of Prussian university reform and its "secularization." If the ecclesiastical authority retreated from the university, it was a result of an ever deeper, more activist involvement of the state in the matter of education generally, and the state power in question was unquestionably monarchical.[18] In view of this history of reform in Europe and its structural limitations, it may be tempting indeed to surmise that the secularization of the academy thus begun despotically in the Old World was destined to have a different, far freer efflorescence in a democratic republic with no established state church, above all, in the United States.

It may be useful to make a note of another peculiar characteristic of German reform that was not to be adopted in the United States. When the new German universities were established, the faculty of theology was not eliminated altogether, as might have been expected, given theology's declining status and its reputation as a holdover from the much maligned old regime and a symbol of ancient iniquities. Instead, even in the most aggressively modern, least clerical of all the new universities, Berlin, the theological faculty was fully instituted with a dramatically transformed outlook, with Friedrich Schleiermacher at the helm, arguably the foremost ecclesiastical luminary of the day. In effect, theology was no longer to be a privileged arena for clerical training (and whatever scholastic exercises that went with it) under the yoke of a particular denominational church sanctioned by the state; rather, theology in the university became, or claimed to have become, a *Wissenschaft* befitting the standard of any modern scholarly discipline, and its norm was not creedal correctness but academic excellence.[19] This reconstitution of theology, which was thus enabled—even necessitated—by the Prussian government's policy of disengaging its church from university affairs, had far-reaching consequences.[20]

Exactly how these German innovations came to permeate the rest of the world, and how they reached the United States, this requires a rather complex narration. What became the "standard" narrative as of the early twentieth century, however, tends to simplify the matter considerably. With the aforementioned German-to-American succession story at the backdrop, it often implies something to the following effect: the spirit of enlightened modernity sallied forth almost of its own accord, when the ideals of critical thinking, universal education, love of truth and humanity, and so on, finally came of age, outgrowing the habit of rote learning and servitude to religion, and thus began to scale the heights of *advanced* knowledge. This narrative, aside from being perilously ungrounded, forgets the history of an earlier period. Upon examining evidence from the first half of the nineteenth century, it is readily apparent that what the world admired most about the German (and especially Prussian) reform movement was the novel scheme to institute a comprehensive, publicly financed, and state-governed educational system, within which the university was to assume an exceedingly important position. The emphasis above all was on the idea of *public* instruction, whose foremost purpose was to fit the entire population for modernity, providing rudimentary skills and discipline to all, while at the higher end nurturing competent leaders and enabling all manner of cultural, scientific, and technological advancements.

In the last decades of the nineteenth century, a number of new universities were founded in the United States, made possible largely by the sudden infusion of enormous private wealth pouring into the cause of "higher education"—the Johns Hopkins University, Cornell University, and the University of Chicago among the most prominent and lasting examples. There is no doubt that the founders and supporters of these institutions championed the principles of academic freedom and advanced learning as their foremost ideals, and they understood these principles to be specifically *German*. Long before these conspicuous events, however, there had been many instances of various state government officials making concerted efforts to establish a comprehensive educational system in the original Prussian sense, even though the results were not always spectacularly successful. One celebrated example was in Massachusetts, where Horace Mann, the state's first secretary of the board of education, implemented a system of compulsory education beginning in 1837, expressly following the Prussian model. The success of Massachusetts caused the state of New York to follow suit.[21] A more ambitious attempt to institute a total system of education, top to bottom, one with a comprehensive administrative structure, was located farther to the west. In this example from the wilderness, moreover, we can discern the material conditions that gave rise to a peculiarly American modality of academic secularity.

In the still sparsely populated Northwest Territory around the western Great Lakes, concerns for public education moved the territorial government of Michigan to appoint a board of trustees for higher education as early as 1817. On that occasion, as Charles Kendall Adams wrote in 1876, "a curiously elaborate plan of a university was adopted by this board." Curious, indeed, in view of the fact that the settler population of the vast area at that time scarcely exceeded six thousand. This "very elaborate scheme for the organization of a university" was to be executed, in due course, in accordance with a territorial law passed the same year; it "not only made the University a part of the school system of the State, but it also provided for the ample support of the University by an extraordinary addition of no less than fifteen per cent to all existing taxation."[22] This law was further amended in 1821, to specify, among other things, the policy regarding religion. The new law declared that "persons of every religious denomination were capable of being elected trustees, and no person, president, professor, instructor or pupil was to be refused admittance for his conscientious persuasion in matters of religion."[23]

With the legal ground thus well prepared, Michigan's state constitution, which was adopted in 1835 in anticipation of imminent statehood, included articles concerning the state's duty to ensure public instruction for all citizens. Fortuitously—or so state officials interpreted it—early in the history of the republic, the federal government decreed that a certain portion of federal lands should be granted to the state for the express purpose of supporting public education. Thus the 1835 state constitution declares: "the Legislature shall take measures for the protection, improvement or other disposition of such lands as have been or may hereafter be reserved or granted by the United States to this State for the support of a University." It further stipulated that "The Governor shall nominate, and by and with the advice and consent of the Legislature, in joint vote, shall appoint a Superintendent of Public Instruction"—a position roughly equivalent to, and clearly modeled after, the Prussian office of Kultusministerium.[24]

Following the promulgation of the new state constitution of 1851, the superintendent of public instruction prepared a voluminous tome, which was printed and distributed to all county and township clerks, treasurers, libraries, and school boards. This six hundred–page document plainly states:

> The System of Public Instruction which was intended to be established by the framers of the constitution [of 1835], the conception of the office, its province, its powers and duties were derived from Prussia. That system consisted of three degrees. Primary instruction, corresponding to our district schools; secondary instruction, communicated in schools called Gymnasia; and the highest instruction communicated in the Universities. The superintendence of this entire system, which was formed in 1810, was entrusted to a Minister of State, called the Minister of Public Instruction, and embraced every thing which belonged to the moral and intellectual advancement of the people.
>
> The system in Michigan was intended to embrace all institutions which had for their objects the instruction of youth, comprising the education of the primary school, the intermediate class of schools, however denominated, and the University.

After decades of thus planning and legislating for a Prussian-style university, the University of Michigan finally took shape more or less as planned, and its first president, Rev. Henry P. Tappan, was duly installed late in the year 1852. In his inaugural address, President Tappan strongly affirmed the state leaders' long-standing commitment to the Prussian model by quoting the above passage in its entirety.[25]

As Charles Kendall Adams observed, it fell singularly upon this first president to implement the long-held plan.[26] It is generally acknowledged that Tappan did much to carry out the plan in earnest, or what he reasonably assumed to be the grand system sanctioned by the duly appointed and elected officials of the state, further bolstered and refined through decades of legislation. In August 1853, the *Detroit Free Press* published the president's address to the graduating class, in the form of a letter sent from Berlin, where he happened to be on a mission. The address offers a plain view of what the Prussian system and its overall objective meant to him:

> Young Gentlemen, what we need most of all in our State, and in our country at large, is to follow the Prussian example. You who have been educated in the University cannot feel indifferent to the educational system of our State, and cannot refuse to lend your aid to the perfecting of that system. We have made a good beginning, but much remains to be done. I hope you will not lose yourselves either in commerce or politics, but in the midst of your pursuits, whatever they may be, will stand shoulder to shoulder, with all the enlightened friends of education in Michigan, to develop every form of education to the most perfect degree. It would be a happy thing for our State if some of our young men could enter the Normal, Artisan, and Agricultural Schools of Prussia, and some the University, that they might become practically acquainted with the working of the system, and then return home to apply the fruits of their observation and experience. It would be a noble thing for the State to send some abroad for this purpose.[27]

In 1863, less than ten years after this address, however, Tappan was summarily removed from his post by a highly controversial move on the part of the university regents. What brought the university to this pass is much too particular and complex for an easy summary.[28] One of the sources of the friction between Tappan and his opponents, however, was substantive and glaring. This had to do with "the policy adopted by President Tappan in the appointment of professors," which Charles Kendall Adams describes as follows:

> From the first [Tappan] maintained that officers of instruction should be selected solely on account of their ability to instruct. When he was pressed to make appointments on denominational grounds, he not only declined to do so, but maintained that such appointments were wrong in principle and highly injurious in practice. "Egregiously do they mistake," declared he, "the character and ends of this institution who imagine that because it belongs to no sect or party in particular, it therefore belongs to all sects and parties conjointly and of equal right. It not only does not belong to any sect or party in particular, it belongs to no sect or party at all. The prime object of a seminary of learning is not like that of a church, to inculcate religion or perform its services, but to afford education.[29]

The idea, as is plain to see, is consistent with the general thrust of the Prussian reform, and Tappan was on excellent grounds to claim that it was fully endorsed by the Michigan state legislature, as spelled out in the state constitution. He was most adamant about this religion-free, denomination-"blind" policy.[30] According to Adams, even as he was preparing to leave Ann Arbor permanently, "President Tappan again reverted to the same policy, and made this very emphatic declaration: 'One thing is certain, no appointment has since been made with any reference to denominational connection.'"[31]

Tappan's policy was an alternative to, and in a sense also in direct opposition to, the policy of religious neutralization that was informally but regularly practiced in the university up to that time. This latter strategy sought to accommodate the fact of religious difference and to ameliorate, if not altogether preempt and efface, any potential for discord among different groups by granting each of the dominant Protestant sects its representation while assuming a measure of toleration toward non-Protestants. In contrast, by strongly asserting that the university belongs to "no sect or party at all," Tappan was effectively proclaiming the *absence of religion* in the university as the norm. The point was not lost on his audience, supporters and detractors alike.

Nor is it surprising that, from the beginning, Tappan dismissed the idea of maintaining a theological faculty within the university. In effect, this American university took a course that deviated significantly from the supposed prototype. Already in his inaugural address of 1852, he asserted:

Our Institution being a State Institution, and, therefore, connected with no particular denomination, cannot establish a Theological School on the University fund. But it is to be hoped that the different denominations will establish professorships in the different branches of theological science in this town. In some of these branches they might unite; in others they would choose to establish separate professorships.[32]

His plan—indeed, his *hope*—was that some kind of theological faculty, individually by separate denominations or ecumenically, would operate *across the street*, but not on university premises. This was something of a new path toward configuring the relation between religion and the university, a seemingly paradoxical arrangement of closest proximity and absolute separation. This solution deviated from the Prussian way, which, as we recall, established a new faculty of *scientific* theology within the university. In contrast, Tappan's plan may be seen as a prototypically *American* solution.

Although Tappan arguably lost his position on account of such novel policies, many American educators of the following generation came to actively adopt, and scrupulously comply with, the same principle of separation. The difference was that, for members of this later generation, only a few decades after Tappan, no argument was needed, apparently, to justify their position.

An opportunity to glimpse this general condition in American universities in the early twentieth century has been provided quite incidentally, thanks to an event that took place thousands of miles away. The World Missionary Conference, which met in Edinburgh, Scotland, in the summer of 1910, was the first large-scale international ecumenical congress of Protestants engaged in foreign missions. In preparation for the conference, eight commissions were appointed, one of which was specifically charged with the task of investigating the "home side of foreign missionary operations," including missionary education in Western Europe and North America.[33] The American correspondent for the commission,[34] as a part of this investigation, sent out a questionnaire to 550 "universities, colleges, schools and academies" in order to ascertain the extent of accommodation made for missionary education at each institution.[35] In addition, a letter was sent to an unspecified number of "leading educators" of the country, inquiring whether, in their opinion, courses dealing "specifically with some phase of the subject

Organic Lemon Sugar Scrub
Org. cane sugar, org. unrefined coconut oil, org. avocado oil,
org. lemon oil

Organic Lavender Sugar Scrub
Org. cane sugar, org. unrefined coconut oil, org. lavender oil

Organic Avocado Lotion
Org. unrefined coconut oil, organic unrefined shea butter,
org. avocado oil, organic vitamin E oil, emulsifying wax
(plant-based)

Organic Shea-Lavender Lotion w/ Sweet Almond
Org. unrefined coconut oil, organic unrefined shea butter,
org. vitamin E oil, org. lavender oil, org. sweet almond oil,

of foreign missions, or with the history, institutions, life or religions of the countries of Africa, Asia, the Levant or Latin America" should be included in the curricula of schools, colleges, and universities.

What is particularly interesting are the answers given by some of those prominent university presidents in response to this inquiry. They replied nearly in unison.[36] Typical is the answer of President James Burrill Angell of the University of Michigan, who wrote:

> I hardly see how a place could be well provided for the study of missions in the curricula of our schools, colleges and universities. It strikes me that that sort of work would have to be left to the Christian Associations or other voluntary religious societies in those institutions; but certainly the work ought to be done in the theological schools, and they should avail themselves of the instruction in the universities in the languages of the countries where we have missions, say Chinese and Japanese, etc.

Opinions of this kind were by no means limited to the officers of public universities. Arthur Twining Hadley, president of Yale, put the matter more pointedly:

> I very clearly do not believe that missions should be included in the curriculum of schools. What we want the schools for is to teach the children to read, to spell, to cipher, and to know how to do certain important things. It would cast grave discredit on missions if their advocates attempted to make the importance of the subject an excuse for urging the substitution of bad methods of education for good ones. If the regular teachers can give the children some idea of the importance of missions in connection with the regular courses in geography or history, that is good; but the attempt to make a special subject of study will injure education and discredit missions.

These strong words—even granting that Hadley in this paragraph is referring specifically to the "curriculum of schools" (i.e., to the education of pre-college age "children")—are still remarkable, coming from the president of a university that houses a divinity school with a long, distinguished, and still active record of missionary work, not to mention one of the most important missionary archives in the world. His extremely guarded stance with respect to missions—or what might be called *actively religious* work—carried over to his stance regarding college education.[37] To be sure, he naturally allows an exception for "divinity schools," but the precision with which he draws this line of exception and exclusion accentuates all the more the anomalous nature of the enclave that is the divinity school. Thus he continues:

> In divinity schools I believe that there is need for special arrangements for the professional training of a certain number of men who look to the mission field as their life work. The instruction of these men of course stands on a different basis from the more general study of missions in the schools or colleges. For such men there is a clear place for such study in a curriculum.

This meticulous demarcation, the sequestering of "a certain number of men" whose instruction "stands on a different basis," which therefore requires "special arrangements"— keeps the rest of the university free of religion. The result, it might be observed, would not be much different from what Tappan proposed at Michigan half a century earlier, namely, that any theological training should take place not within the university but nonetheless "in town" and across the street from the university. For these university presidents at least, there seems to have been no appreciable difference between privately founded and state-funded institutions in this regard. For, in the last analysis, they understood the university's mission to be what nineteenth-century officials always referred to as "public instruction"; for them, there was no turning back to the days when colleges were, supposedly, indolent and secretive private corporations under ecclesiastical control of one kind or another. From this modernist standpoint, perhaps, any actively religious work would seem necessarily denominational, no matter how ecumenical the spirit, and therefore inimical to the university's purpose. In this way of thinking, the Yale president was by no means exceptional.[38]

Even a university officer whose field of specialty might render him more sympathetic to religious causes turned out to be no different in this general attitude. Jacob Gould Shurman—Cornell's third president and successor to the two certified secularist presidents, Andrew Dickson White and Charles Kendall Adams—was a professor of Christian Ethics and Moral Philosophy. Yet he wrote:

> Replying to your letter . . . inquiring whether, in my opinion, the subject of Christian missions should be included in the curricula of schools, colleges, and universities, I would say that, deeply as I am interested in missions and highly as I esteem the work of the missionaries, I do not think it would be possible to make any provision for the study of the subject in the schools,

colleges, and universities in the United States, with the exception of those which are under denominational control.

Although the letter of inquiry requested that each president offer his own opinion—and in confidence, if so desired—it is clear that every one of these officials saw fit to offer his views in light of the overall mission and the governing policies of the institution over which they presided. The consensus among them was that unless an institution happened to be "under denominational control"—which theirs decidedly were not—religion did not and should not have an active life in the university, public *and* private institutions alike, that is, no matter who paid their bills.

Thus it came to be that, despite the overwhelming reputation and influence of the German university system, when it came to the question of religion in the academy, American institutions took a definitive turn away from the example set by the University of Berlin. Academic theology—or what Schleiermacher called *historical* and *philosophical* theologies, in contradistinction to *practical* theology—never developed into a mainstream curriculum in American universities.[39] This may be readily understood if we consider the difference in circumstance. What was possible and expedient in a European monarchy, however "enlightened," was inimical to the polity of the American republic and to the multilayered, shifting, and often conflicting systems of governance that characterized it. But precisely by placing the "theological faculty" either "in town but across the street" or under quarantine in specially marked quarters called "the divinity school," those university leaders could conceivably claim that they remained true to the ideal of *public* instruction, which the American reformers of the earlier generation certainly understood to be the essential principle of the Prussian system.

A well-worn joke, once commonly told among the older generations of religion scholars, would have two strangers casually conversing thus:

"Are you a Catholic or a Protestant?"
"Well, I am an atheist."
"Well, that may be, but are you a Catholic atheist or a Protestant atheist?"

As with all jokes, there is a kernel of truth in this vignette, a core in the middle where laughter stops; and it is precisely because of this silent center that we laugh around it.

So it may be indeed that there are different modalities of being secular, just as there is more than one way of being an atheist. But the further insinuation as to the possible cause or reason for being thus different—that is, the idea that a particular kind of religion induces a particular form of opposition or resistance to it—may be best kept at bay. For, insofar as "the secular" cannot be defined simply as a negative contour of a particular religion (or as an attitude of resistance to all religions, for that matter), grounds for the "variety of secularisms" must be sought somewhere else than in the penumbra of all the namable "religions" that might be thought to exist. By the same token, an ever finer differentiation of the "variety" would not deliver us from the difficulty but instead merely drive us deeper into the bad infinity of particulars. And yet, it is also the particulars—sensibly assembled and in sufficient quantity—that afford us the texture of a historical moment, a feel for the cumulation that constitutes our present situation.

Much of the confusion, contradiction, or inertness of the problems associated with secularism today may prove finally irresolvable. Meanwhile, it may still be incumbent on us to come to terms more squarely with the enormous historical impact of the very notion of "religion" that has been globally introduced into general discourse over the past few centuries. It is probable that a good deal of the unwieldiness of "the secular" stems directly from the stubborn opacity of what we (who?) mean by "religion."

Yearning anxiously for the "post-secular" at this confusing moment, we might be unwittingly drowning our present difficulties under a larger heap of unknown ones. But this may not be inevitable. Contemplating the post-secular in the abstract might lead to a wishful illusion of an exit from the present mire—much as the declaration of "postmodern" at times functioned as an easy way out of the problem that is/was "modern." But, alternatively, we might respond to a call to do some strenuous thinking, in order to scramble these tenuous markers of periodization and territorialization, so that we may better understand the present. The former, a mere contemplation of "post-secular," may give us solace in a fantasy of escape and little else, but the latter, of necessity, would drive us toward scholarship.

Notes

1. Eric Sharpe, *Comparative Religion: A History*, 2nd ed. (La Salle, IL: Open Court, 1986), 123.

2. Ministry of Internal Affairs and Communication, Bureau of Statistics, http://www.stat.go.jp/english/data/nenkan/1431-23e.htm (accessed Aug. 19, 2010).

3. United States Department of State, http://www.state.gov/g/drl/rls/irf/2009/127272.htm (accessed Aug. 19, 2010).

4. https://www.cia.gov/library/publications/the-world-factbook/fields/2122.html (accessed Aug. 19, 2010).

5. "As of December 2006, 182,468 out of 223,970 religious groups were certified by the Government as religious organizations with corporate status, according to the Agency for Cultural Affairs." U.S. Department of State, *International Freedom of Religion Report*. The most recent figure published by the agency (as of December 2007) is similar, at 182,709 religious corporations.

6. *Yomiuri Shinbun*, September 2, 2005, Tokyo morning edition, 17.

7. In practical terms, it might be difficult to avoid such a visit for a whole year, unless one does not have to attend a wedding, funeral, birth or coming-of-age ceremony, or other rites of passage among one's kith and kin, or any school or office excursion and determines to stay home during the entire New Year season. Yet, as the other numbers imply, the large majority of people do not regard such "visits" as religious acts, that is, their significance is not considered religious.

8. To be exact, the question was phrased as follows: "Do you think there is something wrong or strange [おかしいと思う] about having the Shinto and the Buddhist altars in the same house?" *Yomiuri* also publishes an English-language version of the paper, the *Daily Yomiuri,* and its September 3, 2005, edition includes a brief summary of this study, from which the phrasing quoted here—"comfortable with . . ."—is taken.

9. *Asahi Shinbun*, September 23, 1995, morning edition, 21. To the question "Do you think religion is important as you live your life?" 33 percent answered positively and 58 percent negatively, results similar to those recorded by the *Yomiuri* survey conducted ten years later.

10. The constitution does not explicitly mention the phrase "the separation of church and state"—or more literally in Japanese, separation of "government and religion." However, Article 20 "guarantees freedom of religion" to all citizens, prohibiting at the same time "the state and its organs to engage in religious instructions or any other religious activities." Article 89 further prohibits the expending of public monies "for the use and maintenance of any religious bodies."

11. Supreme Court, 31 (4) *Minshū* 553 (July 13, 1977). Interestingly, the chief justice at the time, Ekizō Fujibayashi, known to be a "pious Christian" (obituary in *Yomiuri Shinbun*, Tokyo edition, April 26, 2007, 39), was among the five dissenting judges,

out of fifteen. In addition to the dissenting opinion, he authored a strongly worded addendum, expressing his opposition to the majority.

12. An extensive list and descriptions of the nineteenth- and early twentieth-century law cases is provided in Alvin W. Johnson and Frank H. Yost, *Separation of Church and State in the United States* (Minneapolis: University of Minnesota Press, 1948), 41–73.

13. Robert Michaelsen, *Piety in the Public School: Trends and Issues in the Relationship between Religion and the Public School in the United States* (New York: Macmillan, 1970); Michael Feldberg, *The Philadelphia Riots of 1844: A Study of Ethnic Conflict* (Westport, CT: Greenwood Press, 1975); Paul C. Gutjahr, *An American Bible: A History of the Good Book in the United States, 1777–1880* (Stanford, CA: Stanford University Press, 1999).

14. Laurence R. Veysey, *The Emergence of the American University* (Chicago: University of Chicago Press, 1965) 2.

15. S. Willis Rudy, "The 'Revolution' in American Higher Education—1865–1900," *Harvard Educational Review*, 21: 3 (Summer 1951), 165.

16. I have discussed other aspects of this history in another context. See Tomoko Masuzawa, "The University and the Advent of the Academic Secular: The State's Management of Public Instruction," in Winnifred Fallers Sullivan et al., eds., *Law after Secularism* (Stanford, CA: Stanford University Press, 2011). For a detailed and incisive account of the German university reform and the transformation of theology in the nineteenth century, see Thomas Albert Howard, *Protestant Theology and the Making of the Modern German University* (Oxford: Oxford University Press, 2006). See also Charles E. McClelland, *State, Society, and University in Germany 1700–1914* (Cambridge: Cambridge University Press, 1980); Philip Schaff, *Germany: Its Universities, Theology, and Religion* (Philadelphia: Lindsay & Blakiston, 1857).

17. Bodo Nischan, *Prince, People, and Confession: The Second Reformation in Brandenburg* (Philadelphia: University of Pennsylvania Press, 1994).

18. Friedrich Schleiermacher, *Kurze Darstellung des theologischen Studiums* (Berlin, 1811). The significance of Schleiermacher's leadership for the development not only of the theological faculty but also of the Berlin faculty overall is well documented and analyzed by Howard, *Protestant Theology*, 197–211. See also T. K. Cheyne, *Founders of Old Testament Criticism: Biographical, Descriptive, and Critical Studies* (London: Methuen, 1893).

19. As Howard usefully documents, this development did not originate with the University of Berlin but had an important precedent in Göttingen, especially under the stewardship of Johann Lorenz von Mosheim. Ibid., 104–121.

20. The enormous consequence of the rise of academic theology in Germany cannot be discussed in the present context. Suffice it to remember that, in the early nineteenth century, "theology" covered far wider ground than it does today, and it was either from within the domain of theology or in a competitive dialogue with it that many modern scientific endeavors—archaeological, philological, historical, socioethnological, and philosophical—found their footing. Ward Blanton documents the competitively dialogical relation between philosophy and the nascent biblical studies in his *Displacing Christian Origins: Philosophy, Secularity, and the New Testament* (Chicago: University of Chicago Press, 2007).

21. Mann's *Annual Reports of the Board of Education of the State of Massachusetts* (1837–40) also had a great impact in Britain. See George Combe, [Review of Mann's *Annual Reports . . .*], *Edinburgh Review* 73: 148 (July 1841), 486–502; Combe, "Notes on the New Reformation in Germany; and On National Education, and the Common Schools of Massachusetts" (Edinburgh, 1845); Combe, "Remarks on National Education: Being an Inquiry into the Right and Duty of Government to Educate the People" (Edinburgh, 1847).

22. Charles Kendall Adams, *Historical Sketch of the University of Michigan* (Ann Arbor, MI: The University, 1876), 8.

23. Adams, *Historical Sketch*, 11. All of the territorial laws pertinent to the university are reproduced in *Records of the University of Michigan 1817–1837* (Ann Arbor, MI: The University, 1935).

24. The 1835 state constitution, quoted in Francis W. Shearman [Superintendent of Public Instruction], *System of Public Instruction and Primary School Law of Michigan, with explanatory notes, forms, regulations and instructions; a digest of decisions; a detailed history of public instruction and the laws relating thereto; the history of and laws relating to incorporated institutions of learning, &c. &c.* (Lansing, MI: Ingals, Hedges & Co, Printers to the State, 1852), 18.

25. Henry P. Tappan, *A Discourse, delivered by Henry P. Tappan, D. D. at Ann Arbor, Mich., on the occasion of his inauguration as chancellor of the University of Michigan, December 21st, 1852* (Detroit: Advertiser Power Presses, 1852), 30–31.

26. "Up to the advent of President Tappan, that policy [to shape the university according to the Prussian system] had lain practically dormant. Previous to 1850, when the Medical Department was inaugurated, nothing but the ordinary Classical course had been opened; in a word, there was nothing about the institution on his arrival, to remind one that the Prussian system had ever been so much as thought of, much less recommended and decided upon." Adams, *Historical Sketch*, 16.

27. Address to the graduating class of 1853, folder 1, box 1, Tappan Papers, Bentley Historical Library, University of Michigan.

28. Variously assessing this extraordinary outcome, historians generally conclude that Tappan was ahead of his time but precipitous, too uncompromising and injudicious in his official conduct, and perhaps supercilious and altogether too "Eastern" and European in his demeanor. Veysey, for example, states that Tappan "had prematurely declared that the German institutions could serve as 'literal' models for American higher education. (He moved too fast and was replaced by a docile clergyman.)" Veysey, *Emergence of the American University*, 10. See also Andrew Dickson White, *Autobiography of Andrew Dickson White*, vol. 1 (New York: Century, 1905).

29. Adams, *Historical Sketch*, 18.

30. Andrew Dickson White, describing the 1850s when he began his teaching career at the University of Michigan, writes: "Up to that time the highest institutions of learning in the United States were almost entirely under sectarian control. Even the University of Virginia, which Thomas Jefferson had founded as a center of liberal thought, had fallen under the direction of sectarians, and among the great majority of the Northern colleges an unwritten law seemed to require that a university president should be a clergyman. The instruction in the best of these institutions was . . . narrow, their methods outworn, and the students, as a rule, confined to one simple, single, cast-iron course, in which the great majority of them took no interest." White, *Autobiography*, 271–272.

31. Tappan's emphasis here was that not only he but also other professors were "entirely ignorant" of the "denominational connection" of any of the university officers hired during his administration.

32. *A Discourse Delivered by Henry P. Tappan, at Ann Arbor, Mich., on the occasion of his Inauguration as Chancellor of the University of Michigan, December 21st, 1852* (Detroit: Advertiser Power Presses, 1852), 47–48.

33. The reports of all the commissions, discussed at the conference with approximately twelve hundred delegates, were subsequently published in eight volumes. *World Missionary Conference, 1910*, 8 vols. (Edinburgh: Oliphant, Anderson & Ferrier, n. d. [1911?]).

34. Charles R. Erdman, Presbyterian Church in the U.S.A., Professor of Practical Theology, Princeton Theological Seminary.

35. It is mentioned that, of the 550, 405 responded, with 318 reporting that they had no provision for such courses, 16 reporting a course or courses somewhat overlapping with the topic "in comparative religion or in the history and philosophy of religion,"

and 6 reporting an incidental coverage in connection to other disciplines, such as anthropology, history, sociology, and the like. Cf. *Report of Commission VI*, 79–80.

36. The published report on this aspect of the investigation mentions the result only in a brief paragraph: "On examining the replies from the educators . . . the consensus of opinion seems to be that no separate department of missionary instruction should be established in academic institutions, but that the subject of Christian missions should be treated incidentally, in connection with cognate departments, such as Comparative Religion, History, Sociology, etc." Ibid., 81. It is not stated how many of these letters were sent or to whom. At least some of the letters received in response have been preserved in the Missionary Research Library Collection at the Burke Library Archive at Union Theological Seminary, New York. The ensuing quotations are taken from these original documents, MRL 12: World Missionary Conference, 1910, Series 1, Box 19, Folder 8.

    The inquiry was regarding "the study of Christian Missions," rather than "theology," or "Christian religion." It is conceivable that their answers would have been somewhat different had the question been phrased differently. Nonetheless, it is noteworthy that the "the leading educators" of the time had little difficulty in recognizing the intent of the question and, more to the point, the implications of such a curricular development.

37. The letter continues: "In colleges where the study of history is specialized, there may be opportunity for the study of missions as a separate subject. . . . Whether it should be included in any collegiate *curriculum,* except through the indirect influence of the examination paper, I have some doubt. I am, however, somewhat at a loss as to your interpretation of the word 'curriculum'."

38. Charles Eliot, then in his fourth decade as president of Harvard, delegated the task to an assistant, who wrote briefly as follows: "In reply to your letter of April 24 President Eliot directs me to tell you that he does not think that the study of Missions should be included in college curricula. In his opinion it should be dealt with by the several college religious societies."

    Woodrow Wilson, then the president of Princeton, wrote: "I take pleasure in replying to the question contained in your letter of May 4th. I do not believe that the study of missions should be made a part of the curricula of schools, colleges or universities. I believe that in the study of non-Christian countries and the development of civilization, which makes a part of every college and university curriculum, a place should be made for an exposition of the effect of missions on the development of civilization and that occasion should be made in such courses for a proper appreciation of what missions have accomplished, but I do not believe that the direct study of missions as a means of evangelization belongs outside of a distinctively ministerial training."

David Starr Jordan of the newly established Stanford University wrote: "In response to your kind letter, I would say that outside of theological schools it would hardly seem to be necessary that the study of missions should be included in the work of high schools or colleges. Where special effort is made to prepare men for the mission field, specific work could be included, but in a general way topics of this sort can hardly be made useful in a course of study itself, their value depending entirely on the relation they may have to the aspirations of the individual."

39. This is not to ignore the existence of a very large number of scholars, past and present, who are theologians. I refer here rather to the institutional structure. In the United States, whether theology is or is not really an academic and scholarly discipline remains a matter of debate.

CHAPTER NINE

Religion and Knowledge in the Post-Secular Academy

John Schmalzbauer and Kathleen Mahoney

The university has long been perceived as one of the most secular precincts of American society. In the academy and the media, the secularization narrative dominates accounts of religion's place in higher education.[1] Yet recent scholarship suggests that the secularization narrative may have overstated the extent to which universities have marginalized the teaching and practice of religion. Such scholarship points to the survival and growth of the academic study of religion as well as the vitality of campus religious life. It rejects what historian Martin Marty dubs "complaints and whimpers" about "what went wrong with Christian scholarship."[2]

Yet there is strong evidence that something close to the secularization of the university did occur. Until the late nineteenth century, religion exerted a powerful influence over higher education. Intertwined with the rise of the modern research university, the process of secularization overtook most fields in the early twentieth century. Across the academy, the influence of Freud, Nietzsche, and Darwin cast doubt on religious understandings of reality. As disciplines matured, scholarly inquiry became increasingly specialized. According to historians Jon Roberts and James Turner, the goal was "to think *small*: to ask questions for which there were determinate and publicly verifiable answers." In an age of empiricism and specialization, religious questions became increasingly irrelevant.[3]

In *The Secular Revolution*, sociologist Christian Smith argues that the secularization of higher education was not a faceless process unfolding over time but an organized social movement with identifiable leaders, organizations, networks, and financial resources. By the 1930s, efforts to secularize higher education had largely succeeded, thanks to social scientists such as Lester Ward, organizations like the American Sociological Society, and philanthropists such as Andrew Carnegie.[4]

Despite the success of the "secular revolution," it was not irreversible or complete. Following World War II, religious scholarship staged a brief comeback, reflecting the public piety of the postwar years. More recently, religion has returned to intellectual life in what might be called a "post-secular moment."[5] Like its predecessor, the resurgence of religion has been driven by wider shifts in American culture and around the globe. Since the 1980s, articles on the return of religion have appeared in a dozen disciplines, including art, English, philosophy, music, political science, social work, medicine, history, and sociology. Fifty religious scholarly associations foster the integration of faith and learning, most of them established within the past thirty years, while new centers for the study of religion can be found at Columbia, Virginia, Chicago, Emory, Princeton, and New York Universities and other campuses.[6] In a postmodern era, scholars are challenging the boundaries between faith and knowledge, acknowledging the importance of religion as a human phenomenon and as a way of knowing.

Far from inevitable, the comeback of religion has been realized by organized networks of scholars. Their efforts have benefited from the support of religious professional associations, centers and institutes, journals, and philanthropic foundations.[7] The emergence of multiculturalism, the advent of postmodernism, the rise of the new Christian right, and the role of the sacred in international affairs have also fueled the return of religion to campus.

Some have called the return of religious scholarship a "movement." A closer look reveals not one movement but many. Like most shifts in academic culture, it has been achieved by diverse groups of scholars with competing conceptions of religion and its role in higher education. Reflecting this diversity, the religious resurgence has included believers and skeptics, the spiritual and the religious, those who integrate faith and scholarship and those who approach religion as an object of study. Sometimes they have worked together. Sometimes they have worked at cross purposes.

This essay is a tour of recent efforts to reconnect religion and knowledge, a group portrait of the individuals and organizations behind the growing prominence of religious scholarship. Its purposes are threefold: to document the comeback of religion across the disciplines; to map the networks of scholars and organizations responsible for these developments; and to describe the competing visions animating efforts to heighten religion's place in the academy. It concludes by considering what the return of religion means for American society and the sociology of religion.

The Postwar Religious Revival and Its Collapse

The secularization of intellectual life—even in mainstream settings—was never absolute. Religion became more visible in the 1950s, as theologians made the cover of *Time* and Billy Graham preached on network television. In higher education, the postwar revival led to more religion in the curriculum. In his 1947 book *The College Seeks Religion*, Merrimon Cuninggim wrote that religion held "a larger place in the college's thinking and practice than at any time in the twentieth century." Along the same lines, Will Herberg described the "intellectual rehabilitation of religion" and its prominence in the "'vanguard' journals of literature, politics, and art."[8]

Tied to mainline Protestantism, the postwar religious resurgence was as lasting as its sponsor's hegemony over American culture. When the Protestant establishment declined, its efforts to reconcile faith and knowledge faltered. In the face of student radicalism, "secular theology," and social unrest, organizations like the Faculty Christian Fellowship underwent a collective identity crisis.[9] Some disbanded; others changed their names and missions. Explaining its 1968 transformation from *The Christian Scholar* into *Soundings*, the religious revival's leading journal argued that to "forgo the word 'religion' in preference for 'common human concerns' is not to put on the armor of contemporary atheism or secularism" but to pursue a deeper agenda.[10] The Society for Religion in Higher Education (the journal's sponsoring organization) became the Society for Values in Higher Education in 1975.

In the early 1970s, religion's place in the academy seemed more tenuous than ever. Describing the situation in sociology, Nancy Ammerman writes that in the "pervasively secular" culture of the decade, the topic of religion "had simply passed off [the] radar screens" of many scholars.[11] In other fields, reductionist approaches to knowledge further marginalized religion.

Although new programs were steadily added in religious studies, the field seemed to move in a secular direction. Once dominated by mainline Protestant concerns, scholarly studies of religion underwent a dramatic shift in the 1960s and 1970s. In 1964 the National Association of Biblical Instructors became the American Academy of Religion. Distancing themselves from the Bible and theology curriculum of Protestant divinity schools, members of a new generation of scholars worked to professionalize religious studies. Modeling themselves after the social sciences and history, rather than Protestant theology, scholars articulated an explicitly secular rationale for studying religion. At the same time, they widened their focus to include non-Western religions, ushering in a "post-Protestant" phase of religious studies.[12]

The Return of Religion in the Disciplines

Given these developments, some might expect that religious scholarship would remain on the margins. But growing interest in the sacred for three decades in the humanities and social sciences belies this interpretation.

Increased interest in religion is evident in the growth of religious studies departments. Between 1990 and 2006, membership in the American Academy of Religion (AAR) doubled from 5,500 to 11,000 members.[13] According to the AAR, the number of religion majors increased 31 percent between 1996 and 2005, while overall enrollment in religious studies courses grew by 23 percent. Since 1970 the number of students earning undergraduate degrees in philosophy and religion has doubled. This growth has continued following the events September 11, 2001. According to *Newsweek*, we are witnessing a "religious studies revival."[14]

While portrayed as secular in some accounts, religion departments have continued to take Christian theology seriously; in the year 2000, 45 percent of classes were on Christianity, with nearly 10 percent focusing on Christian theology. Since the 1980s, a range of theological approaches has blossomed in the academy. Among the most outspoken, advocates of radical orthodoxy and post-liberalism have launched a no-holds-barred critique of secular rationality, calling for a full-blown Christian theology that emphasizes the biblical narrative and postmodern theory. A spokesperson for this movement, Duke's Stanley Hauerwas, was named America's Best Theologian by *Time* magazine in 2001 and a fellow of the American Academy of Arts and Sciences in 2003.[15]

So seriously have theological perspectives been taken that some prominent scholars have criticized the American Academy of Religion for its pro-religious outlook and founded an alternative organization, the North American Association for the Study of Religion (NAASR). While leaders of the NAASR have called for a more objective approach to religious studies, others have rejected a perceived dichotomy between advocacy and objectivity, recognizing with Conrad Cherry that the study of religion "requires empathetic participation as well as critical distance."[16] Because the "founding fratricidal conflict" between theology and religious studies remains unresolved, normative religious perspectives continue to have a place in the AAR.[17] Reflecting this normative emphasis, more and more scholars are speaking out of traditions besides Christianity. The 2000 AAR annual meeting featured the panel "Coming Out as a Buddhist and Hindu in the Academy," reflecting a tendency of scholars from many traditions to reveal their own religious identities.[18]

Paralleling the expansion of religious studies, religion has become increasingly visible across the humanities. Nowhere has the return of religion been more dramatic than in philosophy. In a recent article in *Philo*, Quentin Smith chronicles the "desecularization" of American philosophy. Estimating that "one-quarter or one-third of philosophy professors are theists, with most being orthodox Christians," he writes that "it became, almost overnight, 'academically respectable' to argue for theism, making philosophy a favored field of entry for the most intelligent and talented theists." According to Smith, Oxford University Press's 2000–2001 catalogue contains ninety-six books in the philosophy of religion, of which ninety-four take a theistic position. A half dozen philosophy journals currently focus on religion.[19] Founded in 1978, the Society of Christian Philosophers grew to more than one thousand members by 1994, about 12 percent of American philosophers.[20] Though Christian philosophy has enjoyed impressive growth, it remains a minority subculture in a discipline that pays scant attention to religion. As MIT philosopher Alex Byrne notes, "Contemporary Christian philosophers often content themselves with pulling up the drawbridge and manning the barricades" rather than mounting arguments that convince their secular colleagues.[21]

Though less dramatic than in philosophy, a religious resurgence can also be seen in the field of literary studies.[22] As early as 1983, Edward Said remarked on the rebirth of "religious criticism," noting that "when you see influential critics publishing major books with titles like *The Genesis of Secrecy*, *The Great Code*, *Kabbalah and Criticism*, *Violence and the Sacred*,

Deconstruction and Theology, you know you are in the presence of a significant trend."[23] By 1997 John McClure could speak of the "return of religion
in contemporary theory and literature."[24] In a more theological vein, the
1,300-member Conference on Christianity and Literature has explored the
connections between faith and literary criticism, enlisting René Girard,
Denis Donoghue, and the late Wayne Booth.[25]

Even more than the field of English literature, that of history has witnessed
a return of religion. Between 1975 and 2009, the proportion of historians spe-
cializing in religion rose from 1.4 to 7.7 percent. Currently, "religious history"
is the most popular specialization in the American Historical Association.
When Henry May wrote "The Recovery of American Religious History" in
1964, the study of American religion was still the property of liberal Protestant
"church historians" in mainline Protestant divinity schools. By contrast, more
than half of the American religion scholars surveyed in 1993 identified as Catholics (26 percent) or evangelicals (32 percent).[26] Since May's essay, historians
have shifted their focus from white mainline Protestant clergymen to African
American Pentecostals, Orthodox Jews, Japanese American Buddhists, and
Southern evangelical women. By the late 1990s, centers and institutes dedicated
to the study of American religion had been established at Princeton University,
Indiana University, Boston College, and the University of Southern California.
Many were established with the support of foundations.[27]

A major force in mainstreaming American religious history has been the
emergence of the "new evangelical historiography." In books such as *Fundamentalism and American Culture* and *The Democratization of American Christianity*, a network of evangelical historians helped reshape scholarly views of
evangelicalism.[28] By 1991 historian Jon Butler could describe the "evangelical
paradigm" as "the *single* most powerful explanatory device adopted by academic historians to account for the distinctive features of American society,
culture, and identity."[29] Drawing on their autobiographies and confessional
traditions, scholars such as Mark Noll, George Marsden, Edith Blumhofer,
and Nathan Hatch have brought their Christian convictions into the field
of American history.[30] Through organizations such as the Institute for the
Study of American Evangelicals, they have heightened the visibility of religion in the academy. Like the larger project of American religious history,
the institute was supported through grants from Lilly Endowment and the
Pew Charitable Trusts. During the 1990s alone, Pew spent $14 million on
programs focusing on evangelical scholarship.[31]

Across the social sciences, scholars have rediscovered the power of religion. Heralding "the return of the sacred," Harvard sociologist Daniel Bell gave a widely reported lecture at the London School of Economics in 1977, arguing that the exhaustion of secular ideologies had led to a hunger for meaning and transcendence.[32] During the 1980s and 1990s, survey researchers in sociology and political science documented the continuing influence of religion. Such research challenged theories predicting the secularization of modern societies. Chronicling the "desecularization of the world," scholars envisioned a new era "after secularism."[33] Established in 1994, the religion section of the American Sociological Association had 686 members in 2010, larger than thirty-four of the association's forty-nine sections.[34]

Reflecting the heightened role of faith in American politics and across the globe, the study of religion has achieved what Kenneth Wald and his colleagues describe as a "new prominence in political science." Ignored by postwar political scientists, religion has been rehabilitated as an independent variable. Founded in the mid-1990s, the religion and politics section of the American Political Science Association (APSA) is now larger than the sections on public administration, urban politics, and the presidency. In 2006 the APSA established a special task force on religion and democracy in the United States.[35]

Like sociology and political science, psychology has become more open to religion. In a 2003 essay in the *Annual Review of Psychology*, Robert Emmons and Raymond Paloutzian tracked the dramatic growth in the psychology of religion since the late 1970s. Noting the proliferation of books and journal articles between 1988 and 2001, they argued that the psychology of religion has "re-emerged as a full-force, leading edge research area."[36] Founded in 1975, Division 36 of the American Psychological Association (which focuses on the psychology of religion) had more than 1,100 members by the year 2000, making it larger than twenty-nine of the organization's fifty-five sections.[37]

Social workers are also rediscovering religion. While the 1,650-member North American Association of Christians in Social Work advocates "a vital Christian presence" in the profession, the Society for Spirituality in Social Work fosters "connections and mutual support among social workers of many contrasting spiritual perspectives." Between 1995 and 2001, the number of accredited social work programs with courses on religion and spirituality rose from seventeen to fifty.[38] Religious approaches to social work are being published in the top journals. In 2005 the flagship journal *Social Work* featured no fewer than six articles on religion.

The field of medicine is turning its attention to spirituality and healing. The number of medical schools offering religion-related courses has grown from 5 in 1992 to 101 in 2005. At places like the Center for Spirituality, Theology, and Health at Duke University, researchers are exploring the impact of spirituality on blood pressure, depression, and alcoholism. The National Center for Complementary and Alternative Medicine, part of the federal National Institutes of Health, has promoted research on Ayurvedic healing, prayer, and mind-body medicine.[39]

The relationship between religion and the natural sciences is also receiving more attention. Huston Smith notes that "God-and-science talk seems to be everywhere," citing the profusion of science and religion centers (ten across the United States), journals (*Science and Spirit*, *Zygon*, *Theology and Science*), and hundreds of science and religion courses (including eight hundred funded by the John Templeton Foundation's course development program). Like the research on spirituality and health, many of these initiatives have been sponsored by Templeton, including the American Association for the Advancement of Science's Dialogue on Science, Ethics, and Religion.[40] According to Dennis Cheek, there are now more than 150,000 citations in the literature on religion and science.[41]

Across the university, religion has returned to the disciplines. Many have written articles lamenting the *neglect* of religious topics in their disciplines. Others have celebrated the *return* of religion. In most disciplines, faculty interested in religion can point to the existence of religious professional associations and journals as well as high-profile scholars. In almost every corner of academia, religion is making a comeback.

Religion in the Academy: Multiple Movements, Conflicting Agendas

Over the past three decades, scholars have forged connections between religion and their disciplines. Now many of them are working *across* disciplinary lines, addressing the sorts of *meta*-questions that concern the entire university. It is this interdisciplinarity that makes the contemporary resurgence of religion so consequential. By blurring departmental boundaries, religion scholars are resisting a key process of secularization: the differentiation of knowledge into specialized disciplines. If the rise of specialized departments led faculty away from questions of ultimate meaning, the emergence of interdisciplinary discussions of faith and knowledge has helped bring those questions back into the spotlight. Those conversations are happening in centers and cross-disciplinary concentrations. Though departments still have the power to hire, grant tenure, and promote, flexible disciplinary boundaries have changed the *kinds* of knowledge they produce.

Recognizing the heightened visibility of religion *within* and *across* disciplines, some have spoken of an interdisciplinary movement. In 1999 researchers Alexander and Helen Astin wrote that a "movement is emerging in higher education in which many academics find themselves actively searching for meaning."[42] In our 2000 evaluation of Lilly Endowment's work in this area, we reached a similar conclusion, describing the "emergence of a movement to revitalize religion in higher education."[43]

Ten years later, we believe it more accurate to speak of multiple movements rather than a single effort. In our judgment, several different movements (with many variations) have heightened the place of religion in the academy. Sometimes intersecting, they each have a unique justification for the academic study of religion, and each has its own leaders, organizations, and sources of funding.

Most visible are efforts to promote *religion as an object of study*. As noted above, such efforts can be found in individual disciplines, in places like the religion section of the American Political Science Association and Division 36 of the American Psychological Association. In some cases, attempts to promote religious scholarship transcend departmental boundaries, involving university-wide efforts to transform curricula and research.

Nowhere has this effort been more visible than in the creation of religion-oriented centers and institutes.[44] Ten of the most prominent were funded under the Pew Charitable Trusts' Centers of Excellence program, a multiyear initiative begun in 1998. Its goal was to establish an academic foothold for the study of religion at leading U.S. universities, including Boston, Emory, New York, and Princeton Universities and the Universities of Missouri, Pennsylvania, and Virginia. Most of the centers are interdisciplinary in focus.[45] Though some are more active than others, most have continued to operate after Pew phased out its funding.[46]

In addition to social scientific endeavors, scholars in the humanities have made a public case for the academic study of religion. The author of *Religious*

Literacy (2007), Boston University's Stephen Prothero, outlined what "every American needs to know" on the *Daily Show* and in other media outlets. Directing a similar message to the academy, the drafters of the *Wingspread Declaration on Religion and Public Life*, which was sponsored by the Society for Values in Higher Education, concluded that the "study of religion and its public relevance is a crucial dimension to liberal education." Its signers included the editor of the *Journal of American History* and the president of the Association of American Colleges and Universities.[47]

Many of the calls for religion in the academy have focused on nonsectarian approaches to religious education, prizing scholarly objectivity and the separation of facts from values. Recently, some have explored the origins of this objectivist epistemology. In the judgment of Talal Asad and others, the emergence of religion as an academic topic was bound up with the history of Western colonialism. Recognizing the ideological character of "religion as an object of study," the *Journal of the American Academy of Religion* recently commissioned the special issue "The Return of Religion after 'Religion,'" noting that "public talk about the return of religion is taking place at precisely the same time as we see within the academic study of religion a sharp genealogical critique of the category 'religion.'" Others have considered religion's new visibility in the context of feminist theory and liberation theology. Along these lines, a 2007 conference asked, "What new openings for feminism and gender theory are being made by the renewed interest of intellectuals in religion?" Such discussions have raised awareness about the political implications of religious studies.[48]

Equally critical of the ideology of objectivity, another group has played a far more active role in promoting religious scholarship. Envisioning a dialogue between Christian faith and academia, a loose network of scholars has called for overtly confessional approaches to research. Portraying religion as a way of knowing, rather than an object of study, these scholars have incorporated religious beliefs into the content of their scholarship.[49]

The case for confessional scholarship has been articulated mostly by Protestant historians and philosophers, most notably historian George Marsden.[50] The prominence of philosophers and historians is due partly to the heavy presence of Christian scholars in American religious history and the philosophy of religion. Another reason is the ability of philosophers and historians to reflect on the presuppositions and historical origins of the secular university. While historians have described how the university came to exclude religion, philosophers such as Alvin Plantinga and Nicholas Wolterstorff have challenged this exclusion as intellectually untenable.

Given the central role of Christian philosophers and historians in discussions of religion and academic life, it is fitting that the Lilly Seminar on Religion and Higher Education was codirected by Wolterstorff and historian James Turner. Paying special attention to faith and knowledge, the Lilly Seminar explored "the epistemological question of what relation might come to exist between religion and mainstream academic scholarship." Located at Notre Dame, the seminar met six times between 1997 and 1999. Bringing religious academics (Turner, Wolterstorff, Mark Noll, Douglas Sloan) into conversation with others (David Hollinger, Richard Bernstein, Alan Wolfe), the seminar helped raise the profile of religion scholarship. Wolfe went on to write a dozen articles on religion for the *Chronicle of Higher Education* and a cover story on the "opening of the evangelical mind" in the *Atlantic*.[51]

Paralleling efforts to integrate faith and knowledge, a very different group of scholars has called for the *integration of spirituality and higher education*. If George Marsden has served as the unofficial leader of efforts to re-Christianize the academy, education consultant Parker Palmer has been central to the movement for spirituality. A 1998 survey of eleven thousand faculty and administrators identified Palmer as one of the thirty "most influential senior leaders" in American higher education. The *New York Times* has called him a "phenomenon in higher education," and his books are best sellers.[52] In works such as *To Know as We Are Known* (1983), *The Courage to Teach* (1997), and *A Hidden Wholeness: The Journey toward an Undivided Life* (2004), he has described education as a spiritual journey.[53] A practicing Quaker, Palmer has advanced a holistic model of teaching that integrates body, mind, and spirit.[54]

Reflecting this interest in all things spiritual, the Education as Transformation Project at Wellesley College drew eight hundred faculty, students, staff, and administrators, including twenty-eight presidents, to a 1998 conference on "religious pluralism, spirituality, and higher education." Attendees witnessed presentations on classical Indian dance, spirituality and jazz, and Tibetan Buddhism as well as talks by Palmer and Diana Eck. Since then, the project has produced a nine-volume book series on spirituality and higher education. In 2000 the project cosponsored a meeting with the University of Massachusetts, Going Public with Spirituality in Work and Higher Education. Organized by then chancellor David Scott, it featured presentations such as "Science and Spirituality," "Spiritual Intelligence," and "Going Public with Spirituality in the Course Catalogue."[55] At both the University of Massachusetts and Wellesley, efforts to bring spirituality into the classroom have been supported by high-level administrators. Reflecting on the themes of the Education as Transformation Project, Wellesley president Diana Chapman Walsh said that colleges should "envision a whole new place for spirituality in education." In a 2004 piece, project organizer Peter Laurence chronicled the "history of a movement."[56] Using the chancellor's office as a bully pulpit, physicist Scott wrote hopefully of an "integrative university" where questions of ultimate meaning could be brought "into every one of the majors."[57]

The quest for the spiritual is making inroads in national higher-education policy circles. In the past decade, religion and spirituality have been the subject of cover stories in *Liberal Education*, *Academe*, and *Change*.[58] In 2002 the Association of American Colleges and Universities sponsored a conference on spirituality and learning. The keynote speaker was Alexander Astin, of the University of California, Los Angeles (UCLA), the most cited higher-education researcher in the United States.[59] The same year, Astin and his spouse, Helen, signed a statement criticizing the exclusion of spirituality from colleges and universities.[60] Since 2003 they have served as coinvestigators on a massive Templeton-funded project on spirituality in the academy. In a national survey of 112,000 undergraduates, the project documented strong student interest in spirituality and religion. Consistent with this goal, UCLA held a national institute on ways to "incorporate spiritual perspectives into the curriculum and co-curriculum."[61]

The current emphasis on spirituality is an expression of the metaphysical tradition in American culture, the "missing third" of U.S. religious history.[62] Its influence can be seen in the late John Templeton's philanthropic commitment to the reconciliation of spirituality and science. A lifelong Presbyterian, he was influenced by "the New Thought movements of Christian Science, Unity and Religious Science." His foundation reflects these commitments.[63]

Closely related to the quest for spirituality are recent efforts to revive moral and civic education, a cause Templeton has also supported. Since the 1990s, the foundation has funded a variety of college-level character initiatives, including the Institute on College Student Values, *In Character* magazine, the *Journal of College and Character*, the Character Clearinghouse, and the Center for the Study of Values in College Student Development. The guidebook *Colleges That Encourage Character Development* currently lists "405 exemplary college programs in ten categories that inspire students to lead ethical and civic-minded lives."[64]

These initiatives are part of a larger shift that Alan Wolfe has called the "moral revival." In an overview, Wolfe points to the rediscovery of moral development by psychologists, James Q. Wilson's work on the "moral sense," and the rise of communitarianism.[65] Of the movements on Wolfe's list, communitarianism has done the most for the academic study of religion. In philosophy and political theory, Charles Taylor's *Sources of the Self,* Alasdair MacIntyre's *After Virtue,* and Jean Bethke Elshtain's *Democracy on Trial* have made room for religious voices. Though distancing themselves from the communitarian label, Robert Bellah and his colleagues used the biblical and civic republican traditions to articulate a critique of American individualism.[66] Along the same lines, Robert Putnam's *Bowling Alone* and *American Grace* (coauthored with David Campbell) have sparked a lively debate over religion and social capital. From 1995 to 2000, Putnam's Saguaro Seminar included several participants with an interest in religion and public life, such as John DiIulio, Glenn Loury, Martha Minow, Jim Wallis, Stephen Goldsmith, and a young Barack Obama.[67]

A by-product of the emphasis on community was the birth of Campus Compact, the nation's leading service learning organization. A national network of presidents "committed to the civic purposes of higher education," it helped make service learning one of the most widespread curricular innovations of the late twentieth century. By 2010 more than 1,100 presidents had signed on.[68] Church-related colleges and universities have played a central role in the leadership of Campus Compact. As of 1995, 20 percent of member schools were Catholic (Catholic institutions make up about 10 percent of American colleges and universities).[69]

Like other forms of civic education, service learning has blurred the boundaries between morality and learning. As Julie Reuben notes, moral concerns have long been consigned to the nonacademic, extracurricular world of student development, with the "institutional structure [reinforcing] the divide between the Good and the True."[70] The reintegration of the good and the true can be seen in the growing focus on civic and moral education among higher-education policy makers. In 2003 the Carnegie Foundation for the Advancement of Teaching published *Educating Citizens: Preparing America's Undergraduates for Lives of Moral and Civic Responsibility*, a study of twelve colleges and universities that "have made broad institutional commitments to the development of all students' moral and civic development." A disproportionate number of the schools were church-related. In a related study, Helen Astin and Anthony Lising Antonio argued that church-related colleges strengthen civic values and promote character development.[71] Colgate University president Rebecca Chopp observed that the "movement of civic education in this country is vast and sustained," adding that in "recent years educators, educational associations, and students have returned to the long and deep American tradition to educate citizens."[72]

Clearly, religion in higher education has taken many forms. From campaigns for religious literacy to the movement for spirituality in higher education, the return of religion has been accomplished by heterogeneous groups of scholars with divergent visions of academic life. Much of this heterogeneity reflects not only ideological differences over the role of religion in public life but also an increase in religious diversity on American campuses.

The growth of Islamic Studies, Jewish Studies, Buddhist Studies, Hindu Studies, and Sikh Studies has greatly expanded the range of religious traditions represented in American higher education. Such pluralism has enriched academia while creating new challenges. At Columbia University, the creation of a Middle Eastern Studies position honoring the late Palestinian American scholar Edward Said drew sharp criticism from some Jewish groups. Columbia has provided another perspective on Middle Eastern history and culture by establishing a professorship in Israel and Jewish Studies and an institute devoted to the same topic.[73] In the field of South Asian Studies, a different kind of conflict is brewing between Hinduism scholars and Hindu Americans.[74]

To address the challenge of diversity, the Ford Foundation initiated its Difficult Dialogues Initiative in 2005. In a letter signed by the presidents of 15 leading American universities, foundation president Susan Beresford invited proposals for projects that promote "new scholarship and teaching about cultural differences and religious pluralism." With 675 institutions applying, 136 were invited to submit final proposals. In the end, 27 universities received $100,000 grants to "promote campus environments where sensitive subjects can be discussed in a spirit of open scholarly inquiry, academic freedom, and respect for different viewpoints."[75] At the University of Michigan, thirty faculty took part in the seminar "Student Religion, Faith, and Spirituality in the Classroom and Beyond." At Columbia, the initiative has led to several innovative projects, including "Religion versus the Academy," a class taught by Randall Balmer and John Stratton Hawley.[76] Taken together, the Difficult Dialogues courses are a reminder of the contentious nature of religious discourse in the university.

Faculty Reponses to the Return of Religion: Indifference, Anxiety, and Engagement

The most difficult dialogue of all may be between the advocates of religious scholarship and their colleagues. Research indicates most faculty members devote little class time to religion. According to the UCLA spirituality study, 62 percent of students said their professors never encourage discussions of religious or spiritual topics.[77] Religion may also be absent from the vast majority of research agendas. Analyzing four years of scholarly output in one discipline, Nancy Ammerman found only 4 percent of three thousand books reviewed in *Contemporary Sociology* were about religion.[78]

Lack of attention to religion may reflect the religious demography of the faculty. Recent surveys of the professoriate indicate the most popular religious affiliation after Christianity is "none." Though a majority of faculty claim a religious affiliation, they are much less likely to do so than the general population. According to a 2006 survey, 31 percent of faculty identify with no religion. Similarly, the UCLA study found that 37 percent are "not at all religious." The number of nonreligious faculty is even higher at elite institutions. A 2005 survey of scientists at twenty-one top-ranked universities found that half of elite social scientists had no religious affiliation. Though 69 percent identified as "spiritual," only 37 percent described themselves as very or moderately so.[79]

While most faculty have paid scant attention to religious topics, some have criticized efforts to raise the profile of religion in the academy. Several critics have been actively involved in discussions of faith and scholarship. Berkeley historian David Hollinger attended five of the six meetings of the Lilly Seminar. Though appreciative of his colleagues' insights, Hollinger questioned their conviction that religion had been unfairly marginalized in the academy. In "Enough Already: Universities Do Not Need More Christianity," he wrote that the "Lilly group was a seminar in search of a problem."[80]

In some cases, Christian scholars have invited such critiques. By disregarding the "rules of the academic game," they have undercut their own professional credibility.[81] In particular, the emphasis of some evangelical scholars on bringing supernatural explanations into scientific discourse has made their colleagues less open to religious scholarship. Nowhere is this ironic outcome more apparent than in the movement for "intelligent design." As recently as ten years ago, its leaders had high hopes for reshaping the conversation on religion and science. Instead, it has been perceived as a thinly disguised version of creationism. In a 1999 book, philosopher William Dembski exemplified such confidence, predicting that "in the next several years intelligent design will be sufficiently developed to deserve funding from the National Science Foundation."[82] According to a recent study, there is absolutely no support for intelligent design among the nation's elite natural scientists. Rather than building bridges between faith and science, it has led to more anxiety.[83]

The John Templeton Foundation's initiatives on science and religion have also elicited a backlash. In 1999 physicist Lawrence Krauss expressed serious reservations about Templeton's agenda, concluding that "science and religion don't mix."[84] More recently, Richard Sloan of Columbia University called studies of prayer and healing "garbage research."[85] In response to Templeton, some secular scholars have formed organizations and networks of their own. New movements spawn countermovements, and the religion-and-science movement is no exception. In 2006, three dozen faculty, journalists, and academic leaders gathered for a conference sponsored by investor Robert Zeps, the self-described anti-Templeton. Titled "Beyond Belief: Science, Religion, Reason, and Survival," the gathering was a response to the perceived vulnerability of science. Warning that the coming years could be "the twilight for the Enlightenment project," conference organizers asked, could science "create a new rational narrative as poetic and powerful as those that have traditionally sustained societies?" The list of presenters reads like a who's who of the new atheists, including Richard Dawkins, Sam Harris, and Steven Weinberg.[86]

Many of these initiatives have actually heightened the profile of religion. The publications of the new atheists have served to energize religious intellectual life. In 2006 Pulitzer Prize–winning novelist Marilynne Robinson wrote a stinging critique of Dawkins's book, faulting his "simple-as-that, plain-as-day approach to the grandest questions."[87] Across the Atlantic, literary theorist Terry Eagleton published an equally unforgiving review in the *London Review of Books*, calling Dawkins's performance "lunging, flailing, mispunching."[88] Former Human Genome Project director Francis Collins has emerged as Dawkins's chief debating partner.[89] According to Elaine Howard Ecklund's survey of elite scientists, Collins is widely respected by his peers. Recently, Barack Obama made Collins the director of the National Institutes of Health, the largest scientific grant–making agency in the world, a decision that attracted some criticism.[90]

Support for religious scholarship is more widespread if one distinguishes the academic study of religion from efforts to revive Christian intellectual life or promote spiritual development. This focus on the empirical study of religion is one of the most common approaches in the discipline of religious studies. Former American Academy of Religion president Robert Orsi articulated this vision when he warned against "the language of good/bad religion." Instead, scholars should cultivate a radical empiricism that "disentangles normative agendas" from academic scholarship. Orsi's comments have provoked a vigorous debate among historians of American religion.[91]

Systematic surveys and anecdotal evidence suggest that faculty pursue divergent approaches to the study of religion. Ray Hart's 1991 study found that public university religion departments were much less sympathetic to theological studies than their counterparts in church-related colleges and seminaries.[92] More recently, a 2006 survey of introductory religious studies courses uncovered a similar divide between faculty in secular and religious colleges. While 42 percent of religion faculty at church-related schools thought it was essential or very important for courses to "develop students' own religious beliefs," only 8 percent of faculty at secular institutions felt the same way.[93]

From the point of view of students, it may not matter what faculty think they are accomplishing in the classroom. Although professors at religious and secular colleges embrace different goals, students at both types of institutions view the classroom as a place for spiritual discovery. At all four institutions profiled in *Religion on Campus* (including a large public university), students reported growing spiritually in religion classes.[94] Such findings suggest that undergraduates take what they want from the classroom, regardless of faculty intentions.

Surveys of American faculty reveal that a significant percentage of the professoriate sees the spiritual formation of students as a worthy goal. In a 2005 survey conducted by UCLA, 30 percent of faculty agreed that "colleges should be concerned with facilitating students' spiritual development."[95]

In fields such as philosophy, a determined minority of 10 to 30 percent has managed to put religious perspectives back onto the scholarly agenda. In some fields, an even smaller group has made a difference. While these individuals are not likely to carry the day, their mere presence indicates religion's importance.

Conclusion

For decades, scholars have told a widely accepted story of decline, chronicling the exclusion of the sacred from American universities. Strong evidence indicates that a new story needs to be told about religion in the academy, one recognizing the resilience of the sacred in an overwhelmingly secular institution. Over the past three decades, religious scholarship has returned to American higher education. In almost every discipline, faculty can point to the existence of religious professional associations, high-profile scholars, influential books, and religion-oriented centers and institutes.

What is the significance of these developments for sociology? What do they say about the place of religion in American society? In the writings of Peter Berger and other theorists, higher education and the college-educated professions are depicted as the carriers of secularization in the modern world. In recent years, the secularization thesis has come under attack. Yet even critics agree that the academy is the great exception to the vitality of American religion. According to R. Stephen Warner, sociologists have resonated with secularization theory because it fits their own life experiences. Likewise, James Spickard attributes its appeal to "a biographic loss of religiosity on the part of many intellectuals."[96]

What happens to secularization theory when the secularity of the academy is called into question? Over the past two decades, the university has become more open to religious discourse. Across the university, the advocates of religious scholarship have carved out new organizational niches, bringing the sacred into a secular institution. These niches have challenged the structural differentiation of religion and education. They have also resisted the privatization of faith, taking religion into public settings. To be clear, such changes have been limited. In most disciplines, a minority of scholars have turned their attention to religion. Of these individuals, only a few have attempted to integrate their religious convictions into the content of their research. Yet clearly something has changed. Today the academy can no longer be depicted as an island of secularity.

Far from isolated, the university has served as "a bellwether for society's religious revival." Historian Diane Winston notes that "the exclusion of religion from public life" does not adequately describe the place of the sacred in American culture, adding that "'diffusion' may be a better term, signaling the scattering of religious ideas and behaviors." This diffusion can be seen in electoral politics, as candidates from both major parties court the faithful. It is also evident in international affairs, as a resurgent Islam has reshaped geopolitics. In the words of sociologist José Casanova, "we are witnessing the 'deprivatization' of religion" as "religious traditions throughout the world are refusing to accept the marginal and privatized role which theories of modernity as well as theories of secularization had reserved for them."[97] Along the same lines, sociologist Charles Harper and historian Bryan Lebeau write of an era of "de-differentiation" in which previously separated spheres "are increasingly connected and interpenetrating: politics and economics, church and state relations, religion and health, family and media, religion and sports, and so on."[98]

By far the most visible religious group in American politics, evangelicals are one reason religion is making a comeback on campus. Known for their involvement in the new Christian right, they have only recently staked a significant claim in American higher education. Creating a parallel subculture of academic associations and religious colleges, they have built an organizational infrastructure for the integration of faith and learning.[99] This activity is a reflection of the increasing number of evangelicals in the professoriate. In a 2006 survey, 19 percent of American faculty identified as born-again Christians.[100]

Evangelicals have participated in the revitalization of student religious life. In less than a decade, the number of students involved in Campus Crusade for Christ tripled, rising from eighteen thousand in 1995 to sixty-four thousand in 2008. In a sign of increasing religious pluralism, Muslim Student Associations and Mormon Institutes of Religion have also experienced significant growth. The same goes for Hillel and Chabad, mainstays of campus Judaism. In recent years, the university has become a lively religious marketplace. In a reversal of previous patterns, young adults are *less* likely to lose their religion if they go to college. Researchers at UCLA found that undergraduates desire more attention to spirituality in the classroom. Student demand may be one reason for the growth in religious studies.[101]

The resurgence of religion and spirituality has been aided by the diversification of the American faculty. The 2004–2005 UCLA survey on faculty spirituality found that women and African Americans were more likely than others to describe themselves as religious or spiritual. Consistent with this finding, America's most prominent black intellectuals are also some of today's leading religious thinkers, including Cornel West, bell hooks, and Michael Eric Dyson. Likewise, feminist and minority group scholars have challenged the ideology of objectivity, championing women's ways of knowing, queer theory, and Afrocentric epistemologies. Echoing the rhetoric of identity politics, people of faith have demanded a seat at the academic table, arguing that religious ways of knowing are a legitimate form of inquiry.[102]

The responsiveness of higher education to these developments raises questions about the autonomy of the university in a post-secular age. Defending higher education as one of the few American institutions not dominated by religious discourse, historian David Hollinger argues that universities "should not surrender back to Christianity the ground they have won for a more independent, cosmopolitan life of the mind." Already some analysts have warned of a pro-religious bias in the sociology of religion, pointing to the influence of Protestant assumptions on this subfield. Hollinger has raised similar concerns about religious scholars, arguing that "religion is too important to be left in the hands of people who believe in it." Social critics have articulated a parallel critique of the influence of popular spirituality, arguing that a new irrationalism is responsible for the rise of fields like "positive psychology" and "religion and health." From this perspective, higher education is in danger of losing its independence.[103]

As a bellwether, the university is continually buffeted by the winds of public opinion. Yet higher education can also serve as a rudder, steering the American conversation in more productive directions. Because of their training, scholars of religion could play a special role in bridging the conflicts in American society. In our polarized times, fewer Americans have regular contact with those who think differently from themselves. As Bill Bishop argues in *The Big Sort*, the clustering of Americans into ideologically homogeneous neighborhoods is pulling the country apart. While it is possible to exaggerate these conflicts, the battles between tea party activists and progressives suggest that Americans remain divided by culture and class.[104]

Such conflicts often rage on the border between science and religion. According to a 2005 survey, 42 percent of Americans can be classified as strict creationists. Suspicious of scientific expertise, many also question global warming. Given the threat of an ecological catastrophe, it is crucial that scientists talk to their fellow citizens. Sometimes this means speaking to religious audiences. Sociologist Elaine Howard Ecklund points to the need for scientific "boundary pioneers," figures who bridge the domains of religion and science. By increasing the number of bridge builders, the return of religious scholarship may end up lessening the antagonism between faith and science.[105]

In the United States, colleges and universities play a key role in professional education. If the professional project is about "the production of producers," the academy is at the center of law, medicine, and social work. In all of these occupations, practitioners must deal with the challenge of religious pluralism and the boundary between church and state. To the extent that professional schools can provide them with a basic knowledge of religion, they will be better prepared. As a recent Pew survey indicates, lawyers and doctors are not the only citizens lacking in religious literacy. Administered in 2010, it found that only half of Americans knew that Joseph Smith was a Mormon and that Ramadan is the Islamic holy month. In *Our Underachieving Colleges*, Derek Bok writes that "certain bodies of knowledge are essential to enlightened, responsible citizenship." Religion is one of those areas.[106]

The future of this civic conversation will depend on the conduct of the speakers. As this chapter has documented, the return of religious scholarship has been accomplished by a diverse group of faculty and administrators. Reflecting this diversity, they have been motivated by competing visions. Though sometimes overlapping, these visions are not always compatible. In such instances, it is a challenge to maintain the norms of civility and tolerance. Very often, greater contact leads to more conflict, not less. At the same time, we have little choice but to keep talking.

Whatever shape the conversation takes, it is not likely to disappear. In the final analysis, the continuing presence of faith in public life is the best sign that religious scholarship is here to stay. In an era when presidential candidates compete for religious voters, Islam powerfully shapes global politics, and patients turn to spirituality as a therapeutic balm, the influence of religion can no longer be ignored.

Notes

A shorter version of this chapter was published in John Schmalzbauer and Kathleen Mahoney, "American Scholars Return to Studying Religion," *Contexts*, Winter 2008, 16–21.

1. See Lawrence Veysey, *The Emergence of the American University* (Chicago: University of Chicago Press, 1965); Richard Hofstadter and Walter Metzger, *The Development of Academic Freedom in the United States* (New York: Columbia University Press, 1955); George M. Marsden, *The Soul of the American University: From Protestant Establishment to Established Nonbelief* (New York: Oxford University Press, 1994); Douglas Sloan, *Faith and Knowledge: Mainline Protestantism and American Higher Education* (Louisville, KY: Westminster John Knox Press, 1994); James T. Burtchaell, *The Dying of the Light: The Disengagement of Colleges and Universities from Their Christian Churches* (Grand Rapids, MI: Eerdmans, 1998).

2. See Douglas Jacobsen and Rhonda Hustedt Jacobsen, eds., *Scholarship & Christian Faith: Enlarging the Conversation* (New York: Oxford University Press, 2004). See also Mark Noll, "The Future of Religious Colleges: Looking Ahead by Looking Back," in *The Future of Religious Colleges*, ed. Paul Dovre (Grand Rapids, MI: Eerdmans, 2002), 73–94. The Martin Marty quotation comes from Marty's foreword to Jacobsen and Jacobsen, *Scholarship & Christian Faith*, vii.

3. Marsden, *The Soul of the American University*; Sloan, *Faith and Knowledge*; Julie Reuben, *The Making of the Modern University: Intellectual Transformation and the Marginalization of Morality* (Chicago: University of Chicago Press, 1996); Jon Roberts and James Turner, *The Sacred and the Secular University* (Princeton, NJ: Princeton University Press, 2000), 36.

4. Christian Smith, introduction to *The Secular Revolution: Power, Interests, and Conflict in the Secularization of American Public Life* (Berkeley, CA: University of California Press, 2003); Christian Smith, "Secularizing American Higher Education: The Case of Early American Sociology," in Christian Smith, *The Secular Revolution*, vii–159.

5. See Mark Clayton, "Scholars Get Religion," *Christian Science Monitor*, 26 February 2002, available at http://www.csmonitor.com/2002/0226/p12s01-lehl.html; Kathleen Mahoney, John Schmalzbauer, and James Youniss, "Religion: A Comeback on Campus," *Liberal Education*, Fall 2001, 36–41, available at http://www.aacu.org/liberaleducation/le-fa01/le-fa01feature.cfm. See also Alan Wolfe, "A Welcome Revival of Religion in the Academy," *Chronicle of Higher Education* 19 September 1997, B4. On the terms "post-secularism" and "post-secular," see Peter Steinfels, "Swapping 'Religion' for 'Postsecularism,'" *New York Times*, 3 August 2002; John A. McClure,

"Post-Secular Culture: The Return of Religion in Contemporary Theory and Literature," *CrossCurrents*, Fall 1997, 332–347.

6. Sally Promey, "The 'Return' of Religion in Scholarship on American Art," *The Art
Bulletin* 85:3(2003): 581–603; McClure, "Post-Secular Culture"; Quentin Smith, "The
Metaphilosophy of Naturalism," *Philo* 4:2(2001), available at www.philoonline.org/
library/smith_4_2.htm. See also Andreas Andreopoulos, "The Return of Religion in
Contemporary Music," *Literature and Theology* 14:1(2000): 81–95; Kenneth D. Wald,
Adam L. Silverman, and Kevin S. Fridy, "Making Sense of Religion in Political Life,"
Annual Review of Political Science, 8(2005): 121–143; D. W. Miller, "Programs in Social
Work Embrace the Teaching of Spirituality," *Chronicle of Higher Education*, 18 May
2001, A12; Katherine S. Mangan, "Medical Schools Begin Teaching Spiritual Side of
Health Care," *Chronicle of Higher Education*, 7 March 1997; Harry S. Stout and Rob-
ert M. Taylor, Jr., "Studies of Religion in American Society: The State of the Art," in
New Directions in American Religious History, ed. Harry S. Stout and D. G. Hart (New
York: Oxford University Press, 1997), 21, 15; Helen Rose Ebaugh, "Return of the Sacred:
Reintegrating Religion in the Social Sciences," *Journal for the Scientific Study of Religion*,
41:3(2002): 385–395. William Ringenberg estimates that there are about fifty Christian
scholarly associations in the United States in *The Christian College: A History of Protestant Higher Education in America* (Grand Rapids, MI: Baker Academic, 2006), 215.

7. In emphasizing the importance of activists, organizations, and networks in the desecularization of the academy, we follow the lead of Christian Smith, "Preface," introduction to Christian Smith, *The Secular Revolution*, vii.

8. Merrimon Cuninggim, *The College Seeks Religion* (New Haven, CT: Yale University
Press, 1947), 30, as quoted in Sloan, *Faith and Knowledge*, 35; Will Herberg, *Protestant,
Catholic, Jew: An Essay in American Religious Sociology* (New York: Doubleday, 1983), 53.

9. See D. G. Hart, *The University Gets Religion: Religious Studies in American Higher
Education* (Baltimore, MD: Johns Hopkins University Press, 1999). This paragraph
also relies on the analysis of Dorothy Bass in "Church-Related Colleges: Transmit-
ters of Denominational Cultures?" in *Beyond Establishment: Protestant Identity in
a Post-Protestant Age*, ed. Jackson Carroll and Wade Clark Roof (Louisville, KY:
Westminster John Knox Press, 1993), 157–172. See also Sloan, *Faith and Knowledge*;
Amanda Porterfield, *The Transformation of American Religion: The Story of a Late
Twentieth-Century Awakening* (New York: Oxford University Press, 2001); and William R. Hutchison, *Between the Times: The Travail of the Protestant Establishment in
America, 1900–1960* (New York: Cambridge University Press, 1989). Harvey Cox's *The
Secular City* (New York: Macmillan, 1965) helped define the "secular theology" of the
late 1960s.

10.   Sallie TeSelle, "Editorial," *Soundings* 51:1(1968): 2–3.

11.   Nancy T. Ammerman, "Sociology and the Study of Religion," in *Religion, Scholarship, and Higher Education: Perspectives, Models, and Future Prospects*, ed. Andrea Sterk (Notre Dame, IN: University of Notre Dame Press, 2002), 77, 78.

12.   See Conrad Cherry, *Hurrying toward Zion: Universities, Divinity Schools, and American Protestantism* (Bloomington, IN: Indiana University Press, 1995), 112–123. Porterfield discusses the "Post-Protestant" phase of religious studies in *The Transformation of American Religion*, 209–226. See also Hart, *The University Gets Religion*; Bass, "The Independent Sector and the Educational Strategies of Mainstream Protestantism."

13.   *American Academy of Religion Annual Report*, 2000 and 2007. The 2000 annual report was retrieved at http://www.aarweb.org/about/annualreport/AR2000.pdf. The 2007 report is available at http://www.aarweb.org/Publications/Annual_Report/default.asp.

14.   David V. Brewington, "AAR Undergraduate Departments Survey Comparative Analysis of Wave I and Wave II," *Religious Studies News*, May 2008, 14-15. Data on bachelor's degrees is from Lisa Miller, "Religious Studies Revival," *Newsweek*, 12 September 2010, available at http://education.newsweek.com/2010/09/12/religious-studies-thrive-in-troubled-times.html.

15.   See Hart, *The University Gets Religion*, for an account of the secularization of religious studies. The figures on religion courses come from Hillerbrand, "Going Our Way: The 2000 Suvery of Departments of Religion," *Religious Studies News*, March 2004, 6. On Hauerwas, see Jean Bethke Elshtain's profile, "Christian Contrarian," *Time*, 17 September 2001, retrieved from www.cnn.com/SPECIALS/2001/americasbest/TIME/society.culture/pro.shauerwas.html. On radical orthodoxy, see Jeff Sharlet, "Theologians Seek to Reclaim World with God and Postmodernism," *Chronicle of Higher Education*, 23 June 2000, A20; David S. Cunningham, "The New Orthodoxy?" *Christian Century*, 17–24 November 1999, 1127; John Milbank, *Theology and Social Theory* (London: Blackwell, 1993). On post-liberalism, see George Lindbeck, *The Nature of Doctrine* (Philadelphia: The Westminster Press, 1984).

16.   For overviews of these controversies, see Charlotte Allen, "Is Nothing Sacred? Casting Out the Gods from Religious Studies," *Lingua Franca*, November 1996, 30–40; Donald Wiebe, *The Politics of Religious Studies: The Continuing Conflict with Theology in the Academy* (New York: Palgrave Macmillan, 1999); the Cherry quotation comes from *Hurrying toward Zion*, 117.

17.   Rebecca Chopp, "Beyond the Founding Fratricidal Conflict: A Tale of Three Cities," *Journal of the American Academy of Religion* 70:3(2002): 461–474.

18.   The 2000 AAR panel "Coming Out as a Buddhist and Hindu in the Academy" is discussed in Jose Ignacio Cabezon, "The Discipline and Its Other: The

Dialectic of Alterity in the Study of Religion," *Journal of the American Academy of Religion* 74:1(2006): 21–38. For more discussions of insiders' approaches to Hinduism, see "Who Speaks for Hinduism?" in the December 2000 issue of the *Journal of the American Academy of Religion*.

19. Quotations and statistics are taken from Quentin Smith, "The Metaphilosophy of Naturalism," available at www.philoonline.org/library/smith_4_2.htm.

20. The estimate that Society of Christian Philosophers members make up 12 percent of the American philosophical profession is derived from Kelly James Clark's 1993 report, which states that the Society had more than 1,000 members, and the American Philosophical Association's "Selected Demographic Information on Philosophy Ph.D.'s, 1995," which reported 8,300 philosophy Ph.D.'s. The latter is available at http://www.apa.udel.edu/apa/profession/selected.html. Of course, not all the members of the Society of Christian Philosophers hold a Ph.D. in philosophy.

21. Alex Byrne, "God: Philosophers Weigh In," *Boston Review*, January–February 2009, available at http://bostonreview.net/BR34.1/byrne.php.

22. See John A. McClure, "Postmodern/Post-Secular: Contemporary Fiction and Spirituality," *Modern Fiction Studies* 41:1(1995): 141–163.

23. Edward Said, *The World, the Text, and the Critic* (Cambridge, MA: Harvard University Press, 1983), 291. For a discussion of Said's views on religion, see McClure, "Post-Secular Culture," 334–335.

24. McClure, "Post-Secular Culture," 334.

25. See the webpage of the Conference on Christianity and Literature (CCL) at http://www.pepperdine.edu/sponsored/ccl/. The CCL membership figure of 1,300 was taken from www.hope.edu/academic/english/huttar/conference.html. For an analysis of the situation of evangelicals and other Christians in contemporary literary studies, see Harold K. Bush, "The Outrageous Idea of a Christian Literary Studies: Prospects for the Future and a Meditation on Hope," *Christianity and Literature*, 51:1(2001): 79–103.

26. Robert B. Townsend, "Changing Patterns of Faculty Specialization since 1975," *Perspectives,* January 2007, available at www.historians.org/Perspectives/issues/2007/0701/0701new1.cfm; Robert B. Townsend, "AHA Membership Grows Modestly, as History of Religion Surpasses Culture," *AHA Today*, 30 June 2009, available at http://blog.historians.org/news/823/aha-membership-grows-modestly-as-history-of-religion-surpasses-culture. The account of this period is drawn from Stout and Taylor, "Studies of Religion in American Society," 15, 21; Henry May, "The Recovery of American Religious History," *American Historical Review* 70:1(1964): 79–92.

27. For a list of centers and institutes focused on North American religion, see *Centers and Institutes Project 2006* (Indianapolis, IN: Center for the Study of Religion and American Culture, 2006); this list is available at http://www.iupui.edu/~raac/CIP.html. On philanthropy and American religious history, see Michael S. Hamilton and Johanna G. Yngvason, "Patrons of the Evangelical Mind," *Christianity Today*, 8 July 2002, available at www.christianitytoday.com/ct/2002/008/3.42.html. See also Stout and Taylor, "Studies of Religion in American Society," 15, 22.

28. George Marsden, *Fundamentalism and American Culture: The Shaping of Twentieth-Century Evangelicalism, 1870–1925* (New York: Oxford University Press, 1981); Nathan Hatch, *The Democratization of American Christianity* (New Haven, CT: Yale University Press, 1989). The phrase "new evangelical historiography" was coined by Leonard Sweet in "Wise as Serpents, Innocent as Doves: The New Evangelical Historiography," *Journal of the American Academy of Religion* 56:3(1988): 397–416.

29. Jon Butler, "Born-Again America? A Critique of the New 'Evangelical Thesis' in Recent American Historiography," unpublished paper, Organization of American Historians, Spring 1991. Cited in Stout and Taylor, "Studies of Religion in American Society," 19.

30. See the profiles of the evangelical historians interviewed for John Schmalzbauer, *People of Faith: Religious Conviction in American Journalism and Higher Education* (Ithaca, NY: Cornell University Press, 2003).

31. The $14 million figure comes from Michael Paulson, "Evangelicals Find Place at Mainstream Colleges," *Boston Globe*, 20 February 2000, A1. On philanthropy and American religious history, see Michael S. Hamilton and Johanna G. Yngvason, "Patrons of the Evangelical Mind," *Christianity Today*, 8 July 2002, available at www.christianitytoday.com/ct/2002/008/3.42.html. See also Stout and Taylor, "Studies of Religion in American Society," 15, 22.

32. Daniel Bell, "The Return of the Sacred? The Argument on the Future of Religion," in *The Winding Passage: Essays and Sociological Journeys* (New York: Basic Books, 1980), 324–354. See also Fran Schumer, "A Return to Religion," *New York Times Magazine*, 15 April 1984, SM90.

33. Rodney Stark, "Secularization, R.I.P.," *Sociology of Religion* 60:3(1999): 249; Peter Berger, ed., *The Desecularization of the World: Resurgent Religion and World Politics* (Grand Rapids, MI: Eerdmans, 1999). Ebaugh, "Return of the Sacred," 385–395; Nancy T. Ammerman, "Sociology and the Study of Religion," in *Religion, Scholarship, and Higher Education: Perspectives, Models, and Future Prospects*, ed. Andrea Sterk (Notre Dame, IN: University of Notre Dame Press, 2002), 76–88; R. Stephen Warner, "Work in Progress toward a New Paradigm for the Sociological Study of Religion in the United States," *American Journal of Sociology* 98:5(1993): 1044–1093. See also Teresa

Watanabe, "The New Gospel of Academia," *Los Angeles Times*, 18 October 2000. The Spring–Summer 2006 issue of *The Hedgehog Review* was titled "After Secularism."

34. The membership counts of the American Sociological Association's sections can be found at www.asanet.org/sections/CountsLastFiveYears.cfm.

35. The Wald quotation comes from Wald, Silverman, and Fridy, "Making Sense of Religion in Political Life," 121. See also David Leege and Lyman Kellstedt, eds., *Rediscovering the Religious Factor in American Politics* (Armonk, NY: M. E. Sharpe, 1993). The October 2010 membership counts for the APSA's sections can be found at http://www.apsanet.org/sectioncounts.cfm . For more on the Religion and Democracy in the United States task force, see http://www.apsanet.org/section_684.cfm.

36. Robert A. Emmons and Raymond E. Paloutzian, "The Psychology of Religion," *Annual Review of Psychology* 54 (2003): 378–379.

37. The 2000 membership of Division 36 was retrieved from http://research.apa.org/2000membership5.pdf.

38. For the mission and 2001 membership data for the North American Association of Christians in Social Work, see www.nacsw.org/index.shtml and www.nacsw.org/StrategicPlan.htm. On the number of programs with religion courses, see Miller, "Programs in Social Work Embrace the Teaching of Spirituality," A12. On the Society for Spirituality and Social Work, see http://ssw.asu.edu/spirituality/sssw/.

39. On the increase in the number of medical schools with religion-oriented courses, see David G. Myers, "Stress and Health," in *Psychology* (New York: Worth Publishers, 2006). Myers reports that 105 out of 135 medical schools offer courses on spirituality or religion, available at http://www.davidmyers.org/Brix?pageID=52. Information on federal funding for research on alternative medicine (including spirituality and healing) can be found at the webpage of the National Center for Complementary and Alternative Medicine at http://nccam.nih.gov/.

40. Huston Smith, *Why Religion Matters: The Fate of the Human Spirit in an Age of Disbelief* (San Francisco: HarperSanFrancisco, 2001), 72, 73. See the webpage of the Dialogue on Science, Ethics, and Religion at http://www.aaas.org/spp/dser/index.shtml. On the Science and Religion Course Program, see the webpage of the Center for Theology and the Natural Sciences at http://www.ctns.org/news_090102.html

41. Dennis Cheek, "Interdisciplinary Dialogue and Issues in Religion," Metanexus Online, 22 June 2004, retrieved at http://www.metanexus.net/metanexus_online/show_article2.asp?id=8917.

42. Alexander Astin and Helen Astin, *Meaning and Spirituality in the Lives of College Faculty: A Study of Values, Authenticity, and Stress* (Los Angeles: Higher Education

Research Institute, 1999), 1, retrieved from www.fetzer.org/Resources/HERI%20
Fetzer%20Rpt%20w_color.pdf.

43. Kathleen A. Mahoney, John Schmalzbauer, and James Youniss, "Revitalizing
Religion in the Academy: Summary of the Evaluation of Lilly Endowment's Initiative on Religion & Higher Education" (Chestnut Hill, MA: Boston College,
2000), 10. The report is available at http://www.resourcingchristianity.org/Essay.
aspx?ESYID=33904ac8-644a-4139-926c-64fd9f4708d8.

44. See *Centers and Institutes Project 2006,* from the Center for the Study of Religion and
American Culture, Indiana University/Purdue University-Indianapolis, available at
http://www.iupui.edu/~raac/CIP.html.

45. For a list of the Pew Centers of Excellence, see http://web.archive.org/web
/20060220231717/http://www.pewtrusts.org/ideas/index.cfm?issue=17&misc_idea=2.

46. In many cases, Lilly Endowment and the John Templeton Foundation have provided
philanthropic support, illustrating the multiple funding streams available to religious
initiatives.

47. Stephen Prothero, *Religious Literacy: What Every American Should Know and
Doesn't* (San Francisco: HarperSanFrancisco, 2007). Prothero's 2007 appearance
on the *Daily Show* is available at http://www.comedycentral.com/videos/index.
jhtml?videoId=83952. A text of the *Wingspread Declaration on Religion and Public Life*
(including a list of signatories) is available at www.svhe.org/files/Declaration%20
on%20Religion%20and%20Public%20Life.pdf.

48. For an overview of these discussions, see Hent de Vries, ed., *Religion: Beyond a
Concept* (New York: Fordham University Press, 2008). See also Talal Asad, *Genealogies of Religion: Discipline and Reasons of Power in Christianity and Islam* (Baltimore, MD: Johns Hopkins University Press, 1993). Information on the *Journal of
the American Academy of Religion*'s call for papers was issued via the AAR's February
2009 *E-Bulletin,* sent to all members of the organization. For more information on
the 2007 Syracuse University conference, see the event's webpage at http://pcr.syr.
edu/2007/index.htm.

49. For examples of such confessional scholarship, see the individuals profiled in Schmalzbauer, *People of Faith.*

50. Marsden, *The Outrageous Idea of Christian Scholarship* (New York: Oxford University
Press, 1997); Alvin Plantinga, *God and Other Minds*; Nicholas Wolterstorff, *Reason
within the Bounds of Religion* (Grand Rapids, MI: Eerdmans, 1984).

51. For the mission and membership of the Lilly Seminar, see http://www.nd.edu
/~lillysem/. Alan Wolfe, "The Opening of the Evangelical Mind," *Atlantic Monthly,*
October 2000, 55–76; Wolfe, "A Welcome Revival of Religion in the Academy," B4.

52. "Who's Who: Higher Education's Senior Leadership," *Change*, January–February 1998. The *New York Times* quotation comes from the blurb on the back of Parker Palmer's *To Know as We Are Known: Education as Spiritual Journey* (San Francisco: HarperSanFrancisco, 1993).

53. Parker Palmer's *To Know as We Are Known* conceives of education as a form of "spiritual journey" and "spiritual formation." See also Palmer, *The Courage to Teach: Exploring the Inner Landscape of a Teacher's Life* (San Francisco: Jossey-Bass, 1997); Palmer, *A Hidden Wholeness: The Journey toward an Undivided Life* (San Francisco: Jossey-Bass, 2004).

54. Richard Hughes, *How Christian Faith Can Sustain the Life of the Mind* (Grand Rapids, MI: Eerdmans, 2001).

55. The figure of eight hundred attendees comes from the Education as Transformation Project webpage at http://www.wellesley.edu/RelLife/transformation/edu-ngoverview.html. See the webpage of the "Going Public with Spirituality in Work and Higher Education" conference at www.umass.edu/spiritual_conf/.

56. Diana Chapman Walsh, quoted in Peter Laurence, "Can Religion and Spirituality Find a Place in Higher Education?" *About Campus*, November–December 1999, available at http://www.wellesley.edu/RelLife/transformation/CanReligionand-Spirit.doc; Peter Laurence, "Education as Transformation: History of a Movement," *Spirituality in Higher Education Newsletter*, April 2004, 1, available at http://www.spirituality.ucla.edu/docs/newsletters/1/Laurence_Final.pdf.

57. Scott quoted Ali Crolius, "Unsequestered Spirits," *UMass Magazine Online*, Winter 2000, available at www.umass.edu/umassmag/archives/2000/winter2000/hl_spirits.html; Eric Goldscheider, "Religion Journal; Seeking a Role for Religion on Campus," *New York Times*, 2 February 2002, B6. See also the collection of essays at David Scott's webpage, http://www.umass.edu/pastchancellors/scott/papers/papers.html.

58. The Fall 2001 issue of *Liberal Education* focused on religion and higher education. It is available at www.aacu.org/liberaleducation/le-fa01/le-fa01contents.cfm. The January–February 2006 issue of *Academe* on religion can be found at http://www.aaup.org/AAUP/pubsres/academe/2006/JF/. See also the March–April 2006 issue of *Change*, "Religion in the Academy."

59. See the webpage for the "Spirituality and Learning: Redefining Meaning, Values, and Inclusion, in Higher Education" conference held 18–20 April 2002 in San Francisco at http://www.aacu.org/meetings/pdfs/S&LProgram.pdf.

60. "A Position Statement from The Initiative for Authenticity and Spirituality in Higher Education," *Character Clearinghouse*, 23 August 2002, retrieved from http://www.collegevalues.org/spirit.cfm?id=982&a=1.

61. See *The Spiritual Life of College Students: A National Study of College Students' Search for Meaning and Purpose* (Los Angeles: Higher Education Research Institute, UCLA, 2004). Information on the National Institute on Spirituality in Higher Education retrieved from www.spirituality.ucla.edu/national_institute/index.html.

62. This tripartite division of American religion can be found in Catherine L. Albanese, *A Republic of Mind and Spirit: A Cultural History of American Metaphysical Religion* (New Haven, CT: Yale University Press, 2007), 4.

63. See "Biography: Sir John Templeton," posted on the webpage of the Templeton Press at http://www.templetonpress.org/SirJohn/biography.asp.

64. See also the webpage of the NASPA-affiliated *Journal of College and Character* at http://journals.naspa.org/jcc/ and the Institute on College Student Values at http://www.collegevalues.org/Institute.cfm. See also Arthur Schwartz, "It's Not Too Late to Teach College Students about Values," *Chronicle of Higher Education*, 9 June 2000, A68. *The Templeton Guide: Colleges That Encourage Character Development* is available at http://www.collegeandcharacter.org/.

65. For a discussion of the "moral revival," see Alan Wolfe, "Moral Inquiry in Social Science," in *The Nature of Moral Inquiry in the Social Sciences: Occasional Papers of the Erasmus Institute* (Notre Dame, IN: Erasmus Institute, 1999), 1–20; Wolfe, "The Revival of Moral Inquiry in the Social Sciences," *Chronicle of Higher Education*, 3 September 1999, B4.

66. Charles Taylor, *Sources of the Self: The Making of the Modern Identity* (Cambridge, MA: Harvard University Press, 1989); Alasdair MacIntyre, *After Virtue: A Study in Moral Theory* (Notre Dame, IN: University of Notre Dame Press, 1984); Robert Bellah et al., *Habits of the Heart: Individualism and Commitment in American Life* (Berkeley, CA: University of California Press, 1985).

67. Robert Putnam, *Bowling Alone: The Collapse and Revival of American Community* (New York: Simon & Schuster, 2000); Robert Putnam and David Campbell, *American Grace: How Religion Unites and Divides Us* (New York: Simon & Schuster, 2010). For a list of participants in the Saguaro Seminar, see http://www.hks.harvard.edu/saguaro/participants.htm.

68. Robert McClory, "Campus Compact Urges Student Service," *National Catholic Reporter*, 6 October 1995, 13. For the Campus Compact mission and statistics, see www.compact.org; Jennifer Warren, "Students Venturing beyond Ivy Walls for Real Education," *Houston Chronicle*, 4 April 1993, A9.

69. Statistics on Catholic colleges from McClory, "Campus Compact Urges Student Service," 13; Gustav Niebuhr, "Colleges Setting Moral Compasses," *New York Times*, 4 August 1996, EL31.

70. Julie Reuben, "The University and Its Discontents," *Hedgehog Review* 2:(3)2000: 90.

71. Anne Colby et al., *Educating Citizens: Preparing America's Undergraduates for Lives of Moral and Civic Responsibility* (San Francisco: Jossey-Bass, 2003). The quote is from Anne Colby and Tom Ehrlich with Elizabeth Beaumont and Jason Stephens, "Undergraduate Education and the Development of Moral and Civic Responsibility," on the webpage of the Communitarian Network at http://www.gwu.edu/~ccps/Colby.html; Helen S. Astin and Anthony Lising Antonio, "The Impact of College on Character Devleopment," *New Directions for Institutional Research*, Summer 2004, 55–64.

72. Rebecca Chopp, "Living Lives of Integrity and Truth," *Journal of College and Character* 7:6(2006): 5.

73. On the appointment of Rashid I. Khalidi as Edward Said Professor of Arab Studies at Columbia, see Chris Hedges, "Public Lives: Casting Mideast Violence in Another Light," *New York Times*, 20 April 2004. On the establishment of an Israel Studies professorship at Columbia, see Liel Lebovitz, "Battle of the Chairs," *Moment Magazine*, February 2006. For more on the Institute for Israel and Jewish Studies, see http://www.iijs.columbia.edu/.

74. John S. Hawley, "Hinduism Here," in "Spotlight on Teaching," ed. Cynthia Humes, *Religious Studies News*, October 2006, iii, vii. See also the webpage for Hawley's Barnard course "Hinduism Here," which includes "challenges to the course" from the Infinity Foundation, available at http://www.barnard.columbia.edu/religion/hinduismhere/challenges.html.

75. Information on the programs was retrieved from www.fordfound.org/news/more/dialogues/index.cfm. The quotation is taken from the 31 March 2005 letter, retrieved at www.fordfound.org/news/more/dialogues/difficult_dialogues_letter.pdf. The current webpage of the Difficult Dialogues Program is http://www.difficultdialogues.org/.

76. See Matthew L. Kaplan, "Getting Religion in the Public Research University," *Academe*, July–August 2006, available at www.aaup.org/AAUP/pubsres/academe/2006/JA/feat/Kapl.htm. See also Janet R. Jakobsen, "Campus Religious Conflict Should Go Public," *Academe*, July–August 2006.

77. *Spirituality and the Professoriate: A National Study of Faculty Beliefs, Attitudes, and Values* (Los Angeles: Higher Education Research Institute, UCLA, 2006), 1. Available at http://www.spirituality.ucla.edu/docs/results/faculty/spirit_professoriate.pdf.

78. Ammerman, "Sociology and the Study of Religion," 79.

79. Neil Gross and Solon Simmons, "How Religious Are America's College and University Professors?" Social Science Research Council web forum "The Religious

Engagements of American Undergraduates," posted 6 February 2007, available at http://religion.ssrc.org/reforum/Gross_Simmons/; *Spirituality and the Professoriate*, 3, available at http://www.spirituality.ucla.edu/docs/results/faculty/spirit_professoriate.pdf. Data from the Ecklund study was reported in Elaine Howard Ecklund, "Religious Differences between Natural and Social Scientists: Preliminary Results from a Study of 'Religion among Academic Scientists (RAAS),'" paper presented at the Association for the Sociology of Religion annual meeting, August 2005. See also Elaine Howard Ecklund, *Science vs. Religion: What Scientists Really Think* (New York: Oxford University Press, 2010).

80. David Hollinger, "Enough Already: Universities Do Not Need More Christianity," in *Religion, Scholarship, and Higher Education: Perspectives, Models, and Future Prospects*, ed. Andrea Sterk (Notre Dame, IN: University of Notre Dame Press, 2002), 41, 49.

81. For a discussion of the need for Christian scholars to respect the "rules of the academic game," see George Marsden, *The Outrageous Idea of Christian Scholarship*, 44–58. See Thomas Gieryn, *Cultural Boundaries of Science: Credibility on the Line* (Chicago: University of Chicago Press, 1999), for more on how religion relates to the culturally constructed boundary between science and nonscience.

82. William Dembski, *Intelligent Design: The Bridge between Science and Theology* (Downers Grove, IL: InterVarsity Press, 1999), 121.

83. Ecklund, *Science vs. Religion*.

84. Lawrence Krauss, "An Article of Faith: Science and Religion Don't Mix," *Chronicle of Higher Education*, 26 November 1999, A88.

85. Richard Sloan's comments were reported in George Johnson, "A Free-for-All on Science and Religion," *New York Times*, 21 November 2006. See also Richard Sloan, *Blind Faith: The Unholy Alliance of Religion and Medicine* (New York: St. Martin's Press, 2006). On page 60, Sloan notes that "No single organization has been more responsible for the rising interest in religion and medicine than the John Templeton Foundation," noting that the "problem arises when the research supported by foundations is substandard."

86. Johnson, "A Free-for-All on Science and Religion." For more on the "Beyond Belief" conference, see the event's webpage at www.beyondbelief2006.org.

87. Marilynne Robinson, "Hysterical Scientism: The Ecstasy of Richard Dawkins," *Harper's*, November 2006, 86.

88. Terry Eagleton, "Lunging, Flailing, Mispunching," *London Review of Books*, 19 October 2006, available at http://www.lrb.co.uk/v28/n20/eaglo1.html.

89. David Van Biema, "God vs. Science," *Time*, 5 November 2006, available at http://www.time.com/time/magazine/article/0,9171,1555132,00.html. See also Francis

Collins, *The Language of God: A Scientist Presents Evidence for Belief* (New York: Free Press, 2006).

90. Ecklund, *Science vs. Religion*. On the appointment of Collins to lead the National Institutes of Health, see Gardiner Harris, "Pick to Lead Agency Draws Praise and Some Concern," *New York Times*, 8 July 2009, available at www.nytimes.com/2009/07/09/health/policy/09nih.html?scp=3&sq=NIH%20Collins&st=cse.

91. Robert Orsi, "Is the Study of Lived Religion Irrelevant to the World We Live in? Special Presidential Plenary Address, Society for the Scientific Study of Religion, Salt Lake City, November 2, 2002," *Journal for the Scientific Study of Religion*, 42:2(2003): 174. For a different view, see Stephen Prothero, "Belief Unbracketed: A Case for the Religion Scholar to Reveal More of Where She Is Coming From," *Harvard Divinity Bulletin*, 32:2(2004): 10–11, available at www.hds.harvard.edu/news/bulletin/articles/prothero.html.

92. Ray Hart, "Religious and Theological Studies in American Higher Education: A Pilot Study," *Journal of the American Academy of Religion* 59:4(1991): 715–827.

93. The study was conducted by Barbara Walvoord of the University of Notre Dame. The results were reported in Scott Jaschik, "The 'Great Divide' in Religious Studies," *InsideHigherEd*, 20 November 2006, available at http://www.insidehighered.com/news/2006/11/20/religion.

94. Conrad Cherry, Betty A. DeBerg, and Amanda Porterfield, *Religion on Campus* (Chapel Hill, NC: University of North Carolina Press, 2001).

95. *Spirituality and the Professoriate*, 9, available at http://www.spirituality.ucla.edu/docs/results/faculty/spirit_professoriate.pdf.

96. Peter Berger, "Ethics and the Present Class Struggle," *Worldview* 21(1978): 6–11; B. Bruce-Briggs, ed., *The New Class?* (New Brunswick, NJ: Transaction Books, 1979); Warner, "Work in Progress toward a New Paradigm for the Sociological Study of Religion in the United States," 1054; James Spickard, "What's Happening to Religion? Six Sociological Narratives," 2, available at http://www.ku.dk/satsning/religion/indhold/publikationer/working_papers/what_is_happened.pdf, and Spickard, "What Is Happening to Religion? Six Sociological Narratives," *Nordic Journal of Religion and Society* 19:1(2006): 13–29.

97. Diane Winston, "Campuses Are a Bellwether for Society's Religious Revival," *Chronicle of Higher Education*, 16 January 1998, A60; José Casanova, *Public Religions in the Modern World* (Chicago: University of Chicago Press, 1994), 5.

98. Charles L. Harper and Bryan F. LeBeau, "Social Change and Religion in America: Thinking Beyond Secularization," in *The American Religious Experience*, http://are.as.wvu.edu/sochange.htm.

99. Michael Lindsay, *Faith in the Halls of Power: How Evangelicals Joined the American Elite* (New York: Oxford University Press, 2007); Schmalzbauer, *People of Faith*.

100. Neil Gross and Solon Simmons, "How Religious Are America's College and University Professors?" unpublished study retrieved at www.wjh.harvard.edu/soc/faculty/gross/religions.pdf.

101. John Schmalzbauer, "Campus Ministry: A Statistical Portrait," SSRC Web Forum, available at http://religion.ssrc.org/reforum/Schmalzbauer.pdf. Data on Campus Crusade is available at http://campuscrusadeforchrist.com/about-us/facts-and-statistics. See also Jeremy Uecker, Mark Regnerus, and Margaret Vaaler, "Losing My Religion: The Social Sources of Religious Decline in Early Adulthood," *Social Forces* 85:4(2007): 1667–1692; *Spirituality and the Professoriate*, available at http://www.spirituality.ucla.edu/docs/results/faculty/spirit_professoriate.pdf.

102. *Spirituality and the Professoriate*, available at http://www.spirituality.ucla.edu/docs/results/faculty/spirit_professoriate.pdf.

103. Hollinger, "Enough Already," 49; Peggy Levitt, Courtney Bender, Wendy Cadge, and David Smilde, "Toward a New Sociology of Religion," *The Immanent Frame*, 2010, available at http://blogs.ssrc.org/tif/2010/02/15/new-sociology-of-religion/. David Hollinger's remarks appeared on *The Immanent Frame*'s forum "Religion and the Historical Profession," available at http://blogs.ssrc.org/tif/2009/12/30/religion-and-the-historical-profession/. See also Barbara Ehrenreich, *Bright-Sided: How Positive Thinking Is Undermining America* (New York: Picador, 2009); Wendy Kaminer, *The Rise of Irrationalism and Perils of Piety* (New York: Pantheon Books, 1999).

104. Bill Bishop, *The Big Sort: Why the Clustering of Like-Minded Americans Is Tearing Us Apart* (New York: Mariner Books, 2009); Mark Brewer and Jeffrey Stonecash, *Split: Class and Cultural Divides in American Politics* (Washington, DC: CQ Press, 2007).

105. Laurie Goodstein, "Teaching of Creationism Is Endorsed in New Survey," *New York Times*, 31 August 2005, available at http://www.nytimes.com/2005/08/31/national/31religion.html; Ecklund, *Science vs. Religion*, 46.

106. Magali Sarfatti Larson, *The Rise of Professionalism: Sociological Analysis* (Berkeley, CA: University of California Press, 1977), 74. The findings of the Pew Religious Knowledge Survey can be found at http://pewforum.org/Other-Beliefs-and-Practices/U-S-Religious-Knowledge-Survey.aspx. Derek Bok, *Our Underachieving Colleges* (Princeton, NJ: Princeton University Press, 2006), 181.

CHAPTER TEN

Jürgen Habermas and the Post-Secular Appropriation of Religion: A Sociological Critique

Michele Dillon

Jürgen Habermas is undoubtedly the leading social theorist currently alive. His body of work is probably more familiar to philosophers than sociologists, especially in the United States, where there is a long tradition of deep skepticism toward abstract theorizing. His writings, nonetheless, along with those of the late Pierre Bourdieu and Michel Foucault have provided a tremendous amount of intellectual energy to new generations of sociologists. In the Frankfurt School tradition of critical theory, Habermas has tackled major questions focusing on the nature of, and complications to, participatory democracy in an increasingly bureaucratic and consumer society in which the forces of capitalism typically push back against and triumph over the pull of democratic ideals.

Unlike his Frankfurt School predecessors, however, Habermas is committed not just to critiquing the overreach of rationality into all sectors of social life but to offering alternative visions of change. He suggests possibilities for forging a way out of excessive economic, political, and cultural domination, placing hope, in particular, in the possibility of a reinvigorated public sphere in which reasoned civil debate occurs. The emphasis on reason and rationality is pervasive throughout Habermas's writings. Much of his work is an attempt to reorient readers to think of reason not in the instrumental and strategic ways it has come to dominate modern consciousness, or even in terms of a values rationality per se, but rather as a means of argumentation, that is, the giving of reasons for and reasons against any given argument,[1] and thus to use reason to critique the status quo and move beyond its coercive forces to achieve a more argumentatively consensual and a more participatory democratic society.

In the contemporary context of globalizing capitalism, the crafting of an emancipatory agenda is clearly complicated by the multilayered strategic interests and power inequalities that characterize late modernity. But Habermas, at least, offers a vision of emancipatory social action, elaborated primarily in his two-volume *Theory of Communicative Action*.[2] Yet despite, or perhaps because of, his hope for and preoccupation with the possibility of a revitalized public sphere, his writings have given religion short shrift. It is only in recent years that he has formally acknowledged its cultural and practical relevance to contemporary society. In this chapter, I discuss the intellectual significance of Habermas's gesture toward religion and, while welcoming his religious turn, offer a sociological critique of his construal of religion and its implications for post-secular society. Specifically, I argue that Habermas's post-secular–religious turn underappreciates the contested nature of religious ideas, marginalizes the centrality of spirituality, emotion, and tradition to religion, and fails to recognize religion's intertwining with the secular. I argue that Habermas's inattentiveness to how religion manifests and matters in everyday life suggests he doesn't really take religion seriously and, therefore, imports it into the post-secular without taking account of the ways in which religion in all of its richness and complexity complicates his vision of the post-secular. I suggest that Habermas's post-secular–religious turn shows the lingering persistence of his highly cognitive and rational approach to social life and undermines the conceptual promise of a post-secular society for which religion may be an emancipatory resource.

Habermas engages with a wide range of philosophers and social theorists, and the voluminous breadth and depth of his theoretical framework defy easy summary. But his theory of communicative action provides a good sense of his intellectual thrust. Central to the theory of communicative action (TCA) is the claim that critically reasoned deliberation, and not any strategic interest or any appeal to emotion or tradition, is the mechanism that facilitates and propels social action. In the ideal speech situation at the core of Habermas's TCA,[3] social actors seek to reach a common understanding of the situation or question at issue and of plans for mutually agreed, future action.[4] In this idealistic communicative context, each participant uses language to raise validity claims about the propositional truth, normative rightness, and sincerity of statements made by the others.[5] The purpose of reciprocal deliberation is to find, through the use of reasoned back-and-forth argumentation, a reasoned consensus that in turn becomes the basis for action. Communicative action is thus a cooperative process of reasoned interpretive negotiation in which, importantly, "no participant has a monopoly on correct interpretation."[6] It is not who is speaking that matters and whether he or she has high economic, social, political, or cultural status. Rather, it is the soundness of the reasons offered in the particular discussion context, and whether those reasons in and of themselves are strong enough to convince the participants of the reasonableness and validity of the claims being posited.[7]

Habermas's vision of communicative action presents as a highly appealing scenario. It is an especially refreshing idea amid the unilateral and declaratory rhetoric that has come to dominate both public culture and parliamentary debates in recent decades. Nevertheless, it has been criticized on a number of grounds. Most particularly, feminist scholars criticize its marginalization of the power inequalities in social interaction and the different interests, sensibilities, experiences, and language capabilities that individuals necessarily have, bring to, and seek validation of in any communicative context.[8]

Thus while I endorse Habermas's vision of communicative partners engaging in nonstrategic action and cooperatively seeking the truth, I too am concerned that the cognitivist-rational ethos at the core of communicative action ultimately gives short shrift to all those nonrational but highly significant sources of action and meaning in everyday life, all those things that spring from emotion and tradition. In particular, as a sociologist of religion and culture, and as an admirer of Habermas, I have long been concerned that Habermas's TCA sees religion, essentially, as irrelevant to the revitalization of a democratically engaged public sphere. His criteria for communicative action make this so. Since religion comprises strong elements of emotion and tradition, and additionally includes claims about redemption and salvation that cannot be rationally validated, religious discourse as a communicative resource is, for Habermas, not only problematic but highly constricted; religious discourse is "limited in the degree of its freedom of communication."[9]

But even apart from the specifics of the ideal speech situation, religion as a public cultural resource is problematic for Habermas. His embrace of a progressive, evolutionary schema of societal development entails acceptance of the wholesale loss of religious authority. As modern society becomes rationally differentiated, the religious sphere of influence shrinks and gets confined to the nonrational domains of life;[10] by extension, the "authority of the holy is gradually replaced by the authority of an achieved consensus."[11] In short, Habermas posits a polarization between religion and reason or rationality, rather than considering the possibility that religion and reason can coexist and be mutually influential in private and public domains. Just because religious faith (like cultural taste) cannot be rationally defended, this does not mean that all aspects of a religious tradition are closed to reason. Habermas, however, tends to treat religion as a monolithic and reified phenomenon and in doing so does not acknowledge the multiplicity of strands and discourses that are characteristic of both premodern and post-Enlightenment religions. He ignores the place of reason in the various world religions and overlooks how transformations in religion and theology have brought "the critical principles of Enlightenment into religion itself and into theological reflection."[12]

Habermas's conceptual polarization of religion and reason obscures the historically ongoing hermeneutic and interpretive activity involved in understanding revelation and how, as part of this process, diverse religious traditions are open to reasoned self-criticism. In turn, that self-criticism can be used by religious institutions to reorient how they conceptualize the public sphere (e.g., affirming the autonomous relation between civil law and religious morality), their role within the public sphere (as a public non-creedal, moral voice), and, importantly too, to reframe their theology to present policy arguments on moral issues (e.g., abortion)[13] that fit with the argumentative expectations and constraints of the secular public domain. In the modern era, the Catholic Church's Second Vatican Council (1962–1965) and its subsequent elaboration of a public Catholicism are illustrative of religious institutional self-reflexivity and of the convergence of religion and reason.[14]

Habermas is not alone among scholars in positing the illegitimacy of "the authority of the holy" in the public sphere,[15] and whether, when, and how religious ideas can reasonably enter public debate are valid and much debated questions among philosophers and constitutional scholars.[16] From a sociological rather than a political philosophical perspective, however, it is nonetheless surprising that Habermas, someone who has long been engaged in dialogue with theologians,[17] remained so aloof for so long from conceding the possible value of religious discourse to political culture and action. One would have expected him to be interested in the progressive theological writings of his fellow Europeans, such as Jacques Maritain, who elaborated an eloquent model of religious and political differentiation that accommodates rather than excludes religious discourse.

Moreover, as someone specifically interested in discourse, law, and democracy,[18] he would have benefited from sociological sensitivity to the practical ways in which religious institutions and organizations reframe their respective theologies in order to more fully engage in public discourse about law and morality. Since the early 1970s, the U.S. Catholic bishops, for example, have a long record of using secular reasoning and American cultural themes in elaborating their stance on abortion,[19] and their influential, politically liberal statements in the 1980s on nuclear war and economic justice also relied heavily on secular moral arguments. These issues were all extensively debated by American publics in the 1980s, a time when Habermas was a frequent visitor to the United States. The church has similarly engaged in various public moral debates in several European countries since the 1970s; even in heavily Catholic Ireland, the bishops notably grounded their opposition to divorce not in Catholic doctrine but in secular social scientific arguments about its negative economic and social effects.[20]

The Catholic Church, of course, is wedded to particular religious norms and moral viewpoints and is unlikely to change its opposition to abortion or divorce. Therefore, the participation of the Church in public discourse about these issues does not approximate the high bar of sincere openness to the potentially better-reasoned argumentative claims of other debate participants as is required of communicative action.[21] Nevertheless, the content of the bishops' arguments, the diverse fora in which they present them (e.g., in the United States, in Congressional testimony, Supreme Court briefs, general statements addressed to the public at large), and their civil and reasoned style of presentation must surely be seen as evidence of the translation of religious values into a culturally accessible and reasoned public discourse. Yet time and again, even when Habermas nodded to the enduring pull of religious influences, given, as he noted, the Enlightenment's inability "to quieten or to dry up the need for consolation,"[22] he held steadfastly to his core viewpoint that religious language eludes "expression in philosophical language and await[s] translation into justificatory discourses."[23] In sum, until the dawn of the twenty-first century, Habermas discounted the rationality and emancipatory potential of religious discourse and avoided considering how a religious discourse, notwithstanding its—of necessity—limited rationality, might nonetheless contribute to a rational critique of society.

Enter the Post-Secular

It was, then, a stirring sight to see Habermas sit down with Cardinal Ratzinger in 2004 for a philosophical dialogue. It is hard not to miss a breath at the image of both men in conversation, one the arch-defender of reason and rationality, described by Habermasian scholar Thomas McCarthy as the "last great rationalist,"[24] and the other, renowned as Prefect of the Congregation for the Doctrine of the Faith (and subsequently as Pope Benedict XVI), for his steadfast theological defense of Catholic tradition and moral teaching. At the same time, the twinning of the two Germans made for a fitting tableau: through their long careers, both have shown little interest in sociological realities and have remained intellectually aloof from lived experience.

It was, in any case, an interesting conversation. Among other points, Habermas noted that the Enlightenment project of modernization had gone somewhat awry, has become derailed.[25] In particular, as he had previously elaborated,[26] he noted that globalizing economic markets defy the control of consensual rational judgments, and he lamented not only the extent of global socioeconomic inequality but the mass political indifference toward it.[27] This indifference is part of a longer depoliticization process resulting from modernization and increased affluence and consumerism, highlighted by Habermas decades earlier.[28] For Habermas, the threat posed by current globalizing forces to potentially "degrade the capacity for democratic self-steering," both within and across nations,[29] makes the need for public communicative reasoning all the more necessary. He thus looks to discover new (i.e., underappreciated) political cultural resources for the democratic revitalization project. Hence, "a contrite modernity," one characterized by several social pathologies that need fixing, may benefit, Habermas argued, from religious-derived norms and ethical intuitions. He conceded that these religious resources can help human society deal with "a miscarried life, social pathologies, the failures of individual life projects, and the deformation of misarranged existential relationships."[30]

Many sociologists have elaborated on the perils of globalization and the increased polarization between classes and regions as the profit logic of capitalist markets inexorably trumps normative considerations.[31] Yet only Habermas looks to the religious domain rather than pushing for attentiveness to a rearticulated political ideology of, for example, global social democracy,[32] as a way of reorienting societal thinking about modern socioeconomic pathologies. In his view, "The translation of the likeness of the human to the image of the divine into the equal and absolutely respected dignity of all human beings"[33] offers a way of using religious values to reorient society's values toward principles of economic and social justice.[34] Clearly, Habermas's new affirmation of the relevance that religious ideas and ethics have for contemporary political debate marks a major transformation in his thinking. I very much welcome this more inclusive view of religion as a potentially emancipatory political and cultural resource, a resource that can open up and enhance rather than retard public discourse, and energize the creation of more deliberative and more participative social institutions.

Habermas's view of religion's potential as a remedial cultural resource for contemporary societal ills is shared by many religious leaders. For example, more than one hundred diverse religious leaders meeting in Rome in June 2009 ahead of the G8 summit collectively affirmed the urgent need for political leaders to recognize the relevance that religious ideas and moral values have in shaping the social fabric. They strongly emphasized that economic and political decisions, devoid of awareness of their moral consequences, cannot serve the common good. These themes are further elaborated in Pope Benedict's encyclical *Caritas in Veritate* (Charity in Truth) and are in line with a long tradition of Catholic social teaching originating in the late nineteenth century, through which Catholic leaders, drawing on natural law reasoning, have cautioned against industrial policies that marginalize workers and ignore the needs of the economically downtrodden.[35]

Habermas's new regard for religion, articulated across several venues since 2001, leads him to embrace the term "post-secular society" in order to demarcate the current moment. He is not the only one to use this language, and there has been a tremendous amount of hairsplitting over what exactly the term means and how it is related to the secular, secularization, secularism, secularistic, and post-secularism.[36] The gain in popularity of post-secular terminology comes in the wake of the postmodern, the postcolonial, and the post-national. Many scholars would concur that there really is something qualitatively different about the post-1970s era, enough to warrant a new term that differentiates the modern era (roughly defined as the period encompassing 1770–1970) from the postmodern. As David Harvey has argued, "There has been a sea-change in cultural as well as in political-economic practices since around 1972. This sea-change is bound up with the emergence of new dominant ways in which we experience space and time"[37] and has produced what he refers to as "the condition of postmodernity." Similarly, the post-national captures the changing legal and political status of the nation-state in the context of the rise of transnational or supranational entities (e.g., the European Union), and the postcolonial offers a dynamic way of rethinking the cultural agency, transformative identities, and differentiated histories of previously colonized peoples.[38]

It is not compellingly evident that the term "post-secular" is newly warranted. After all, sociologists still have a hard time conceptualizing and especially measuring secularization, something that is surely related to the secular. By extension, it is challenging to assess whether or not secularization has in fact occurred given that there is so much differentiated evidence for and against its sociological reality; even the most secular societies, such as the United Kingdom, still have, for example, public rituals affirming the symbolic and cultural influence of religion on government. If we are unsure about the secular, it may be intellectually premature to talk about the post-secular (although it is certainly a stimulating way to change the conversation).

Yet it makes sense for Habermas—as Habermas, and with his Habermasian worldview—to construe a post-secular society. His understanding of progressive societal evolution and his deep intellectual commitment to the triumph of reasoned argumentation—to communicative action rather than strategic action—suggest that he has long construed the West as essentially secular since the Enlightenment. But now that, as he states, the Enlightenment project has been partially derailed and reason subsumed by strategic market interests and political indifference, it is appropriate for him to rethink the secular. Hence, in my reading of Habermas, the post-secular provides him with a useful analytical device for acknowledging not so much the persistence of religion as the partial failure (derailing) of the Enlightenment, a failure that by default brings religion back and into the secular. The post-secular denotes that the secular, like the Enlightenment, fell short of its originally intended destination. It is not that secularization has not occurred; it is just that there are some complications that the persistence of religion has thrown on its tracks. Overall, Habermas is clear that, despite his recognition of religion's continuing relevance, "the data collected globally still provide surprisingly robust support for the defenders of the secularization thesis."[39]

There is some ambiguity in Habermas's use of post-secular language. He argues that the term "post-secular society" applies only to those affluent societies "where people's religious ties have steadily or rather quite dramatically lapsed" since the mid-twentieth century. In this designation, he includes European countries and Canada, Australia, and New Zealand. Yet Habermas also argues (in the same passage) that even in Europe, "sociological indicators . . . of [the] religious behavior and convictions of the local populations" have not changed so dramatically as to "justify labeling these societies post-secular" despite their trends toward deinstitutionalized religion.[40] The confusion with Habermas's definition emerges because while he talks about "post-secular society," it seems he really intends to talk about a post-secular Zeitgeist, "a change in consciousness."[41] Thus, he subsequently clarifies, "Today, public consciousness in Europe can be described in terms of a post-secular society to the extent that at present it still has to adjust itself to the continued existence of religious communities in an increasingly secularized environment."[42] Driving this post-secular consciousness, Habermas argues, is the resurgence of religion in Europe, evidenced by the increased participation of churches in public policy debates in some "secular societies" and the increased visibility of religion in local immigrant communities (principally Muslim) as well as religion's increased global presence, especially manifested through various fundamentalist movements.[43] In short, for Habermas, the term "post-secular" can be applied to *secularized* societies in which "religion maintains a public influence and relevance, while the secularistic certainty that religion will disappear worldwide in the course of modernization is losing ground."[44]

Because the "post-secular" recognizes the public relevance of religion and of religious ideas in informing civic discourse, I would argue that it is applicable to the United States, notwithstanding differences in U.S. secularism compared to that of Europe or Canada. Although religion has maintained a relatively steady and exceptionally strong hold for Americans, churchgoing Americans typically show a highly autonomous (virtually secular) attitude toward religious obligations and church teachings and, like their affluent peers in Europe and Canada, for example, presume to live in a secular society. Thus, while their religious ties have not necessarily lapsed, they make their own choices about how and when to be religious; their religious beliefs and practices are determined largely by their own authority (acting as modern, self-oriented individuals) than by the coercive power of an external religious authority. Moreover, the United States is secular in that it is a constitutional republic with a strict separation of church and state, and public consciousness of this separation dominates legal opinion and legislative and policy debates notwithstanding the visibility of religion in politics and public culture. In my view, the term "post-secular" is more theoretically robust if we can use it to help us understand the more general relevance of religion as a public cultural resource in all modern democratic societies regardless of their varying degrees or levels of secularism and secularization.

Post-Secular Obligations, Tensions, and Complications

Habermas, of course, is not one to self-present as a sociological observer. Therefore, he is ultimately less interested in the criteria for differentiating between what is and what is not a post-secular society than in the normative questions the post-secular poses to societal participants and institutions.[45] Anchoring the normative question for Habermas is his long-standing intellectual preoccupation with the crafting of a public discourse that achieves civility amid a plurality of cultural and, now too, religious worldviews. He argues that post-secular society is not only characterized by but requires a changed consciousness of the relevance of religion in society. Notwithstanding his own previous disregard of religion,[46] he now criticizes what he calls the Enlightenment fundamentalist perspective for devaluing religion as an inferior intellectual formation.[47] He argues instead that political and cultural pluralism requires acceptance of the legitimate public intervention of religious groups and organizations in civic debates, on abortion, stem cell research, immigration, climate change, and the like.

Post-secular society requires acknowledgment of the persistence of religion, but it also pushes religion to occupy a highly rational space. In particular, the post-secular imposes highly constraining obligations on religious individuals. It requires them to be reflexively self-conscious of their own beliefs. This means, in part, that when "religious citizens," as Habermas calls them, participate in public debate, they must necessarily do so by translating their religious norms into a secular idiom.[48] Post-secular society thus still privileges rational as opposed to faith-based argumentation, and it privileges an understanding of citizenship that is stripped of any manifest religious influence. Habermas imposes a heavy burden on religious individuals: they have to discard the specifically religious vocabulary that penetrates their experiences, worldviews, and everyday language, and they have to be self-reflexive in the process. It thus seems as if religious individuals enter the public sphere as second-class citizens; their communicative competence as citizens is diluted by their religious background experiences, assumptions, and vocabularies. Habermas emphasizes that "secular citizens in civil society . . . must be able to meet their fellow religious citizens as equals."[49] They are, nonetheless, less burdened: Secular citizens are required only to acknowledge the persistence of religion and the rights of religious citizens to hold religiously informed, but secularly translated, views and to not discount a fortiori religious utterances;[50] their reasoned communicative competence is not in doubt.

Nonetheless, in a remarkable conciliatory gesture toward religion, Habermas acknowledges that "the persons who are neither willing nor able to divide their moral convictions and their vocabulary into profane and religious strands must be permitted to take part in political will formation even if they use religious language."[51] How this religious language will be received or interpreted by "secular citizens" and whether the unexamined background assumptions secular citizens may hold about religion will distort the post-secular dialogical and will-formation processes are questions unaddressed by Habermas. Yet this concession to religious language, given his prior emphasis on its limited communicative rationality, clearly marks a major departure for Habermas. It is also a major blow against the highly secularistic understanding of civic life that has been so insistently present in some intellectual circles.

I very much welcome Habermas's newly accommodating stance toward religion. There are tensions, nonetheless, in his appropriation of religion. For example, while Habermas affirms the post-secular relevance of religious ideas, there is ambiguity regarding which religious ideas should be privileged in orienting post-secular consciousness and deliberation. The boundaries demarcating what counts as a religious idea are less distinct and the content comprising particular religio-moral ideas are more differentiated than Habermas acknowledges. Because religions are living traditions, their doctrines and ideas are highly differentiated and nuanced, and they shift and evolve over time. Related to this dynamic evolution, the meanings attached to any particular religious tradition are not always straightforward or unambiguous. As the renowned Catholic theologian David Tracy argues, "An insistence on the plurality of ways within every great religion is an ethical and religious responsibility."[52]

Some specific religious beliefs can certainly be translated into a broadly understood secular discourse; it is relatively easy, for example, to translate the religious idea of divinely created human life into a secular claim regarding the dignity of the individual and human rights. Nonetheless, the implications of this and of any other religious idea (e.g., the Catholic thesis of a "consistent ethic of life") for social and political action are highly contested even among people who share a broadly similar religious identity.[53] While we can think of religious groups or denominations as interpretive communities, considerations other than cool rationality alone typically influence the selectivity by which some ideas are given a particular practical interpretation or greater interpretive force than others. Religious ideas, similar to nonreligious ideas, develop in, and out of, particular historical, social, cultural, political, and institutional contexts, and hence they are not as pure as some might like to presume; the theological histories of, for example, usury and divorce,[54] abortion,[55] and women's ordination[56] in the Catholic Church are cases in point. The sociohistorical encrustations that any religious tradition invariably carries mean that the appropriation of religion into civic discourse is not a straightforward matter of simply retrieving from some historical vault a set of rationally pure principles, arguments, or interpretations whose meanings and action outcomes are pre-given, unambiguous, and uncontested.

Aside from the discursive ambiguities posed by the differentiated and contested nature of religious ideas, a second tension emerges from Habermas's narrow conceptualization of religion. He construes religion primarily in cognitivist terms—as ideas and ethical knowledge claims, and ones that can be translated into secular argumentation. Religion, however, is not just about ideas and cognitive sense. It is also about emotion and tradition, and these matter at both the micro- and the macro-level. For many individuals, religion is primarily about the spiritual aspects of life and how emotion, mystery, and the sacred intertwine with embodied everyday lived experiences.[57] Yet emotionally embodied experiences and traditions, and how they matter to individuals, often defy rational translation. This is not because religious or spiritual individuals lack reflexive consciousness; quite the contrary, many exemplify a high degree of self-reflexivity.[58] The tension stems, rather, from the fact that the visceral emotion many attach to religion or spirituality inhibits the translation of feelings and experiences into a rationally coherent secular idiom.

In a nod to the spiritual dimensions of religion, Habermas intimates that "faith in a higher or cosmic power" acts as a buffer against hopelessness, "uncontrolled contingencies," and existential despair.[59] This, by and large, is empirically true. It is also the case, however, that there are different ways of construing, interpreting, and using faith, even in largely similar religious-cultural contexts such as the United States, and these differences reflect, and have varied consequences for, how religious and spiritual individuals live their lives. For example, whereas church-centered religious individuals are more likely to use religious resources as a way of re-equilibrating their feelings of life satisfaction in response to despair, individuals who favor deinstitutionalized spiritual practices are more likely to see adversity as an opportunity for personal and spiritual growth.[60] In any event, it is uncertain whether religious or spiritual responses to existential despair enhance the reflexivity of citizen engagement and more deliberative democratic participation.

Religion also has emotional salience at the macro-level. Typically, religion serves as a cultural anchor orienting the emotionally charged community of memory[61] that underpins a community's or a society's collective identity. These memories and the habits and traditions they embody shape individuals' and groups' sensibilities toward religion as well as toward particular social and political issues. The diverse meanings attached to religion, however, whether as faith, spirituality, or culture, and their broader possible relevance in illuminating religion's significance as a resource in dealing with the pathologies of modernity, do not always compose a standpoint that is accessible to others who have not had similar experiences and traditions or who do not share the same interpretive repertoire.

Yet Habermas's post-secular society requires participants to genuinely appreciate beliefs and ways of life that they themselves reject and to talk with, rather than against or independent of, those with whom they disagree. For him, tolerance means that "believers of one faith, of a different faith and non-believers must mutually concede one another the right to those convictions, practices, and ways of living that they themselves reject."[62] The Canadian philosopher Charles Taylor[63] advocates a similar approach. He argues that ours is a *secular* age— that is, we are living in a time in which religious belief is one among many options and possibilities, though the default position is one, he argues, of unbelief; "the presumption of unbelief . . . has become dominant" in several different milieus and "hegemonic in the academic and intellectual life."[64] Nevertheless, the reality of many options, of many belief positions, means, Taylor argues, that "We all learn to navigate between two standpoints: an 'engaged' one in which we live the best we can the reality our standpoint opens us to; and a 'disengaged' one in which we are able to see ourselves as occupying one standpoint among a range of possible ones, with which we have in various ways to coexist."[65]

While I fully endorse Habermas's and Taylor's normative commitment to a civil society in which active tolerance of religious and cultural differences is realized in practice, this ideal is burdened by substantial challenges. Independent of whether individuals and groups are or are not religious, an engaged tolerance of difference does not come easily. Most of us are too embroiled in our own everyday reality and the immediacy of its here-and-now demands to be able to fully recognize our reality as one of many possible realities.[66] Many of us realize we have to coexist with others and that some others are not like us because intersecting differences in religion, race, gender, social class, sexuality, and so on, mark everyday experiences, worldviews, and language use. But this coexistence, in any case, mostly requires our passive acceptance of pluralism rather than a reflexive engagement toward our own particular standpoint.[67] Moreover, the normalcy of our own particular views is typically reinforced by the commonsense and professional norms of the circles in which we move[68] and by the iconic cultural symbols that reaffirm our group and community attachments.[69]

These everyday sociological constraints do not mean it is impossible to maintain the double register required of post-secular communication; some people are able to reflexively engage and disengage simultaneously across different standpoints. This is exemplified perhaps in sociology by Robert Bellah,[70] who self-presents as a "Christian sociologist," and beyond social science, by Francis Collins, an avowed evangelical and distinguished biologist who is currently the director of the U.S. National Institutes of Health (NIH). Nevertheless, as evident in the range of public comment on Collins's appointment to the NIH,[71] maintaining the public legitimacy of different identities simultaneously is not without tensions. Because of the communicative tensions that arise from acknowledging different realities simultaneously, individuals and groups tend to choose, especially in public debates, polarizing stances on emotionally charged contested issues. We know from the ongoing abortion debate in the United States, for example, one now further complicated by the possibilities offered by reproductive genetic technologies,[72] that it is not always possible for well-intentioned and reasonable people to fully engage with one another's points of view despite some shared adherence to salient values. Thus, the relation between beliefs and openness to alternative beliefs and competing explanations is more complicated than Habermas and Taylor fully acknowledge.

Religion clearly adds an extra layer of intensity to the challenge confronted in bridging differences. While it may be indicative of a post-secular sensibility that large proportions of churchgoing Americans tell pollsters that there are many pathways to truth,[73] we do not see this tolerance fully translated into political debates and policy outcomes on abortion, assisted suicide, gay marriage, and immigration rights, among other pressing issues. We should also note that despite the American ethos of religious pluralism, there are substantial numbers of "exclusive Christians" who have a very singular understanding of truth and of what that truth can tolerate.[74] The controversy surrounding the building of an Islamic cultural center in New York City, near the site of the Twin Towers destroyed by terrorists on September 11, 2001, and its ripple effects in fostering anti-Muslim feelings in communities and workplaces across the United States[75] underscore the raw emotional ways in which various truths get entangled in contested symbols and in the contested meanings of particular symbols and values (e.g., religious freedom). These entanglements contribute to derailing the possibility of reasoned communication about the validity of the truths at issue.

Similarly, across Europe, where one might expect a secular republican culture to welcome the freedom of expression of different standpoints, this is not so. Take, for instance, the local activism against the building of mosques. With the rise in the number of mosques in England, sites designated for new mosques literally become contested sites. Their symbolism threatens English notions of authentic Englishness, such that locals express "unease at minarets competing in the urban landscape with the spires and stones of centuries-old cathedrals."[76] Relatedly, the European parliamentary election in June 2009 saw a rise in the fortunes of the far-right British National Party, a party that, among other ethnocentric policies, opposes the "creeping Islamification" of Britain.[77]

We see similar instances of anti-Muslim activism in Germany. Germany has more than three million Muslims, and recent years have seen an expansion in mosque building there too: there are approximately 150 mosques in the country and around two thousand prayer rooms in old warehouses and other industrial spaces. Many Germans don't seem to mind working alongside Muslims, but they see the building of mosques as a clear cultural threat. In Bavaria, for example, the most religious and conservative state in Germany, residents in one working-class community organized a petition against the legality of a proposed mosque, declaring that its presence was a threat to

Bavarian life. The petition stated: "Bavarian life is marked by the drinking of beer and the eating of pork. In Muslim faith, both are unclean and forbidden."[78] Similarly, while French authorities oppose the *hijab* on the grounds that it is contrary to French values and their ideals of women's dignity,[79] it is surely also—and maybe even especially—because the image of a *hijab*-wearing woman walking down a French street is a visceral offense to subjectively collective French feelings about what is normal and what it means to be French. In short, in particular sociocultural contexts, religious attachments are more likely to stimulate emotion rather than communicative rationality, a point underscored by the fact that Islamic symbols have become sources of passionate debate even in Switzerland and Denmark, countries more typically associated with cool rationality than emotion.

Therefore, we can, in principle, accept the possibility that reasoned communication about and across religious and cultural differences is the only rational way to deal with difference. This principle is undermined, however, by the collective emotions that surround and penetrate attachment to and perceptions of particular convictions and ways of life. It is hard to engage in reasoned argument with individuals, groups, and whole societies for whom religious and cultural difference constitutes an emotional issue of individual and collective identity rather than, as for Habermas, an abstract cognitive issue to be determined by rational argumentation. The examples noted here point to the challenge encountered in "allowing for the expression of differences in public space,"[80] a key component identified by Bouchard and Taylor[81] as necessary to the accommodation of cultural differences in secular society. One might have thought that in a secular or post-secular age, secular or post-secular consciousness would not be threatened by either the increased visibility of Islamic faith or by, as is also the case in Europe, the formal acknowledgment of the historical legacy of Christian faith in the European Union's constitution. If the symbolism of religion and of religious difference is so threatening, success with the post-secular task of reasoned deliberative engagement across these differences seems far off.

It may well be that Habermas introduces the post-secular as a way forward from the cultural divisiveness of religion. But religion impedes the full realization of the post-secular, mutually reasoned communication he envisages because both as an individual spiritual identity and as a political-cultural phenomenon it tends to encompass a good deal of emotion. The emotional dimensions of religion and their intertwining with spirituality and tradition thus call into question the conceptual viability of the post-secular. Dialogue across differences is never easy. We can welcome and make much of the recent Habermas-Ratzinger intellectual exchange on the possibilities for the bridging of religious and secular claims. Nonetheless, the basic impediment to both religious-secular and inter-religious discourse is such that, as Ratzinger (Pope Benedict) himself recently noted, "In theological terms, a true dialogue is not possible without putting one's faith in parentheses."[82]

Therefore, while Benedict and other religious leaders, as well as scholars such as Habermas, emphasize the full importance of reaching a better cultural understanding of religious ideas and their societal implications, these conversations will invariably be hampered by underlying faith differences that cannot be compartmentalized in the name of rationality. These differences cannot simply be sequestered as if they are epiphenomena; different beliefs, rather, as Max Weber elaborated, produce different worldviews and make some courses of action appear more reasonable than others. In sum, the idea that religious believers and secularists "can live together in a self-reflective manner," as Habermas envisages,[83] is attractive but hard to imagine. It is not the living together but the reflexive self-reflection—and the new political and cultural outcomes that it might envision—that are more elusive.

Religious Citizens and Secular Citizens

Another tension with the post-secular appropriation of religion is that although Habermas expresses conciliatory recognition of the cultural value of religion, it seems he does not fully apprehend how religion—even at its most rational—matters or gets worked out in everyday life. Although individuals for the most part are well able to differentiate their religious and their non-religious habits and vocabularies, they do not necessarily think of themselves either as *secular citizens* or as *religious citizens*. Yet Habermas[84] as well as some other philosophers[85] use these terms—"secular citizens" and "religious citizens"—as if in fact they delineate separate, clear-cut, bounded identities in contemporary society. As cultural scholars and feminist theorists highlight, however, individual and group identities usually entail the simultaneous holding of multiple, intersecting, and often contradictory, identities and identity-formation experiences.[86] Thus, despite his new recognition of religion, it still seems that Habermas sees the religious and the rational as starkly different and polarized domains. His dichotomization of religious and secular citizens suggests that individuals who have religious affiliations and beliefs are nothing else, essentially, but religious believers, rather than modern citizens who fully participate in a secular society while simultaneously holding religious beliefs and highly rational beliefs.

Similarly, Habermas talks of "religious communities"[87] as if they are sectlike groups cut off from mainstream society and who somehow are just emerging as novel participants in civil society. This interpretation ignores a long history of participation by churches and religious groups in public policy debates. It also ignores the discursive strategy of, for example, the Catholic bishops in the United States, who, when collectively elaborating the Church's position on various issues, speak to the public at large by addressing their "fellow citizens" and not simply their fellow believers or fellow religious citizens.

Postulating a polarized classification of religious citizens and communities and secular citizens and communities might be an apt characterization of individuals and groups at the fundamentalist extremes of some secular-religious continuum. But this does not seem to be what Habermas had in mind in distinguishing between religious and secular citizens. In fact, his construal of the post-secular excludes fundamentalist traditions; as he states, "A receptive and dialogical relation is only possible towards non-fundamentalist traditions that do not close themselves off from the modern world."[88] Habermas groups together Pentecostals and radical Muslims as fundamentalist, and he is also indisposed toward New Age syncretic movements and new religious Chinese and Japanese sects.[89] Thus he implies that dialogue is possible only with mainstream participants in mainstream institutionalized religions (e.g., Catholicism, mainline Protestantism, Judaism). Yet, especially for mainstream religious adherents, the sharp distinction between religious and secular citizens is inappropriate; in most everyday contexts, and for most of these moderate religious individuals and groups, being religious and being secular are mutually reinforcing orientations.

Religious-based ideas and movements have been significant mobilizing forces in driving social and political change. But if we were to look at the civil rights movement, for example, we would be hard pressed to say who in that movement was a religious citizen and who was a secular citizen. Many nonreligious individuals are mobilized by religious-cultural ideals, and many religiously involved individuals pursue civic goals that may have little or no bearing on their religious beliefs. When the Archbishop of Canterbury called for legal accommodations for Muslims in England, it was hard to say whether he was acting as a religious citizen or as a secular citizen. Similarly, when American politicians support federal vouchers for religious schools or government funding of faith-based social service organizations, it is hard to say whether they are acting as religious citizens or as secular citizens. Whether in the context of Europe or the United States, a polarized frame that artificially distinguishes religious citizens from secular citizens does little to help advance our understanding of the public cultural relevance of religion.

The increased salience, moreover, of a deinstitutionalized spirituality and of increasing numbers of individuals in Europe and the United States who describe themselves as "spiritual but not religious"[90] suggests that Habermas would also need to think about how the post-secular might deal with "spiritual citizens." Houtman and Mascini elaborate on what they call the post-Christian spiritual turn in Europe,[91] where, despite the secular decline in institutionalized religion, spiritual beliefs persist. The Danes and the Swedes, for example, though among the most secular of Europeans, nonetheless embrace a nonrational spirituality; close to half of the Swedes (46 percent), for example, "affirm the existence of some kind of spirit or force."[92]

It is further noteworthy that whether we look at post-Christian Europe or at the United States, skepticism toward church authority exists in tandem with skepticism toward science and technology. Contrary to the modernization-secularization thesis, we are witnessing not a rationalist but a spiritual turn that rejects both institutionalized "religious faith and scientific reason as vehicles of truth."[93] Yet the new forms of spirituality,[94] some of which have links to the "California syncretism" of which Habermas is leery,[95] do not necessarily provide the reasonable justificatory arguments Habermas requires of "religious citizens" who wish to engage in civic discourse. Hence post-secular society might encounter more civic challenges than previously appreciated; it not only must have a non-triumphant attitude toward the secular but must also make room for its "spiritual" citizens, notwithstanding their strong tendencies to reject the rational dimensions of both institutionalized religion and secular science.

In sum, there are tensions in Habermas's conceptualization of religion. These derive from his underappreciation of its interpretive differentiation, its noncognitive spiritual and emotional dimensions, and its everyday intertwining with, rather than separation from, the secular. While these gaps suggest that Habermas misunderstands the complexity of religion, they also suggest he does not really take religion seriously. If, as Habermas intends, religion is to be accommodated in post-secular society, then he would need to fully examine what religion is so he can assess whether and how it can be accommodated. Habermas has to be open to the possibility that while he may now look to religion to help reorient a contrite modernity, religion may not be the emancipatory cultural resource he imagines. How, after many years of dismissing religion's compatibility with reasoned communication, can religion suddenly be compatible with reasoned deliberation? It seems an ad hoc move for Habermas to simply construe a post-secular society that is obliged to be inclusive of religion when critical elements of religion detract from the communicative rationality and post-secular consciousness he requires. The dilemma for Habermas is that while he looks to religion to provide society with cultural resources and a solidarity that can stare down and redeem the pathologies of modernity through reasoned deliberative communication, the cultural strength of religion derives, in part, precisely from the aspects of religion that complicate reasoned communication.

Notwithstanding the ways in which religion complicates communicative reason and a post-secular consciousness, Habermas is optimistic about the reflexive integration of religion into contemporary society. It can be facilitated, he argues, largely through the actions of the state: "It is in the best interest of the constitutional state to act considerately toward all those cultural sources—including religion—out of which civil solidarity and norm consciousness are nourished."[96] At first blush, it seems reasonable to expect the state to act considerately toward religion and the role it might play in helping to redress some of the pathologies of modern society. However, it is not at all self-evident what it means for the state to act considerately. Sociologists, following Weber and Marx, are accustomed to thinking of the state not as a considerate actor but as one that instrumentally serves particular interests and fosters particular solidarities. Nonetheless, it is the neutrality of the state that Habermas emphasizes despite the fact that, as he also acknowledges, the state may remain "bound up with the religion prevailing in the country."[97] He thus seems to imply that the modern constitutional state is so thoroughly rational that it is able to hover above the vested institutional and cultural interests that permeate the society in which it acts.

But as Robert Bellah and Talcott Parsons make clear,[98] even in the most modernized of societies, generalized value commitments inform how the state and other institutions frame the questions at issue; thus "the neutrality of a democratic state is always conditioned by its past, and, in particular, by its religious past."[99] In the context of the United States, Protestantism and its culturally derived discourse of individual freedom and individual self-reliance strongly influence American law and social policy.[100] Similarly, when the French parliament bans the burqa on the grounds that this "radical" practice of Islam is incompatible with French citizenship and French values,[101] it is acting more considerately toward some interests and traditions than others; it is hardly impartial or universally considerate. So too the outrage among the British political elite in response to the Anglican archbishop's suggestion of legal accommodations for religious Muslims[102] underscores the cultural limits to what is considered normative and normal.

If we were able to empirically examine the actions of the state, whether in the United States or in European countries, the preponderance of evidence would probably indicate that when the state is perceived as acting considerately, it most likely serves the cultural-religious influences it knows best. Particular religious-cultural understandings of individual and collective identity, of political deliberation, and of community norms get translated into state-sanctioned laws and public policies. Post-secular possibilities, therefore, will invariably be constrained by political and cultural tensions over what is normal and what is strange and threatening.

Conclusion

Habermas has long been preoccupied with the constellations of modernity and the ways in which some of the obligations and promises of democracy are undermined by capitalist forces and crises. Rather than just diagnosing or despairing over modernity's woes (e.g., poverty, inequality, political apathy), however, Habermas instead sees knowledge as having an emancipatory purpose, a resource that can be used to help free society from the various forms of oppression that are detrimental to the common good.[103] He thus outlines empowering visions of societal change that tend to challenge his readers to reexamine and rethink the intellectual and moral duties of citizenship. For him, communicative reason and its realization through the ideal speech situation offer the only non-oppressive way out of oppression. He is thus committed to a vibrant and inclusive public sphere in which reasoned debate takes place around questions and issues that have no predetermined outcomes.

Habermas's commitment to communicative rationality led him for many decades to dismiss the potential relevance of religious resources in reorienting public discourse. It is only in recent years that he has affirmed the role of religion as a cultural resource for a "contrite modernity" trying to deal with its numerous social pathologies.[104] He has thus argued that post-secular society must acknowledge the persistence of religion and craft a public sphere in which secular and religious citizens meet and mutually engage one another as equals.[105] Religious citizens, nonetheless, carry the burden of translating their religious ideas and norms into a secular idiom; for Habermas, if religion is to be relevant to, and incorporated into, public discourse, it must not dilute or derail communicative rationality.

It is a welcome development when scholars like Habermas who have previously ignored the possible emancipatory relevance of religion rethink their assessment. Religion is a social and cultural force whose significance demands serious intellectual appraisal, even if embarking on that path causes discomfort to some who may see any incorporation of religion as an entirely regressive move. The public faces of religion too often present as authoritarian, defensive, and uncivil. Yet there is much in religion that can be drawn on to resist the colonization of society by an excessively intrusive and strategic rationality that defies ethical consideration of any larger communal good. The doctrines and ethical theses within many religious traditions can help steer reasoned debate about a wide range of emancipatory and life politics issues, whether on economic justice, abortion, reproductive technologies, universal health care, or environmental stewardship.[106]

Further, the theological differentiation and nuances within any given religious tradition mean that we should be careful not to dismiss, a priori, religious voices from traditions more frequently associated with resisting rather than transforming modernity. Some evangelical leaders, for example, have been at the forefront in articulating religiously derived arguments in support of environmental preservation; the communicative resources their arguments contain would be lost to diverse publics, however, if it were just (some) evangelicals who were to listen to their claims.

Similarly, while there is much that is rational in religion, there is also much that is not rational; emotion, mystery, and the pull of ritual and tradition are all part of many individuals' religious and spiritual experiences as well as of their cultural identities. These experiences and traditions have somehow to be woven into culturally accessible public vocabularies that can enrich post-secular society and its way forward. The communicative burden should fall not only on religious individuals to develop secular frames by which to communicate with the nonreligious. Secular discourses and citizens also need to become reflexively open in order to aid in the translation and interpretive processes between religious and secular claims.

The great emancipatory feature about Habermas's ideal speech situation is that no one has a monopoly on the correct interpretation—not the secular philosopher nor the erudite pope nor the charismatic politician. The philosopher and the cardinal should sit down together. The obligation is on all of us to listen for, and to, good reasons to do things that we might not want to do and to argue back with even stronger reasons why we should do what we do not want to do. We live at a time in which public discourse has become shrill and often nonsensical, and relatively cohesive interpretive communities (e.g., the French nation, Anglicans worldwide, U.S. Supreme Court justices), though always pluralistic and differentiated, have themselves become fraught with interpretive tensions over the good. It is indeed urgent that we use all the emancipatory resources we can identify to shift the terms and substance of our current debates, and with a view toward creating societies and communities that better serve our core ideals of human dignity, equality, pluralism, and tolerance.

Thus I welcome Habermas's affirmation of a post-secular society that can benefit from religion's multilayered political and cultural relevance. I agree that religious voices have a fully legitimate place in the public sphere and that communicative rationality should be the high bar toward which all public discourse aims (though it must invariably fall short). I strongly applaud the intellectual efforts to articulate why and how civil society should accommodate religious traditions and arguments. I caution, however, that generalized claims about religion are often at odds with the on-the-ground, everyday lived realities of religion. Religion has much complexity; it includes theological pluralism within as well as across religious traditions, emotion, and collective memory along with diverse spiritualities and experiences that are not easily contained within institutionalized traditions. Moreover, religion simultaneously and mutually intertwines with the secular.

It is important to recognize that religion is not a panacea for anything, at either the individual or the societal level. Its reincorporation into the public sphere will indeed invigorate public debates but not always in terms of the civility and rationality we would like. Recognizing religion's complexities derived from its sociohistorical, cultural, and emotional embeddedness means that we can temper idealized expectations of religion yet appreciate its emancipatory possibilities. By extension, we should also temper our understanding of what the post-secular can accomplish, both conceptually and in practice. Thus, we can incorporate religion as a public cultural resource without setting it up to fail as a redemptive force for democratic societies wrestling with the political, social, and cultural challenges of late modernity.

Notes

I appreciate the comments on an earlier draft of this chapter from David Little, Eduardo Mendieta, and other participants in the Yale University Symposium on Exploring the Post-Secular, April 2009. I also am grateful to the editors and an anonymous reviewer for their helpful comments.

1. Thomas McCarthy, "Translator's Introduction," in *The Theory of Communicative Action*, vol. 1, *Reason and the Rationalization of Society*, by Jürgen Habermas, trans. Thomas McCarthy (Boston: Beacon Press, 1984), x.

2. Jürgen Habermas, *The Theory of Communicative Action*, vol. 1, *Reason and the Rationalization of Society*, trans. Thomas McCarthy (Boston: Beacon Press, 1984), and Habermas, *The Theory of Communicative Action*, vol. 2, *Lifeworld and System: A Critique of Functionalist Reason*, trans. Thomas McCarthy (Boston: Beacon Press, 1987).

3. Habermas, *The Theory of Communicative Action*, vols. 1 and 2.

4. Habermas, *The Theory of Communicative Action*, vol. 1, 86.

5. Ibid., 75.

6. Ibid., 100.

7. Ibid., 17–18.

8. Elisabeth Frazer and Nicola Lacey, *The Politics of Community: A Feminist Critique of the Liberal-Communitarian Debate* (Toronto: University of Toronto Press, 1993). Iris Marion Young, "Communication and the Other: Beyond Deliberative Democracy," in Seyla Benhabib, ed., *Democracy and Difference: Contesting the Boundaries of the Political* (Princeton, NJ: Princeton University Press, 1996), 120–135.

9. Jürgen Habermas, "Transcendence from Within, Transcendence in This World," in Don Browning and Francis Schussler Fiorenza, eds., *Habermas, Modernity, and Public Theology* (New York: Crossroad, 1992), 233.

10. Jürgen Habermas, *Legitimation Crisis* (Boston: Beacon Press, 1975), 120.

11. Habermas, *The Theory of Communicative Action*, vol. 2, 77.

12. Francis Schussler Fiorenza, "The Church as a Community of Interpretation," in Don Browning and Francis Schussler Fiorenza, eds., *Habermas, Modernity, and*

Public Theology (New York: Crossroad, 1992), 66–91, 74. Michele Dillon, "The Authority of the Holy Revisited: Habermas, Religion, and Emancipatory Possibilities," *Sociological Theory* 17 (1999): 290–306.

13. Michele Dillon, "Cultural Differences in the Abortion Discourse of the Catholic Church: Evidence from Four Countries," *Sociology of Religion* 57 (1996): 25–36.

14. Michele Dillon, *Catholic Identity: Balancing Reason, Faith, and Power* (New York: Cambridge University Press, 1999).

15. For example, Richard Dawkins, *The God Delusion* (New York: Mariner Books, 2008).

16. See, for example, Robert Audi, *Religious Commitment and Secular Reason* (New York: Cambridge University Press, 2000); John Rawls, *Justice as Fairness: A Restatement*, ed. Erin Kelly (Cambridge, MA: Harvard University Press, 2001); Ronald Dworkin, *Is Democracy Possible Here? Principles for a New Political Debate* (Princeton, N.J.: Princeton University Press, 2008).

17. Don Browning and Francis Schussler Fiorenza, eds., *Habermas, Modernity, and Public Theology* (New York: Crossroad, 1992). Jürgen Habermas, *Religion and Rationality: Essays on Religion, God, and Modernity*, ed. and trans. Eduardo Mendieta (Cambridge, MA: MIT Press, 2002).

18. For example, Jürgen Habermas, *Between Facts and Norms: Contributions to a Discourse Theory of Law and Democracy* (Cambridge, MA.: MIT Press, 1996).

19. For example, Dillon, "Cultural Differences in the Abortion Discourse of the Catholic Church," 25–36.

20. Michele Dillon, *Debating Divorce: Moral Conflict in Ireland* (Lexington, KY: University Press of Kentucky, 1993).

21. Habermas, *Theory of Communicative Action*, vol. 1.

22. William Outhwaite, *Habermas: A Critical Introduction*, 2nd ed. (Stanford, CA: Stanford University Press, 2009), 157, 193 n. 24.

23. Ibid., 158.

24. Thomas McCarthy, "Translator's Introduction," vi.

25. As quoted in Virgil Nemoianu, "The Church and the Secular Establishment: A Philosophical Dialog between Joseph Ratzinger and Jurgen Habermas," *Logos* 9 (2006): 25.

26. Jürgen Habermas, *The Postnational Constellation* (Cambridge, MA: MIT Press, 2001).

27. Nemoianu, "The Church and the Secular Establishment," 25.

28. Jürgen Habermas, *Legitimation Crisis* (Boston: Beacon Press, 1975).

29. Habermas, *The Postnational Constellation*, 67.

30. Nemoianu, "The Church and the Secular Establishment," 26.

31. See, for example, Anthony Giddens, *Runaway World: How Globalization Is Reshaping Our Lives* (New York: Routledge, 2003); David Held, *Global Covenant: The Social Democratic Alternative to the Washington Consensus* (Cambridge: Polity Press, 2004); Leslie Sklair, *Globalization: Capitalism and Its Alternatives* (Oxford: Oxford University Press, 2002).

32. For example, David Held, *Global Covenant: The Social Democratic Alternative to the Washington Consensus* (Cambridge: Polity Press, 2004), 163.

33. Nemoianu, "The Church and the Secular Establishment," 27.

34. Although Habermas and Talcott Parsons were writing in very different sociohistorical and theoretical contexts, Habermas's willingness to look to religious orientations as a possible reference point in thinking about solutions to modernity's social pathologies is not radically different from Parsons's view of religion. Parsons argued that precisely because of the complex technical and moral problems confronting modern society, there is all the more need of "moral orientations toward the problems of life in this world" (Talcott Parsons, "Christianity and Modern Industrial Society," in *Sociological Theory and Modern Society* [New York: Free Press, 1967], 385-421, 420). Recognizing the emerging religious pluralism of a globalizing society, he carefully noted the cultural as opposed to the religious-doctrinal value of Christianity's values of tolerance and equal rights in helping to address contemporary problems (ibid., 421).

35. See, for example, Charles Curran, *Catholic Social Teaching: A Historical, Theological, and Ethical Analysis* (Washington, DC: Georgetown University Press, 2002). There is a generally unrecognized similarity in tone and substance between the Vatican's critique of economic inequality, consumer culture, and the dehumanization of the individual and that of Horkheimer and Adorno (*The Dialectic of Enlightenment*, ed. Gunzelin Schmid Noerr, trans. Edmund Jephcott [Stanford, CA: Stanford University Press, 1972–2002]), Habermas's intellectual forebears. Although Catholic social teaching and critical theory are anchored in very different philosophical traditions and are committed to different objectives, both nonetheless are influenced by historical consciousness of World Wars I and II and the threats to human society posed by the dominance of technical rationality and various forms of economic, political, and cultural totalitarianism. Thus, Catholic teaching has long condemned excessive liberal individualism as well as state socialism and its subordination of individual rights (e.g., Curran, *Catholic Social Teaching*, 9).

36. James Beckford, "Post-secularity: Fashion or Foible?" Unpublished paper presented to the Society for the Scientific Study of Religion, November 2009.

37. David Harvey, *The Condition of Postmodernity: An Enquiry into the Origins of Cultural Change* (Cambridge, MA: Blackwell, 1990), vii.

38. See, for example, Stuart Hall, "What Is This Black in Black Popular Culture?" in Gina Dent, ed., *Black Popular Culture* (Seattle: Bay Press, 1992).

39. Jürgen Habermas, "Notes on Post-secular Society," *New Perspectives Quarterly* 25 (2008): 3.

40. Ibid., 1.

41. Ibid., 3.

42. Ibid., 3.

43. Ibid., 3–4.

44. Ibid., 4. The larger context for Habermas's discussion of the post-secular is also informed by ongoing debates in political philosophy about social justice (e.g., John Rawls, *Justice as Fairness: A Restatement*, ed. Erin Kelly [Cambridge, MA: Harvard University Press, 2001], and Francis Schussler Fiorenza, *Rights at Risk: Confronting the Cultural, Ethical, and Religious Challenges* [New York: Continuum, 2010]) and, more pragmatically, by the increased presence of Islam in Europe and the more general integration of culturally diverse immigrants into European societies, and the dilemmas these changes pose for ensuring universal civil rights in pluralistic secular societies.

45. Habermas, "Notes on Post-secular Society," 5.

46. Habermas, *Theory of Communicative Action*, vols. 1 and 2.

47. Habermas, "Notes on Post-secular Society," 9.

48. Nemoianu, "A Philosophical Dialog between Joseph Ratzinger and Jurgen Habermas," 27.

49. Habermas, "Notes on Post-secular Society," 11.

50. Ibid., 12.

51. Ibid., 11.

52. David Tracy, *Plurality and Ambiguity* (San Francisco: Harper & Row, 1987), 95–96.

53. For example, William D'Antonio, James Davidson, Dean Hoge, and Mary Gautier, *American Catholics Today: New Realities of Their Faith and Their Church* (New York: Rowman and Littlefield, 2007).

54. John Noonan, *A Church That Can and Cannot Change: The Development of Catholic Moral Theology* (South Bend, IN: Notre Dame University Press, 2005).

55. Kristin Luker, *Abortion and the Politics of Motherhood* (Berkeley: University of California Press, 1984).

56. Michele Dillon, *Catholic Identity*.

57. Meredith McGuire, *Lived Religion: Faith and Practice in Everyday Life* (New York: Oxford University Press, 2008).

58. For example, Michele Dillon and Paul Wink, *In the Course of a Lifetime: Tracing Religious Belief, Practice, and Change* (Berkeley: University of California Press, 2007).

59. Nemoianu, "A Philosophical Dialog between Joseph Ratzinger and Jurgen Habermas," 26. Habermas, "Notes on Post-secular Society," 2.

60. Dillon and Wink, *In the Course of a Lifetime*.

61. Robert Bellah, Richard Madsen, William Sullivan, Ann Swidler, and Steven Tipton, *Habits of the Heart: Individualism and Commitment in American Life* (Berkeley: University of California Press, 1985).

62. Habermas, "Notes on Post-secular Society," 6.

63. Charles Taylor, *A Secular Age* (Cambridge, MA: Harvard University Press, 2007).

64. Ibid., 12–13.

65. Ibid., 12.

66. Cf. Peter Berger and Thomas Luckmann, *The Social Construction of Reality: A Treatise in the Sociology of Knowledge* (New York: Anchor Books, 1966).

67. Language itself, as Foucault would note ("Truth and Power," in Paul Rabinow, ed., *The Foucault Reader* [New York: Pantheon, 1984], 51–75), impedes reflexivity and social transformation. It is symptomatic of the challenges encountered in crafting a pluralistic society that integrates social and cultural differences that even Charles Taylor and Gerard Bouchard's well-intentioned report on Quebec secularism and cultural integration notes at the outset its use of the male pronoun. It states, "In the interests of stylistic clarity, the masculine form of pronouns has been used throughout this report and includes without discrimination both men and women" (Gerard Bouchard and Charles Taylor, *Building the Future: A Time for Reconciliation*, Report Commissioned by the Government of Quebec, 2008, 6). Notwithstanding their disclaimer, the use of the male pronoun may, nonetheless, contribute to a nonreflexive understanding of male and female differences and one that reinforces acceptance of practices that subordinate women to men. By extension, we can appreciate the practical challenges encountered in accommodating the Otherness of religious differences.68. For example, see Berger and Luckmann, *The Social Construction of Reality*.

69. For example, Emile Durkheim, *The Elementary Forms of Religious Life*, trans. Carol Cosman (Oxford: Oxford University Press, 2001[1912]).

70. Robert Bellah, "Response to 'Religion in the Public Sphere' by Jürgen Habermas," Kyoto Laureate Symposium, University of San Diego, March 4, 2005, unpublished manuscript (Berkeley: University of California, Department of Sociology).

71. Sam Harris, "Science Is in the Details: Faith, Knowledge and the Nomination of Francis Collins," *New York Times*, July 27, 2009, A21.

72. For example, John Evans, *Contested Reproduction: Genetic Technologies, Religion, and Public Debate* (Chicago: University of Chicago Press, 2010).

73. For example, Pew Forum on Religion and Public Life, *The U.S. Religious Landscape Survey: Religious Beliefs* (Washington, DC: Pew Research Center, 2008).

74. Robert Wuthnow, *America and the Challenges of Religious Diversity* (Princeton, NJ: Princeton University Press, 2005).

75. See, for example, Laurie Goodstein, "American Muslims Ask: Will We Ever Belong?" *New York Times*, September 6, 2010, A1, 3, and Steven Greenhouse, "Muslims and Rising Tensions," *New York Times*, September 24, 2010, B1, 4.

76. Jane Perlez, "A Battle Rages in London over a Mega-mosque Plan," *New York Times*, November 4, 2007, A13.

77. Stephen Castle, "A Rightist Harnesses British Discontent," *New York Times*, June 10, 2009, A6.

78. Mark Landler, "In Munich, Provocation in a Symbol of Foreign Faith," *New York Times*, December 8, 2006, A3.

79. Katrin Bennhold, "A Veil Closes France's Door to Citizenship," *New York Times*, July 19, 2008, A1, 8. Steven Erlanger, "Parliament Moves France Closer to a Ban on Facial Veils," *New York Times*, July 14, 2010, A6.

80. Habermas, "Notes on Post-secular Society," 17.

81. Bouchard and Taylor, *Building the Future*.

82. Rachel Donadio, "In Letter, Pope Puts Focus on the Limits of Interfaith Dialogue," *New York Times*, November 24, 2008, A7.

83. Habermas, "Notes on Post-secular Society," 12.

84. Ibid., 11–12.

85. For example, Robert Audi, *Religious Commitment and Secular Reason*.

86. See Patricia Hill Collins, *Black Feminist Thought: Knowledge, Consciousness, and the Politics of Empowerment* (New York: Routledge, 1990), and Stuart Hall, "Cultural Identity and Disapora," in *Identity: Community, Culture, Difference* (London: Lawrence & Wishart, 1990), 222–237.

87. Habermas, "Notes on Post-secular Society," 3.

88. Jürgen Habermas, "An Interview with Jürgen Habermas," by Paul Gillespie, *Irish Times*, June 11, 2010, 2.

89. Habermas, "Notes on Post-secular Society," 2–3.

90. Dick Houtman and Stef Aupers, "The Spiritual Turn and the Decline of Tradition: The Spread of Post-Christian Spirituality in 14 Western Countries, 1981–2000," *Journal for the Scientific Study of Religion* 46 (2007): 305–320. Pew Forum on Religion and Public Life, *The U.S. Religious Landscape Survey*.

91. Dick Houtman and Peter Mascini, "Why Do Churches Become Empty, While New Age Grows? Secularization and Religious Change in the Netherlands," *Journal for the Scientific Study of Religion* 41 (2002): 455–473.

92. Rodney Stark, Eva Hamberg, and Andrew Miller, "Exploring Spirituality and Unchurched Religions in America, Sweden, and Japan," *Journal of Contemporary Religion* 20 (2005): 14.

93. Houtman and Aupers, "The Spiritual Turn and the Decline of Tradition," 307.

94. Wade Clark Roof, *Spiritual Marketplace: Baby Boomers and the Remaking of American Religion* (Princeton, NJ: Princeton University Press, 1999).

95. Habermas, "Notes on Post-secular Society."

96. Habermas, as quoted in Nemoianu, "The Church and the Secular Establishment," 27.

97. Ibid., 6.

98. Bellah, "Response to 'Religion in the Public Sphere' by Jürgen Habermas"; Talcott Parsons, "Christianity and Modern Industrial Society."

99. Bellah, "Response to 'Religion in the Public Sphere' by Jürgen Habermas," 3.

100. For example, Mary Ann Glendon, *Abortion and Divorce in Western Law* (Cambridge, MA.: Harvard University Press, 1987).

101. Bennhold, "A Veil Closes France's Door to Citizenship." Erlanger, "Parliament Moves France Closer to a Ban on Facial Veils."

102. John Burns, "Top Anglican Seeks a Role for Islamic Law in Britain," *New York Times*, February 8, 2008, A10.

103. Jürgen Habermas, *Knowledge and Human Interests* (Boston: Beacon Press, 1968–1971).

104. Habermas, "The Church and the Secular Establishment."

105. Habermas, "Notes on Post-Secular Society."

106. Cf. Giddens, *Runaway World*, 214–231.

CHAPTER ELEVEN

Religion and Secularization in the United States and Western Europe

John Torpey

Largely as a result of the attacks of September 11, 2001, the subject of religion has returned to the Western social science agenda with considerable force. In the immediate aftermath of (and obviously prompted by) the attacks, Jürgen Habermas argued that we have entered into a "post-secular" age,[1] in which the claims of religion have to be addressed by liberal democracies in a more serious manner than had been the case theretofore. Meanwhile, Charles Taylor has insisted in his celebrated recent book *A Secular Age* that we live in a time in which the intrinsically secularizing "immanent frame" has become a perfectly reasonable option and perhaps even the "default setting" for many people in the contemporary world.[2] In yet a third view, Peter Berger, long a leading advocate of secularization theory, reversed course and claimed shortly before the turn of the millennium that "the world is as furiously religious as it ever was, and in some places more so than ever."[3] The views of these three observers suggest three quite different perspectives regarding the extent of religiosity in the world today and hence call into question the adequacy of the theory of secularization as an account of religion's place in the contemporary world.

At the very least, it is fair to say that the notion that secularization is a necessary concomitant of "modernization" is in substantial disarray. Indeed, from having once seemed one of the few incontrovertible truths in the social sciences, it now seems to have more detractors than defenders. A considerable measure of this reversal of fortune has resulted from giving more serious consideration to American experience, once widely regarded as "exceptional" (that is to say, deviant) from the standpoint of a European trajectory assumed to be the norm. This development in social science thinking about religion has had the consequence of (further) decentering the European experience as paradigmatic of "modernity." Just as Europe has been "provincialized" in much recent historiographical discussion, Europe has also increasingly come to be seen as "exceptional" in religious terms.

But the exceptionalisms attributed to the United States and to Europe, respectively, are of course very different in terms of their points of reference. The idea of American exceptionalism—referring especially to the weakness of the socialist impulse or of the welfare state—was always premised on a comparison with Western Europe (and perhaps Japan) as societies sharing the United States' general level of socioeconomic development but taking very different paths with regard to the role of the state in social life. The exceptionalism perpetrated by contemporary Western Europe, by contrast, is based on a comparison not only with the United States but with more or less the entire world. The alleged deviancy here concerns Western Europe's unrepentant secularism in the face of the vibrancy of religion elsewhere in the world.

Against this background, some have concluded that secularization theory maintains its relevance, but only (or at least chiefly) with regard to Western Europe. From this perspective, what needs explaining is not how religion dies out as societies modernize but rather why religion died out in Western Europe while remaining furious in the manifestly modern United States and even more so in other modern or modernizing places.

Prima facie evidence suggests that there is a genuine puzzle here: Why has much of Europe turned out differently from other places with respect to its religiosity—or, more directly, its secularity? And what might this tell us about religiousness and secularization in the modern world more generally? We will explore this problem in the remainder of the paper. But first, we should note that the profusion of exceptionalisms in these discussions reminds one of Aristide Zolberg's cautionary question, "How many exceptionalisms?" and his salutary answer, in which he reminds us that there are as many exceptionalisms "as there are cases under consideration" and recommends comparative historical analysis as a corrective to this self-evidently "absurd" conclusion.[4]

This paper seeks to explore the meaning of secularization and its applicability to the American and European worlds, and thus to develop an assessment of the usefulness of the secularization thesis. To anticipate, suffice it to say that much in this analysis depends on how we define religion and on what we mean by "secularization." We shall see that there is considerable uncertainty about the meaning of the concept of religion, which unavoidably detracts from efforts to assess its prevalence in different times and places. About the concept of secularization there is considerably greater clarity, which greatly facilitates our understanding of the extent to which this process has taken hold in various settings. Against this background, the available evidence indicates that there is, indeed, a significant difference between Western Europe and the United States with regard to religious participation and interest, and this variation offers a valuable reminder that we must avoid the tendency to assume unilinear processes on the basis of grand claims about historical trajectories. Secularization has taken place in these modern contexts—but not uniformly, and with lots of ups and downs across the centuries. Our baseline expectation should be that religiosity will persist, and that it is the decline of religion in specific historical settings rather than its staying power that most requires social scientists' attention.

The persistence of religiosity in various places results in part because different areas of the world have become imbued with a "latent" religiosity that endures even as the active religiosity of a region's inhabitants may shift. The religious *longue durée*, with its spatial and cultural dimensions, thus continues to shape everyday religiosity despite the overt preferences and inclinations of the participants. Notwithstanding the "conservative" impact of latent religiosity, however, we may now be witnessing a major transformation in global religion as a result of the spread of voluntaristic Protestantism to places where it had previously been marginal or unfamiliar. In the process, the center of gravity of world Christianity is moving to the global South and challenging traditional, top-down ways of doing things in the cultures in which it is becoming implanted. But let us first explore what social scientists mean when they use the term "religion" in the first place.

What Is Religion?

The question "What is religion?" is one of the most vexatious and perhaps unanswerable questions in social science. Is religion fundamentally about belief or practice, doctrine or experience? What is its relationship to magic? Is religion necessarily communal, or can it also be individual? Must the rewards sought by the religious be otherworldly only, or may they be "this-worldly" as well? Is it even possible to develop a definition that is valid across all times and places? Some critics doubt whether, although it might be thought possible, it is desirable to advance a universal definition of religion because of the ways in which such a procedure is itself caught up in time-bound preoccupations, rendering any universal definition a kind of performative contradiction. Indeed, one wonders whether it is useful to deploy a concept about which there is so little agreement. Without a common understanding of the term, how do we know we are discussing the same thing(s) when we speak of "religion"? Without a common definition, efforts to determine whether there is "more" or "less" of it in any given context will inevitably resemble attempts to nail pudding to the wall.

The difficulty inherent in the problem of defining religion is exacerbated by problems of cultural difference. For example, in chapter 2 in this volume, Richard Madsen raises serious questions about the extent to which what "we" regard as religion is also regarded as such by "them."[5] Since Madsen is talking principally about the Chinese as he explores this problem, one is reminded of Weber's insistence that a valid social scientific analysis is one that must be logically accepted "even by a Chinese." Madsen's point is that it is not at all clear that the Chinese in question would regard as "religion" that which, say, the Jesuit missionary understands by that term. What for the Catholic was a religious issue might well have been regarded by the Chinese as a scientific or philosophical matter. As this example suggests, there may be an incommensurability between "their" understanding and "ours" that precludes us—at least to some extent—from playing the same "language game" when we talk about religion. This is a major conundrum that plagues any attempt to analyze what religion is and how much of it there is around.

In a number of contributions to this discussion (in addition to chapter 2, see chapter 6, by Bryan Turner, as well), there is a certain tendency to distinguish between the characteristics of Eastern religions—particularly Confucianism (not universally regarded *as* a religion), Taoism, Hinduism, Buddhism—and those of Western religions such as Christianity, Judaism, and Islam, and to view them as largely incomparable. Not altogether surprisingly, given the centrality of "faith" and "books" in the Abrahamic traditions, Western analysts tend to focus on belief and other mental states as manifestations of religiosity. Rodney Stark and Roger Finke, for example, assert in no uncertain terms that religion is about belief in the transcendent and cannot be understood coherently in any other way.[6] The supernatural is inevitably involved, although churches may or may not be. William James famously stressed religious experience—the states of mind associated with the religious—not so much to downgrade the significance of religious practice but as a counterpoint to a focus on the religious institutions he often seems to have regarded as unnecessarily burdensome.[7]

Where Eastern religions are concerned, the tendency is to argue that belief cannot be the central component defining religiosity and to stress the importance of practices and rituals. Eastern religions are sometimes said to be more bound up in practices of worship (whether of gods or ancestors) and less preoccupied with religious ideas. Compounding the distinctiveness, these practices and rituals typically occur in the absence of the sorts of institutions that often environ them in Western religions, and with less fretting about orthodoxy or exclusive forms of membership. There may be occasional visits to a temple, but there is as a rule no congregation and correspondingly no priesthood directly responsible for the pastoral care of a specific flock. There is no church to belong to, and hence no way to count participation in the ways this is typically done with regard to Western religions, such as by using measures of church attendance or involvement in other activities associated with churches and their congregations. Hand-wringing about orthodoxy is harder to generate when there is no canonical text to assert as a standard ne plus ultra. Religious practice in these contexts may amount to little more than veneration of an amulet purchased at a flea market in the hope of securing good fortune in this world. This sort of religiosity seems relatively little distinct from magic, even if there are no efforts to coerce spiritual forces as opposed to simply worshipping them.

Or perhaps magic and religion are not so easily distinguishable, notwithstanding Durkheim's famous dictum that "there is no church of magic."[8] Weber tended to set the two on a continuum, with placement determined largely by the ethical quality of the practice in question and especially a doctrine's proximity to or distance from an "ethic of brotherliness." Paradoxically, Weber argued that Calvinism and its notion of an elect few extinguished the ethic of brotherliness at the same time that it remorselessly drove magic out of religion.[9] Confucianism lacks the magical elements of, say, Taoism, but in many quarters Confucianism has not been seen as a religion, as distinct from a catalog of practical and ethical maxims.

There appears to be a certain "Orientalism" inherent in these positions, however. For one thing, needless to say, practice is a crucial element of religiosity in the West as well as in the East; meanwhile, many Eastern religions are as much bound up with certain ideas (viz., karma or nirvana) as are Western religions. Meanwhile, Pentecostalism, which is seizing populations both "East" and "West," is not a particularly doctrinal phenomenon; its hallmarks are faith healing, speaking in tongues, and emotionalism—combined with a Manichaean conception of the struggle between God and the devil. Religions inevitably involve both beliefs and practices.

The notion of an irreconcilable opposition of "belief" and "practice" is thus simply misguided. Both are expressions of efforts to make sense of human life in symbolic terms. One does not engage in religious practice without some set of beliefs in a higher power or powers capable of bestowing sought-after rewards, even if one may also be doing other things—such as displaying wealth and prosperity—at the same time. Otherwise, why call them "religious" at all? Martin Riesebrodt has recently insisted that religions inevitably invoke a "promise of salvation" involving the intercession of superhuman powers. His definition is meant to avoid the "absurd" understanding of religion "according to which soccer games, shopping at a supermarket, or barbecues are religious phenomena."[10] This proposal is sensible enough, but we must still bear in mind that the rewards promised may be as much in this world as in another. Conceptions of salvation depend "upon what one wants to be saved from, and what one wants to be saved for."[11]

More importantly, perhaps, positing an East/West distinction paralleling that between belief and practice may obscure from us the profound changes that are taking place in these putative world regions as a result of what David Martin[12] and Olivier Roy[13] have called the "de-territoralization" of religion—that is, the appearance and in certain cases the efflorescence of religious traditions in places where these had previously been largely unknown or at least in a distinct minority. While East Asia has long been host to limited outside infusions of Christianity, for example, there is now under way in China a major expansion of Christianity associated especially with an insurgent Pentecostalism gripping tens of millions of people. Conversely, Europe is presently seeking to digest a significant inflow of Muslims from its Mediterranean and Anatolian peripheries. In his inaugural address, President Barack Obama described the United States as a country of "Christians and Muslims, Jews and Hindus . . . "; such a characterization would have seemed odd only a generation ago. The interpenetration of East and West due to the migration of both persons and religious proclivities is leading to the recasting of the religious topography in each. The culture zones assumed by Samuel Huntington to be the bases of clashing civilizations increasingly play host to relatively novel populations bearing unfamiliar religious traditions or accept novel religious influences that are transforming the character of the religious in these different zones.

In addition to the ways in which religious hybridization and de-territorialization may cloud our preconceptions of the nature of religiosity, we need to consider what one might call the "para-religions." By this I mean such phenomena as civil religion, political religion,[14] and so-called secular religion. Something about these phenomena compels people to designate them as religions. With the notion of civil religion, for example, Rousseau advocated a devotion to country that would rival that to faith; in his account, "to die for one's country . . . becomes martyrdom." Even if one insists that religion consists in faith in a transcendent being or realm, Rousseau's conception of civil religion[15] fits because he saw this brand of patriotism as service to the state's "tutelary gods"—even if adherence was enforced by the authorities. The civil religion of which Robert Bellah spoke in his noted 1967 essay "Civil Religion in America" is a rather broader interpretive schema that, he argues, provides the major signposts by which Americans make sense of their individual situation. Yet Bellah held that all countries have some kind of civil religion "through which [they interpret their] historical experience in the light of transcendent reality."[16] Indeed, he regards this as a "sociological simplicity," flowing unavoidably from a Durkheimian conception of society. Against this background, it is not difficult to see why Weber saw the modern nation-state and its demand for the highest sacrifice as a serious competitor to salvation religion.

From the standpoint of a sturdy Durkheimianism, however, mere "spirituality" begins to run off the far edge of the canvas of religion. Spirits and phenomena such as spirit possession are run-of-the-mill elements of folk religion and present few difficulties for a definition of religion. The problem arises with the kind of spirituality associated with New Age ideas and practices: yoga (in the absence of its traditional intellectual concomitants), crystals, goddess worship, and the like. The difficulty has especially to do with the individualized character of such putative "religion." Bellah and his *Habits of the Heart* coauthors famously needled this form of faith in the example of

Sheilaism, the creed supposedly followed by an interviewee named Sheila.[17] (Another version has been associated with the name of Cindy Crawford.) This sort of "individualized religion" seems to fly in the face of the tensions with the world that Weber, at least, took as a central feature of salvation religions. Steve Bruce puts the point succinctly: "[O]nly a religion that has an authoritative reference point outside the individual is capable of providing a challenge to any status quo."[18] Others, however, see New Age spirituality as a legitimate resident in the house of religion, stressing its affirmative qualities along the lines that Durkheim emphasized when he noted that religion fortifies the believer for the challenges of life.

Despite these many disagreements and conundrums about what "counts" as religion, there seems to be little disagreement that religiosity around the world has become less confined institutionally than was previously the case. Nearly half a century ago, Robert Bellah argued that this deinstitutionalization of religion is a characteristic feature of the contemporary stage of religious evolution. Indeed, he regarded the growing individualization of religion as part and parcel of the historical stage of "modern religion" as such. In this framework, individualization in the religious domain is simply a product of human social evolution, and one reflecting humans' greater autonomy relative to their environment. At the same time, deinstitutionalization means that "religious action in the world becomes more demanding than ever," placing the burden of finding salvation increasingly on the individual.[19]

Alternatively, one might conceive of individualized religion simply in terms of the mysticism that Ernst Troeltsch suggested a century ago was one of the three principal manifestations of Christian religious organization. Rather than a specifically evolutionary development, then, individualized religion might be regarded as forming part of a perennial triangle with "church" and "sect," the other organizational forms that Christianity has taken historically. This is surely the conclusion suggested by Courtney Bender's important work on "the new metaphysicals," who—as heirs of the Transcendentalists and other "spiritual but not religious" movements in American history—turn out not to be so new after all.[20] One might further think of these different forms of religious organization as reflecting variations in religious "temperature." Churches, the embodiment of the routinization and institutionalization of charisma, are "cool"; sects, driven by the religious zeal of their members, are "hot"; and mysticism, which transforms worship and doctrine into "a purely personal and inward experience" is "warm"[21]—edifying and uplifting, perhaps, but lacking an adequately social dimension that many analysts regarded as crucial to genuine religion.

Troeltsch's approach suggests not so much a stage theory of religious development as a constantly shifting dynamic among the three different organizational forms. Needless to say, sectarianism within Christianity is not purely a product of the Protestant Reformation, nor has mysticism/spirituality been a product exclusively of the recent past. In this connection, José Casanova has suggested in a private communication that we should regard the post-secular not as a stage *after* secularism but instead as the *opposite* of secularism understood as an intellectual-political project. That is, "the post-secular" can only mean the abandonment of the "stadial" consciousness associated with the ideology of secularism and its expectation of the (welcome) demise of religion. We would be well advised to abandon the teleological conceptions that entail predetermined trajectories and outcomes; these invariably are proved wrong in the shorter or longer run.

Ultimately, a satisfactory definition of religion arguably revolves around two principal axes. The first question is whether or not the practice or activity in question contains a social dimension on the basis of which one might judge and mount a challenge to existing social arrangements, including one's place in the social order. Some of the challenges generated by religion are as likely to be nourished by resentment as by a magnanimous desire for justice. Meanwhile, the spiritual may be noninstitutional, but it need not be entirely antisocial and rarely appears in utterly anti-institutional form. The other question is whether the activity or practice involves supernatural powers to whom or to which appeal may be made to bring about a more desirable, alternative state of affairs for the individual or the social order, in this world or in the next. Religion is about hope that someone or something stronger than the self will set things right, however that may be understood.

Against this background, we must now seek to determine what is meant by "secularization."

What Is Secularization?

In attempting to come to grips with the meaning of the concept of secularization, we are in a somewhat odd position: secularization has arguably been better defined than the phenomenon whose decline the term is supposed to characterize. José Casanova's approach, now a standard widely applied to understanding the problem at hand, sensibly breaks the concept down into three elements: the differentiation thesis, the decline-of-religion thesis, and the privatization thesis.[22] The differentiation thesis, also defended in nuanced fashion by David Martin,[23] maintains that religion is no longer married to institutional power in the way that, for example, European monarchs once ruled by "divine right." The decline-of-religion thesis posits that religious belief and practice have declined in the lives of those who might once have believed. Finally, the privatization thesis holds that religious belief is reduced to a private matter, lacking the significance it had previously had in the lives of societies. These distinctions offer valuable assistance in trying to evaluate whether secularization has in fact occurred in any given context.

Yet each is problematic in its own way as well. The differentiation thesis, which Casanova and Martin take to be the defensible core of the concept of secularization, tells us that churches and other institutions, especially the state, have become decoupled but doesn't necessarily tell us in what way that is the case. As is widely known, although the laws of both France and the United States require the separation of church and state, the "wall of separation" between the two institutions that is supposedly characteristic of the United States differs fundamentally from the secularist (*laïc*) stance of the French state, which is generally thought to be more antagonistic to religion than anything associated with American constitutional practice. Neither resembles very much the state support for religion that has been typical of the Scandinavian countries and Germany, despite the fact that the (Lutheran) church has forfeited much of its former significance when it comes to policy making in these countries (think of the Kulturkampf). All of these cases, in other words, reflect the differentiation of throne and altar, but they involve very different stances toward the place of the church in official and social life. There is a variety of constellations relating religious to secular powers, ranging from hostility and suppression (e.g., in Soviet-type societies) to state support in the form of tax collection or state sanctioning of allegedly deviant religions (Germany). The arrangement in the United States is a seemingly contradictory amalgam: strict constitutional prohibition of established religion combined with a tradition of voluntarism and a religious "free market" that is meant as much to protect religion from the state as to protect the state from religion.

The situation is similar with regard to the notion of secularization as the decline of belief and practice. There is indeed considerable evidence for claims of declining religiosity understood in this way, particularly in Western Europe and in some of the formerly Communist countries of Eastern Europe. Weber proposed that, with the advance of science and rationalization, religion would be cast increasingly into the realm of the irrational. Despite Charles Taylor's objections to the notion that we should understand religious decline in terms of various "subtraction stories" (i.e., science and reason would rise, and religion would be "subtracted"), Taylor largely supports the view that religion has come to be regarded as irrational. The "secular age" he depicts is one in which people can now, for the first time in the realm of Latin Christendom, opt for a secular, nonbelieving sensibility, and this indeed may be widely regarded as the default setting. But as a claim about "modern" societies generally, the notion of an inevitable decline in belief or practice is clearly misguided. It is this version of the secularization thesis that tends to be most widely held, however, especially by the general public and by more militantly atheistic intellectuals. Making sense of the contemporary world entails understanding that it is wrong.

Casanova shows at considerable length that the idea that religion has been privatized in modernity is also wrongheaded.[24] Indeed, as we noted at the outset, much of the return of religion to the social scientific agenda is a product of the raging public relevance of religion. Can a president support abortion and still speak at the graduation of one of the country's leading Catholic universities? Can a female student wear a veil to school in a secular political order? What (if any) is the religious basis of Islamist extremism? Can creationism be taught in public schools? Should the state recognize shari'a as a legitimate source of jurisprudential decision making? All of these questions highlight the problematic relationship between religion and public order. At the same time, there is something to the notion that religion is increasingly thought of as a private rather than a public matter. In contrast to earlier times, in many contexts, religiosity and religious identification have shed their status as sources of difference and conflict in public spaces. Still, it is not entirely clear what it means to say that religion is "privatized." Does such privatization refer to the inner life only of the individual? To that of a family? To small conventicles of believers who shun public relevance or indeed the outside world as such?

I would like to propose an additional way of thinking about religion and secularity that has profound implications for contemporary life. This concerns a distinction that might be made between *active* and *latent* religiosity.[25] Active religion is the sort of piety that one observes in houses of worship, at religious festivals and pilgrimages, and in the everyday religious practices of the faithful. Latent religion, by contrast, manifests itself more subtly, especially through the organization of public space and time, but also in terms of the sensibilities underlying particular regions and states. With regard to the organization of public space and time, for example, the officially observed Sabbath takes place on Sundays in Christendom but on Friday nights and Saturdays in Israel (even if exceptions may be made for believers of different faiths, they are precisely that—exceptions). Christian holidays tend to be observed in predominantly Christian realms, Muslim holy days in Muslim-dominated polities. As far as sensibilities are concerned, the United States is an overwhelmingly Protestant milieu, whereas Western Europe alternates between Catholic and Protestant areas—just travel from Berlin to Munich sometime and observe the changes in architecture as you proceed southward. Another way of exemplifying this point is to argue that punk rock, which made an aesthetic of ugliness, flowered mainly in Protestant contexts (the United States, the United Kingdom, the Netherlands, Germany, and Scandinavia); such a subcultural movement appears to have had little resonance in the non-Protestant world (with the possible exception of Japan, which is sometimes thought to share the secularity of post-Protestant Western Europe). Protestant asceticism nurtured a musical style with limited appeal in other contexts.

Latent religiosity is arguably the source of some of the most important political conflicts in the contemporary world and help account for their relative intractability. As a result of underlying sensibilities rather than of any deep commitment to Christianity, the construction of a mosque often becomes a very contentious matter in countries historically dominated by Christian churches.[26] Countries where this sort of issue arises may regard themselves as secular (indeed, as hypersecular), but the spaces and periods that are given over to religious observance reflect a persistent undertone favoring one (or more) faith(s) over another. It is this historical formation by particular religious traditions that shaped Samuel Huntington's notion of "civilizations," and it is no coincidence that he draws on Weber in developing this conception. This is not to say that Weber would have agreed with

Huntington's political conclusions, of course, but it is to say that the world religions have shaped different areas of the world in profound and enduring ways over the *longue durée* and that these influences persist despite more recent efforts to separate throne and altar and to accommodate novel populations of immigrants. It was this latent religiosity that sparked the debate over the inclusion of some reference to Christianity in the European constitution, despite the largely secularized character of the populations that make up the countries of the European Union. Latent religiosity, the geological substratum left behind by centuries of religious influence, complicates problems arising from religious pluralism, notwithstanding the stated intentions of the parties involved.

Secularization may occur in any or all of the three dimensions outlined by Casanova without doing much to mute the significance of these deeper currents of religion. Casanova's trinitarian approach to understanding the concept of secularization makes the concept considerably more precise as well as more empirically manageable. It also tends to render the place of religion in public life more accessible to modification by means of law and public policy. My addition of a distinction between active and latent religiosity foregrounds an aspect of religion, and hence of secularization, that is less readily amenable to such measures. This is not necessarily to say that the manifestations of latent religiosity cannot be overcome; the Hagia Sophia was first a Christian church, then a mosque, and now, in keeping with the Kemalist project of Turkish *laïcité*, a museum. The site of the Babri Mosque in Ayodhya offers a less encouraging example of the conflict potential that may arise from latent religiosity.

We should perhaps add by way of conclusion that there are a number of different issues under discussion here arising from concepts whose common root word is "secular." Secular*ism* is an ideology, a set of beliefs about a possible state of affairs that one seeks either to bring about or to defend. That state of affairs might be referred to as "secularity." Secularization, however, is a *process* with multiple determinants, various dimensions, and contingent outcomes depending on the case in question. It is worth stressing that it is the decline of belief, the separation of church and state, and the privatization of faith—not their opposites—that constitute the puzzles we must decipher. For good reasons, Weber regarded the rise of a heartless Calvinism as a bizarre historical anomaly—an unlikely triumph of procedural rationalism over human warmth and loyalty, and one with deeply disturbing implications for humanity. Weber took for granted that blood was thicker than water and that people would naturally incline to assist those to whom they were close rather than put themselves in the "cold skeleton hands" of bureaucratic rationalism. It was the cultural breakthrough to impersonalism (with all its historical ramifications) that required explanation, not the historical predominance of kinship ties over impersonal procedures. And so it is with the social scientific study of religion: *not the persistence of religion, but its abeyance in particular times and places is what needs explanation and clarification.*

Why Does Secularization Occur?

Having discussed what secularization *is*, we need to consider what might cause it. One of the most intriguing and perplexing developments in the recent sociology of religion concerns the understanding of the consequences of religious pluralism. Pluralization was once thought to lead to a decline in the plausibility of religious belief *tout court* on the grounds that if more than one religion is said to be true, then none of them can be true.[27] In a stark reversal of this viewpoint, however, more recent approaches have sought to demonstrate that, far from weakening faith, pluralism actually strengthens it. This is one of the central propositions of the "religious economies" or "supply-side" approach to religion that has emerged in recent years. It is difficult not to see this approach as the intellectual concomitant in the study of religion of the "market fundamentalism" of the pre–financial crash era. The main bête noire of the religious economies approach is religious establishment (i.e., monopolization) or state interference in the religious market more broadly. The supply-siders suggest that as long as the market is free (i.e., the state stays out of the way), a variety of religious suppliers will contend for souls and so remain at the cutting edge of religious marketing and entrepreneurship. Critics have noted, however, that this conception of a marketplace of faith tends to presuppose that people regard different faiths as equally available "options"—how many Protestants abandon their faith for Catholicism, much less Islam, Judaism, and so on?—and yet fails to note that they might view irreligion as an option as well. Meanwhile, in China, where there are currently five officially recognized faiths, the state's intrusion into the religious market appears to have stimulated rather than suppressed religiosity and indeed may have led to greater pluralization rather than less.[28] Furthermore, the conception of a marketplace of religion does not map well onto premodern contexts in which religious monopolies held the field; variations in religious vitality in such contexts could hardly be explained by the same independent variable (i.e., establishment). In all events, Chaves and Gorski's searching review of relevant research found the supply-siders' contentions "not supported" by the available data.[29] Notwithstanding the supply-siders' insistence, state intervention in religious life—more the norm than the exception—is not unambiguously predictive of spiritual torpor.

Despite doubts about the general predictive capacity of the supply-side approach, however, there is considerable consensus around the notion that religious establishment tends to have long-term negative consequences for religious vitality. This has been especially true in predominantly Protestant contexts. Yet it is not clear how this idea can be applied in contexts in which there is no church per se to establish. Hinduism, for example, for all its association with Indianness, is thought by some to be not a single religion at all but simply a congeries of religions indigenous to India.[30] The attempt of the Hindu-nationalist Bharatiya Janata Party (BJP) to promote some primordial Hindutva is thus an intrinsically problematic enterprise—more nailing pudding to the wall, one might even say. By definition, religious establishment seems likely to lead to secularization only in parts of the world in which churches in the strict sense of authoritative dispensers of salvation are a common form of religious organization.

The widespread critique of the secularization thesis notwithstanding, some continue to defend the thesis that "modernization" in the form of economic and other forms of security brings in its train a decline in religious belief and participation. This perspective has returned with particular force in the work of Pippa Norris and Ronald Inglehart.[31] Drawing on the many years of data now available from the World Values Survey, they find that in those contexts in which the vulnerability of the populace has been diminished by economic prosperity and social welfare policies intended to relieve distress in hard times, the demand for religiosity has declined. Similarly, Riesebrodt sees religion as a means of "coping with contingency," given humans' inability to contend with forces greater than themselves.[32] Where uncertainty and, indeed, chaos prevail, the search for solace persists.

Focusing on these sorts of considerations, David Martin has argued in a series of publications that the explosion in the Third World of Pentecostalism and its charismatic cousins reflects an epochal shift among the downtrodden from what he calls "the trajectory of 1789" to that of 1776.[33] In other words, the Catholic-dominated world and the characteristic patterns of anti-clericalism that emerged in response to the anciens régimes associated with it—both in Europe and in the colonial world—are being supplanted by the voluntaristic patterns associated with sectarian Protestantism and its chief contemporary geo-religious bastion, the United States.

If one regards Marxist socialism as one form of eschatological belief that offered the meek the prospect of inheriting the earth if they were willing to struggle for it politically, in this argument Pentecostalism offers some of the same possibilities on the basis of individual effort, discipline, and self-control. Although Martin is careful to note that one cannot expect a one-to-one correspondence between religion and politics, his studies of the spread of Pentecostalism around the world can be thought of in terms of a contest between Marxism and Methodism.[34] Due to Pentecostalism's emotionalistic, nondoctrinal character, Martin sees it as at least a partial descendant of Methodism, which pioneered these tendencies some two centuries ago. He argues that Pentecostalism is a means by which the "wretched of the earth" respond to their plight, at least under certain circumstances, in religious rather than political terms. The Pentecostals pull themselves up by their bootstraps with little in the way of doctrine or intelligentsia to guide them, stressing self-discipline, health, and wealth.

Martin correctly observes that much of this activity is simply off the radar of a heavily secular Western intelligentsia, not least because of the weak ideational character of the former and the predilection of the latter to follow specifically intellectual trends. He also takes issue with the inclination of Marxists such as E. P. Thompson to denigrate religiously inspired self-restraint as mere "capitalist work discipline,"[35] arguing that instead such self-remaking can mean the crucial difference between utter impoverishment and small-scale respectability and even savings. The difference, of course, is that this is an individualistic or familial response to chaos and marginality, not a theoretical or political one. Martin insists that Pentecostalism is empowering for those who embrace it, even if it does not energize a "working class" designated by intellectuals to play the leading role in the redemption of a fallen world. Although it is by no means universally apolitical or conservative, the tendency of Pentecostalism is to withdraw from worldly affairs into its own protective shell. Martin suggests that Pentecostalism is a self-help system for the uprooted rural masses that will keep their noses to the grindstone and their menfolk out of the public house and the brothel. Writing against the grain of a secularized Western academy, Martin is seeking to rescue the abused Guatemalan housewife, the Nigerian businessman-preacher, the charismatic Korean healer, the favela-dwelling peasant from the Brazilian countryside, and even the deluded follower of Jimmy Swaggart from the enormous condescension of urbanity.

While Martin regards Islam as anything but voluntaristic, one might see the same dynamic at work among the so-called Islamic Calvinists who now run a once-hypersecular Turkey. Parallel developments have also taken place in other parts of the Islamic world, where the retreat of states and the decline of Arab nationalism and socialism have given rise to self-help movements of Islamic coloration, such as Hamas in Gaza and Hizbollah in Lebanon.[36] The demise of one eschatology—a secular variant promising that the meek would inherit the earth in their lifetimes—may have given wing to another, in which the rewards are deferred to another life.

As a sclerotic Soviet Communism in its waning years ceded the field of utopian dreams to a surge of religiously inspired movements, this picture made considerable sense. Daniel Bell had proposed such a scenario already in the late 1970s, viewing both Marxism and modernism as exhausted and ripe for replacement by transcendental yearnings.[37] Now that economic crisis has lent some renewed legitimacy to statist solutions of social problems, including in the United States, however, one wonders whether this image of developments will maintain its plausibility. The specter of a surging but very much top-down China,[38] which has now surpassed Japan as the world's second-largest economy and dramatically raised Chinese living standards, raises doubts about any untrammeled hegemony of the voluntarist path. Perhaps the two *modi*—the bottom-up approach generated by sectarian Protestantism and the top-down approach of gerontocratically managed capitalism—are fated to confront each other in Africa, Latin America, and Asia itself as contending models of improvement and uplift.

Secularization in Europe and the United States

Now that we have addressed what secularization is and what may cause it, we may address the question of whether it has actually taken place—in Europe, the United States, and elsewhere. This is unavoidably an historical and comparative question. The language of "exceptionalism" notwithstanding, each case has its own peculiarities that must be teased out in order to make sense of the patterns of religiosity or its decline.

Two paradigms, in particular, have been proposed to characterize tendencies toward secularization in Europe: "believing without belonging," initially proposed as a characterization of the United Kingdom,[39] and "belonging without believing," mainly for Scandinavia but also relevant to Germany. The general conclusion is that Europeans—with the exception of, say, Ireland, Greece, and Poland—have become a decidedly unchurched or nonparticipating population (although religious participation, if not belief, has also declined considerably in Ireland as the Celtic tiger advanced economically over the past quarter-century). The exceptions are cases in which religiosity and nationhood have strongly overlapped.

It may nonetheless be the case that there remains significant "demand" for religion; Stark and Finke insist that there is considerable evidence of new sectarian activity.[40] Defining religion fundamentally in terms of belief, they are inclined to dismiss the notion that religious demand has weakened—as far as they are concerned, only the supply is poor. Along similar lines, Andrew Greeley has produced substantial evidence of belief in God, the afterlife, and the like, among Europeans.[41] Yet Norris and Inglehart dismiss his claim that religion is "relatively unchanged" in the traditionally Catholic countries of the continent as "a triumph of hope over experience, and sharply at odds with the evidence."[42] Nor is there much indication that Greeley's spiritual superior (he is a Catholic priest as well as a sociologist), Pope Benedict XVI, would share this sanguine view of matters.

Similarly, David Martin argues that most European contexts are infertile fields for supporting new religious growths due to the significant cooling of the continent's religious temperature, although there are missions by some Pentecostalist and other groups that evangelize among European populations, often those of the European periphery (such as Portugal, southern Italy, and—bizarrely—Sweden).[43] Martin[44] and Mark Noll suggest that the "hot" religiosity offered by Pentecostalism appeals primarily to the uprooted and upwardly mobile poor streaming into the urban areas of the global South. Noll, one of the Christianly *engagé* scholars described by John Schmalzbauer and Kathleen Mahoney in chapter 9 in this volume, argues that the non-European (and non-Islamic) world is proving amenable to the voluntaristic Protestant message because "globalization and other factors have created societies that resemble in many ways what Americans experienced in the frontier period of their history."[45] Martin's nuanced and ideographic approach jibes with Norris and Inglehart's statistically substantiated view that religiosity chills when basic ("materialist") needs are met, while it is the more vulnerable and marginalized who seek religious succor. Some see the persistence of a religious impulse in the spread among European populations of New Age spirituality and other individualized religions, especially among the better-educated. Others insist that this sort of "warm" religion is effectively no religion at all and hence reject the notion that the flourishing of such practices can stave off the demise of religion's hold on the indigenous European population.[46]

These arguments shed considerable light on the secularization of contemporary European life. Yet they also raise questions insofar as a very substantial degree of the decline of religiosity in Europe is a product of the post–World War II period. After a couple of generations in which religiosity has taken a backseat compared to its earlier significance in, say, the Netherlands or Germany, it may appear that this is a fundamental, irreversible decline. But perhaps it will turn out to be a contingent product of the extraordinary prosperity of the postwar years, just as European unification has come to seem increasingly problematic as Germany flexes its political muscles in response to the economic crisis. We must be careful about interpreting whatever might be happening to us now as the "end of history," whether religiously speaking or otherwise.

We must also bear in mind that Europe is no longer more or less exclusively white and Christian. As a result of relatively large-scale immigration from predominantly Muslim countries, a growing proportion of the European population has Islamic roots. Martin's notion of "de-territorialization" is thus useful for thinking about religiosity in contemporary Europe, where Muslims constitute the major contribution to an apparent upsurge in religious identification. In the United States, Muslims are simply among the latest newcomers on the religious block; they merely add to the string that began "Protestant-Catholic-Jew," without making a major addition to the overall level of religiosity (there are also relatively fewer Muslims in the United States than in Western Europe). In Europe, however, the Muslim presence is responsible for the reactivation of the continent's otherwise latent identification with its Christian roots. For all the ugly anti-Muslim sentiment that it stirred up, the contretemps that arose around the so-called

Ground Zero mosque seems likely to fade with the ebbing of the commemoration of 9/11 and the Republican Party's efforts to exploit the issue for electoral purposes.

From a long historical viewpoint, more Americans are churched now than were at the time of the American Revolution, and rates of religious participation in church services have generally been high relative to recent Western European experience.[47] Still, trends in the United States with regard to religiosity hardly suggest unproblematic religious persistence. Gallup polls have for decades found that about 40 percent of Americans report that they go to church each week, considerably more frequently than their Western European counterparts. Yet these self-reports have also been found to be exaggerated, and a more realistic figure for such attendance is probably around 30 percent or less.[48] Some see this as characteristic of the differences between Americans and Western Europeans; the former feel that the "right" answer is to say that one has been to church, while the latter do not. Consistent with the notion of social desirability bias in favor of expressed religiosity, a recent survey found that atheists are at the bottom of Americans' list of groups that share their view of the world—a list that also included Muslims.[49] Americans are also much more likely than their European counterparts to belong to a religious organization, which approximately 60 percent do. This figure is actually down from a 1960 level of about three-quarters.[50] These numbers are substantial indeed.

Viewed from the perspective of one hundred years or so, the United States is without question a considerably more secular place than it once was in terms of the differentiation of church and other institutions. Institutions of higher education, for example, many of them founded with an explicitly religious purpose, are much less likely to expect daily prayer or other religious devotion from their students. Indeed, the secular research university tends to be the object of considerable hostility among strong believers. Meanwhile, the centuries-long predominance of a white, Anglo-Saxon, Protestant elite has been shaken since at least the election of John F. Kennedy in 1960. There has also been a growing contingent of nonbelievers, to the extent that President Obama explicitly acknowledged them in his inaugural address.[51] Still, those growing numbers who have abandoned religion resemble their European counterparts in the sense that they often partake of the same elements of "vicarious religion" noted by Grace Davie—such as the religious consecration of such moments of passage as birth, marriage, and death.[52]

If Barack Obama's inaugural speech is any indication, American culture seems increasingly constituted by and accepting both of unfamiliar religions and of unbelief. Given that Robert Bellah's arguments about American civil religion rested on the empirical foundation of an analysis of presidential inaugural speeches, Obama's address seems a significant datum. As Norris and Inglehart note, religion in the United States remains strongest among the poorest and most vulnerable segments of the society. There is also a regional inflection of religiosity in the United States; the Northeast and the West Coast tend toward irreligion, while the Midwest and the South tend toward greater religiosity. A country of some three hundred million inhabitants, the United States displays marked divergencies among some of its constituent populations, and some of those groups betray a more "European" set of attitudes toward religion. We might also note that the United States tends on many, many measures to be within a broadly "European" range of preferences and policies.[53]

In the end, however, the perception is correct that Americans are more religious, in the sense of the traditional measures of participation and belief, than their counterparts in Western Europe. Yet this fact has not necessarily mollified the more religiously concerned in the recent past. After a period of extensive debate about whether the public square was "naked"[54] and Americans had come to inhabit a "culture of disbelief,"[55] "god talk" has arguably attained a renewed acceptability in public discourse. Surely some would argue that this has led to an overemphasis on religiosity in public affairs, and this perception seems likely to be the source of the recent spate of stridently antireligious polemics by Richard Dawkins, Christopher Hitchens, and Sam Harris. Even liberals have sought to indicate that they are comfortable with religion, objecting to the notion that religiosity is the exclusive province of the right and seeking to refurbish the long-standing link in American life between progressive politics and religious commitment.[56]

One wonders at present about the consequences of the economic downturn for American religiosity. It is not at all clear that economic difficulties lead to increased churchgoing, as some people are inclined to assume and as the argument concerning religiosity and insecurity may suggest.[57] Nor has American religion been notable for its resistance to the depredations of American capitalism; the religious elitism of sectarian Protestantism is frequently seen as allowing for a view of economic life that happily countenances leaving those who fail to their own devices.[58] This stance has been less characteristic of American Catholicism, however, and in this regard American religiosity bears echoes of the corporatism of Catholic social teaching that has undergirded European statism and its relatively more skeptical attitudes toward the market.

Whether religion has more than prayer to offer in the depths of a severe economic recession remains to be seen. Some surely have seen the economic crisis as an occasion for reflection on "what really matters" and on how we came to find ourselves in such a mess. Barack Obama's interpretation of his religion clearly betrays a disposition requiring public service and a need to focus special attention on the needs of the poor and oppressed, though he has soft-pedaled that religiosity as president. As in the previous administration, churches and other faith-based institutions are being counted on to provide food, shelter, and other forms of assistance as the economy crumbles and state sources of support are exhausted or lacking. If churches are not seen as refuges from the storm, they are unlikely to find new recruits. But religious organizations have been providing this sort of assistance on both sides of the Atlantic for a long, long time.[59]

Conclusion

Charles Taylor's portrayal of a "secular age" in the realm of Latin Christendom (aka "the West") in which it is as plausible—perhaps even more so—not to believe in God as it is to do so captures a fundamental aspect of the modern era.[60] Jürgen Habermas's suggestion that we have more recently entered into a "post-secular" age[61] points to the return of the public significance of religion, especially among intellectuals for whom this was previously off the radar, and the corresponding need to rethink the relationships between faith and politics. Yet neither of these approaches tells us very much about the medium-term trajectory of belief and religiosity or about their specific patterns in the countries of the West or elsewhere. It is perhaps not coincidental that the worry about secularity among these two writers issues from North America, whereas that about the return of religion emanates from a Western European commentator.

Those who see a divergence in trends and fundamental dispositions between the United States and Western Europe are not wrong, but these differences can certainly be overstated.[62] While there is more active religiosity in the United States among ordinary people and elites, both

Western Europe and the United States are at least latently Christian, and this fact—along with their common domination by "white" ethnoracial groups—helps to sustain the notion of a community of outlook and interest across the Atlantic. While the active religiosity propagated by Americans spreads around the world into the unlikeliest places, Western Europeans tend to find its more enthusiastic manifestations an acute embarrassment. Former British prime minister Tony Blair's conversion to Catholicism—a voluntaristic act—seemed only to confirm the image of Britain as lying in the middle of the Atlantic rather than immediately off the French coast.

Without necessarily accepting the views of the "supply-side" analysts of religion, then, close examination of the "two exceptionalisms" suggests that religious demand is relatively consistent across time and that the anomaly to be explained today is the fairly pervasive irreligion of Western Europe. Against this background, Alexis de Tocqueville appears as the patron saint of the return of religion to a central place in the social scientific agenda, for he insisted—against the dominant assumptions of Enlightenment-inspired thinkers eager to replace religion with reason—that "faith alone is the permanent state of humanity."[63] "Alone among living things, Man experiences both a spontaneous disgust for existence and an immense desire to exist: he despises life and fears unbeing. These contradictory instincts drive his soul incessantly towards the contemplation of another world, and it is religion which will take him there. Religion, then, is only a particular kind of hope, and it is also as natural to the human heart as hope itself."[64] What are more transitory and less universal are the active forms that this hope may take, although these forms tend to be overdetermined by the latent religiosity in different historical contexts.

Notes

This is a revised and expanded version of a paper that appeared previously as "A (Post)Secular Age?: Religion and the Two Exceptionalisms," *Social Research* 77, no 1 (Spring 2010): 269–296. Thanks to an anonymous reviewer of this volume for provocative comments that helped me widen the reach of this version.

1.   Jürgen Habermas, "Faith and Knowledge," in *The Future of Human Nature* (Malden, MA: Polity, 2003).

2.   Charles Taylor, *A Secular Age* (Cambridge, MA: Harvard University Press, 2007).

3. Peter Berger, "The Desecularization of the World: A Global Overview," in *The Desecularization of the World: Resurgent Religion and World Politics* (Washington, DC: Ethics and Public Policy Center; Grand Rapids, MI: William B. Eerdmans Publishing Co., 1999), 2.

4. Aristide Zolberg, "How Many Exceptionalisms?" in I. Katznelson and A. Zolberg, eds., *Working-Class Formation: Nineteenth-Century Patterns in Western Europe and the United States* (Princeton, NJ: Princeton University Press, 1986), 455.

5. Richard Madsen, "What Is Religion? Categorical Re-Configurations in a Global Horizon," in Philip Gorski, David Kyuman Kim, John Torpey, and Jonathan VanAntwerpen, *The Post-Secular in Question* (New York: New York University Press, 2011).

6. Rodney Stark and Roger Finke, *Acts of Faith: Explaining the Human Side of Religion* (Berkeley: University of California Press, 2000).

7. William James, *The Varieties of Religious Experience* (New York: Penguin, 1985 [1902]).

8. Emile Durkheim, *The Elementary Forms of the Religious Life* (New York: Free Press, 1965 [1915]), 60.

9. Max Weber, "Religious Rejections of the World and Their Directions," in Hans Gerth and C. Wright Mills, eds., *From Max Weber: Essays in Sociology* (New York: Oxford University Press, 1946), 332–333 .

10. Martin Riesebrodt, *The Promise of Salvation: A Theory of Religion* (Chicago: University of Chicago Press, 2010), 76–77.

11. Max Weber, *Economy and Society*, vol 1, trans. Guenter Roth and Claus Wittich (Berkeley: University of California Press, 1978), 526.

12. David Martin, *Pentecostalism: The World Their Parish* (Malden, MA: Blackwell, 2002).

13. Olivier Roy, *Globalized Islam: The Search for a New Ummah* (New York: Columbia University Press, 2004).

14. See, for example, Eric Voegelin, *The Political Religions* (Lewiston, NY: Edwin Mellen Press, 1986 [1938]).

15. Jean-Jacques Rousseau, *The Social Contract and Discourses* (New York: E. P. Dutton, 1973), 272–273.

16. Robert Bellah, *The Broken Covenant: American Civil Religion in Time of Trial* (New York: Seabury, 1975), 3.

17. Robert Bellah et al., *Habits of the Heart: Individualism and Commitment in American Life* (Berkeley: University of California Press, 1985).

18. Steve Bruce, "Secularization and the Impotence of Individualized Religion," *Hedgehog Review* 8, nos. 1 and 2 (Spring and Summer 2006): 43.

19. Robert Bellah, "Religious Evolution," in *Beyond Belief: Essays on Religion in a Post-traditional World* (Berkeley: University of California Press, 1991 [1964]), 43.

20. In addition to Bender's analysis in chapter 3 in this volume, see her *The New Metaphysicals: Spirituality and the American Religious Imagination* (Chicago: University of Chicago Press, 2010); see also Leigh Schmidt, *Restless Souls: The Making of American Spirituality* (New York: HarperCollins, 2005).

21. Ernst Troeltsch, *The Social Teachings of the Christian Church*, trans. Olive Wyon (Louisville and London: Westminster John Knox Press, 1992 [1912]), vol. 1, 993.

22. José Casanova, *Public Religions in the Modern World* (Chicago: University of Chicago Press, 1994).

23. David Martin, *On Secularization: Toward a Revised General Theory* (Burlington, VT: Ashgate, 2005).

24. Casanova, *Public Religions in the Modern World*.

25. Though he never used these specific terms, I owe this distinction to conversations with Aristide Zolberg.

26. A number of observers have noted that those who object to the mosque proposed near Ground Zero in New York City, who often claim Christian inspiration, do not object to the salacious activities available in the same neighborhood that might also trouble a good Christian.

27. See, for example, Peter Berger, *The Sacred Canopy: Elements of a Sociological Theory of Religion* (New York: Anchor Doubleday, 1967).

28. See Joachim Gentz, "The Religious Situation in East Asia," in Hans Joas and Klaus Wiegandt, eds., *Secularization and the World Religions* (Liverpool: Liverpool University Press, 2009).

29. Mark Chaves and Philip Gorski, "Religious Pluralism and Religious Participation," *Annual Review of Sociology* 27 (2001): 274.

30. See Heinrich von Stietencron, "Hinduism," in Hans Joas and Klaus Wiegandt, eds., *Secularization and the World Religions* (Liverpool: Liverpool University Press, 2009).

31. Ronald Inglehart and Pippa Norris, *Sacred and Secular: Religion and Politics Worldwide* (New York: Cambridge University Press, 2004).

32. Riesebrodt, *The Promise of Salvation*, 172.

33. David Martin, *Tongues of Fire: The Explosion of Protestantism in Latin America* (Cambridge, MA: Blackwell, 1990), and Martin, *Pentecostalism*.

34. Martin is taking the side of Elie Halevy, who argued that the rise of Methodism prevented revolution in England, in a dispute that engaged such historians as Eric Hobsbawm and E. P. Thompson.

35. E. P. Thompson, *The Making of the English Working Class* (London: Penguin, 1968 [1963]).

36. See Susanne Hoeber Rudolph and James Piscatori, eds., *Transnational Religion and Fading States* (Boulder, CO: Westview Press, 1997).

37. Daniel Bell, "The Return of the Sacred?" *British Journal of Sociology* 28: 4 (Dec. 1977): 419–449.

38. Ian Johnson, "The Party: Impenetrable, All-Powerful," *New York Review of Books* 57: 14 (Sept. 30, 2010).

39. See Grace Davie, *Religion in Britain Since 1945: Believing without Belonging* (Cambridge, MA, and Oxford: Wiley-Blackwell, 1994).

40. Rodney Stark and Roger Finke, *Acts of Faith: Explaining the Human Side of Religion* (Berkeley: University of California Press, 2000).

41. Andrew Greeley, *Religion in Europe at the End of the Second Millennium* (New Brunswick, NJ: Transaction, 2003).

42. Inglehart and Norris, *Sacred and Secular*, 88. See also Detlef Pollack, "Die Wiederkehr des Religiösen: Eine neue Meistererzählung der Soziologen," *Herder Korrespondenz Spezial—Renaissance der Religionen* (Oct. 2006): 6–11.

43. Martin, *On Secularization*.

44. Martin, *Pentecostalism*.

45. Mark A. Noll, *The New Shape of World Christianity: How American Experience Reflects Global Faith* (Downers Grove, IL: IVP Academic, 2009), 189.

46. See, for example, Steve Bruce, "Secularization and the Impotence of Individualized Religion," and Detlef Pollack, "Die Wiederkehr des Religiösen."

47. Roger Finke and Rodney Stark, *The Churching of America: Winners and Losers in Our Religious Economy* (New Brunswick, NJ: Rutgers University Press, 1992); see also Claude Fischer, *Made in America: A Social History of American Culture and Character* (Chicago: University of Chicago Press, 2010).

48. C. Kirk Hadaway, Penny Long Marler, and Mark Chaves, "What the Polls Don't Show: A Closer Look at U.S. Church Attendance," *American Sociological Review* 58 (1993): 741–752.

49. See Penny Edgell, Joseph Gerteis, and Douglas Hartmann, "Atheists as 'Other': Moral Boundaries and Cultural Membership in American Society," *American Sociological Review*, 71:2 (2006): 211–234.

50. See Steven Pfaff, "The Religious Divide: Why Religion Seems to Be Thriving in the United States and Waning in Europe," in J. Kopstein and S. Steinmo, eds., *Growing Apart? America and Europe in the Twenty-first Century* (New York: Cambridge University Press, 2008), 28.

51. See Michael Hout and Claude S. Fischer, "Explaining the Rise of Americans with No Religious Preference: Politics and Generations," *American Sociological Review* 67 (April 2002): 165–190.

52. Grace Davie, *Europe: The Exceptional Case: Parameters of Faith in the Modern World* (London: Darton Longman & Todd, 2002).

53. See Peter Baldwin, *The Narcissism of Minor Differences: How America and Europe are Alike* (New York: Oxford University Press, 2009).

54. See Richard John Neuhaus, *The Naked Public Square: Religion and Democracy in America*, 2nd ed. (Grand Rapids, MI: Wm. B. Eerdmans, 1986).

55. See Stephen Carter, *The Culture of Disbelief: How American Law and Politics Trivialize Religious Devotion* (New York: Basic Books, 1993).

56. See, for example, E. J. Dionne, *Souled Out: Reclaiming Faith and Politics After the Religious Right* (Princeton, NJ: Princeton University Press, 2008), and Michael Lerner, *The Left Hand of God: Healing America's Spiritual and Political Crisis* (New York: HarperCollins, 2006).

57. Frank Newport, "No Evidence Bad Times Are Boosting Church Attendance," Gallup Polls, available at http://www.gallup.com/poll/113452/Evidence-Bad-Times-Boosting-Church-Attendance.aspx. Interestingly, this finding replicates one from the early 1990s; see Ari L. Goldman, "Religion Notes: God and Misery," April 4, 1992, available at http://query.nytimes.com/gst/fullpage.html?res=9E0CE2DD1E3BF937A35757C0A964958260&n=Top/Reference/Times%20Topics/People/G/Goldman,%20Ari%20L.&scp=2&sq=religion%20economic%20downturn&st=cse.

58. See Robert Bellah, "Max Weber and World-Denying Love: A Look at the Historical Sociology of Religion," *Journal of the American Academy of Religion*, 67: 2 (1999): 277–304, and José Casanova, "Secularization Revisited: A Reply to Talal Asad," in David Scott and Charles Hirschkind, eds., *Powers of the Secular Modern: Talal Asad and His Interlocutors* (Stanford, CA: Stanford University Press, 2006).

59. See, for example, Anders Bäckström and Grace Davie, eds., *Welfare and Religion in 21st Century Europe*, vol. 1: *Configuring the Connections* (Burlington, VT: Ashgate, 2010).

60. Taylor, *A Secular Age.*

61. Habermas, "Faith and Knowledge."

62. See N. J. Demerath, "Excepting Exceptionalism: American Religion in Comparative Relief," *Annals of the American Academy of Political and Social Science* 558 (1998): 28–39.

63. Alexis de Tocqueville, *Democracy in America*, trans. and ed. Harvey Mansfield and Delba Winthrop (Chicago: University of Chicago Press, 2000 [1835–1840]), 284.

64. Letter to Sophie Swetchine, February 26, 1857, quoted in Hugh Brogan, *Alexis de Tocqueville: A Life* (New Haven, CT: Yale University Press, 2006), 53.

CHAPTER TWELVE

Spiritual Politics and Post-Secular Authenticity: Foucault and Habermas on Post-Metaphysical Religion

Eduardo Mendieta

Let's note that the God whose death was announced by Nietzsche is not necessarily the God in which many of us still believe—I consider myself a Christian, but I am pretty sure that the God who died in Nietzsche is not the God of Jesus. I even believe that exactly thanks to Jesus I am an atheist. The God who died, as Nietzsche himself says somewhere in his work, calling him "the moral God," is the first principle of the classic metaphysics, the supreme entity which is supposed to be the cause of the material universe—and which, by the way, needs that special discipline which is called "*theodicea*" [theodicy], a series of arguments that try to justify him/her/it in face of the evils we see everywhere in this world.
—Gianni Vattimo

Introduction

One of the virtues of Charles Taylor's work has been to show that we have become secular not *against* religion but *because* of religion. Already in his numerous essays, collected in two volumes, Taylor had written about what he called the "expressivist tradition" and the Romantic tradition of valorizing the subjective and inwardness.[1] In his 1989 *Sources of the Self*, Augustine plays a pivotal role in the emergence of this expressivist and Romantic tradition that then gives way to the culture of authenticity.[2] For Taylor, expressivism and authenticity are inextricably linked to the "moral topography" of inwardness that he claims was first discovered by Augustine. In his *Malaise of Modernity*, published in the United States under the title *The Ethics of Authenticity*, Taylor traced and diagnosed three major malaises, or paradoxes of modernity.[3] One of these paradoxes has to do with the centrifugal forces unleashed by the paradigm of expressivism and Romantic inwardness. On the one hand, authenticity, that is, truthfulness to one's inner convictions, has resulted in a culture that valorizes individuality, uniqueness, and what Foucault would call, following the ancient Stoics, "frankness," or what Habermas called "subjective truthfulness." On the other, the explosion of mass culture, brought about in part by industrialization and thus the success of instrumental reason, has synergized with the imperative of authenticity in such a way and to such a degree that inwardness itself is sacrificed on the altar of consumption and fashion. This paradox is sublimely captured in jeans and perfume commercials that command us to be original, be unique, wear this—and of course everyone does, and so a large number of people look expectedly very much alike and not at all original and distinct. These themes continue to resonate in Taylor's most recent work. In his *Varieties of Religion Today*, which is an engagement with William James's classic work on religion, Taylor notes that religious pluralism and denominationalism more specifically are logical consequences of Western culture's basic concept of inwardness.[4] In general, it could be said that Taylor has been arguing not just that we have become secular precisely because of religion but that religion has remained vital and unsurpassable, unassimilable, because our foundational concept of the self was made possible by religion and in turn produces religious diversity. Or, in other words, by becoming secular, we also produce ever more diverse forms of experiencing religion, which is another way of saying producing ever more diverse ways of engaging in reflexivity. The secular age is thus also, perforce, profoundly religious. And religious fervor as well as freedom, freedom of faith and personal conviction, is the mark of that secularity. In his book *Atheism in Christianity: The Religion of the Exodus and the Kingdom*,[5] Ernst Bloch argues that "only an atheist can be a good Christian; only a Christian can be a good atheist." In a similar vein, Charles Taylor can be read as arguing that only a good secularist can be a good Christian, and only a Christian can be a good secularist. We can read him as claiming something like this only if we acknowledge that at the core of Taylor's genealogy of modernity and the secular age is recognition of the self-reflexive concept of the subject that essentially was inaugurated by Augustine.

When we discuss in the same breath, as if paradoxically, both secularism and the never-having-gone-away character of religion, that is, that we will never be able to exhaust religion or sublimate it into either ethics or art, we are in fact discussing the subject or agent that has a particular configuration because of the convergence of Greek, Roman, and Christian thinking. Secularism and post-secularism have as a common point of reference the question of the constitution of certain forms of subjectivity and agency. At the core of Taylor's work is a genealogy of subjectivity, agency, and inwardness that excavates its "religious" sources. Here, Taylor is very close to both Foucault and Habermas, who also have offered competing, sometimes conflicting, but ultimately converging genealogies of modern subjectivity and agency. All three, for instance, share the phenomenological critique of Cartesian and Kantian disembodied subjectivity that reduces inwardness to transparent epistemic certitude at the price of rendering the subject a prisoner of its own mind. They also share the hermeneutical critique of the de-historicized, de-socialized subject that would seem to be born fully matured and ready for complex epistemic transactions without having undergone a learning and socialization process. They all, in general, share a commitment to the valorization of what Taylor has called "radical reflexivity" and to the belief that this is what makes the modern subject distinct from other forms of subjectivity or agency.

There are, however, disagreements too. Habermas's move from Freudian psychoanalysis to developmental psychology, in the tradition of Jean Piaget, and moral psychology, in the tradition of Lawrence Kohlberg, puts him on entirely different ground from that of Taylor and Foucault, who reject the biologism and scienticism presupposed by both forms of "developmental" psychology. Habermas's adoption of functionalist and systems models of societal development, such as those generally associated with Max Weber and Niklas Luhmann, also set him apart from both Taylor and Foucault, who problematized any and all views of the putative progressive rationalization of society, or the view that all social progress is but further rationalization of social structures and organizations. Habermas's contributions to political philosophy, since the sixties, have been about the rationalization and domestication of political power by means of juridification (lawmaking) or public deliberation in a robust but "naked" public sphere.[6]Implicit in such an approach was the goal of purifying debate in the public sphere of nonrational or irrational appeals, such as those that are identified with religious or faith pronouncement. Taylor and Foucault, in different ways, rejected such purification projects. We know, furthermore, that Taylor was very critical of Habermas's position on subjectivity to the extent this had been articulated in his *Theory of Communicative Action*. In his essay for the Festschrift edited for his sixtieth birthday, Taylor accused Habermas of having adopted an "acultural" analysis of modernity, one that instrumentalizes a cultural self-understanding that is the product of a first-person perspective that has to give an account of its belonging to a particular culture's self-reflection.[7]

This thumbnail sketch of convergences and divergences among Foucault, Habermas, and Taylor allows us to foreground three fundamental issues that frame the question of secularity and post-secularity, in which the question is whether they are incompatible or concomitant, whether, in fact, one implies the rejection or overcoming of the other. The three issues are as follows: First, what is the relationship between religion and "the political"? Indeed, the approving use of the term "post-secular" incites visceral reaction because it is taken to suggest that now religion can and should be mingled with the state. The post-secular conjures up the specter of a theocracy, or at the very least, the fear of the erosion of the wall of separation between church and state. Second, what is the relationship between social structures and rationality, or, more precisely, does the "rationalization" of social institutions mean their "secularization"? Indeed, since Max Weber, social theory has operated on the assumption that the rationalization of social structures (economy, state, university, family, etc.) has meant eviscerating them of religious contents and forms. We can say that rationalization means desacralization. Third, what is the role of the religious, of religion in general, in the constitution of modern subjectivities and agency? Since Niccoló Machiavelli and Thomas Hobbes, both subjectivity and political agency have been articulated without reference to religion. In fact, political modernity was born at the moment when political agency could be conceptualized without reference to either faith or religious justifications. At the same time, however, at least since Machiavelli and Hobbes, religion has been thought of as an expression of subjective self-relationality. To confess a faith, to proclaim a belief, is to take a stance vis-à-vis others. Religion thus became an instance, an exemplar of self-reflexivity at the same time that it was constitutive of that subjectivity. Each issue, in summary, represents a problem or a conundrum. The first issues we can call, along with Pierre Manet, the "Theological-Political" problem of the West.[8] The second we can call the problem of the rationality of religion. The third we call the problem of the religious sources of subjective reflexivity and intersubjective relationality.

In the following, I can address only one of these problems, namely, the problem of the religious sources, or religious determinations, of subjective reflexivity—which henceforth I will use as shorthand for not simply subjective awareness but intersubjective relationality as such. I want to defend the claim that the post-secular (post-secularity in general) allows us to gain a more expansive and substantive understanding of subjective reflexivity insofar as a post-secular consciousness and attitude can be the foundation for what I will call "post-secular authenticity." "Post-secular" here means post-metaphysical, and thus post-foundational.[9] I understand, and hope to illustrate, the post-secular, following Taylor and Habermas, as that type of abstemious and parsimonious philosophical and ethical attitude that dispenses with grand metaphysical and ontological commitments. But most importantly, the post-secular when conjoined with authenticity, means the affirmation of a type of subjective reflexivity and intersubjective relationality that neither dispenses with nor affirms a priori either the significance or irrelevance of religion for modern subjects. If by authenticity we can mean a way of constituting one's subjectivity, of claiming it sovereignly, then post-secular authenticity means constituting one's subjectivity without either hate or love of religion. In order to make plausible this claim, I will stage a possible dialogue between Habermas and Foucault, with Taylor as the moderator, on the question of religion. This dialogue will require that we do a lot of reconstruction and recovering of material that is not well known or is barely known. The aim, however, is not to show how one can convince the other, or how the one offers arguments against the other, or how the one is deaf to the other's analysis. Instead, I hope to illuminate the ways in which their respective engagements with the question of religion, with which their names are not generally associated, evidently with the exception of Taylor, allow us to confront what I called the problem of the religious sources of subjective reflexivity. In the end, what I will have accomplished by triangulating Habermas, Foucault, and Taylor is to trace a line of reasoning that shows how secularity and post-secularity are linked internally to post-secular authenticity.

How Religion Made Us Modern

More than two decades after Michel Foucault's death and numerous publications by Jürgen Habermas, it could be easily said that their philosophical and theoretical differences have grown and become even more incommensurable. Habermas's works over the past two decades on law, international politics, the rule-of-law state, the liberal state, and moral cognitivism have surely made him even more of a difficult dialogue partner for a Foucault who went in the opposite direction, namely, toward an ethics of existence and a hermeneutics of the subject that seemingly eschews the macro and global and sticks to the micro-level of the constitution of subjects. Yet here I claim that, unexpectedly and surprisingly, notwithstanding these two decades of temporal distance, it is at this juncture in Habermas's thinking that he and Foucault could most easily, productively, and perhaps with great sympathy, engage each other's thinking. At the center of this juncture is the question of religion. In the past decade, Habermas's preoccupation with religion has grown, to the extent that it has become a major concern and coagulating core of his recent work. Since 2001, when he gave his speech on faith and knowledge at the acceptance of the German Publishers and Booksellers Association's Peace Prize, Habermas has been writing a series of pointed essays on the role of religion in contemporary society and the public sphere.[10] During the fall of 2008, Habermas gave a series of lectures at Yale University. In the fall of 2009, he gave a seminar at Stony Brook University titled "From Political Theology to the Political Philosophy of Religion." This seminar was be capped with a public dialogue among Judith Butler, Habermas, Taylor, and Cornel West and a workshop dedicated to a growing manuscript by Habermas on "religion in the post-secular, multicultural world society."[11] What marks Habermas's recent work on religion is its post-Orientalist and post-Occidentalist tenor, and how it contributes to a new approach to questions of subjectivity and agency.[12] I will argue that it is this tenor, this orientation, this perspective that joins Foucault and Habermas, in unexpected ways, in their respective, and equally idiosyncratic, approaches to religion. In order to reach this goal, I will have to engage in a bit of reconstruction and synopsis of Foucault's work on religion, which I will then follow by an overview of Habermas's recent contributions on religion.

Foucault's Spiritual Politics

Jeremy Carrette's collection of Michel Foucault's "Religion and Culture" writings[13] as well as his monograph *Foucault and Religion: Spiritual Corporality and Political Spirituality*[14] have provided us with excellent points of entry into Foucault's immense and still generative contribution to the study of religion. Indeed, we philosophers tend to be ignorant of the profound impact Foucault's work has had on religious studies, and this may have to do with the general antireligion and anticlerical prejudices of the U.S. philosophical establishment. However, in his lengthy introduction to the twentieth-anniversary edition of his *Body and Society: Men, Women, and Sexual Renunciation in Early Christianity*,[15] Peter Brown surveys the work that has been done in the aftermath of Foucault's work and as a reaction to his own book, which he confesses was explicitly influenced by Foucault. Be that as it may, Foucault's references to and analysis of religious issue and themes are spread throughout his books. Yet it can be shown that Foucault's preoccupation with religion intensified in the second half of the seventies, during what has been called his "genealogical period."[16] We know, for instance, that the original plan for his *History of Sexuality*, which was to have five volumes, excluding the introductory volume, was revised to include only three volumes. One of these volumes, titled *Les Aveux de la chair* (Confessions of the Flesh) was to deal with Christianity, in particular, the problem of the flesh and the purification of desire.[17] "The Battle for Chastity," an essay published in 1982, seems to have been a chapter of this projected volume.[18] Here, however, I would like to focus specifically on his Collège de France lectures from 1977–1978, titled, perhaps misleadingly, *Security, Territory, Population*, in order to illustrate both the growing preoccupation with religion and the novelty of Foucault's approach to it.[19] We can make the argument that both his Tanner Lectures, "'*Omnes et Singulatim*': Toward a Critique of Political Reason,"[20] as well as what would become *Les Aveux de la chair*, have their roots or earliest formulations in this course.

Security, Territory, Population is the first of a two-part set of lectures that Foucault thought dealt with the history of "governmentality" and the "birth of biopolitics." At the heart of this two-year cycle of lectures were the concept of government of others and of oneself and the provocative thesis that the state, in fact, may have been a crystallization of governmentality, rather than the other way around. It is these sets of lectures that show us, more explicitly and lucidly, why Foucault may be rediscovered as a key political philosopher of the twenty-first century, and why his work on sexuality needs to be placed under the larger philosopheme of governmentality. But before we can turn to the 1978 course, we need to note that the 1975–1976 course, *Society Must Be Defended*, had announced Foucault's new methodological departure.[21] This new method, which he called the "genealogical method," would seek to explore subjugated knowledges in order to reveal the circuits and fissures through which and at which power is applied, contested, and made to circulate synergistically. One of the central methodological points of this genealogical approach was the denunciation and renunciation of the Hobbesian conception of sovereignty. This conception presupposes that power is unitary; it is repressive; it is negative and privative; it is deployed by a sovereign over subjects; it can be identified with a certain "substance" (the violence of the army, or the force of the police, the censure of the censors). In short, it is a model that conceives sovereign power as something "someone" exerts over individuals in discrete or quantifiable forms. The genealogical analysis of power unmasks its capillarity and defused character through an analysis of its effects on the periphery of social existence, the mundane and pedestrian ways in which we monitor, control, and regulate ourselves by submitting to certain norms, regulations, and disciplines. The genealogical method begins with the fact of given practices and techniques of social regimentation and normalization, suspending and bracketing the question of a sovereign that exerts its will over subjects. Instead of who and what, the genealogical approach asks about practices and relations.

In the 1975–1976 course, Foucault introduces the concept of biopolitics and biopower as forms of control and submission that bypass or are different from the Hobbesian model of governance.[22] In contrast to the Hobbesian form of governance, which has the power to put to death and to let live, biopolitical governance makes live and lets die.[23] It is within the context of this provocative analysis of the transformation of political power that Foucault offers his chilling analysis of racism. It is chilling because Foucault shows both the singularity and also the inescapability of the genocidal racisms that would emerge with modernity.[24] Racism, biological racism, the kind of racism that both justifies and compels, making it a duty and a necessity, the extermination of another race, appears in Foucault's analysis of the emergence of biopolitics as the modern correlate of a new form of governance. Racism is the means by which biopolitical power reclaims political power's grip over death. Racism allows, nay commands, the imperative to kill, but now in the name of the security and preservation of the population and not of some king or sovereign. Pivotal in this new power to make live and to be commanded to put to death is the emergence of the population as the target of political power. Biopolitical power makes live by attending, nurturing, enhancing, and protecting the health of the biological body of the mass of subjects, that is, the population. Biopolitical power thus is deployed over the living body of a mass of bodies that is simultaneously collective and singular. Killing, the selecting out, the excising, and the ultimate extermination of threats to that biological mass, the body politic of the population, is now seen as one of the uncircumventable goals of biopolitical power. Under biopolitical power, then, the health of the population has as its nefarious complement genocidal killing. Adumbrated in this lecture course, however, are two problematics that are extremely important for our immediate concerns. On the one hand, there is the problem of the population, namely, of what is a population and how it is to be treated and dealt with by political power. On the other, there is the problem of the appearance of a concern with government that is not reducible to the exertion of a sovereign will. Foucault's invention, or discovery, of biopolitical power forced him to deal with the problem of how new forms of governance had emerged.

The *Security, Territory, Population* lecture course of 1977–1978 begins exactly with a reinstatement of the methodological claims of the 1975–1976 lecture course: the need to think past the Hobbesian model of sovereignty to a new form of governance that deals with populations as a "biological factum" and as a set of processes to be managed, in accordance with principles dictated by the very logic of that biological organism. In the fourth lecture, from February 1, 1978, Foucault claims that the actual subject of the lectures is the "arts of government," or what he calls "governmentality." By "governmentality," Foucault meant three things, at the very least: First, the "ensemble of institutions, procedures, analysis, reflections, calculations, tactics" that are deployed or come to bear upon a "population," and for which political economy is the primary form of knowledge, and uses the apparatuses of security as a technical instrument. Second, "governmentality" means a line of force or tendency within the West that has led to the preeminence of the power of government over all other forms of power, such as sovereignty, discipline, and so on. It is to be underscored that here Foucault is indicating that there is a history of governmentality within which we have to locate the different modalities of political power. Additionally, and surprisingly, at least here, Foucault seems to be indicating a narrative of forms of government that seems to have a telos, namely the telos of "government." Third, and finally, by "governmentality," Foucault means the processes by which the state of justice (a modality of the Hobbesian form of sovereignty) became the administrative state. This is a process in which the state is "governmentalized"—that is, we have a line of development that does not lead to "*etatisation*" but to the "governmentality" of the state. It is at the conclusion of this fourth lecture and overview of what he means by "governmentality" that Foucault announces that the rise of this new form of power, of a governmentalized state, in which we have moved from a state of justice to an administrative state, had its roots in the Christian pastorate. Foucault then proceeds to devote the next five lectures to a study of the Christian pastorate and pastoral power.

About half, then, of *Security, Territory, Population* is devoted to an analysis of pastoral power. These lectures represent one of Foucault's most sustained, focused, and provocative analyses of Christianity and what he calls religious power. Evidently, what he claims in those lectures has to be supplemented with what he went on to claim about Christianity and Augustine in the last two volumes of *The History of Sexuality* (and the fourth volume that was never published, as noted above), and in particular with what he says about Augustine and the art of writing as a form of care of the self in his *Hermeneutics of the Subject* lectures from 1981–1982.[25] Most importantly, I want to argue, now that we have access to these lectures from the period when Foucault is moving toward a full-fledged analysis of the genealogy of the subject, we can have a better understanding of why he would be interested in what was going on in Iran during the late seventies, which would culminate in the Iranian revolution that brought Khomeini to power. But I will return to this shortly. For the moment, I want to briefly survey some of the key claims in these lectures.

The pastorate, which has its roots in Judaism, is characterized by three main elements: first, it aims at salvation; second, it entails submission to God's law; and third, it demands submission to a particular truth. For the Hebrews, the pastor guides to salvation, prescribes or reveals the law, and teaches the truth. Christianity takes over this pastorate and modifies it through four new principles: First, we have the principle of analytical responsibility, which means that the pastor is responsible for each sheep and the entire flock. Second, there is the principle of exhaustive and instantaneous transfer according to which everything that every sheep does is the pastor's responsibility and vice versa. Or, in other words, when the pastor fails, the sheep are harmed. Third, there is the principle of sacrificial reversal, in which the pastor must sacrifice himself for the flock and the flock for the shepherd. Fourth, and finally, we have the principle of alternate correspondence by which the pastor must not always be completely virtuous lest he should be unable to teach the flock. In general, however, these principles lead to a very distinct form of the Christian pastorate in which there is complete submission of one individual to another, of the sheep to the pastor. This thoroughly individualized relation of submission, however, does not have a telos external to it. It is not as with the Greek submission to a teacher or master, in which submission is for the sake of edification, or glory, or virtue. Here submission is its own goal. One submits in order to arrive at a state of obedience. Finally, under the Christian pastorate, education is a daily teaching that aims at the spiritual direction of one's conscience. It is an education that leads to the discovery of an internal, secret, personal truth.[26]

In this way, then, the Christian pastorate gave birth to a new form of power, a power whose unique manifestation is that of individualization. The Christian pastorate gave rise to a unique form of religious power, a power that circulates and is produced by the processes of individualization that take place in and through the relationship between pastor, sheep, and flock. If we look closely at how the Christian pastorate was a form of religious power that individualized, we note that it achieved this through its analytical identification of each sheep, each devoted soul, the subjection of each sheep to the pastor, for the sake of achieving the state of obedience, and how it instigated subjectification, by commanding the discovery and confessing of an individual and private "truth." Through this analysis, Foucault arrives at the following formulation: the history of the Christian pastorate, which is yet to be written and which he himself does not hazard to undertake, is the history of human individualization in the West. And, most importantly, this history of individualization is a prelude to and precondition for the emergence of modern governmentality.

Foucault is quick to acknowledge that the history of the Christian pastorate was not marked by smooth implementation and transitions but is instead shot through with conflicts, contestations, and what he called rebellions of "counter-conduct." He identifies five forms of counter-conduct that led to the diverse forms and modalities of the Christian pastorate: asceticism, religious communities, mysticism, scripture, and eschatological beliefs. Each one of these practices, beliefs, and forms of congregation were avowed forms of counter-conduct that directly challenged the Christian pastorate. In this way, then, we have the history of the Christian pastorate as also the history of resistances to it, of its counter-conducts. Inasmuch as these forms of "tactical resistance" confronted the religious power of the Christian pastorate, they also revealed the extent to which Christianity ". . . is not an ascetic religion, it is not a religion of community, it is not a mystical religion, it is not a religion of Scripture, and, of course, it is not an eschatological religion."[27] As Foucault noted, however, inasmuch as counter-conducts directed themselves to the pastoral power of Christianity, they remained internal to or tactical vis-à-vis Christianity. They did not stand in a relation of exteriority but rather sought to challenge one or many elements of the matrix of Christian pastoral power. From this line of analysis, we can safely arrive at the following claim: that the history of the Christian pastorate, which is the history of Western individuation, is also the history of resistance to it. Within its very history there is concealed a counter-history, or a history of tactics of resistance that led to a pluralization of forms of both subjection and subjectification.

An important passage from a round table of May 1978, barely a month after Foucault finished his *Security, Territory and Population* lectures, captures succinctly what is at stake in Foucault's analysis of the Christian pastorate. The passage reads: ". . . isn't the most general of political problems the problem of truth? How can one analyze the connection between ways of distinguishing true and false and ways of governing oneself and others? The search for a new foundation for each of these practices, in itself and relative to the other, the will to discover a different way of governing oneself through a different way of divvying up true and false—this is what I would call 'political spirituality.'"[28] We could thus say that Foucault's approximation to a history of the Christian pastorate was a study of the political spirituality that Christianity enabled. Or, perhaps most pointedly, the question of political spirituality is really about the ways in which agents are formed and constituted through the exertion of a religious power that is immediately countered and resisted by tactics of counter-conduct through which those subject try to establish new practices of governing themselves.

The phrase "political spirituality" is provocative not only because it focuses our attention on these insurgent and contestational forms of individuation and subjectification but also because this is the phrase Foucault used to sum up what was both promising and unique in developments in Iran during the fall of 1978. We are fortunate now to have access to the ten or so different texts on Iran that Foucault wrote in the fall of 1978 and spring of 1979 because of the judicious scholarship of Janet Afary and Kevin B. Anderson.[29] In "What Are the Iranians Dreaming About?" Foucault closes with the following passage: "For the people who inhabit this land, what is the point of searching, even at the cost of their own lives, for this thing whose possibility we have forgotten since the Renaissance and the great crisis of Christianity, a *political spirituality*. I can already hear the French laughing, but I know that they are wrong."[30] In other words, the Iranians were dreaming of new ways of governing themselves, of giving birth to new modalities of subjectification that recapture the novelty and insurrectional spirit of Europe's own transit through that <u>stage of the aesthetics of the self</u> during the Renaissance, the Reformation, and the Counter-Reformation. It is also noteworthy that Foucault's cycle of texts on Iran closes with a brief text titled "Is It Useless to Revolt?" which is from May 1979 and thus was written after Khomeini had come to power and established an Islamic republic, and thus had already begun the implementation of codes of conduct in accordance with the Quran. There is a particularly important sentence that echoes the sentiments of the ones just quoted: "If societies persist and survive, it is because behind all the consent and the coercion, beyond the threats, the violence, and the persuasion, there is the possibility of this moment where life cannot be exchanged, where power becomes powerless, and where, in front of the gallows and the machine guns, men rise up."[31]

For Foucault, the Iranian revolution was particularly fascinating because it exhibited what he called a "spiritual politics," that is, a form of political counterpower through which agents try to fashion new forms of government of others and themselves.[32] The Iranian revolution was also particularly important for Foucault because it allowed him to see the ways in which religion remained an "irreducible" dimension of societies. We now know that Foucault was severely critiqued for his uncritical enthusiasm for the Iranian revolution. We also know that he refused to address the subject after his last brief essay. Yet, along with Afary and Anderson, we can agree that the Iranian revolution was not only of political but also of philosophical, and thus ethical, import to Foucault. He approached it not just as an activist and a journalist but also as a philosopher who saw in it a partial validation of some of his own theoretical insights. What is also significant about Foucault's writings on the Iranian revolution is that in them Foucault declaredly refused to reduce the religious to either a mere form of Iranian archaism or evidence of a postcolonial strategic instrumentalization of religion. In other words, Foucault refused to see the resurgence of Shi'ism in terms of either functional instrumentalization or ideological Machiavellianism.

What may not need underscoring, because it may appear obvious, is that for Foucault, "spiritual politics" is a way of referring to what Charles Taylor called "radical reflexivity." Foucault coined the phrase "spiritual politics" in the context of thinking about forms of governmentality, that is, forms of subjection and subjectivation. For him, every regime of government, every modality of governmentality, is shadowed by forms of both subjectification and subjectivation, through which we submit but also relate to ourselves through the ways in which we submit or refuse to submit. As Foucault claimed, his work on the Christian pastorate was just another genealogy of the modern subject. It is significant that in his genealogical analysis of the Christian pastorate, as already noted, stress is laid on how the Christian pastorate also gave birth to forms of resistance that challenged the attempts by normalizing society to subjugate them. At the heart of the subjection-subjectivation dynamic of the Christian pastorate was a relation of reflexivity that manifested itself most explicitly in what Foucault called "spiritual politics," a politics in which the subject positions itself at the most extreme point on the horizon of normalization in order to both resist and counter the order to subjectivation—spiritual politics, in other words, is that region or liminal space in which the subject witnesses to its "incalculable and intractable" freedom in order to give birth to itself.

Habermas' Post-metaphysical Reason and Post-Secular Consciousness in a Multicultural World Society

We must begin by acknowledging that Habermas's preoccupation with religion is neither new nor aleatory to his philosophical project. Already in his dissertation on Schelling, there is an evident treatment of religion.[33] In fact, one of his earliest published essays, a compressed version of his dissertation, attempts to trace the ways in which Schelling's theologically influenced reflections were appropriated by the post-Hegelian philosophical aftermath.[34] The essays collected in his *Philosophical-Political Profiles*, in particular those dealing with the Jewish influence on German idealism and historical materialism, are suffused with attention to the religious tonalities of German philosophy.[35] During the seventies, Habermas was in intense debate and dialogue with political theologians, such as Dorothe Sölle,

Johann Baptist Metz, Jürgen Moltmann, and, of course, Helmut Peukert. We can go on like this, marking decade by decade, over the past half century, Habermas's sustained engagement with questions of religion and the enduring relevance of religion in philosophy as well as social theory in general.[36] Yet, given the distinct nature of these engagements, it would be useful to offer a typology.

Throughout his intellectual itinerary, Habermas has approached the question of religion from at least three very distinct perspectives: the philosophical, the sociological, and, more recently, the political. The adoption of each one of these distinct perspectives can be said to correspond to different stages in the evolution of Habermas's theoretical project. Thus, from the fifties through the late sixties, Habermas's concern with religion adopted a strictly philosophical perspective. From this perspective, the religious was considered not just as that which philosophy must disavow and overcome but that which remains philosophy's point of departure and indispensable dialogue partner. From the early seventies through the early nineties, Habermas's concern with religion took a strictly sociological perspective. This is the period that corresponds to the formulation and development of his theory of communicative action. In the avowed goals of the project, articulated in the conclusion to volume 2 of *The Theory of Communicative Action*, the theory of rationality turns into a theory of modernization and societal rationalization that must give an account of both pathologies and inchoate paths toward remedying those very pathological rationalizations of society. In the same way that philosophy is assimilated into a theory of social rationalization, which culminates in modernity, religion is assimilated into a phylogeny of social rationalization, which could be said to culminate with the putative secularization of all subsystems of the social system. From the early nineties, since the publication of *Faktizität und Geltung*,[37] Habermas has devoted most of his theoretical attention to political questions. Over the past decade, therefore, Habermas has been approaching the question of religion from the political perspective, namely, in terms of how its endurance, persistence, and revitalization translate into an uncircumventable challenge and potential resource. Each period and perspective resulted in a different level of appreciation and evaluation of religion. The earliest period corresponds to a respectful distancing and valorization that refused to either dismiss religion or entirely appropriate it within the philosophical vocabulary, leaving no remainder. The second period corresponds to the now heavily criticized view that religion would become mere anachronistic and atavistic remains from an earlier phylogenetic stage in the evolution of society. The third period corresponds to a far more positive consideration of the religious. I would like to add that Habermas's more recent contributions to the assessment of the political valences of religion are couched not just in terms of challenges to liberal democracies but simultaneously, and with equal consideration, in terms of global challenges. The cosmopolitan intent of Habermas's contributions to the positive evaluation of religion is unmistakable, and this intent has become the more pronounced in his most recent writings.

Before I discuss Habermas's fall 2008 lectures at Yale University, I'd like to briefly consider what I take to be a neglected aspect of his contributions to the analysis of religion vis-à-vis constitutional democracies. In the speech presented in a dialogue with then cardinal Joseph Ratzinger, as well as in subsequent essays on religion collected now in *Between Naturalism and Religion*, Habermas has articulated an argument that seeks to valorize the role of religious views and convictions within modern democracies.[38] At a philosophical level, first, Habermas argues that religion has been and continues to be a source of "semantic meanings" that can provide moral resources to modern post-secular societies that they themselves can neither provide nor exhaust. Religion is an indispensable source of meanings that give both coherence and substance to the worldviews that are woven in particular life-forms. At a more political-philosophical level, second, Habermas argues that the secularist orientation of deliberative and constitutional democracies cannot and should not deliberately or disproportionately burden those members of the polity whose religious identities are significant to them. Participation in the public sphere should not be based on the preliminary disavowal and dispossession of one's religious convictions, not just because this imposes a particular hermeneutic burden on religious citizens but also because it can deprive and impoverish the public discussions that have to deal with questions of the good life that the procedural and deontological orientation of deliberate democracies cannot always address. An aspect of this argument that is not immediately evident is that for Habermas, the secularist bias of modern secular states really aims at fracturing or severing an important phenomenological and hermeneutical dimension of the socialization of post-conventional subjects. The self-reflexivity of subjects demanded by the post-conventional societal situation is short-circuited when contemporary secular states demand that social agents dissociate themselves from their otherwise meaningful and determining religious convictions before they can enter the public sphere or the space of democratic deliberation. For Habermas, the issue is not just of the relationship between the life-world and the societal systems, in which the latter threatens to colonize the former, leading to the desiccation and impoverishment of the former. It is also about the relationship between modes of "individuation through socialization" in which forms of agency and subjectivity are rendered more or less self-reflexive. Thus, for Habermas, and we will return to this point later on, post-metaphysical reason requires that it also become post-secular, just as post-conventional forms of subjectivity require that religion not be ruled out of order from the outset. Just as religion, in the West in the form of the Judeo-Christian tradition, gave birth to particular forms of subjectivity and agency (which Taylor analyzes in his masterful study), modern subjectivity and agency have matured to the level that they neither dismiss nor privilege religion as having a particular dangerous or atavistic semantic meaning. Post-secularity is related to post-conventional agency, as post-metaphysical reason is related to a post-Occidentalist and post-secular global consciousness.[39]

A quick overview of Habermas's fall 2008 Yale lectures reveals, furthermore, that Habermas is preparing himself to offer us a systematically integrated analysis of religion that brings together philosophy, social theory, and politics. Whereas his earlier contributions seemed to be episodic or occasional interventions, the Yale lectures reveal that Habermas is aiming to offer us an overarching analysis that is more theoretically unified and integrated with his earlier theoretical formulations. On one level, we have a reworking of the communicative theory of rationality in terms of a post-metaphysical and post-secular reason that eschews any kind of privileging of the Western path to modernity. If *The Theory of Communicative Action* was about a theory of reason as a theory of societal rationalization qua modernization of society, in his recent manuscripts, Habermas appears to be arguing that we must uncouple the Western path to modernity from global or different civilizational paths to modernities. In this way, a contemporary theory of rationality can only be a theory of different forms of modernity and not just one unitary mode of societal rationalization. In this way, Habermas's own philosophical work on post-metaphysical reason catches up with its sociological crystallization. If we take seriously the post-metaphysical aftermath of the linguistic turn, then reason can appear only in a post-secular guise.

At the social theoretical level, Habermas has taken on one of the central tenets of Western sociological theory, namely, the secularization thesis. At the core of Western sociological theory is the coupling of societal modernization with secularization. Habermas is sanguine enough to recognize that the resurgence and resilience of religion provide us with enough counterexamples for the claim that religion has been on the path to growing obsolescence and eventual disappearance. In fact, Habermas challenges the validity of five putative aspects of secularization. Those who defend the secularization thesis urge us to consider these five claims: First, that as levels of social security have increased and improved, religion as a social mechanism for dealing with insecurity has decreased. Second, that the functional differentiation of social subsystems has relegated religion to more circumscribed spheres of social interaction. Third, scientific-technical progress and development have led to the increasing and irreversible "disenchantment" of the world that has accordingly made appeals to religion less urgent or credible. Fourth, the structural differentiation of the life-world coupled with the functional differential of the social system have led to the liberation of the individual from proscriptive behavioral patrons. Fifth, the evident fact of religious pluralism has made religious comprehensive doctrines less acceptable in larger or encompassing social contexts. Habermas contends that the missionary expansion of the major monotheistic religions, fundamentalist radicalization, the emergence of postmodern or post-theistic forms of religion, and the political instrumentalization of religion give the lie to those five claims, or aspects of supposed secularization. As Habermas maintains: "post-secular society must adjust itself to the continued existence of religious communities in a secularized environment."[40] I would add, retrieving earlier Habermasian insights, as society has undergone processes of secularization, religion itself has been modernized, transformed, to make it more contemporaneous with a growing "secular environment." Thus as society has been modernized, religion has also been modernized. And just as there is a post-metaphysical reason of modernity, there is a post-theistic and post-secular religion of world society.

One of the most noteworthy and promising aspects of Habermas's recent work on religion is the way in which he links the study of the "resilience and resurgence" of religion to the methodological imperative to uncouple the postulate of social evolution from any specific model of social evolution that may be ascribed solely to the West. Understanding how religion continues to endure and play a decisive and irreducible role in contemporary world society requires that we localize, even provincialize, certain patterns of secularization that have been distinct to and distinguishing of the West. Thus, in contrast to the two methods that have dominated social analysis in the past century, namely, the systems theory and the radical culturalism approaches, Habermas champions a comparative study approach. Neither the systems theory nor the radical culturalism approaches do justice to local dynamics or the uniqueness of the new global multicultural society. The comparative study method, argues Habermas, is able to combine attention to systems development as well as rationalization of life-worlds in a way that does not gloss over differences or assimilate all processes into projection and colonization by one developmental logic or social subsystem. Post-secular consciousness is not just consciousness that is post-metaphysically enlightened; it is also, and perhaps just as importantly, a type of social reflexivity that guides a social theory that is open to the factum of a multicultural world society.[41]

In his 1983–1984 lectures on *The Philosophical Discourse of Modernity*, Habermas wrote the following on Foucault: "Genealogical historiography can only take over the role of a critique of reason qua antiscience if it escapes from the horizon of just those historically oriented sciences of men whose hollow humanism Foucault wants to unmask in his theory of power."[42] In order to accomplish this, Habermas continued, Foucault had ". . . *put an end to global historiography* that covertly conceives of history as a macro-consciousness. History in the singular has to be dissolved, not indeed into a manifold of narrative histories, but into a plurality of irregular emerging and disappearing islands of discourse. The critical historian will first dissolve *false continuities* and pay attention to ruptures, thresholds, and changes in direction."[43] It is clear that Foucault's critique of reason qua genealogical study of the Western Christian pastorate would lead to putting an end to a global macrohistory of religion in the service of opening our consciousness to other islands of discourse. It is also clear that this is Habermas's aim when he urges us to graduate post-metaphysical reason to its post-secular maturity.

Conclusion: Post-Secular Authenticity and Post-Occidentalism

Taylor closes his essay for Habermas's sixtieth birthday with the following sentence: "a better understanding of our Western modernity should enable us better to recognize the alternative modernities which are developing in other parts of the world, to free them from the distorting grid of a bogus universality and from our ethnocentric prison."[44] Part and parcel of a better understanding of Western modernity is acknowledgment of the centrality of inwardness or radical reflexivity. For Taylor, then, the project of challenging Eurocentrism and ethnocentrism is married to recognizing the importance of radical reflexivity in understanding our own culture. Here Taylor converges with Foucault's project of a problematization of self-understanding. Notwithstanding Taylor's critical remarks about Foucault (many of which can be rejected in light of all the work by Foucault that Taylor did not know and could not have known when he wrote his criticisms), both seem to agree that in order to engage in an analysis of our contemporary situation, we need to understand the way in which we have become the kinds of subjects who can ask about the very character of their contemporary situation. This is exactly what Foucault is arguing in his celebrated essay on Kant that carries the name of Kant's own essay: "What Is Enlightenment?"[45] This question, which asks about our historical ontology, is simultaneously a question about who the asking subject is. Furthermore, genealogy, in general, is always about how a particular ensemble of concepts makes any sense to a contingent historical subject.[46]

Taylor's critique of Habermas, enunciated in the early nineties, is no longer valid, especially now that Habermas has taken distance from the functionalist and systems theoretical (or Weberian and Luhmannian) aspects of his work from the 1980s. Habermas's work, however, ever since his hermeneutical stage in the fifties and sixties, has been informed by a preoccupation with reflexive agency. Already in his debate with Gadamer, Habermas announced the norm of a post-conventional subject who can and must take a reflexive relation to all meaning of the life-world, no less than of its very "modernity." As Habermas argued in the last chapter of *The Theory of Communicative Action*, which delineates the tasks of critical theory in light of the failure of the total critique of reification and functionalist reason, that part of a critique of pathological modernity was the self-reflection on the very conditions that made such self-understanding possible. The tasks of a critical theory include thus giving an account of the kind of subjects who reflect on their modernity, that is, their own contemporaneity. At the heart of this modern subject is what he calls a "post-conventional orientation" toward both moral and cognitive meanings, which is just another way of saying that modern subjects are reflexive agents par excellence. In his most recent work, Habermas has expanded his understanding of what this reflexive agent entails vis-à-vis semantic meanings that remain significant and unextinguished for modern societies. For Habermas, a reason that is reflexive is one that adopts a post-metaphysical stance toward both its own genealogy and the contents of its own deferred and localized universality. Such a post-metaphysical attitude requires that reason also adopt a parsimonious and abstemious relation vis-à-vis that which informs it without at the same time being able to either assimilate it or dispense with it.[47] It is attitude and consciousness that I claim can be called "post-secular authenticity." It names the kind of agency-subjectivity that has come of age and neither fears nor dismisses a symbolic reservoir that gave birth to it without being at the same time sublimated, or *aufgehoben*. A post-secular authenticity, that is, reflexive agency, is also one that has freed itself from its "ethnocentric prison" so that it can now encounter other cultures on the other side of Eurocentric arrogance.

While it is too soon to fully access the changes in Habermas's position on modernity, secularity, and the modern post-conventional and post-metaphysical subject, it is nonetheless possible to sketch the general contours of what may be called a Habermasian concept of post-secular authenticity.[48] If we bring together the insights developed in his most recent essays, those collected in *Between Naturalism and Religion* as well as those now in volume 5 of *Critique of Reason*, his collected philosophical essays, we are able to trace the pillars of such a concept.[49] My proposal is that Habermas's inchoate notion of post-secular authenticity is made up of at least seven main notions: First, the notion of an existential, ontological, and corporeal incertitude. Humans are biological creatures whose existence must be continuously secured and whose basic vulnerability is both a weakness and a mark of the possibility of its freedom. Our creatureliness is rooted in our neoteny.[50] We are born incomplete and thus always at the mercy of those around us. Second, but related to the basic philosophical anthropological notion of our existential insecurity, is our equiprimordial corporeal vulnerability. We are corporeal in that we are our bodies, while at the same time we are not totally defined by them. In the language of Helmut Plessner, we have *Körper* (bodies) but are *Leib* (flesh). Our entry into the social world is mediated by our fleshy existence—our flesh is the face of our vulnerability. Being one self, thus, presupposes that we come to terms with our existential incertitude and our corporeal vulnerability. Third, and without implying that freedom is rooted in our biological makeup, which could lead to a "naturalist fallacy," freedom is an expression of our fundamental biological openness. In contrast to Martin Heidegger, Habermas does not think that the communicative subject is not a biological creature. If for Heidegger, Dasein is never an animal, for Habermas, the human is always an animal, that is, a biological creature, whose basic characteristic is its incompleteness, its mangled character. Now, as we are corporeality related, flesh in relation, our freedom is not given but accomplished. At the heart of Habermas's political philosophy and theory of rationality is the concept of communicative or dialogical freedom. One could say that both negative and positive freedoms derive from a more originary form of freedom, namely, communicative freedom.[51] To be oneself, then, is not something one can accomplish alone. To be oneself, to live in accordance with one's own life plan, requires precisely an encounter with others. To be oneself is always already a relation. To be oneself is precisely to come to oneself by way of others, those who both enable or constrain our possibilities. It should be noted here that the pivot of communicative freedom is where social phylogeny intersects with individual ontogenesis, for freedom is singular but also historical. It is singular because individuals alone can be free, but free in accordance with historical possibilities. We are never free in the same way, and freedom is marked by a historical index that reveals how it is a product, a creation. To paraphrase Richard Rorty, freedom is not found or given, but made, and its making is a collective endeavor. Fourth, freedom registers the social or dialogical dimension of human action, just as it is also the expression of what is most individual and private. Communicative freedom depends on the possibility of "expressivist relationality." We are ourselves precisely because we can express our sense of what it means to be ourselves in a given set of social circumstances. To be a creature of language, or to be a creature that is *languaged*, spoken in communicative action, means not just that one enters a space of reasons in which what alone is true and right is what must be called to account vis-à-vis the objective and social worlds. Truthfulness is just as equiprimordial. Every speech act always raises the validity claims of effectiveness, truth, rightness, and truthfulness. When we speak-act, we refer to an objective world, a social world, and a subjective world.[52] Post-secular authenticity is the making explicit of this fundamental dependence of every speech act on the possibility of social agents expressing their subjective worlds. Fifth, and in tandem, there is no truthfulness or expressiveness without the possibility of aesthetic creativity, for creativity is the possibility of discovering what it is that is subjective. If to be oneself is coming to oneself, this coming is a creative endeavor. One is never simply oneself. One becomes oneself. This becoming oneself is a project in which freedom, expressiveness, and creativity are intermingled. Sixth, the communicative and dialogical agent at the heart of discourse ethics is one who, as in the Kantian tradition, can discern and know the moral. The post-secular authentic subject is essentially a moral agent whose moral actions can be universalized from within the real communicative context. Communicative freedom has as its other Janus face moral universalizability. Finally, and seventh, since communicative freedom is a social and thus historical accomplishment, it always implies what I would call "dialogical cosmopolitanism."[53] Every cultural formation is always the promise that some unique configuration between the objective, social, and subjective worlds has been accomplished that can illuminate our basic corporeal, social, and moral vulnerability.

Our triangulation of Foucault, Habermas, and Taylor has allowed me to illustrate more clearly how it is that we became modern not against religion but precisely because of religion. The staging of this dialogue has also allowed me to foreground in particular how it is that one of the ways in which we have become modern was precisely by coming to recognize that individual and social creativity are nourished by securing and expanding freedom of belief and unbelief. Our gods are as much our invention as we ourselves are the invention of the gods we believe in, or refuse to believe in. If gods did not exist, we would have to invent them, not so as to domesticate ourselves, to make ourselves into docile creatures, but rather precisely as an exercise of our freedom. By the same token, if gods were taken to exist beyond our human creativity, we would have to kill them in order to regain our freedom.[54] Post-secular authenticity names our contemporary maturity (*Mündigkeit*, to echo Kant and Foucault). It is a maturity that says, dare to live without fear of the gods but also without hate toward them. It is a maturity that recognizes the singularity and privacy of our encounter with that universal voice in each heart that calls us to be ourselves with and through others.

Notes

Epigraph, Gianni Vattimo, "Is Religion an Enemy of Civilization?" (Oslo speech, February 2009).

1. Charles Taylor, *Human Agency and Language*, vol. 1 of *Philosophical Papers* (New York: Cambridge University Press, 1985).

2. Charles Taylor, *Sources of the Self: The Making of the Modern Identity* (Cambridge, MA: Harvard University Press, 1989).

3. Charles Taylor, *The Ethics of Authenticity* (Cambridge, MA: Harvard University Press, 1992).

4. Charles Taylor, *Varieties of Religion Today: William James Revisted* (Cambridge, MA: Harvard University Press, 2002).

5. Ernst Bloch, *Atheism in Christianity*, trans. J. T. Swann (London: Verso Books, 2009 [1968]). This is a reissue of the 1972 Herder and Herder translation, with a new introduction by Peter Thompson

6. I have in mind here Habermas's *The Structural Transformation of the Public Sphere: An Inquiry into a Category of Bourgeois Society*, trans. Thomas Burger with the assistance of Frederick Lawrence (Cambridge, MA: MIT Press, 1989), and the criticisms in Craig Calhoun, ed., *Habermas and the Public Sphere* (Cambridge, MA: MIT Press, 1992), esp. chapter 9, by David Zaret. The reference to a naked public sphere is appropriated from Richard John Neuhaus, *Naked Public Square: Religion and Democracy in America* (Grand Rapids, MI: W. B. Eerdmans Publishing Co., 1984).

7. Charles Taylor, "Inwardness and the Culture of Modernity," in Axel Honneth et al., eds., *Philosophical Interventions in the Unfinished Project of Enlightenment* (Cambridge, MA: MIT Press, 1992), 88–110.

8. See Pierre Manet, *An Intellectual History of Liberalism*, trans. Rebecca Balinksi (Princeton, NJ: Princeton University Press, 1994), chapter 1.

9. I use "post-foundational" in the sense overviewed by Oliver Marchart in his *Post-foundational Political Thought: Political Difference in Nancy, Lefort, Badio and Laclau* (Edinburgh: Edinburgh University Press, 2007).

10. This speech is now in Jürgen Habermas, *The Future of Human Nature* (Cambridge: Polity, 2003).

11. The public dialogue is now in Eduardo Mendieta and Jonathan VanAntwerpen, eds., *The Power of Religion in the Public Sphere* (New York: Columbia University Press, 2011). The papers presented at the workshop and Habermas's reply are

gathered in Craig Calhoun, Eduardo Mendieta, and Jonathan VanAntwerpen, eds., *Habermas and Religion* (Cambridge: Polity, 2012).

12. See Eduardo Mendieta, "A Postsecular World Society?: An Interview with Jürgen Habermas," in *The Immanent Frame*, http://blogs.ssrc.org/tif/2010/02/03/a-postsecular-world-society/ (accessed Jan. 14, 2011). See also Mendieta, "Rationality, Modernity and Secularization," in Barbara Fultner, ed., *Habermas: Key Concepts* (Durham, NC: Acumen, 2011), 222–238.

13. Michel Foucault, *Religion and Culture*, ed. Jeremy R. Carrette (New York: Routledge, 1999).

14. Jeremy R. Carrette, *Foucault and Religion: Spiritual Corporality and Political Spirituality* (New York: Routledge, 1999).

15. Peter Brown, *Body and Society: Men, Women, and Sexual Renunciation in Early Christianity* (New York: Columbia University Press, 2008 [1998]).

16. See Todd May, *The Philosophy of Foucault* (Montreal and Kingston: McGill-Queens's University Press, 2006), chapter 3.

17. See Didier Eribon, *Michel Foucault*, trans. Betsy Wing (Cambridge, MA: Harvard University Press, 1991), 320, and David Macey, *The Lives of Michel Foucault* (New York: Pantheon, 1994), 466. For a thorough and insightful analysis of the different versions of the plan for "The History of Sexuality," see Stuart Elden, "The Problem of Confession: The Productive Failure of Foucault's *History of Sexuality*," in *Journal for Cultural Research* 9, no. 1 (January 2005): 23–41. Elden cites Foucault's third-person description of the forthcoming fourth volume, *Les Aveux de la chair*, on p. 32.

18. See Michel Foucault, *Politics, Philosophy, Culture: Interviews and Other Writings, 1977–1984*, ed. Lawrence D. Kritzman (New York and London: Routledge, 1988), 227–241.

19. Michael Foucault, *Security, Territory, Population: Lectures at the Collège de France, 1977–78*, trans. Graham Burchell (New York: Palgrave Macmillan, 2007).

20. See Michel Foucault, *Power: Essential Works of Foucault, 1954–1984*, ed. James D. Faubion (New York: New Press, 2000), 298–325.

21. Michael Foucault, *"Society Must Be Defended": Lectures at the Collège de France, 1975–1976*, trans. David Macey (New York: Picador, 2003). For an extensive analysis, see Stuart Elden, "The War of Races and the Constitution of the State: Foucault's 'Il faut défénder la société' and the Politics of Calculation," *boundary 2* 29, no. 1: 125–152.

22. See Chloë Taylor, "Biopower," in Dianna Taylor, *Michel Foucault: Key Concepts* (Durham, NC: Acumen, 2011), 41–54.

23. This is the formulation we also find in Michel Foucault, *The History of Sexuality*, vol. 1: *An Introduction*, trans. Robert Hurley (New York: Pantheon, 1978), 135–159.

24. See Eduardo Mendieta, "'Hacer Vivir y Dejar Morir': Foucault y la Genealogía del Racismo," *Tabula Rasa*, no. 6 (January–June 2007): 137–152. Available at www.unicolmayor.edu.co/investigaciones/tabularasa.html.

25. Michael Foucault, *Hermeneutics of the Subject: Lectures at the Collège de France, 1981–1982*, trans. Graham Burchell (New York: Picador, 2004).

26. Foucault, *Security, Territory, Population*, 169–172.

27. Ibid., 214.

28. Michael Foucault, *Power: Essential Works of Foucault, 1954–1984*, ed. James D. Faubion (New York: New Press, 2000), vol. 3: 233.

29. Janet Afary and Kevin B. Anderson, *Foucault and the Iranian Revolution: Gender and the Seductions of Islamism* (Chicago: University of Chicago Press, 2005).

30. Ibid., 209.

31. Ibid., 263–264.

32. See Karen Vintges, "Freedom and Spirituality," in Dianna Taylor, ed., *Michel Foucault: Key Concepts* (Durham, NC: Acumen, 2011), 99–110.

33. Jürgen Habermas, *Das Absolute und die Geschichte: Von der Zwiespältigkeit in Schellings Denken* (Bonn: Bouvier, 1954).

34. See Jürgen Habermas, *Theorie und Praxis: Sozialphilosophische Studien* (Frankfurt: Suhrkamp, 1971), ch. 5.

35. Jürgen Habermas, *Philosophical-Political Profiles*, trans. Frederick G. Lawrence (Cambridge, MA: MIT Press, 1983), ch. 2.

36. For an overview, see Eduardo Mendieta, *Global Fragments: Globalizations, Latinamericanisms and Critical Theory* (Albany: State University of New York Press, 2007), ch. 8.

37. Jürgen Habermas, *Faktizität und Geltung: Beiträge zur Diskurstheorie des Rechts und des demokratischen Rechtsstaats* (Frankfurt: Suhrkamp, 1992).

38. Jürgen Habermas, *Between Naturalism and Religion: Philosophical Essays* (Cambridge: Polity, 2008).

39. See Jürgen Habermas et al., *An Awareness of What Is Missing: Faith in a Postsecular Age* (Cambridge: Polity, 2010), esp. Habermas's chapter and reply.

40. Jürgen Habermas, "Essay on Faith and Knowledge: Postmetaphysical Thinking and the Secular Self-interpretation of Modernity" (manuscript, 2009).

41. In addition to Mendieta, "A Post-secular World Society?" see Jürgen Habermas, *Europe: The Faltering Project*, trans. Ciaran Cronin (Cambridge: Polity, 2008), esp. chs. 5 and 6.

42. Jürgen Habermas, *The Philosophical Discourse of Modernity*, trans. Frederick Lawrence (Cambridge, MA: MIT Press, 1987), 249.

43. Ibid., 251.

44. Charles Taylor, "Inwardness and the Culture of Modernity," 108.

45. See Michel Foucault, *The Politics of Truth*, trans. Lysa Hochroth and Catherine Porter (Los Angeles: Semiotext(e), 2007), as well as Michel Foucault, *The Government of Self and Others: Lectures at the Collège de France, 1982–1983*, trans. Graham Burchell (New York: Palgrave Macmillan, 2010).

46. See discussion of Foucault's historical ontology and genealogies of subjectivity in Eduardo Mendieta, "The Practice of Freedom," in Dianna Taylor, ed. *Michel Foucault: Key Concepts* (Durham, NC: Acumen, 2011), 111–124.

47. See Jürgen Habermas, *Postmetaphysical Thinking: Philosophical Essays*, trans. William Mark Hohengarten (Cambridge, MA: MIT Press, 1992).

48. There are a series of unpublished manuscripts on faith and reason that Habermas made available to a workshop on all of his work on religion that was held October 23–24, 2009, at the Institute for Public Knowledge, at New York University. The workshop was organized by Craig Calhoun, Jonathan VanAntwerpen, and Eduardo Mendieta. The results of the workshop will be published in Craig Calhoun, Eduardo Mendieta, and Jonathan VanAntwerpen, eds., *Habermas and Religion* (Cambridge: Polity, 2012).

49. Jürgen Habermas, *Philosophische Texte*, 5 vols. (Franfurt: Suhrkamp Verlag, 2009).

50. Habermas developed most of these ideas in his *The Future of the Human Species* (Cambridge: Polity, 2003) and *Between Naturalism and Religion*, chs. 6 and 7.

51. I expand on the concept of communicative freedom in "Habermas on Cloning: The Debate on the Future of the Species," *Philosophy and Social Criticism* 30, no. 5–6 (2004): 721–743, and "Communicative Freedom and Genetic Engineering," *Logos* 2, no. 1 (Winter 2003): 124–140.

52. Jürgen Habermas, *The Theory of Communicative Action*, vol. 1: *Reason and the Rationalization of Society*, trans. Thomas McCarthy (Boston: Beacon Press, 1983), 329.

53. On "dialogical cosmopolitanism," see the introduction to Mendieta, *Global Fragments*, as well as Eduardo Mendieta, "From Imperial to Dialogical Cosmopolitanism," *Ethics & Global Politics* 2, no. 3 (2009): 241–258. See also the

discussion of Habermas's cosmopolitanism in Eduardo Mendieta, "Interspecies Cosmopolitanism: Towards a Discourse Ethics Grounding of Animal Rights," in Cynthia Willett and Leonard Lawlor, eds., *Recenterings of Continental Philosophy*, vol. 35, SPEP supplement 2010 of *Philosophy Today* 54, 208–216.

54. These ideas are developed further in Eduardo Mendieta, "Secularization as a Postmetaphysical Religious Vocation: Gianni Vattimo's Post-secular Faith," in Silvia Benso and Brian Schroeder, eds., *Between Nihilism and Politics: The Hermeneutics of Gianni Vattimo* (Albany: State University of New York Press, 2010), 149–164.

CHAPTER THIRTEEN

Time, World, and Secularism

Craig Calhoun

Secularism is often treated as a sort of absence. It's what's left if religion fades. It's the exclusion of religion from the public sphere. But then it is seen as somehow in itself neutral. This is misleading. We need to see secularism as a presence. It is something, and therefore not entirely neutral, and in need of elaboration and understanding. It shapes not only religion but also culture more broadly. Whether we see it as an ideology, as a worldview, as a stance toward religion, as a constitutional approach, or as simply an aspect of some other project—of science or a philosophical system—secularism is something we need to think through, rather than merely the absence of religion. By the same token, post-secularism can hardly mean "after secularism," though it might signal an end to taking it for granted that a clear, stable, and consistent demarcation has been established between secular and religious dimensions of life.

Secularism, moreover, is only one of a cluster of related terms. Reference to the secular, secularity, secularism, and secularization can in confusing ways mean different things. There is no simple way to standardize usage now, no possibility of policing the association of each term with only one concept. But the fact that the different terms have a common linguistic root shouldn't obscure the fact that they operate in different conceptual frameworks with distinct histories. Although they sometimes inform one another, we should try to keep distinct such usages as reference to temporal existence, to worldliness, to constitutions distinguishing religion from politics, or to a possible decline in religion.

It is helpful to unpack some of the range of references. These have a longer and more complex history than is implied by a secularization narrative starting in the seventeenth or eighteenth centuries: secularism is not simply a creature of treaties to end religious wars, or the rise of science, or the Enlightenment. It is informed by a long history of engagements with the temporal world and purposes that imply no transcendence of immanent conditions. We need to understand this history in order to clarify contemporary discussions of religion and public life. Moreover, current discussions too often work within a sharp binary of secularism versus religion, and this too is problematic. Not least, such an approach obscures the important ways in which religious people engage this-worldly, temporal life; the important senses in which religion is established as a category not so much from within as from "secular" perspectives such as that of the state; and the ways in which there may be a secular orientation to the sacred or transcendent.

"Secularization" and Other Misleading Terminology

Secularism is clearly a contemporary public issue in its own right. France proclaims secularism, or *laïcité*, not simply as a policy choice but as part of its national identity. It is, however, a "Catholaïcité" shaped like French identity not just by generally Christian history but also by Catholic culture, its struggle against and ascendancy over Protestantism, and then the challenge brought by revolutionary and republican assertions of the primacy of citizenship over devotion. There remains a cross atop the Pantheon, a sign not only of its history as a church before it became a monument to the heroes of the secular state but also of the compromises between religion and *laïcité* that shape France today. These are informed by a specific history of anticlericalism, itself shaped not just by a long history of priestly involvement in politics, education, and other dimensions of social life but also by a strong reactionary effort to intensify that involvement during the nineteenth and early twentieth centuries. Thus secularism shapes the French response to Islamic immigrants, but hardly as a neutral category unrelated to its own religious history.

A version of French *laïcité* was incorporated into the design of Attaturk's Turkey and, not surprisingly, was also changed by the context. It was packaged into Attaturkism as an essential sign of modernity and as a demarcation not only from domestic Islamist politics but also from the Arab and Persian countries in which Islam has played a greater public role—at least until recently. A different model of secularism is a central part of the constitutional and policy formation in which India deals with religious diversity. In this case, secularism is identified not with distance from religion but with equity toward religions, including equitable state subsidies for Hindus, Muslims, and others. Still another secularism is embodied in the U.S. Constitution, which in prohibiting laws establishing churches has protected religious difference and helped to create a sort of marketplace of religions in which faith and active participation flourish. The reformulation of constitutional doctrine as separation of church and state later created its own controversies. And a broader secularism is attacked by parts of the American religious right as an element of the notorious "secular humanism." In each of these contexts, secularism takes on its own meanings, values, and associations; it is not simply a neutral antidote to religious conflicts.

Indeed, over a longer time frame, much of the most important thinking about the secular has been religious thinking about the relationship among God, the larger cosmos, and the world as we engage it in mortal and material life. Having an idea of the secular doesn't presume a secularist stance toward it. The Catholic Church, for example, distinguishes priests with secular vocations from those in monasteries or other institutions devoted wholly to contemplation and worship of God. A secular vocation, it should be clear, is not a vocation to promote secularism. It involves, rather, a calling to ministry in this world, to help people deal with temporal existence and maintain a religious orientation to their lives in this secular world.

The idea of secularization, by contrast, is a suggestion that there is a trend. It is a trend that has been expected at least since early modernity and given quasi-scientific status in sociological studies advancing a secularization hypothesis. This is often simply the prediction of a long-term, continuous decline in religious practice and diminution in the number of believers. This seems not to have occurred, save in Western Europe. A less tendentious version is embedded in the idea of a differentiation of value spheres. Religion may continue to exist, but in modernity it ceases to integrate economic, political, and other dimensions of life; it is one semiautonomous realm, perhaps protected from the others but also limited in its influence. In classic formulations such as Max Weber's notion of the disenchantment of the world, "secularization" refers also to the growing capacity of secular explanations and secular institutions. There is reality to secularization in this second sense, though not in simplistic expectations of a, pardon the pun, secular decline in religion.[1]

There has been an enormous expansion in the construction of institutions for worldly purposes. These are often demarcated from spiritual engagements, sometimes with restrictions on explicit religious practices. They not only pursue goals other than promoting religion; they operate outside the control of specifically religious actors. Much of social life is organized by systems or "steering mechanisms" that are held to operate independently of religious belief, ritual practice, or divine guidance. Markets are a preeminent example. Participants may have religious motivations; they may pray for success; they may form alliances with coreligionists. But despite this, economists, financiers, investors, and traders understand markets mainly as products of buying and selling. It may take a certain amount of faith to believe in all the new financial instruments they create, but this is not in any strict sense religious faith. For most, it is not faith in divine intervention but rather faith in the honesty and competence of human actors, the accuracy of information, the wisdom of one's own investment decisions, and the efficacy of the legal and technological systems underpinning market exchange. In short, it is a secular faith. Or, put another way, people understand what markets are by means of a social imaginary in which the relevant explanations of their operations are all this-worldly.

Not only markets but also a variety of other institutions have been created to organize and advance projects in this world. Schools, welfare agencies, armies, hospitals, and water purification systems all operate within the terms of a secular imaginary. Of course, some people's actions may be shaped by religious motives, and religious bodies may organize such institutions in ways that serve their own purposes. But even for those who orient their lives in large part to religious or spiritual purposes, activities in relation to such institutions are widely structured by a secular imaginary. Cause-and-effect relationships are understood in this-worldly terms as matters of nature, technology, human intention, or even mere accident. This is part of what Charles Taylor means by describing modernity as a "secular age."[2] It is an age in which lots of people, including religious people, make sense of lots of things entirely or mainly in terms of this-worldly cause and effect. In Taylor's phrase, they think within "the immanent frame." They

But what of my experience? Do I see things as separate or as connected? What is the daily experience.

see nonmetaphysical, nontranscendent knowledge as sufficient for grasping a world that works entirely of itself. One of the themes of Taylor's *A Secular Age* is working out how people come to see this immanent frame as the normal, natural, tacit context for much or all of their action, and how this changes both religious belief and religious engagement in the world.

A secular imaginary has become more prominent, and a variety of institutions exists to do things in this world. In this sense, one might say that secularization has been real. But discussions of secularization generally are not limited to this sense; they present modernity as necessarily involving a progressive disappearance of religion. Particularly outside Europe, this simply hasn't happened, and there is almost no evidence of it happening. Even in Europe, the story is more complex. Certainly it is not simply a linear pattern revealing continuous religious decline. On the contrary, the later nineteenth century saw a renewal in popular devotions such as pilgrimage and veneration of Mary and the Sacred Heart even while it also saw more explicit unbelief. Widespread withdrawal from religious practice dates especially from the second half of the twentieth century—more or less the era of the welfare state. The differentiation of value spheres—religious, political, economic—that Max Weber described as basic to modernity may be the more basic pattern, bringing a compartmentalization of religion. But we should be clear that this pattern was ideological, not simply a natural evolution. Moreover, differentiation is not disappearance. Declaring oneself an unbeliever is different from accepting an order of society in which religion matters prominently in some affairs more than in others, on some days of the week more than on others.

Many accounts of secularization take the form of what Taylor has called "subtraction stories." That is, they suggest that religion used to fill a lot of space and that religion has been removed from some of the space, leaving everything else untouched. This is another sense of seeing the secular as the absence of religion rather than something, a presence, needing analysis. For the importance of secular institutions has grown through historical transformations, not simply through a process of subtraction. Secular institutions have facilitated some purposes and impeded others. They have taken forms that empowered some people more than others.

Many secularization narratives present religion as simply an illusory solution to problems that could in modernity be met by more realistic solutions. But even without taking a position on the truth of any particular religion, one can recognize that religious practice takes many forms other than advancing propositions that may be true or false. From marriages to mourning, from solidifying local communities to welcoming newcomers in large cities, from administering charities to sanctifying wars that made charities more necessary, religion involves a range of actions and institutions. Changes in religion, including reductions in religious belief or organized religious participation, cannot accordingly be mere subtractions. They are parts of more complex transformations.

In order to get a better picture of this process, it is helpful to reduce the extent to which discussions of the secular, secularism, and secularization start with either the Peace of Westphalia or the Enlightenment.

"The Secular" through Time

The root notion of the secular is a contrast not to religion but to eternity. It is derived from *saeculum*, a unit of time important to Etruscans and adapted by the Romans after them. For example, the lives of children born in the first year of a city's existence were held to constitute its first *saeculum*. The succession of *saecula* was marked with ritual. While some ancient texts held that this should be celebrated every 30 years, making the *saeculum* roughly equivalent to the notion of generation, more said every 100 or 110 years, reflecting the longest normal duration for a human life. The latter usage dominated as calendars were standardized, and the *saeculum* became roughly a century.

It is worth noting that already in this ancient usage there is reference both to the natural conditions of life and to the civil institution of ritual and a calendar. Each of these dimensions informed the contrast drawn by early Christian thinkers between earthly existence and eternal life with God. For many, it should be recalled, this was something that would come not simply after death but with the return of Christ after a thousand years, a millennium, or ten *saecula*. Here too an older idea was adapted. The Etruscans thought ten *saecula* to be the life span allotted to their city. Romans celebrated the thousandth anniversary of the founding of Rome with great ritual in 248. This marked the beginning of a *saeculum novum*, though Rome's situation in this new era quickly became troubled. Christians started a new calendar, of course, marking years before and after the birth of Christ and investing metaphysical hopes (and fears) in the millennium expected in the year 1000. Here the succession of *saecula* counted the time until Christ's return and the end of history. In a very important sense, this was not what later came to be called "secular time." It was temporary, a time of waiting, not simply years stretching infinitely into the future.

Likewise, when Saint Augustine offered his famous and influential distinction separating the City of God from the City of Man, he did not mean to banish religion from "secular" affairs. On the contrary, his image of the City of God is the Church, religious people living in secular reality, and the contrast is to those who live in the same world but without the guidance of Christianity. Augustine wrote shortly after the sack of Rome in 410, an event that (not unlike the attacks of September 11, 2001) underscored the vulnerability of even a strong state. Some argued that Christianity helped bring on the attacks. Augustine not only insisted that Christian suppression of pagan religion was not to blame; he argued that Christian faith was all the more important amid worldly instability. He urged readers to look inward to find God, emphasizing the importance of this connection to the eternal for their ability to cope with the travails of the temporal world. They—even a Christian emperor—needed to resist the temptation to focus on material gains or worldly pleasures. One reason the pagans were often corrupt is that they lacked the advantage of Christianity. So Augustine distinguishes a spiritual orientation from an orientation to worldly things.

Augustine criticizes pagan religion for its expectation that gods can be mobilized to protect or advance the worldly projects of their mortal followers. Christians, he says, look to God for a connection to what lies beyond such "secular" affairs. God shapes human affairs according to a plan, but this includes human suffering, tests that challenge and deepen faith, and demands for sacrifice. Knowing this helps Christians escape from the tendency to desire worldly rather than spiritual gains. We need, says Augustine, to put this world in the perspective of a higher good.[3]

Augustine's discussion, along with others of the early Christian era, is informed by fear of an entanglement in worldly, sensual affairs. This is a theme dating back at least to Plato, a reflection of the prominence of ascetic and hermetic traditions in early Christianity and an anticipation of the prominence of monastic life in the Middle Ages. Caught up in the material world, we lose sight of the ideal and run the risk of corruption. This is an anxiety that comes to inform ideas of the secular. It is not merely the world of human temporality in which we all must live until the Second Coming. It is the world of temptation and illusion.

The contrast of sensuous and corrupt to ideal and pure is mapped onto that of secular to eternal. For one thread of the ensuing conceptual history, the secular is associated more with the fallen than simply with the created. Asceticism, retreat from worldly engagements, and monastic disciplines are all attempts to minimize the pull of worldly ends and maximize focus on ultimate ends. In this context, Christianity has long had special issues with sex and bodily pleasures. These run from early Christian debates about marriage and celibacy, reflected in Paul's instructions to the Christians of Corinth, through the tradition of priestly celibacy, to nineteenth-century utopian communities like the Shakers. The issue remains powerful in the current context, in which the fault lines of politically contested debates over religion and the secular turn impressively often on issues of sexuality and of bodies: abortion, homosexuality, sex education, and promiscuity have all been presented as reflections of a corrupt secular society in need of religious improvement.

Yet this very idea of subjecting the secular world to religious action is different from simply keeping it at a distance. The two notions have subsisted side-by-side through Church history. Both parish ministry and monastic discipline have been important. There are "religious" priests in orders that call for specific liturgical practices. There are "secular" priests who have not taken vows specific to any of these orders and who live "in the world." But religious priests may also serve parishes or go out into the world as missionaries. This isn't the place to try to untangle a complex and sometimes contested distinction, but we should note that its meaning has shifted with contexts and over time. For example, in some colonial settings, indigenous priests were more likely secular and resented what they saw as preferential treatment for priests in religious orders who were more likely to be European. More generally, secular priests were important to a growing sense of the positive value of engagement with the world. Overlapping the era of the Reformation, this period included figures like Bartholomew Holzhauser whose communitarian—perhaps even communist—Apostolic Union of Secular Priests formed in the aftermath of the Thirty Years War for the purpose of leading a renewal of religious life among laypeople.

This development coincided with what Taylor has called a new value on "ordinary happiness." A variety of this-worldly virtue received new levels of praise; new moral value was attached, for example, to family life.[4] Priests were called to minister to the affairs and moral conditions of this world, not only to the connections of people to the transcendent. In no sense uniquely

Catholic, this trend runs from the seventeenth century through missionary work that emphasized hospitals and schools as much as conversion and salvation to the recent dramatic expansion in the role of churches—not least large Evangelical churches—as service-delivery institutions. That is, they may espouse biblically literalist, or fundamentalist, or enthusiastically celebrationist theologies and religious practices, but they are also organized, in very large part, to deliver secular services in the world: marriage counseling, psychotherapy, job placement, education, help for immigrants. They are, in that sense, secular-while-religious. All the more so are those religious mobilizations that seek not just to serve people in their worldly lives but also to change the world itself, not least through politics.[5]

There is also a long and overlapping history around humanism and indeed humanitarianism. This appears in theological debates over the significance of the humanity of Christ, in late medieval and early Modern humanism, and in questions about the spiritual status of New World peoples. The Valladolid controversy, for example, famously pitted Bartolomé de Las Casas against Juan Gines de Sepùlveda and made clear that answers to religious questions had secular consequences: "Do the natives have souls?" "Should we think about them as needing to be saved?" "Are they somehow like animals and thus to be treated as mere labor?" Versions of these debates were intertwined with missionary activity throughout the era of European colonialism. They also influenced the idea of humanitarianism as a kind of value and a virtue linked to progress in this world. Informed by the idea of imitating Christ, by the nineteenth century, to be a good humanitarian was to be somebody who helps humanity in general and advances progress in society. This was an ultimately secular project, though it might have religious motivation for many participants. And this remains important in humanitarian action today: emergency relief in situations of natural disaster or war and refugee displacement is an important project for religious people and organizations (as well as others), but it is organized very much in terms of ministering to the needs of people in the secular world.

Some of the same ideas can inform ethics—and spiritual engagements—that do not privilege the human. Seeing environmentalism as stewardship of God's creation is a religiously organized engagement with (quite literally) the world. The Deep Ecology movement even introduces new metaphysical ideas, new notions of immanence. Others approach environmental issues with equal dedication but entirely within the immanent frame.

Religion, Politics, and the State

Throughout the Christian era, a key question was how the Church—and, after successive splits, the various churches—would relate to states and politics. It's an issue that goes back to the first century of the Christian Era. It forms the context for *The Book of Revelations*, written in the aftermath of the Jewish Wars. It shapes centuries of struggle over papal and monarchical power and, ultimately, issues with Marsilius of Padua in the doctrine of the Two Swords. Of course, this notion of distinct powers in different spheres was honored more in doctrine than ever in reality. Which is to say that the pope and the monarchs of Europe, who represented a kind of secular counterpart to church power, didn't live up to the notion of separate-but-equal for very long.

The Reformation brought an intensification of religion's relationship to politics. This produced considerable violence within states as religious minorities were persecuted, sometimes on a large scale as in France's St. Bartholomew's Day Massacre in 1572. It also shaped 150 years of interstate war. Of course, the "religious wars" that wracked Europe through the fifteenth and early sixteenth centuries were also wars of state building. In other words, they expanded secular power even when they were fought in the name of religion. Indeed, the conclusion of these wars in the 1648 Peace of Westphalia is often cited as the beginning of a secular state system in Europe. It is claimed as the beginning of modern international relations, understood as a matter of secular relations among sovereign states.

This is profoundly misleading. The Peace of Westphalia did not make states secular. It established the principle of *cuius regio eius religio*—who rules, his religion.[6] What followed was a mixture of migration, forced conversion, and legal sanctions against religious minorities. European states after the Peace of Westphalia were primarily confessional states with established churches. Members of some minorities moved to European colonies abroad, including English settlers who fled religious persecution only to set up state churches of their own in American colonies they dominated. Colonial-era governments (which often had established churches) further developed the category of religion—that is, reference to a set of bodies of partially analogous cultural practice and belief—in order to take account of the religions of the people they governed.[7]

There is much more to this story, of course, including different formations and transformations of nationalism. Sometimes closely related to religion, this was increasingly a secular narrative establishing the nation as the always already identified and proper people of a state and thereby a secular basis for legitimacy. It became harder for monarchs to claim divine right and more important for them to claim to serve the interests of the people. Where the power of absolutist states was closely tied up with religious claims to authority (and the daily domination of religious authorities)—as in France—revolution took up the mantle of secularism.

The European path to relatively strong secularism—and, in some countries, eventually irreligion—was not a direct one from the Peace of Westphalia. It was, rather, shaped by struggles against the enforced religious conformity that followed the 1648 treaties. The alignment of church with state after the Reformation produced relative peace in the early eighteenth century followed by growing conflicts over new philosophical and scientific ideas and challenges to the intellectual as well as sometimes the temporal authority of churches.

Though the Enlightenment came to be identified with secularism and free thought, it was shaped in significant ways by intellectual innovations among religious thinkers.[8] The Scottish moralists included some secularists like Hume, but more broadly the Scottish Enlightenment was shaped by a call for moderate religion, rejecting the "enthusiasm" of seventeenth-century Puritans and other militants not only because it brought political turmoil but also because it was rooted in appeal to personal conviction and experience outside the realm of intersubjective validation. Many participants called for grounding religious discussion in scholarship, not just personal revelation. Like German and other northern European Protestant counterparts, many emphasized the authority of the Bible but held that its texts were hardly transparent. They studied Hebrew, Greek, and sometimes Aramaic in order to understand the Bible better. This didn't succeed in banishing biblical literalism or claims to direct inspiration—to this day, many so-called fundamentalists are deeply suspicious that the "higher criticism" (to use a later phrase) means putting the norms of secular scholarship above commitment to fundamental Christian truths. But this began an argument within largely religious contexts that influenced religious developments and sometimes dovetailed with more secular attitudes toward the Bible as a historical text.[9]

Other participants in the Scottish and, more generally, British Enlightenment tended toward Deism, with more or less faith in Providence. Most were not hostile to religion even if they objected to both sectarianism and enthusiasm. Their followers were prominent among the American founders and were influential in the U.S. Constitution's guarantee of freedom of religion through its prohibition on the government establishment of religion. In England, the collusion of the established church in repressing popular protest brought Thomas Paine more readers of *The Age of Reason* than he had in America. And elsewhere too the role of churches in authoritarian politics helped to discredit religion and produce sharply secularist responses.

It is worth remembering that Catholic intellectuals also flourished in the Age of Enlightenment. Though the Jesuit order was identified with militant and sometimes intolerant defense of the faith, in this period it became increasingly scholarly and more deeply influenced by the cosmopolitan character of its work—as well as entangled controversially in politics. France produced numerous polemics against priests and religion before the Revolution and more afterward. The French Enlightenment was more directly antireligious than that of Protestant countries—perhaps because most Protestant countries had enough religious pluralism for confutative struggles to be played out among religious protagonists. But Catholic intellectuals were also active in the eighteenth century, not only in rebuttal of the Enlighteners outside the Church but also in pursuit of Church reform and theological advancement.

Anticlericalism was important in the French Revolution, but it was really in the late nineteenth century that the doctrine of *laïcité* took deep root. Right-wing Catholic nationalists and monarchists attempted to regain ground lost in 1789 and to suppress republican, radical, and indeed secular thought (not least after the insurrections of 1848 and 1871). They had considerable if unstable popular support, which they abused with anti-Semitic mobilizations like that of the notorious Dreyfus affair (as well as with financial machinations that eventually led to scandals). They were sufficiently hostile to the Republic that when the Republic triumphed decisively, it made *laïcité* not merely policy but a part of its vision of French national identity. This stronger version of secularism was the product of unchurching struggles—struggles against priestly authority—that continued through the nineteenth and into the twentieth century. These gave a more militant form to secularism and positioned it as a dimension of social struggle and liberation.

Struggles against clerical domination intensified largely because leaders of established churches tied religion closely to conservative political projects. The struggle against this, as José Casanova has argued as clearly as anyone, is central to what has made Europe particularly secular. It contrasts with situations in which there is more of an open marketplace for religion. This is one reason, perhaps ironically, the U.S. separation of church and state has been conducive to high levels of religious belief and participation.

More generally, such secularizing struggles confronted not only ancient state churches but new church-state partnerships forged in the wake of 1648. Indeed, Enlightenment-era intellectuals contributed to a misleading secularization story by presenting religion as simply the dark shadows of ancient superstition. But the intense focus on religion was not simply ancient. It was in many ways the product of the Reformation. Renaissance intellectuals—largely humanists and classicists—would have been shocked by the frequency with which their seventeenth- and eighteenth-century heirs quoted the Bible and insisted on doctrinal religious conformity. Religious engagement has ebbed and flowed, among both intellectuals and broader populations. It is crucial to recognize that it was made much stronger by the Reformation and by religion's entanglement in politics after as well as before 1648. Religious and secular action were constantly entangled in the making of modern Europe, at every level including motivation, organization, and ideology. The one-directional story told by Carl Schmitt and similar thinkers of a long-standing, nearly unquestioned political theology that gave way to modern secular states is simply not true.

It was not linear "progress" that produced modern, doctrinaire secularism but first an intensified project of religious domination and then reaction and resistance to it. The project of domination was not confined to a separate spiritual realm; that would involve the kind of thinking about differentiated spheres that developed in the course of modern social thought. It included the politics of states that were growing powerful enough to shape the life of whole nations, and it included intervention in ever more active pursuit of scientific knowledge. It was the struggles against such claimed authority that produced a strident, militant *laïcité*.

We see confused echoes of these struggles in today's European panics over Islam, which often strike a chord among populists and intellectuals alike that is not well-recognized. On the one hand, there are frequent contrasts of Enlightenment reason to unenlightened versions of faith. And many are indeed committed to an idea of comprehensive rationality, the supremacy not just of logic and empirical research but also of systematic, thorough, and exclusive reliance on them. This European history and concept-formation also informs the *laïcité* of other countries where anxiety over religious-political rule is strong—not least Turkey—though transposing it into a new context changes at least some of its meaning. Yet to take such commitments as though they are the whole story—their virtues a sufficient explanation for holding them—is to obscure both the more specific European history and the extent to which reliance on these ideas is informed by anxiety over specific manifestations of religion, notably Islam but also evangelical Christianity. As I suggested, the same issues were at the forefront of the Scottish Enlightenment. The great philosophers were proponents in various combinations of reason and research, but they were also opponents of religious enthusiasm. Enthusiasm always seemed to them to encourage not only belief on bases not subjected to rational criticism but failures of discipline. Enthusiasm encouraged both strong convictions and a willingness to express them directly in action. This was dangerous not only in religion but in politics, where it might seem to give warrant to radicals seeking to mobilize the "lower orders" in wholesale transformation of social institutions.[10]

Secularism can also designate a framework for religious pluralism, but this is by no means always the case. If Europe's trajectory was state churches followed by militant *laïcité*, the United States, India, and a number of other postcolonial states produced much stronger practices of religious pluralism. In fact, postcolonial societies around the world have given rise to most of the regimes of religious pluralism and religious tolerance. These are much less directly products of the European Enlightenment than is sometimes thought. They are shaped by particular contexts, and usually more by the pursuit of equitable and nonviolent coexistence among religions than by a notion of unbelief versus belief. They are institutionalized in very different models of state neutrality: if separation of church and state is the rule in the United States, the Indian state subsidizes religion but seeks to do so without bias for or against any.[11] And there is attempted neutrality, which need not be secularism, in the attempts of some self-declared Islamic republics to resist taking the side of either Shi'a or Sunni.

Nondominant religions may actually be disadvantaged by apparently neutral regimes that mask tacit understandings of legitimate religious identity. In other words, the secular may be constructed with one kind of religion in mind, such that it legitimates that kind of religion but doesn't do a good job of being neutral toward other kinds of religions or projects. Arguably, European secularism remains tacitly Christian in this sense, even while relatively few Europeans are committed Christians. This is important, because ideas of citizenship have been constructed in secular terms in most of the societies of the world.

This is also an issue with regard to how secularism gets mobilized in other projects. For example, the assertion of secularism may seem to be just an assertion of neutrality. But when it is written into a constitution, it typically reflects events that are not neutral: a new party coming to power, a revolution, or conflicts with international actors in other states. So there's always a political context, and one needs to ask of particular secular regimes what they express in that political context and how they shape distributions of power and recognition.

In a more general sense, the category of religion reflects not so much the self-understanding of the religious as the gaze on a plurality of religious practices—particularly from the standpoint of states. It is often argued that the root of the term "religion" is Latin for "binding."[12] But it is not the experience of being bound together with others or with God that gives us the category so much as the recognition of multiple different ways of being bound and organizing the ritual practices, moral understandings, and beliefs that follow from this. This idea was developed already in Rome, as imperial authorities recognized that other peoples had practices and beliefs not commensurate with those of Roman custom.[13] It was echoed in the Mughal, Ottoman, and other empires. The category of religion groups together objects—religions—understood as cultural phenomena. It thus includes those considered false religion—errors—not only the true and correct. It is a reference to phenomena in the secular world, even when articulated by someone who is religious as well as by someone who believes all religions to be erroneous.

Awareness of "other religions" was thus an awareness of systems of belief and practice partially analogous to one's own or that are prevalent in one's own society. It coexisted with other notions, like that of the infidel—one who lacked faith or at least the proper faith or, as importantly, failed to adhere faithfully to the proper practices. Faced with new divisions among Christians in the era of the Reformation, the idea of religion as a category gained importance, not least in pleas for religious tolerance but also in the attempt to separate religion from politics, especially interstate politics and war.

This awareness informed the Peace of Westphalia and with it the founding myth of modern international relations. This is grounded in the view that both religions and states exist as objects in the secular world. Each state is sovereign, without reference to any encompassing doctrine such as divine right. Carl Schmitt saw this as the transfer of an idea of the absolute from theology proper to political theology, rendering each state in a sense an exception but also beyond the reach of any discourse of comparative legitimacy. The Peace of Westphalia produced a division of the international from the domestic modeled on that between the public and the private, and it urged treating religion as a domestic matter. Both diplomatic practice and eventually the academic discipline of international relations would come to treat states as externally secular—that is, they attempted to banish religion from relations between states.

So thoroughly did the academic field of international relations absorb the idea that interstate relations were essentially secular that it became all but blind to religious influences on international affairs.[14] As Robert Keohane explains, "the attacks of September 11 reveal that all mainstream theories of world politics are relentlessly secular with respect to motivation. They ignore the impact of religion, despite the fact that world-shaking political movements have so often been fueled by religious fervor."[15] After all, it is not as though religion was not a force in international politics between 1648 and 2001 and somehow erupted out of the domestic sphere to shape international politics only in this era of Al Qaeda and other non-state movements. And of course it is not only Muslims who bring religion into international politics, as though they were simply confused about the proper modern separation. Consider, to the contrary, recent U.S. legislation mandating an international defense of religious freedom. As Saba Mahmood has indicated, the ostensible secularism or at least neutrality of the legislation obscures the fact that it is strongly informed by specific religious understandings.[16] Much the same goes for the demonization of Islam in the name of a secular national security.

But if the field of international relations is extreme, it is not alone. In general, social science is a deeply secular project, secular almost by its very definition. Particularly in the North American context, the group of fields called "the social sciences" became a separate faculty within the arts and sciences partly on the basis of a late nineteenth-century determination to separate itself from religion and moral philosophy.[17] More generally, in their very pursuit of scientific objectivity (and status), the social sciences (some more than others) have tended to approach religion less than one might have expected, based on its prominence in social life, and often only in ostensibly value-free external terms, leaving more hermeneutic inquiries to other fields. They also subscribed to the secularization narrative longer than dispassionate weighing of the evidence might have suggested.

Social science discussion of secularism centers largely on the role of religion in politics. What should be the role of religion in politics, if any? How autonomous should the state be from religion? How autonomous should religion be from the state? Certainly some social scientists join in the so-called New Atheism espoused by a variety of scientific authors seeking a more stringent secularism in reaction to religious movements. But this is more a matter of personal ideology than of research and scholarly argumentation.

Situated in the context of a dominant interest in the relationship of religion to politics, secularism is easily backgrounded. It is in this context that it is commonly treated as an absence more than a presence. But there is growing recognition that constructions of the secular and governmental arrangements to promote secularism both vary a good deal. Constitutional regimes approach the secular in very different ways, as a look at the United States, India, France, and Turkey quickly suggests. Questions of freedom of religion, of the neutrality of the state toward religion, of the extent to which religious laws should be acknowledged by secular states all put the varied structures of secularism on the research agenda. Likewise, there is growing recognition that secularism is not simply a universal or a constant in comparative research. On the contrary, secularism takes different shapes in relation to different religions and different political and cultural milieus. I have discussed mainly the development of European secularism in a history dominated by Christianity, but distinct issues arise around secularism among Jews and in Israel, among Muslims in different regions, among Buddhists, among Hindus, and in countries where more than one of these or other religions are important.

Ideas of the secular concern not only the separation of religion from politics but also the separation—or relation—between religion and other dimensions of culture and ethnicity. For some people, religion appears as a quasi-ethnic secular identity. Being Muslim, being Christian, being Hindu, being Jewish are mobilized as secular identities, like ethnic identities. People who don't practice the religion in any active way sometimes claim religious identities as secular markers, as do some people who explicitly declare themselves unbelievers. Likewise, recent use of the idea of "civilization" in reference to both "the clash of civilizations" and "dialogue of civilizations" has often situated religion as a central feature of a broader cultural complex and identity. This renews a sense of religion as culture, reversing the efforts of religious reformers who have sought to purify religion by separating it from nonreligious beliefs and practices.

Reform and purification movements in Europe in the late medieval and early modern period sought to separate proper Christian practice from pre-Christian inheritance: from magic, from superstition. Such purification efforts have continued, particularly among religious intellectuals, and not only within Christianity. This new policing of the proper content of religion also intensified religion's boundary with the secular as well as with other religions and other spiritual practices. It may have made explicit professions of unbelief more likely.[18]

Attempts to enforce doctrinal orthodoxy also raise issues about the extent to which "a" religion is unitary and the extent to which different national or other cultures shape versions of such an ostensibly unified religion. Do all Catholics in the world believe the same things? North American Catholics are a little bit shaky on this. Or are there strong national differences but limited capacity to recognize them? The Islamic *ummah*, or community of believers, ostensibly a unit of common submission to teaching and law, is divided not just between Shia and Sunni but also on national lines. What's distinctive in Indonesia, or in Pakistan, or in Yemen? Again, intellectual resources for thinking through the relationships among "secular" culture, varied religious practices, and proclamations of religious unity are important but often underdeveloped. Catholicism and Islam offer just two examples. We could add the upheavals of the Anglican Communion to this picture, or tensions over who is recognized as a Jew in different contexts. In general, it is unclear how much we can separate religion from culture, ethnicity, national identity, or a variety of other concepts constructed in secular terms. Or, put another way, how "the secular" is constructed shapes not only how religion is conceptualized but how culture more generally is understood.

But even people who are serious about their religious commitments and practices can be unclear about the relationship between the use of a religious label to denote religion as such or to denote a population. Muslim attitudes toward the relation of religion to politics, for example, are shaped not just by religious ideologies but also by resentment of external political domination. Such resentment is common among Muslims, but it is misleading to see it as an attribute of Islam per se.[19] Indeed, it is striking how much of what goes on among, or is ascribed to, Muslims is understood by ostensibly secular Westerners as integral to Islam. More room needs to be made for attention to the secular institutions of the "Islamic" world.

Questions continue to be raised as to whether Islam can be separated from politics. Debates about this, however, are shaped by previous debates over the division of religion and politics in Christendom. Aspects of European history are now projected onto and reworked in Islam. This isn't only a question about alleged theocracy or about clerical rule of one kind or another. It is also a question that shapes the whole idea of what counts as modern. The separation of religion from politics has come to all but define the modern for some.

Ironically, there are also concerns that this very separation has gone too far. Twenty-five years ago, this was the theme of Richard John Neuhaus's *The Naked Public Square*. More surprisingly, it has emerged in the recent writings of Jürgen Habermas,[20] which have generated discussions of "postsecularism." The term is confusing because it often isn't clear whether those who use it intend to describe a change in the attitudes of a large population or only a shift from their own previous, more doctrinaire, secularism. The stakes of the discussion are whether the democratic public sphere, first, loses the capacity to integrate public opinion if it can't include religious voices and, second, is deprived of possible creative resources, insights, and ethical orientations if it isn't informed by ideas with roots in religion.

Both John Rawls and Jürgen Habermas have reconsidered their previous arguments that the public sphere has to be completely secular in order to be neutrally accessible to all. Both have been advocates for a mainly processual, nonsubstantive treatment of public discourse. They argue that constitutional arrangements and normative presuppositions for democracy should focus on achieving just procedures rather than pursuing a particular substantive definition of the good.[21] Rawls initially excluded religious reasons from public debates; late in his life, he reconsidered and argued that they should be included so long as they could be translated into secular terms.[22] Habermas has gone further, worrying that the demand for "translation" imposes an asymmetrical burden; he is also concerned not to lose religious insights that may still have liberatory potential.[23] Habermas seeks to defend a less narrow liberalism, one that admits religion more fully into public discourse but seeks to maintain a secular conception of the state. He understands this as requiring impartiality in state relations to religion, including to unbelief, but not as requiring the stronger *laïc* prohibition on state action affecting religion, even if impartially. Indeed, he goes so far as to suggest that the liberal state and its advocates are not merely enjoined to practice religious tolerance but—at least potentially—should be cognizant of a functional interest in public expressions of religion. These may be key resources for the creation of meaning and identity; secular citizens can learn from religious contributions to public discourse (not least when these help clarify intuitions the secular has not made explicit). But, Habermas insists, it remains the case that a direct appeal to the absolute, a transcendent notion of ultimate truth, is a step outside the bounds of reasoned public discourse.

Habermas's argument presumes that such absolutes, or higher-order values, are absent from ordinary rational discourse and introduced only by religious beliefs (or close analogues such as nationalist politics informed by Schmitt's political theology). But here I would follow Taylor in suggesting that all normative orientations, even those that claim to be entirely rational, in fact depend on higher-order values.[24] Being completely rational can be one such value. Some higher values are very this-worldly, as, for example, in economic discussions in which either some indicator of utility or some hedonic principle of human happiness is clearly the higher value on which the entire discussion is organized and has a standing apart from any of the mere incremental values. So it is not clear that reference to higher values clearly demarcates religious from secular reason. The question of how "secular" the public sphere can and should be remains contested.

Secular Transcendence

The relationship between eternity and the temporal lies at the root of the idea of the secular. The secular world, this world, is the world of temporal change and also finitude. Transcendence implies reaching beyond this world to eternity and to God. But we should not ignore the possibility of another sense of transcendence, that of reaching beyond the limits of what actually exists, beyond the now and the identification of the real with the actual. To engage the possible and the future may arguably entail some version of what Kant called "the transcendental," that is, the capacity to know objects even before we experience them.[25] But I am concerned here not so much with the transcendental conditions of knowledge as with the capacity to imagine the future and orient oneself toward it (a capacity that I think also entails imagining the past and the continuity of the world beyond oneself as a specific subject).

In considering "the immanent frame," Taylor examines the rise of insistence on the adequacy of this-worldly explanation and understanding of all phenomena including human life.[26] Such thought seeks both meaning and causation in the world of senses and human action. Taylor suggests that life itself may be foreshortened by assumptions about what is possible and what counts as explanatory. Ruling out theocentric explanations is part of this. More generally, attempts to purge philosophy of metaphysics raise similar questions. The issue is not just the viability of particular explanations that rely on God or Gaia or *Geist*. It is a preference for reductionistic and decontextualizing explanations, and frequently explanations that resist reliance on ideas of "meaning." This preference is not entailed by insistence on this-worldly explanations; it is a sort of epistemic elective affinity. Ironically, it often has the effect of limiting the idea of the human even in philosophies (and scientific thought) that would appear to support humanism.

The limits are of various kinds. Mechanistic explanations bring some. An insistence that consciousness is a phenomenon of discrete, individual minds brings others. So does a sharp distinction between poetry and the reliance on unambiguous constative statements to represent (let alone evoke) truth. So does giving rational consistency paramount value. But my main focus here is on the tendency to equate the real with the actual. This inhibits attention to the past, the future, the centrality of poiesis, and important aspects of human being-in-the-world. It makes it much harder to recognize and appreciate the ways in which some "values," or what Taylor calls "hypergoods," give order to human life and action.

If we reduce "value" to "desire," for example, we can effectively work within the limits of reductionist explanations. Desires are as immediate as projected outcomes; they can be understood in purely material terms. But a value is something different insofar as it suggests a determination to make certain preference orderings in the future. Even desire is more complicated than often imagined. The model of desiring, say, food or even specific foods doesn't exhaust what we mean by the word. Desire for a life with my wife and family, for example, extends beyond possession and beyond experience of current pleasures. It places a value not only on what I might acquire but also on what I might be and what I might create. It includes current "tastes" but also anticipations—for example, that while I do not desire to be old, I prefer to be old in my marriage than without it. It includes commitments, world-making promises in Hannah Arendt's sense, and also hopes (including for forgiveness when promises are broken). But value also has other meanings, as, for example, valuing freedom isn't the same as wishing for the freedom to pursue any particular course of action (though how we think about it is surely informed by concrete images and desires). Even so, we could understand, or try to understand, freedom as simply one potential good among many—alongside dinner, a good night's sleep, and remembering your wife's birthday. When I sit in a faculty meeting and wish to be free of it, the meaning is of this sort. But the point of the idea of hypergoods is to remind us that the work done by values like freedom is not just of that sort. Beyond the concrete freedoms we wish, we may—most of us probably do—value freedom in a way that gives order to our other values and desires and thus to our actions, our lives, and our imaginings of possible futures.

We could say that freedom is a sacred value. The exaltation of specific values is one plausible meaning of "sacred." Whether equating the sacred to hypergoods is an adequate exploration of the concept is not my primary question here, but my sense is that it is not. This is only part of what the sacred means to us. The sacred is a matter of awe in a way that hypergoods may not necessarily be.

In any case, hypergoods, even if not sacred, reach beyond the immediate and beyond the immanent. They describe a way in which we are oriented beyond not only what we have now but also what we are or what we can achieve. Wanting ourselves to have better wants is a part of this. To be sure, valuing rational explanations and "being reasonable" are not transcendent in the way valuing God's will is. But what, say, of valuing universal justice or care for all who suffer or, for that matter, the beauty of the world? Universal justice and care for all who suffer are clearly aspirational. They can be located only in the future and, I think, only in a particularly hypothetical future, since it is not at all clear that faith in this future would be rationally justified. The beauty of the world is different. There is more than enough beauty in the world to inspire awe and wonder and longing and attachment. Yet every day, some of it vanishes; recurrently, we fear its loss, or loss of our access to it. This is part of the meaning of mortality, as well as part of the anxiety in a strong environmental consciousness.

Our relationship to the beauty of the world transcends the existing, even though it is intensely related to it. We understand that this beauty belongs to the world, not only to our experience of it.[27] As immediate as experience of it can be, its very magnificence and our awe and wonder are related to the fact that it is part of the world that existed before us and will exist after us—although anxiety about how long the world will endure may inflect and perhaps intensify our sensitivity to this beauty. This may offer a version of the experience of "fullness" that Taylor evokes. Taylor exemplifies this with a lovely passage from Bede Griffiths—troubling to some readers because of its apparent sentimentality—which indeed engages the beauty of the world. For Griffiths and perhaps for Taylor, the experience of fullness points to something beyond the world; it is a fusion of the immediately material with the cosmic and spiritual. Without denying that experience (or interpretation), I want to evoke the possibility of a transcendent experience of the beauty of the world that does not depend on fusion with something beyond the world but, rather, relies on the extent to which the world itself is beyond us, is enormous, and is, at least in the aspect of its beauty, whole. With a nod to Griffiths's efforts to fuse East and West, we might say it is integral. But we should be cautious here. The integration in question may not be a matter of logical consistency. The opposite of "fragmented" need not be "systematically integrated."

We may grasp the beauty of the world as involving innumerable connections without necessarily apprehending it as systematic. Thus by the "wholeness" of the world's beauty, I want to designate the sense of connections that constitute something larger. The connections are not only of classification, nor of cause and effect. They are of diverse and not necessarily commensurable sorts. We cannot abstract particulars fully from their contexts and connections. I mean to suggest something integral rather than fragmented, and thus not something complete in the sense of plenitude. By contrast, Taylor's metaphor of fullness could be read—against his own inclination—as signaling the kind of Neoplatonic completeness (and indeed hierarchy) traced by Arthur Lovejoy in his account of the great chain of being. That would be a matter of all spaces being filled in, recognizing connections especially in hierarchy, rather than of the ubiquity of connections and omnipresence of spiritual meaning.[28]

What I hope to evoke is the possibility of dramatic, moving connections that are nonetheless multiple and not readily commensurable. We could evoke this through the distinction between a polytheistic sense of the gods and the at least reductionistic versions of monotheism. In any case, monistic system building is not the only way in which we apprehend large-scale connections.

Connections are different from equivalences, and connections are not only matters of cause and effect. They involve shared culture and common histories. They involve the closeness to specific settings and versions of being-in-the-world that Heidegger described as "dwelling." This may involve a recognition of others as belonging in some of the same settings even without a sense of being the same as them or feeling fond of them. At a global scale, thus, we might helpfully think of a cosmopolitanism of connections, rather than one only of universal categorical equivalences. And at a local level, we may create the conditions of peaceful coexistence better through recognition of fellow-belonging despite difference than through a search for universalistic common denominators.[29]

In any case, there may be something transcendent in our connection to the beauty of the world. We reach beyond the moment, beyond our individual lives, and beyond a fragmented sense of existence. Something of the same transcendent connection may be forged in relation to the sorrows of the world. Think, for example, of the empathy felt for victims of the 2010 Haitian earthquake (or any of a host of other disasters). We respond not simply to recognition that those suffering are human. Our sense of common humanity is often represented as membership in a set of more or less equivalent individuals—this is the logic of human rights, for example. But that is not the only way in which we apprehend the human. We apprehend it in analogies, contexts, and connections. The suffering human beings who are represented as interchangeable masses in many media images are also connected to us by intertwined histories such as colonialism and slavery, by recognition of analogous roles like those of parent and child, and by the awareness that we have a capacity to act to mitigate suffering or to fail to act.

Our potentially transcendent relationship to the world depends in important ways on recognition that it exists without us. Yet we may also recognize that the world is in part made by human action (not only damaged by it), and indeed that we participate in that action, albeit usually in rather small ways. For example, it matters both that the consequences of the 2010 Haitian earthquake were so devastating because of conditions the United States helped to create—poverty, political instability, and the growth of Port-au-Prince precisely at an ecologically unsustainable site on a tectonic fault line—and that as individuals we have genuine options to care or not care, help or not help.

Connection to history and to projects of making the future is potentially a source of secular transcendence. By this, I mean two things. First, both consciousness of the past and anticipation of the future enable people to recognize the institutional arrangements and other features of the present as contingent rather than essential or necessary. This invites an awareness of larger (or at least other) possibilities. It may also suggest connections to people, culture, ideas, and threads of experience that transcend the immediately given. Second, people may work actively to transcend the limits of existing social conditions or culture. They may do this as individuals, but social movements are particularly important to this effort. They both depend on a sense of the possibility of transcending the given and (at least sometimes) reinforce this with experiences of transcendent solidarity.

Participating in a movement brings to many both a heightened sense of the possibility of transforming conditions others take as unalterable and a heightened sense of connection to others in the movement. These connections are not necessarily—and are generally not primarily—connections to humanity as whole. Nor are they necessarily "oceanic" feelings of connection to everything. They are connections to others who join in shared actions, to specific individuals and larger groups. They evoke the sense not so much of equivalence or sameness as of connection despite difference and of being in something together. Likewise, the sense of possibility need not be the anticipation of perfection. There may be mountains beyond mountains, movements beyond movements. Movements link the general sense of potential transcendence we gain from taking the historicity of human existence seriously to engagement in particular transformations. We wish to overcome capitalist exploitation, or environmental deprivation, or war—and usually specific capitalist abuses, specific degradations of the environment, and specific conflicts.

Similar thoughts might inform a different theological understanding. We might engage God less as the Absolute or the One at the center of the Neoplatonic order and more as being "in the struggle with us." Likewise, we might explore the extent to which transcendent connections to music and art are not to those categories as such but to much more specific works and events of performance or contemplation. These are mediated by history and culture even though they may take us beyond the limits of historical circumstances and cultural categories. But my main point is to urge us to think of both experiences of and commitments to transcendence in this-worldly, temporal life. A secondary point, which I have not developed, is that this need not be understood in the register of the "aesthetic." It may be much more directly connected to action in the world. In this regard, many modern versions of "the secular" and "the immanent frame" are importantly antihistorical. They suggest that we must accept the world as it is. They may argue especially against the hope that God offers something better in eternal life. But implicitly, their frameworks argue also against the hope that we can make this into a better world. This is ironic, since many of these self-declared secularists are in fact committed to making the world better through science, technology, and social reform. But the potential of these projects is often hemmed in by the tendency to treat too much of the existing as necessary and inevitable.

Conclusion

Distinctions between the religious and the secular are embedded in a modern era that also imposes a range of other differentiations, notably that of public and private. Many of these are closely linked to states and their administrative practices—indeed, in both colonial and domestic administration, states helped to create the very category of religion as one that would subsume a whole class of ostensibly analogous phenomena. But the differentiation of states from market economies, sometimes understood to be self-moving, is also powerful. These differentiations shape modern social imaginaries that in turn help to make the world. That is, by distinguishing politics from religion, or the economy from both, we inform our material practices and the way we build institutions in the world. Thus, the distinctions take on a certain material reality, but they can also be obstacles to a better intellectual analysis. The distinction between the secular and the religious is a case in point. It obscures both the ways in which religious people engage the temporal world and the ways in which states and other this-world institutional structures inform the idea of religion itself.

Max Weber famously argued that the differentiation of value spheres—religious, economic, political, social, aesthetic—was basic to modernity. The notion of value spheres is informative, but we should also be clear that the differentiations reflect (and reproduce) tensions among projects, not just values. The making of the world is pursued by both religious and nonreligious projects. There is contention among these projects over the nature of institutions. Some of that contention is between the religious and the nonreligious. Part of the advance of what we call "the secular" stems from creating new domains of this-worldly efficacy and action. Science is important in this way, not just as a clashing value system or ideology. Medicine is not just another domain of knowledge but now meddles with the very nature of life through genetic engineering. The economy, the state, and social movements all involve world-making projects. These may contend with one another as well as with specifically religious projects. But the expansion of reliance on this-worldly institutions and practices is an expansion of the secular even when it is compatible with or carried out by religious people.

Finally, we should recognize the prominence of a secularist ideology that goes beyond affirming the virtues of the ostensibly neutral. The demarcation between religion and the secular is made, not just found. The secular is claimed by many not just as one way of organizing life, not just as useful in order to ensure peace and harmony among different religions, but as a kind of maturation. It is held to be a kind of developmental achievement. Some people feel they are "better" because they have overcome illusion and reached the point of secularism. That ideological self-understanding is itself powerful in a variety of contexts. It shapes even the way in which many think of global cosmopolitanism as a kind of escape from culture, nation, and religion into a realm of apparently pure reason, universal rights, and global connections. We might, by contrast, think of cosmopolitanism as something to be achieved through the connections among all the people who come from and are rooted in and belong to different traditions, different social structures, different countries, different faiths. There is a profound difference between an ideology of escape and the idea of interconnected *ecumenae*.

In any case, secularism is not simply the Other to religion. It is a phenomenon in its own right that demands reflexive scholarship, critique, and open-minded exploration.

Notes

1.   The idea of a secular trend, after all, is of a pattern of change that moves linearly through time—and thus a reminder of the centrality of temporality to the notion of the secular.

2.   Taylor, *A Secular Age* (Cambridge, MA: Harvard University Press, 2007). See also Michael Warner, Jonathan VanAntwerpen, and Craig Calhoun, eds., *Varieties of Secularism in a Secular Age* (Cambridge, MA: Harvard University Press, 2010).

3.   Some five hundred years after Augustine, the great Muslim thinker Abu Nasr al-Farabi also used the idea of the city to explore the issue of virtue and imperfection in the world. Influenced even more by Neoplatonism than Augustine was, he saw life in terms of emanations from the universal and perfect one, descending into a plural and imperfect temporal world. His vision did not include the mediation of the Church, of course, nor come as close to binary distinction between matters of world and soul, but did insist as much as Augustine's on the necessity of the perfect in order to put the quotidian in perspective.

4.   Charles Taylor, *Sources of the Self: The Making of the Modern Identity* (Cambridge, UK: Cambridge University Press, 1989).

5.   See James Davidson Hunter, *To Change the World* (Oxford: Oxford University Press, 2010). Hunter argues that such engagement with the world rightly follows from Christian commitments, but that it is often distorted by a model of producing secular change by combat over belief and moral conviction and by seeking secular power, rather than by a commitment to "faithful presence" honoring the Creator of all.

6.   Spain, though associated more with empire in histories of the seventeenth century, had actually pioneered in this trend, expelling and forcibly converting Jews and Muslims under those most Catholic monarchs Ferdinand and Isabella and pursuing national integration and even a specifically Spanish— not papal—inquisition.

7.   There has been much discussion in the field of comparative religion of the formation of the category that defines it, including its colonial-era roots and the importance of international assemblies purporting to represent the world's religions. See, for example, Tomoko Masuzawa, *The Invention of World Religions: Or, How European Universalism Was Preserved in the Language of Pluralism* (Chicago: University of Chicago Press 2005).

8.   See David Sorkin, *The Religious Enlightenment: Protestants, Jews, and Catholics from London to Vienna* (Princeton, NJ: Princeton University Press, 2010); Eric Nelson, *The Hebrew Republic: Jewish Sources and the Transformation of European Political Thought* (Cambridge, MA: Harvard University Press, 2010); Michael Allen Gillespie, *The Theological Origins of Modernity* (Chicago: University of Chicago Press, 2008); Joshua Mitchell, *Not by Reason Alone: Religion, History and Identity in Early Modern Political Thought* (Chicago: University of Chicago Press, 1993); Eldon Eisenach, *Two Worlds of Liberalism: Religion and Politics in Hobbes, Locke, and Mill* (Chicago: University of Chicago Press, 1981).

9. Henning Graf Reventlow, *The Authority of the Bible and the Rise of the Modern World* (Philadelphia: Fortress Press, 1985).

10. Here we see the link between figures such as Hume in the Scottish Enlightenment and Burke's famous response to the French Revolution. But we should not equate this with conservatism in the sense of a "right wing." Even the early anarchist William Godwin insisted on gradualism, resisted enthusiasm (which he thought as likely to take the form of church-and-king mobs as Jacobinism), and abhorred the idea that the undisciplined lower orders would participate directly in politics. See Alex Benchimol, "Cultural Historiography and the Scottish Enlightenment Public Sphere: Placing Habermas in Eighteenth-Century Edinburgh," in Alex Benchimol and Willy Maley, eds., *Spheres of Influence: Intellectual and Cultural Publics from Shakespeare to Habermas* (Bern, Switzerland: Lang, 2007), and Don Herzog, *Poisoning the Minds of the Lower Orders* (Princeton, NJ: Princeton University Press, 1998).

11. See Alfred Stepan's review in "The Twin Tolerations," and the various chapters in Rajeev Bhargava, ed., *Secularism*. In regard to the U.S. case, note that though Jefferson spoke of a separation of church and state, that formulation does not appear in the Constitution, enters Supreme Court jurisprudence only in the 1870s, and comes to the foreground only after the Second World War.

12. Though cases are also made for other etymologies.

13. Somewhat similarly, the Roman idea of "nation" was shaped not by self-reflection but by reference to the distinctive cultures of others, including conquered peoples and enemies. These were nations partly because inclusion was reckoned in terms of descent rather than citizenship. See Patrick J. Geary, *The Myth of Nations: The Medieval Origins of Europe* (Princeton, NJ: Princeton University Press, 2002).

14. Elizabeth Shakman Hurd, *The Politics of Secularism in International Relations* (Princeton, NJ: Princeton University Press, 2007).

15. Robert O. Keohane, "The Globalization of Informal Violence, Theories of World Politics, and 'The Liberalism of Fear'" in C. Calhoun, P. Price, and A. Timmer, eds., *Understanding September 11* (New York: New Press 2002), 72.

16. "Politics of Religious Freedom: Minority Rights, Sovereignty, and Gender." Speech at the American Academy of Religion, Montreal, 9 November 2009.

17. See Julie Reuben, *The Making of the Modern University* (Chicago: University of Chicago Press, 1996).

18. This is an important contention of Taylor's *A Secular Age*.

19. See Tariq Ramadan, "Manifesto for a New 'We,'" 7 July 2006, available at http://www.tariqramadan.com/spip.php?article743.

20. Richard John Neuhaus, *The Naked Public Square* (Grand Rapids, MI: Eerdmans, 1984); Habermas, *Between Naturalism and Religion* (Cambridge: Polity, 2008).

21. Compare Alastair MacIntyre, *Whose Justice, Which Rationality* (South Bend: Notre Dame University Press, 1988) and *After Virtue* (South Bend, IN: Notre Dame University Press, 1981).

22. John Rawls, "The Idea of Public Reason Revisited," *University of Chicago Law Review* 64, no. 3 (Summer 1997): 765-807.

23. See Jürgen Habermas, *Rationality and Religion: Essays on Reason, God, and Modernity* (Cambridge, MA: MIT Press, 2002) and "Religion in the Public Sphere," in *Between Naturalism and Religion*.

24. See the discussion of "hypergoods" in Taylor, *Sources of the Self*.

25. Immanuel Kant, *The Critique of Pure Reason* (orig. 1781; London: Penguin, 2008).

26. Charles Taylor, "The Immanent Frame," in *A Secular Age*, 539-93 (Cambridge, MA: Harvard University, 2007).

27. I am using the phrase "beauty of the world" rather than, say, "experience of the sublime" precisely to emphasize reference to aspects of the world itself that we experience, rather than of our experience as such. I have in mind something of the orientation to nature suggested by the nineteenth-century New England transcendentalists among others. This is not nature as a system, though thinking of nature that way need not preclude access to the beauty of the world.

28. Arthur O. Lovejoy, *The Great Chain of Being* (Cambridge, MA: Harvard University Press, 1936).

29. Such a conclusion fits, for example, with Varshney's findings about the presence or absence of intercommunal violence in Indian cities.

About the Contributors

COURTNEY BENDER is Associate Professor of Religion at Columbia University. She is the author of *The New Metaphysicals: Spirituality and the American Religious Imagination* (University of Chicago Press, 2010), and *Heaven's Kitchen: Living Religion at God's Love We Deliver* (University of Chicago Press, 2003).

CRAIG CALHOUN is president of the Social Science Research Council and University Professor of the Social Sciences at New York University. His most recent book is *Nations Matter: Culture, History, and the Cosmopolitan Dream* (Routledge, 2007).

MICHELE DILLON is Professor of Sociology and Chair of the department at University of New Hampshire. She is the author of several books and articles on religion, culture, and institutional change and president-elect of the Society for the Scientific Study of Religion, past president of the Association for the Sociology of Religion, and past chair of the American Sociological Association section on the sociology of religion. She will be the Tipton Distinguished Visiting Professor in Catholic Studies at the University of California, Santa Barbara, for 2011–2012.

PHILIP S. GORSKI is Professor of Sociology at Yale University. His research focuses on religion and politics in early modern and modern Europe and the United States. He is currently completing a book on American civil religion.

DAVID KYUMAN KIM is Associate Professor of Religious Studies and American Studies at Connecticut College, Senior Advisor at the Social Science Research Council, editor-at-large of *The Immanent Frame*, and coeditor of the Stanford University Press series RaceReligion. Author of *Melancholic Freedom: Agency and the Spirit of Politics*, he is currently writing *The Public Life of Love*.

RICHARD MADSEN is Distinguished Professor of Sociology at University of California, San Diego. He is the author or coauthor of twelve books on Chinese culture, American culture, and international relations, including his best-known works *Habits of the Heart* (University of California Press, 1995) and *The Good Society* (Knopf, 1991), which he coauthored with Robert Bellah, William Sullivan, Ann Swidler, and Steven Tipton.

KATHLEEN MAHONEY is a consultant working with foundations and non-profit organizations. She is the recent past president of Porticus North America Foundation and author of *Catholic Higher Education in Protestant America: The Jesuits and Harvard in the Age of the University* (Johns Hopkins University Press, 2003).

TOMOKO MASUZAWA is Professor of History and Comparative Literature at University of Michigan. She is the author of *In Search of Dreamtime: The Quest for the Origin of Religion* (University of Chicago Press, 1993) and *The Invention of World Religions: Or How European Universalism Was Preserved in the Language of Pluralism* (University of Chicago Press, 2005).

EDUARDO MENDIETA is Professor of Philosophy at State University of New York, Stony Brook. He is the author of *Global Fragments: Critical Theory, Latin America and Globalizations* (State University of New York Press, 2007) and *Adventures of Transcendental Philosophy: Karl-Otto Apel's Semiotics and Discourse Ethics* (Rowman & Littlefield, 2002).

JOHN SCHMALZBAUER is Associate Professor of Religious Studies and Blanche Gorman Strong Chair in Protestant Studies at Missouri State University. He is the author of *People of Faith: Religious Conviction in American Journalism and Higher Education* (Cornell University Press, 2003).

JAMES K. A. SMITH is Professor of Philosophy at Calvin College in Grand Rapids, Michigan. He is the author or coauthor of a number of volumes, including *Thinking in Tongues: Pentecostal Contributions to Christian Philosophy* (Eerdmans, 2010) and *The Devil Reads Derrida: and Other Essays on the Church, the University, Politics, and the Arts* (Eerdmans, 2009). He is currently writing a book on Charles Taylor's analysis of our secular age.

JOHN TORPEY is Professor of Sociology at the Graduate Center of the City University of New York. He is the author or editor of half a dozen books, including the recent *Making Whole What Has Been Smashed: On Reparations Politics* (Harvard University Press, 2006).

BRYAN S. TURNER is Presidential Professor of Sociology and Director of the Committee on Religion at The Graduate Center of the City University of New York. He edited the *New Blackwell Companion to the Sociology of Religion* (Blackwell-Wiley, 2010) and published *Religion and Modern Society* (Cambridge University Press, 2011).

JONATHAN VANANTWERPEN is Director of the Religion and the Public Sphere program at the Social Science Research Council and a visiting scholar at New York University's Institute for Public Knowledge. He is coeditor of *The Power of Religion in the Public Sphere* (Columbia University Press, 2011), *Rethinking Secularism* (Oxford University Press, 2011), and *Varieties of Secularism in a Secular Age* (Harvard University Press, 2010).

HENT DE VRIES holds the Russ Family Chair in the Humanities and is Professor of Philosophy at Johns Hopkins University, where he is also Director of the Humanities Center. His principal publications include *Philosophy and the Turn to Religion* (Johns Hopkins University Press, 2000), *Religion and Violence: Philosophical Perspectives from Kant to Derrida* (Johns Hopkins University Press, 2006), and *Minimal Theologies: Critiques of Secular Reason in Theodor W. Adorno and Emmanuel Levinas* (Johns Hopkins University Press, 2005).

Index

Abington School District v. Schempp, 196

Academic secular, 200

Anscombe, G. E. M., 80

Aquinas, Thomas, 93

Aristotle, 79–84, 88–90, 92–95, 97–99, 101, 102

Asad, Talal, 7, 224

Asceticism, 342

Asia: academic attention to, 205; as new center of wealth, 17, 295; religious marketplace in, 143; secularization in, 137–138

Axial age, 36, 39

Bellah, Robert: on civil religion, 145, 227, 285, 299; *Habits of the Heart*, 57, 285; *Religion in Human Evolution*, 33–36; on religion in the public sphere, 268; on religious evolution, 153, 286; on Sheilaism, 57; sociology of religion, contribution to, 4, 144, 262

Bender, Courtney, 365

Berger, Peter: on globalized elite culture, 160, 166, 177, 232; on plausibility structures, 164; on religious experience, 56; shift in position on secularization, 2, 138, 279; sociology of religion, contribution to, 144; *The Heretical Imperative*, 56

Bloch, Ernst, 308, 330

Bourdieu, Pierre, 144, 153, 172–175

Buddhism: commodification of, 139; and definitions of religion, 23 35; in Japan, 192–194; in the Song Dynasty, 24; in Tibet, 30, 37, 225; Western religions, compared to, 282–283

Calhoun, Craig, 365

Cambridge, MA, spirituality in, 47, 52–53, 58–61

Campus Crusade for Christ, 233

Casanova, José, 6–7, 140–141, 287–289, 346–347

Catholicism: Blair, Tony, 301; Cardinal

sources of reflexivity, 307–311; Taylor, Charles, 307–311, 320, 326–329

Franciscans, 25

French Revolution, 86, 346, 363

Functionalism, 3, 96–98

Germany: church and state in, 141, 198, 288; functionalism in, 99; Islam in, 263–264; Protestantism of, 145, 290; secularization in, 296–297; the university in, 196–198

Globalization theory, 154

Gorski, Philip S., 365

Granet, Michel, 38

Greek philosophy, 34, 39. *See* Aristotle.

Habermas, Jürgen: and Cardinal Ratzinger, 11, 145–146, 254, 265; Foucault, Michel, 307–311, 325; on post-secular society, 255–259, 261–262; on religious reason in the public sphere, 144–146, 252–253, 265–266, 312, 320–324; Taylor, Charles, 261–262, 326; *The Theory of Communicative Action*, 250–251, 256, 310, 321, 323, 326–327; on translation of religious reasons, 259–260

Habits of the Heart (Robert Bellah et al.), 57, 285

Harvey, David, 16, 144, 157, 255, 275

Hebrew, 34, 345, 362

Heidegger, Martin, 169, 328

Heretical Imperative, The (Peter Berger), 56

Hillel, 233

Hinduism, 137, 228, 282, 293

Hitchens, Christopher, 8, 19, 160, 299

Humanitarianism, 343

Huntington, Samuel, 37, 285, 290

Husserl, Edmund, 159, 177

Immanent frame, the: and environmentalism, 343; and historicism, 360; neutrality of, 123, 279, 338–339, 355; and political liberalism, 124; and theology, 37

Individualism: and American religion, 35, 227; and New Age movements, 39; and new media, 151; Niebuhr, Reinhold, 128; and religious authority, decline of, 153; and sociology, 100; spirituality and religious individualism, 48–49, 51, 54, 57

Individualized religion, 139, 286

International Religious Freedom Report, 192

Inwardness, 307–309, 326

Iranian Revolution, 318–320

Islam: academic attention to, 13, 136–137, 228; in Europe, 263–264, 269, 336–337, 347–348; Huntington, Samuel, 37–38; and international relations, 27, 233, 235; and the Internet, 150–151; Iranian revolution, 318–320; Islamic Calvinists, 301; Obama, Barack, 108–109, 113–116; sources of authority in, 150; *Ummah*, diversity of, 352–353; in the United States, 263, 350; and US-Muslim relations, 108–109

James, William, 52, 55, 136, 283, 308

Japan, 189, 192–195, 278, 280, 290, 295

Jaspers, Karl, 36, 38

Jay, Martin, 54, 72, 74

Jesuits, 24–27, 40, 190

Kant, Immanuel: Durkheim, Émile 77–84, 87–88, 95, 99; *Religion within the Boundaries of Mere Reason*, 147–148; and sociology, 8–10

Taylor, Charles: *A Secular Age*, 123, 136, 163–164, 261–262, 279, 339; focus on religion, 13, 227; Foucault, Michele, 307–311, 326–329; on fullness, 357; grand narrative, 34; on Habermas, Jürgen, 307–311, 326–329; and the immanent frame, 37, 123, 279, 338–339, 355; intellectualism, critique of, 172–174; on ritual, 161–162, 173–174; on religious tolerance, 261–262, 264; secular, on meanings of the, 163–164; on secularization, 289, 307–308, 342; on subtraction stories, 166, 289, 339

Theory of Communicative Action, The (Jürgen Habermas), 250–251, 256, 310, 321, 323, 326–327

Tibet, 30, 37, 225

Torpey, John, 367

Transcendence: in the axial age, 38, 39; belief in, 165; and definitions of religion, 175–177; secular transcendence, 354–360; and secularization, 141–142, 152, 227, 336

Troeltsch, 49, 55, 286–287

Turner, Bryan S., 367

University of Michigan, 202–204

Urban piety, 137

VanAntwerpen, Jonathan, 367

Victorian moralism, 9

de Vries, Hent, 367

Weber, Max: conflict theory, 3; on the differentiation of value spheres, 339, 360; neo-Kantian, 9–10; *The Protestant Ethic and the Spirit of Capitalism*, 15, 29, 142, 147; *The Sociology of Religion*, 143, 148–150; value freedom, 10

West, Cornel, 234, 312

Zedong, Mao. *See* Chairman Mao.

Žižek, Slavoj, 13, 22